Ireland's Great Famine

The author and publishers acknowledge with gratitude the financial support
of the National University of Ireland's Publications Scheme.

A note on the jacket illustration

The jacket illustration is one of the best known of the *Famine Sketches* depicting
the Great Bengali Famine of 1943–4 by local artist Zainul Abedin (1917–76). In
1943, as a member of the Anti-Fascist Writers and Artists Association, Abedin
'took on the role of a chronicler with paper and brush, trudging the streets and
lanes (of Calcutta), with his stock of cheap paper, ink and brushes'. Much
reproduced in Communist Party newspapers and periodicals at the time, the
sketches, which highlighted the divide between the destitute masses and the
wealthy few, made Abedin's reputation. The crows in the sketch, like the
raven in Irish mythology, signify death.

No doubt such scenes were commonplace in Ireland in 1846 and 1847, but
they were never recorded in the same graphic terms. Nor do later artistic works
depicting the Irish famine capture the horrors of famine in the way the works
of Abedin and his fellow artists did the Bengali famine (for more on Abedin
see Sarkar 1988).

Ireland's Great Famine
Interdisciplinary Perspectives

CORMAC Ó GRÁDA

with the collaboration of
Andrés Eiríksson,
Timothy Guinnane,
Joel Mokyr, and
Kevin O'Rourke

UNIVERSITY COLLEGE DUBLIN PRESS
Preas Choláiste Ollscoile Bhaile Átha Cliath

First published 2006
by University College Dublin Press
Newman House
86 St Stephen's Green
Dublin 2
Ireland
www.ucdpress.ie

Chs 1, 2, 7, 9–14 © Cormac Ó Gráda, 2006
Chs 3, 5 © Cormac Ó Gráda and Joel Mokyr, 2006
Ch. 4 © Cormac Ó Gráda and Andrés Eiríksson, 2006
Ch. 6 © Cormac Ó Gráda and Timothy Guinnane, 2006
Ch. 8 © Cormac Ó Gráda and Kevin H. O Rourke, 2006

ISBN 1-904558-57-7 pb
978-1-904558-57-6

1-904558-58-5 hb
978-1-904558-58-3

Cataloguing in Publication data
available from the British Library

The right of Cormac Ó Gráda to be identified as
the author of this work has been asserted by him

Typeset in Ireland in Adobe Garamond,
Janson and Trade Gothic by
Elaine Burberry, Bantry, County Cork
Text design by Lyn Davies
Index by Jasne Rogers
Printed in England on acid-free paper by
MPG Books Ltd, Bodmin, Cornwall

In memory of three great scholars of the Great Famine

Austin Bourke (1913–95)

Donal Kerr (1927–2001)

Thomas P. O'Neill (1921–96)

'Maireann na crainn ach ní mhaireann na lámha a chuir iad'.

Contents

Acknowledgements

I would like to thank the editors of the relevant journals and volumes for permission to reproduce here versions of earlier work, some of it with other scholars, which appeared in the following publications: 'The famine: an introduction', in Cormac Ó Gráda, Richard Paping and Eric Vanhaute (eds), *The European Potato Crises of the 1840s* (Brepols, 2006); 'Poor and getting poorer' (with Joel Mokyr), *Economic History Review* XXXVII (2) 1988: 209–35; 'Famine disease and famine mortality' (with Joel Mokyr), *European Review of Economic History* 6 (3) 2003: 339–64; 'Mortality in the NDU during the Great Irish Famine' (with Timothy W. Guinnane), *Economic History Review* LV (3) 2002: 487–506; 'Mass migration as disaster relief: lessons from the Great Irish Famine' (with Kevin H. O'Rourke), *European Review of Economic History* 1 (1) 1997: 3–25; 'The famine, the New York Irish, and their bank', in Antoin E. Murphy and Renée Prendergast (eds), *Contributions to the History of Economic Thought: Essays in Honour of R. D. C. Black* (London, 2000), pp. 227–48; 'The Great Famine and other famines', in C. Ó Gráda (ed.), *Famine 150: Commemorative Lecture Series* (Dublin, 1996), pp. 129–57; 'Famine, trauma, and memory', *Béaloideas* 69, 2001: 121–44; 'Making Irish history in the 1940s and 1950s: the saga of the Great Famine', *The Irish Review* 12, 1992: 87–107; 'Making famine history in Ireland in 1995', *History Workshop Journal* 42, 1996: 87–104.

My thanks also to Andrés Eiríksson, Tim Guinnane, Joel Mokyr, and Kevin O'Rourke for allowing me to publish some our joint labours in this form. Over the years I have accumulated heavy academic debts, some of which I have acknowledged elsewhere. Here, I want to record my gratitude to three famous famine scholars no longer with us, who helped me in many ways, and who are still missed by many: Austin Bourke, Donal Kerr, and Thomas P. O'Neill. I dedicate this book to their memory.

CORMAC Ó GRÁDA
December 2005

Abbreviations

AER	*American Economic Review*
AgHR	*Agricultural History Review*
AICP	Association for the Improvement of the Condition of the Poor (New York)
BPP	British Parliamentary Papers
CUP	Cambridge University Press
DEM	*Dublin Evening Mail*
EEH	*Explorations in Economic History*
HER	*Economic History Review*
EIC	East India Company
EISB	Emigrant Industrial Savings Bank
EREH	*European Review of Economic History*
FAD	Food Availability Decline
FJ	*Freeman's Journal*
HC	House of Commons
HIS	*Irish Historical Studies*
HO	Home Office
ICHS	Irish Committee of Historical Sciences
IEC	Incumbered Estates Court
IESH	*Irish Economic and Social History*
IHS	*Irish Historical Studies*
IPA	Institute of Public Administration
IPUMS	Integrated Public Use Manuscript Sample
JEH	*Journal of Economic History*
JPE	*Journal of Political Economy*
JRSS	*Journal of the Royal Statistical Society*
JSSISI	*Journal of the Statistical and Social Inquiry Society of Ireland*
LEC	Landed Estate Commission
MUP	Manchester University Press
NA	National Archives (London)
NAI	National Archives of Ireland

NDU	North Dublin Union
NFRP	National Famine Research Project
NGO	Non-government organisation
NLI	National Library of Ireland
NUI	National University of Ireland
NYPD	New York Police Department
OUP	Oxford University Press
P&P	*Past and Present*
PDR	*Population and Development Review*
PP	Parliamentary Papers
PRIA	*Proceedings of the Royal Irish Academy*
PS	*Population Studies*
PUP	Princeton University Press
QJE	*Quarterly Journal of Economics*
RDE	R. Dudley Edwards's academic diary
RMT	Recovered Memory Theory
SII	Subjective Impoverishment Index
TCD	Trinity College, Dublin
UCD	University College Dublin
UCLA	University of California, Los Angeles

Introduction

The Great Famine was the defining event of nineteenth-century Irish history, and nineteenth-century Europe's greatest natural disaster. Besides being directly responsible for the premature deaths of one million people, it prompted many hundreds of thousands more to emigrate. In the Houses of Parliament at Westminster the famine prompted the repeal of the Corn Laws, the creation of the Irish Incumbered Estates Court, and the tightening up of legislation governing passenger transport on the high seas. At the time, some people in high places blamed the famine on the fecklessness and the fertility of the Irish poor; others, then and since, saw only genocidal intent. Most historians today reject both views. Instead they attribute the famine to a combination of economic backwardness, an inadequate and inhumane response from the government of the day, and bad luck – though the relative importance of these factors is still debated. The Great Famine also left its mark on both Ireland and on the Irish abroad in the long run, and scarred Anglo-Irish relations for over a century. 'That one million people should have died in what was then part of the richest and most powerful nation in the world is something that still causes pain as we reflect on it today', declared the British Prime Minister Tony Blair in 1997.[1]

For an event with such deep and enduring ramifications, it seems fair to say that until the 1980s the Great Famine remained under-researched. Since then the surge of scholarly publications about the famine, much of it spawned by its 150th anniversary in the mid-1990s, has more than made up for any earlier 'silence' on the topic. The literature on the famine is now enormous. The graph below describes holdings of all famine-related books published since the 1850s in the US Library of Congress, broken down by decade of publication. The Irish share of the total in the recent past is truly staggering.

The surge in publications, which both anticipated and outlasted the sesqui-centennial commemorations, seems now to be subsiding. This would seem a good time, then, to release the present collection of essays, all of which except one

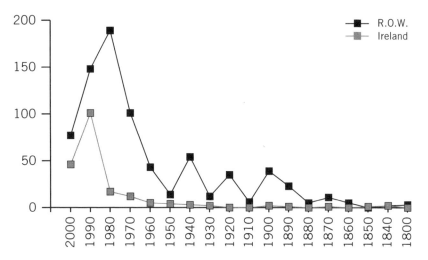

Figure 1 **Books on famine in the Library of Congress catalogue, 1800–2005**

were written between the early 1990s and 2004. They are presented here more or less as written, although a few have been pruned to minimise repetition. Three of the essays have not seen the light of day before: the others are scattered over a wide range of publications at home and abroad. Together, they offer a particular, but also (I hope) a wide-ranging and interdisciplinary perspective on the famine.

Chapter 1 offers a brief analytical narrative of the famine. It draws on my own earlier work, particularly on *Black '47 and Beyond* (Princeton University Press, 1999) and *The Great Irish Famine* (Cambridge University Press, 1995), and on the famine chapters in *Ireland before and after the Famine* (2nd edn, Manchester University Press, 1993) and in *Ireland: A New Economic History* (Oxford University Press, 1994). However, it also incorporates the results of recent work by other scholars on the topic and adds some comparative perspectives.[2]

Chapter 2 (co-written with Joel Mokyr) offers some socio-economic context for the Great Famine. Its analysis of trends in poverty in Ireland in the previous half-century or so is based on a number of proxies for living standards, ranging from the average consumption of items such as tea and tobacco to anthropometric measures of health and well-being. Inspired in part by the famous British 'standard of living debate', the chapter is a reminder that the impact of industrialisation on most of Ireland was very different than on the industrialising regions of Great Britain. We argue that the sometimes conflicting stories implied by the different measures or proxies for living standards are a measure of increasing income and wealth inequalities in pre-famine Ireland.

Chapter 3 (co-written with Andrés Eiríksson) emerged from research done in conjunction with the Irish Famine Network, an informal forum for researchers established in 1993 and active for a few years thereafter.[3] Its focus is the impact of the famine on Ireland's ten thousand or so landed proprietors. These proprietors ranged from owners of a few hundred acres to major landowners such as the Duke of Devonshire, the Marquess of Downshire, and Trinity College. Irish landlords wielded enormous power. At the aggregate level, there are statistics on the thousands of smallholders they evicted in the late 1840s and estimates of the changes in their aggregate rental income (Donnelly 1995; O'Neill 2000; Ó Gráda 1974). At the local level, many well-documented examples survive of both brutish and humane behaviour by individual landlords during the famine. Relying mainly on an analysis of properties processed through the Incumbered Estates Court, chapter 3 argues that the economic damage inflicted on landlords by the famine was less than usually claimed in the past. The Incumbered Estates Court was established in 1849 to free up the sale of lands belonging to indebted and insolvent landowners. It turns out that nearly all landlords forced to dispose of some or all of their lands in the wake of the famine were already in dire financial straits before it. Only the costs and the red tape surrounding litigation had protected them from their creditors. Had the Incumbered Estates Court been in place prior to 1845, many of these landlords would already have succumbed before the blight struck. The Incumbered Estates Court was a by-product of the famine, but landlord indebtedness was not.

Chapter 4 (also co-authored with Joel Mokyr) is a study of what the famine's million or so victims died of. It is based largely on the reworking of a famous but flawed source, the Tables of Death produced by William Wilde for the 1851 census. Wilde's data offer a detailed estimate of total mortality and of the main causes of death between 1841 and 1851. Institutions such as workhouses, hospitals and prisons provided some of Wilde's data. On the whole, those data are reliable, but the same cannot be said for the returns culled from household census forms. Householders were asked to list members of the household who had died during the previous decade, but this meant that deaths in households that did not survive the famine for one reason or another were excluded. The combination of institutional and individual returns yields an incomplete and biased count of famine fatalities. An added problem is that the medical diagnostics are fallible. Nevertheless, Mokyr and I argue that some useful results can be generated from Wilde's tabulations. We also take the opportunity to make some broader comparative points about the causes of famine mortality. The Irish pattern is replicated, broadly speaking, in sub-Saharan Africa in the recent past and in India in the 1940s, but not in environments such as Leningrad or the western Netherlands during the Second World War, where infectious diseases were no longer endemic in normal times (compare Livi-Bacci 1991: 47).

Chapter 5 (which I wrote with Tim Guinnane) analyses workhouse management during the famine. The essay is part of an attempt to establish plausible yardsticks for public servants and elected officials charged with famine relief. Obviously, the problems facing poor law union guardians and workhouse masters in Tralee or Ballina in the west of Ireland were not those facing their colleagues in, say, Wexford or Newtownards in the east.[4] Here the focus is the North Dublin Union workhouse, which was responsible for relieving the destitute of the northern half of the capital city. Dublin escaped lightly during the famine. Even so it suffered excess mortality and a considerable influx of destitute country people seeking charity and work.[5] Our analysis of the union's admission registers finds that the workhouse was competently run, and that most of those who perished there during the famine were already in poor health on admission. The same, alas, cannot be said for the management of several other unions.[6]

Chapter 6 is also about the famine in Dublin. It describes how the demand for, and supply of, potatoes in the capital responded to the onset of *Phytophthora infestans* (potato blight). It is based largely on an analysis of press reports of the prices and qualities of potatoes sold in on the market in Little Green Street on the city's north side before and during the famine.

The next three chapters concern famine emigration. The exodus of hundreds of thousands of famine victims is an important part of the tragedy of the late 1840s. The historiography highlights the dangers of the Atlantic crossing and the cold welcome received by the emigrants in the New World. On balance, however, the emigrants were the lucky ones, when compared to those even poorer than they were, and who could not afford to leave. Chapter 7, which was co-written with Kevin O'Rourke, argues that had emigration to North America not been available as a safety valve, excess mortality in Ireland itself (and perhaps in Britain too) would have been even higher than it was. Chapter 8 describes the conditions faced by the famine Irish in one important destination, New York City. For most immigrants, New York was only a temporary destination, and some of the Irish who remained on there in the 1850s were almost certainly locked in by poverty and ignorance. The plight of those trying to make a living in ghettos like the crime-ridden Sixth Ward – the Bloody Oul' Sixth – was indeed a hard one (compare Burrows and Wallace 1999: 743–8; Anbinder 2001, 2002). The popular historiography of the city and its Irish-born inhabitants in this era resonates of Tammany Hall, the Bowery Bhoys, and gang rivalries – all markers of the city's 'maleness'. Yet in the 1850s a significant majority of New York's Irish-born inhabitants were women. Most of them remained there by choice, since there was ample demand in the city for domestic servants. The vibrancy of the immigrants' networks of churches and schools and the beginnings of Irish participation in mass politics are also part of the New York Irish story. Chapter 9 is about the New York Irish and their bank, the Emigrant Savings Bank, founded by comfortably off, philanthropic Irishmen in 1850 at the instigation of the Tyrone-born Bishop (later Archbishop) John Hughes.[7]

Chapter 10 is based on a public lecture delivered in Dublin in 1996, one of a series jointly sponsored by Teagasc (Ireland's state-run agricultural research and advisory service) and University College Dublin. The text seeks to retain the somewhat informal character of the original lecture, so it is reproduced as delivered, except for the addition of a few contextual footnotes. The chapter describes Ireland's famine in comparative and Third World perspective, and seeks to explain how Ireland's famine resembled and differed from present-day famines.[8] Chapter 11 offers some reflections on the tensions between the history, folklore, and collective memory of Ireland's famine. Its reappraisal of the Irish Folklore Commission's oral-historical holdings on the famine acknowledges their power to conserve vivid narratives of the catastrophe, but suggests some previously unsuspected lacunae and biases as well.[9] It also claims that the 'collective memory' jogged by the sesquicentennial commemorations, by turning the descendants of all survivors into 'vicarious victims', over-simplified the grim realities of the Famine in several respects. This is not to deny the useful role of the commemorations in highlighting the injustices associated with present-day famines, and in prompting a great deal of worthwhile historical research.

Finally, chapters 12 and 13 are mainly historiographical. The first describes the conception, creation, and release of a classic of Irish collaborative historical scholarship, *The Great Famine: Studies in Irish History*, edited by R. Dudley Edwards and T. Desmond Williams of UCD. Published in early 1957, *The Great Famine* was the long-delayed outcome of a government-financed project to mark the famine's centennial with an academic history. It thus dates from an era when university departments were more feudal in structure and the pressure to publish far less than today. However, I acknowledge here something I should have noted in 1991: that the resources available to researchers half a century ago were also far fewer than today (compare Cullen 1998: 170; Lee 2000). Moreover, the record of subsequent collective publication ventures, in Ireland and elsewhere, gives pause. At the very first conference of contributors to a *New History of Ireland* in late December 1968, the late F. X. Martin 'stressed the need to adhere scrupulously to the time-table' of a project that would not reach completion until 2004, while *The Agrarian History of England and Wales*, completed as recently as 2000, began with 'a meeting chaired by R. H. Tawney in 1956', and publication of the volumes of the Cambridge Economic History of Europe straddled the period between 1952 and 1989.[10] Nor has the scholarly volume envisaged by the publicly funded National Famine Research Project of the mid-1990s seen the light of day.[11] After many adventures along the way, *The Great Famine* eventually saw the light a dozen years behind schedule. Much better late than never, however: a measure of its staying power is that a new 1994 paperback edition is still selling copies. My essay is partly an exercise in what a colleague dubbed 'gossip with footnotes' about Irish historians. Probably for that reason, it attracted a good deal of attention from historians.[12]

I wrote chapter 13, originally commissioned by *History Workshop Journal*, during a stay at New York University's Ireland House in the spring of 1996, at the height of the sesquicentennial events. Its object was to capture the tone and scope of what it dubbed the 'new famine history'. The 'new' research it describes highlighted the catastrophic dimensions of a tragedy rather marginalised in Irish 'revisionist' historiography, and was less apologetic in its stance towards those wielding power and influence in the 1840s.

Reading and writing these studies of Ireland's famine involved learning about famines elsewhere. In recent years, some of my research has focused on the broader history of famine. As suggested more than once in what follows, the Irish famine had much in common with famines throughout history. Many of the features described in mordant detail in an early graphic depiction of famine, referring to northern Mesopotamia in AD 499–501 (Wright 1882: 29b–34b), were replicated in Ireland in the 1840s. They include high food prices ('there was a dearth of everything edible . . . everything that was not edible was cheap'); desertion ('others their mothers had left . . . because they had nothing to give them); public action ('the emperor gave no small sum of money to distribute among the poor'); unfamiliar substitute foods ('bitter-vetches . . . withered fallen grapes'); allegations of migration ('many villages and hamlets were left destitute of inhabitants'); infectious diseases ('many of the rich died, and not of hunger'). Famines vary more by cause than by symptom, however, and the factors leading to that famine in Edessa (now Urfa in eastern Turkey) a millennium and a half ago were quite different from those operating in Ireland in the 1840s. Its context, its dimensions, and its legacy make *An Gorta Mór* distinctive and worthy of further study.

CHAPTER ONE

Ireland's Great Famine

The proximate cause of the Great Irish Famine (1846–52) was the fungus *Phytophthora infestans* (or potato blight), which reached Ireland in the autumn of 1845. The fungus destroyed about one third of that year's crop, and nearly all that of 1846.[1] After a season's remission, it also ruined most of the 1848 harvest. These repeated attacks made the Irish famine more protracted than most. Partial failures of the potato crop were nothing new in Ireland before 1845, but damage on the scale wrought by the ecological shock of potato blight was utterly unprecedented (Solar 1989; Bourke 1993a; Clarkson and Crawford 2001). However, the famine would not have been nearly so lethal had Ireland's dependence on the potato been less. The experience of other European economies in the 1840s is telling in this respect. In Ireland the daily intake of the third or so of the population mainly reliant on the potato was enormous: 4–5 kilos daily per adult male equivalent for most of the year. After allowing for non-human consumption and provision for seed, the 2.1 million acres (or 0.8 million hectares) under potatoes in the early 1840s produced over two kilos per man, woman and child. In France, by comparison, the average daily intake of potatoes was only 165 grams in 1852; in Norway in the early 1870s, 540 grams; in Holland about 800 grams in the 1840s; in Belgium 640 grams. A few European regions – Belgian Flanders, parts of Prussia and Alsace – came closer to the Irish norm, however (for sources see Ó Gráda 1999: 18, 237 and the case studies in Ó Gráda, Paping, and Vanhaute 2006). Table 1.1 (based on Bourke 1993a: 90–113; Mokyr 1981) gives a sense of the potato's importance in the Irish rural economy.

In Ireland the potato's initial impact was as a seasonal garden crop in the seventeenth century, complementing a diet based mainly on oatmeal and dairy products. The precise contours of its subsequent diffusion are controversial, but its consumption rose over time, and by the 1840s poverty had reduced the bottom one third or so of the population to almost exclusive dependence on it for sustenance. Before the potato assumed such dominance, it arguably lessened

Table 1.1 **Allocation of the potato crop in the early 1840s**

A *Human consumption in Ireland*

Occupation	Population (m.)	Annual consumption (m. tons)
Labourers	3.3	3.9
Cottiers	1.4	0.8
Small farmers	0.5	0.3
Large farmers	0.25	0.1
Textile workers	0.75	0.4
Other workers	0.85	0.4
Professional et al.	0.95	0.3
Total	8.2	6.2

B *Other uses*

Animal consumption: pigs	2.6
Animal consumption: cattle	1.8
Animal consumption: horses and other	0.3
Exports	0.2
Seed and wastage	2.5

the risks of severe famine in a country where earlier famines (in 1649–52 and 1740–1) had wrought devastation that was probably at least on a par, relatively speaking, with that of the 1840s.

Human consumption accounted for only half of Irish potato production: this meant that in the event of failure the portion normally reserved for pigs and hens acted as a crude buffer stock. Ireland's moist climate, moreover, gave it a comparative advantage in potato cultivation, and potato yields were high: about 15 metric tonnes per hectare. The potato tended to alternate with grain in the crop rotation, and played a useful role in preparing the soil for grain crops, of which oats was the most important. However, the potato's low yield-to-seed ratio exacerbated the impact of repeated shortfalls. Its importance in the Irish diet, coupled with an inadequate and inhumane policy response from the authorities, made the consequences of repeated shortfalls in the 1840s devastating (Bourke 1993a; Mokyr 1981; Rosen 1999).

Ireland was a very poor country in 1845, income per head being about half that in the rest of the United Kingdom. The regional contrast between the northeast, which was undergoing rapid industrialisation at this time, and the west and the south was marked. Moreover, while there were some signs of a rise in urban- and middle-class living standards, the half-century or so before the famine was a period of increasing impoverishment for the landless poor (see chapter 2 below). Population rose from about five million in 1800 to seven million in 1820 and 8.5 million in 1845. A rising emigration rate and a falling birth rate offered only partial relief to increasing population pressure (Boyle and Ó Gráda 1986). Moreover, demographic adjustment was weakest in the western and southern areas most at risk. The collapse of a largely home-based textile industry exacerbated the situation in some rural areas, particularly in north Connacht and south Ulster; the result was increasing dependence on the potato and increasing recourse to seasonal migration during the summer months. The nutritional content of the potato and widespread access to heating fuel in the form of turf eased somewhat the poverty of Ireland's three million 'potato people', who were healthier and lived longer than the poor in other parts of Europe at the time. One indication of this, based on evidence from military and prison archives, is that adult Irish males from the lower end of the socio-economic scale on the eve of the famine were at least as tall as, if not taller than, their English peers (Ó Gráda 1991; Mokyr and Ó Gráda 1996). However, their poverty meant that when the potato failed, there was no prospect of trading down to a cheaper alternative food (Ó Gráda 1994a: 80–97). Nowhere else in Europe had the potato, like tobacco a gift from the New World, made such inroads into the diet of the poor. It bears noting that the potato also failed throughout Europe in the 1840s. This brought hardship in many places, and excess mortality in the Low Countries and in parts of Germany. Yet nowhere was Ireland's cataclysm repeated (Solar 1997; Ó Gráda et al. 2006).

The first attack of potato blight inflicted considerable hardship on rural Ireland, though no significant excess mortality. The catastrophe of the Great Irish Famine really dates from the autumn of 1846, when the first deaths from starvation were recorded. By mid-October 1846 four of the country's 130 workhouses were already full, and three months later the workhouses – established under the Irish Poor Law of 1838 – held nearly 100,000 people. By the end of 1846 three in five already contained more inmates than they had accommodation for, and many were turning away would-be inmates (Ó Gráda 1999: 50–2). Of those still with spare capacity, a third or so were in less affected areas in the northeast and east. Ominously, however, several more were located in areas already threatened with disaster, but lacking the resources and the political will to cope. Good examples are the workhouses of Ballina, Ballinrobe, Ennistymon, Gort, Kilrush, Swinford and Westport.

At first there were the food riots and 'moral economy' protests often associated with famines, but these subsided as hope and anger gave way to despair (Eiríksson 1997b; see also Ó Murchadha 1998: 98–9,170–5). The number of crimes reported by the police force peaked in 1847, at more than three times the pre-famine (1844) level. However, the nature of crime shifted: incidents of cattle- and sheep-rustling rose eleven-fold, and burglaries and robberies quintupled, while the number of reported rapes dropped by two thirds. Inmates with no previous conviction formed a rising proportion of the prison population and, in Dublin, proportion of inmates from the distant provinces of Connacht and Munster rose sharply. A further indication of the changing nature of crime was that the mean height of both male and female prisoners in Dublin's Newgate prison rose during the famine. Some prison inmates, it is claimed, committed petty crimes in order to gain access to prisoners' rations; and that much of famine-era crime was driven by desperation is also suggested by the deaths of some of the perpetrators in prison from famine-related causes (Ó Gráda 1994a: 202–4; 1999: 188–91).

The famine did not impact much on Irish politics. The aging leader of Catholic Ireland, Daniel O'Connell, was in poor health at the height of the crisis and died in Genoa in May 1847. An electorate restricted to middle- and upper-class voters increased the representation of O'Connellites in Westminster in the general election of July 1847, but the Irish MPs exerted little pressure on Lord John Russell's weak and divided Whig administration. Nor did extra-parliamentary opposition achieve much: the 'rising' of 1848 was an improvised, tragic-comic affair that lasted less than a week.

Ireland's representatives in Westminster were beholden to a tiny, economically privileged electorate. In June 1847 only two of them opposed a clause inserted into the Poor Law Amendment Act (1847), which drastically reduced the relief entitlements of rural smallholders. Henceforth households occupying more than about 0.1 hectare of land were excluded from public relief. Given the attachment of the poor to their mini-holdings, this clause is usually deemed to have exacerbated mortality. Nor was there much political solidarity within Ireland: in 1849–50 the so-called 'rate-in-aid', a property tax imposed by the authorities in London on richer Irish regions in support of the poorer, provoked strong resentment from political spokesmen in loyalist Ulster (Grant 1990).

The human carnage reached its peak during the winter and spring of 1846–7, but the crisis continued to cost lives for another three or four years. Like all major famines, the Irish potato famine produced many instances of roadside deaths, of neglect of the very young and the elderly, of heroism and of anti-social behaviour, of evictions, and of a rise in crimes against property. Like all famines, it produced its grotesque cameos of life turned upside down and of bonds of friendship and kinship sundered:

- In May 1847 two teenage girls sold their hair for 2s 3d (about three times the daily wage of an unskilled worker) to a hairdresser in Clonmel, County Tipperary, 'an original and extraordinary mode of seeking relief' (Ó Gráda 1999: 40).
- In west Kerry a local poet described how young women might venture out at night without fear of harassment from the young blades of the neighbourhood (Ó Gráda 1994b: 73).
- In Ballykilcline in County Roscommon an entire family succumbed to famine fever and was not discovered for a week: the men who carried the corpses 'got weak and had to be given whiskey' (Ó Gráda 1999: 40).
- In Ballymote in County Sligo by February 1847 beggars were being refused at door after door, 'quite a new feature in the Irish peasant's character' (Swords 1999: 140).
- In the same vein is the account of a young boy employed on a public works scheme next to a Caherdaniel graveyard, who continued working as his father's corpse arrived for burial. The steward fired him for his heartlessness, but the story was later told as evidence of how the famine destroyed 'the good nature in people's hearts' (Póirtéir 1996: 158–9).
- In May 1847 a mail car traveller sought to help a 17-year-old girl whose child had perished on the roadside between Glin and Tarbert. Unwilling to leave the body with nobody to watch over it, the girl too died 'under the broad canopy of Heaven' (Curtin 2000: 111).
- In the city of Cork, Denis Lane was found dead in his prison cell after his arrest for 'forcibly taking meal from carmen' (Ó Gráda 1994a: 204; 1999: 40).
- Deaths on the highway gave rise to the term 'road sickness'. In Ballydehob in west Cork in January 1847 'a poor man named John Coughlan from Kilbronoge . . . was on his way to one of these new roads, that lead to nothing save death, when he fell from exhaustion and . . . was numbered with the other victims of the Board of Works' (Hickey 2002: 169).
- In May 1847 Thomas Mahon of Ennis relief committee received a letter from 'Captain Starlight', accusing him of inflicting 'lingering death by starvation' on the poor of the town. 'Captain Starlight' berated Mahon and his committee for their meagre dole of 'a quart of a pint of porridge and a penny brown loaf for a poor creature for 24 hours'. 'Tempt your dogs

with it', he added, 'and in a month you'll have no dogs' (Ó Murchadha 1998: 118–19).

• There were even rumours of cannibalism, at least in the more restricted sense of the flesh of victims being eaten by survivors: in Mayo a starving man was reported to have 'extracted the heart and liver . . . [of] a shipwrecked human body . . . cast on shore' (*The Times*, 23 May 1849).[2]

Such cameos can offer only hints of the horrors witnessed and endured in Ireland in these years. The famine was widely reported in the contemporary press at first, both in Ireland and abroad. It elicited a massive response in terms of private donations for a time, especially through the agency of the Roman Catholic Church worldwide and the Society of Friends. Philanthropists in Britain were also moved by Irish suffering, until compassion fatigue set in. Even the Choctaw Nation in faraway Oklahoma subscribed $170 for famine relief. Accessible narrative accounts of the tragedy include Edwards and Williams (1956), Woodham-Smith (1962), Ó Gráda (1994a: ch. 8; 1999), and Donnelly (2001).

Public action

Much of the historiography of the Irish famine addresses this issue. Critics of the stance of British policy makers during the Irish famine, both in the 1840s and today, castigated them for not doing more. Accusations of tightfistedness were common: for example, the guardians of Fermoy's workhouse in November 1846 pleaded with ministers 'who gave twenty million to emancipate the slaves, who were never so much to be pitied as the people of this country are at present' (*Cork Constitution*, 7 Nov. 1846). In the *Cork Constitution* a month later a correspondent from devastated Skibbereen 'could not help thinking how much better it would be to afford [the poor] some temporary relief in their own homes during this severe weather, than thus sacrifice their lives to carry out a miserable project of political economy' (cited in Ó Gráda 1996: 104). Towards the end of the crisis, the Rev. Sidney Godolphin Osborne 'looked on the Crystal Palace and thought of Kilrush Workhouse, as I have seen it and now know it to be'. He felt 'as a Christian, and the subject of a Christian government, utter disgust' (Murphy 1996: 79). Such reactions anticipate modern critiques of relief policy by the likes of Thomas P. O'Neill (1956) and Christine Kinealy (1994).

On the other hand, influential and callous laissez-faire ideologues such as Nassau Senior in the *Edinburgh Review* and Thomas Wilson in the *Economist* urged ministers to err in the direction of economy. Referring to the policies pursued, Senior fully approved of the 'experiments . . . made . . . on so large a scale, and pushed to their extreme consequences with such a disregard for the sufferings which they inflict', which he described to his friend Alexis de Tocqueville to be 'as precious as those of Majendie',[3] while Wilson preached in the *Economist* that 'it [was] no man's business to provide for another', and that redistribution would only shift resources from 'the more meritorious to the less' (cited in Ó Gráda 1999: 52). Meanwhile, the abrasive Henry Brougham reminded the House of Lords of times 'when it was more difficult to do nothing than to do something, although the trying to do something were almost certain mischief' (cited in Ó Gráda 1993: 127–8). Supporters of the same policy-makers, then and now, make the points that: (a) the backward character of Irish agriculture made disaster inevitable; (b) much was done in an era when parsimony and callousness were 'exhibited as much to the English as to the Irish poor'; and (c) given widespread corruption in the areas worst affected, further expenditure would have saved few lives (e.g. Daly 1986: 114). In a classic variant of (a), the late E. R. R. Green (1984: 273–4) described the famine as 'primarily a disaster like a flood or an earthquake', by way of implying that state intervention could not have prevented most of the mortality.

The choice of appropriate relief measures for Ireland was widely debated in the press and in parliament in the 1840s. Some of the debates have quite a modern resonance (compare Drèze and Sen 1989). At first the government opted for reliance on the provision of employment through public works schemes, the cost of which was to be split between local taxpayers and the central government. The schemes consisted for the most part of small-scale infrastructural improvements; relief considerations constrained their size and location. At their height in the spring of 1847 the works employed 700,000 people, or one in twelve of the entire population. The public works did not contain the famine, partly because they did not target the neediest, partly because the average wage paid was too low (McGregor 2004),[4] and partly because the works entailed exposing malnourished and poorly clothed people (mostly men) to the elements during the worst months of the year.

Exasperated by the ineffectiveness and rising cost of 'workfare', and concerned that it was diverting labour from more productive uses in the agricultural sector, early in 1847 the authorities decided to phase out the public works and switch to food aid. The publicly financed soup kitchens which replaced the public works were designed to target those most at risk directly. The food rations were in effect non-transferable and non-storable. They reached three million people daily at their peak in early 1847, an extraordinary bureaucratic feat. Doubts remain about the effectiveness of a diet of thin meal-based gruel on weakened stomachs, but mortality seemed to fall while the soup kitchens operated.

The drop in food prices during the summer of 1847 prompted the authorities in London to treat the famine henceforth as a manageable, local problem. The main burden of relieving the poor was then placed on the workhouses established under the Irish Poor Law of 1838. This meant that the worst hit areas bore the heaviest fiscal burdens. In principle those requiring relief were supposed to pass 'the workhouse test', i.e. refusal to enter the workhouse was deemed evidence of being able to support one's self. In practice, most of the workhouses were ill equipped to meet the demands placed upon them, and in the event about one quarter of all excess famine mortality occurred within their walls. Workhouses in the worst affected unions began to fill up in late 1846, and mortality within their walls rose in tandem. Local histories highlight mismanagement and the impossible burden placed on local taxpayers by the government; and, indeed, the high overall proportion of workhouse deaths due to contagious diseases is an indictment of this form of relief. Several excellent studies of individual workhouses are available. These paint a mainly negative picture of workhouse management, highlighting venality, overcrowding and incompetence. They also demonstrate, however, how risky employment in the workhouse was: a significant proportion of those so employed perished of famine-related diseases (O'Neill 1956; Kinealy 1994; Ó Murchadha 1997).

Measurable yardsticks of union performance are available: a poorly managed union might be one that was relatively late to open, or in which mortality from infectious diseases was relatively high, or in which the overall death rate was relatively high (Guinnane and Ó Gráda 2002b). For instance the workhouse in Enniskillen, County Fermanagh opened on 1 December 1845. Enniskillen, 96th in terms of poor law valuation per head, was only 123rd of 130 to open. The late opening of the workhouse left little time for 'non-crisis' admissions before the famine. Moreover, a high proportion of the Enniskillen dead (about 56–57 per cent) perished from infectious diseases. This meant either that they entered the workhouse in a very bad state, in which case they should have been admitted sooner or catered for elsewhere, or else that they contracted an infectious disease within the workhouse from another inmate. Some workhouse managements sought to segregate the diseased from the healthy; some did not bother. In July 1847 Enniskillen's guardians voted against building a fever hospital, whereupon its medical officer remarked: 'Now that is all over, I have only to say there are 24 persons lying of fever in the house, and the rain is dripping down on them at this moment' (Guinnane et al. 2004: 15). The percentages succumbing to marasmus and dropsy (or what today is called hunger oedema), both famine-related conditions indicating severe malnutrition, were also high in Enniskillen relative to neighbouring and similarly circumstanced unions. Whether inmates succumbing to these diseases acquired them in the workhouse due to inadequate diet, or arrived in a dying state and on the verge of starvation, cannot be known, however. The very high mortality in some workhouses in 1850 and 1851 is evidence of the long-lasting character of the famine in some western areas (Eiríksson 1997a; Ó Murchadha 1998).

Traditional accounts of the famine pit the more humane policies of Sir Robert Peel's Tories against the dogmatic stance of Sir John Russell's Whig administration, which succeeded them. Peel was forced out of office in July 1846 when his party split on the issue of the Corn Laws. The contrast between Peel and Russell oversimplifies. Though Peel was more familiar with Ireland's problems of economic backwardness than Whig ideologues such as the Chancellor of the Exchequer, Charles Wood, the crisis confronting Peel in 1845–6 was mild compared to what was to follow. Moreover, Peel broadly supported the Whig line in opposition, and it was left to his former Tory colleagues to mount a parliamentary challenge against Russell and Wood. It was left to the Tory leader, Lord George Bentinck, to accuse the Whigs of 'holding the truth down', and to predict a time 'when we shall know what the amount of mortality has been'; then, Bentinck added, people could judge 'at its proper value [the Whigs'] management of affairs in Ireland'.

Assessment of the public policy response cannot ignore the apocalyptic character of the crisis that it faced. Nonetheless, the government's obsession with parsimony and its determination to make the Irish pay for 'their' crisis cannot but have increased the death rate. The same goes for the insistence on linking relief with structural reform (for example by making the surrender of all land-holdings a strict condition for relief). At the height of the crisis the policy stance adopted by the Whigs was influenced by Malthusian providentialism – the conviction that the potato blight was a divinely ordained remedy for Irish over-population. The fear that too much kindness would entail a Malthusian lesson not learnt also conditioned both the nature and extent of intervention (Gray 1999). This stance rationalised caution, circumscribed relief, and shifted the responsibility to Irish property owners. Compassion on the part of the British elite was in short supply.

Though Ireland was a highly bureaucratised polity by mid nineteenth-century standards, administrators in Dublin and London still faced the challenge of how best to identify and relieve the destitute in remote areas. Critics of relief could point to many instances of red tape, incompetence and corruption. The case of the workhouses has already been mentioned; cheating and favouritism were also features of the public works and, to a lesser extent, the soup kitchens. On the other hand, the authorities had the benefit of a numerous and able police force and of hard-working and well-informed clergy of all denominations. And relieving officers ensured that many abuses were short lived (Kerr 1996; Ó Gráda 1999: ch. 2).

Demographic consequences

The Irish famine killed about one million people, or one eighth of the entire population. This made it a major famine, relatively speaking, by world-historical standards. In pre-1845 Ireland famines were by no means unknown – those caused by a combination of war and poor harvests in the early 1650s and arctic weather conditions in 1740–1 may have killed as high a share of much smaller populations (Lenihan 1997; Dickson 1998) – but those that struck during the half-century or so before the Great Famine were mini-famines by comparison. The excess death toll of a million is an informed guess, since in the absence of civil registration excess mortality cannot be calculated directly (Mokyr 1985; Boyle and Ó Gráda 1986). The record of deaths in the workhouses and other public institutions is nearly complete, but the recording of other deaths depended on the memory of survivors in households where deaths had taken place. In many homes, of course, death and emigration meant that there were no survivors. The estimate does not include averted births, nor does it allow for famine-related deaths in Britain and further afield (Mokyr 1981; Neal 1998). On the basis of an analysis of a large sample of surviving baptismal registers, Joel Mokyr put the drop in the birth rate at the height of the crisis at one third. Some parish register data from Clare, a badly affected county, suggest that this is not far fetched: in 17 parishes where the surviving records are of good quality, births in 1847–9 were 38 per cent fewer than in 1844–6. The decline was the product of several factors: reduced fecundity, reduced libido, the separation of spouses, and a lower marriage rate.[5]

Within Ireland mortality was regionally very uneven. No part of the island escaped entirely, but the toll ranged from one quarter of the population of some western counties to negligible fractions in Down and Wexford on the east coast. The timing of excess mortality varied too, even in some of the worst hit areas. In west Cork, a notorious black spot, the worst was over by late 1847, but the deadly effects of the famine ranged in Clare until 1850 or even 1851. Infectious diseases – especially typhoid fever, typhus and dysentery/diarrhoea – rather than literal starvation were responsible for the bulk of mortality. By and large, the higher the death toll in a county or province, the higher the proportion of starvation deaths. And while the population of Irish towns and cities rose by 7.3 per cent between 1841 and 1851,[6] that of rural Ireland dropped by nearly a quarter.

Karl Marx was almost right when he claimed that the Irish famine killed 'poor devils only', but many who were not abjectly poor and starving died of famine-related diseases. Medical progress, by shielding the rich from infection, has made subsequent famines even more class-specific. As in most famines, the elderly and the young were most likely to succumb, but women proved more resilient than men. In the six west Cork parishes surveyed by the poor law inspector J. J. Marshall in late 1847 men were 33 per cent more likely to succumb than women. The lower excess death rate of women was due to physiological rather than cultural factors (Hickey 2002: 215–17; Ó Gráda 1999: 101–4; Mokyr and Ó Gráda 2002).[7]

The famine also resulted in emigration on a massive scale. Again precise estimates are impossible. Though the emigrants were also victims of the famine, their departure improved not only their own survival chances, but also those of the majority who remained in Ireland. True, the Atlantic crossing produced its own carnage, particularly in Quebec's Grosse-Isle, but most of those who fled made it safely to the other side. There thus is a sense in which migration was a crude form of disaster relief, and that more public spending on subsidised emigration would have reduced the aggregate famine death toll (Ó Gráda and O'Rourke 1997). Most of those who emigrated relied on their own resources, though some landlords helped through direct subsidies or by relieving those who left of their unpaid rent bills (Norton 2005). For the most part, the landless poor simply could not afford to leave.

While migration saved lives in Ireland, it led to increased mortality across the Irish Sea. In England and Wales mortality was 100,000 above trend in the 1846–8 period: however, its distribution between arrivals from Ireland and natives succumbing to famine diseases is not known. There was also a drop in the birth rate in England and Wales in the late 1840s, indicating that the crisis was not solely an import from John Bull's Other Island. In Scotland, virtually all the excess mortality was in the cities. In Glasgow burials doubled in 1847. This might be seen as the result of the influx of destitute Highlanders, but immigration into Glasgow from Ireland easily exceeded that from the Highlands. So the Irish famine may also have been mainly responsible for the fever deaths causing excess mortality in Scotland (Neal 1998; Ó Gráda 1999: 112–13).

Whether migration relieves or exacerbates famine depends on the context. In nineteenth century India a rise in migration was seen as one of the surest symptoms of famine, and in Bengal in 1943 mass migration into the cities indicated that 'the famine [was] out of control' (Famine Inquiry Commission 1945: 2). In the Bengali case, migration may have made an already serious crisis worse; in Ireland, however, migration was both symptom and palliative.

A hierarchy of suffering

Like all famines, the Irish famine produced its hierarchy of suffering. The rural poor, landless or near landless, were most likely to perish, and the earliest victims were in that category. Farmers found their effective land endowment reduced, since their holdings could no longer yield the same quantity of potatoes as before. They also faced increased labour costs, forcing them to reduce their concentration on tillage. Between 1847 and the early 1850s hundreds of thousands of smallholders and landless or semi-landless labourers were evicted by hard (and sometimes hard-pressed) landlords and by unsentimental land agents. Proprietors employed bailiffs to carry out the evictions and demolish cabins, while the police stood by (O'Neill 2000). Thus it is hardly surprising that although the recorded labour force fell by nearly one fifth between 1841 and 1851, the number of bailiffs rose by over one third (see chapter 11 below).

Landlords' rental income plummeted by as much one-third while the crisis lasted, while their outlays on poor relief rose. Naturally, historians have linked the high bankruptcy rate of landowners in the wake of the famine to these pressures: in the words of one, 'up to one quarter of all land changed hands as a result of famine-induced bankruptcy among landowners' (Proudfoot 1995: 43). A corollary is that landlords who were spared were too impoverished to buy up the properties that came on the market in the wake of the crisis, leaving the way open to *nouveau riche* shopkeepers and lawyers. These arguments contain a strong element of *post hoc ergo propter hoc*. In reality most of the sales processed through the Incumbered Estates Court from 1849 on were of estates so financially embarrassed that debts accruing from the famine can have accounted but for a small fraction of the total. Alas, the proprietors of such estates were poorly equipped to help their tenants when the famine struck (see chapter 3 below; also Ó Gráda 1999: 128–9).

It is natural to focus on agriculture and on the countryside, but no sector of the economy was unscathed. Banks had to cope with bad debts and massive withdrawals of deposits. Retail sales declined. Pawnbrokers found their pledges being unredeemed as the crisis worsened. Least affected were those businesses and their work forces who relied on foreign markets for their raw materials and their sales. Many clergymen, medical practitioners, poor law officials, and others in contact with the poor paid the ultimate price, dying of infectious diseases.

The relative impact of the famine on different occupational groups may be inferred from comparing the 1841 and 1851 censuses. The overall decline in the labour force was 19.1 per cent. There were 14.4 per cent fewer farmers, and 24.2 per cent fewer farm labourers. Not surprisingly, given their vulnerability, the number of physicians and surgeons dropped by 25.3 per cent. The small number of coffin makers (8 in 1841, 22 in 1851) is a reminder that during the famine most coffins were not made by specialist coffin makers. It is difficult to identify any significant class of 'winners' in the 1840s, though the census indicates increases in the numbers of millers and bakers, of barristers and attorneys, and of bailiffs and rate collectors. The huge fall in the numbers of spinners and weavers was partly a consequence of the famine, partly due to other causes (Ó Gráda 1999: ch. 4; 2001a).

The famine was also very uneven regionally. Its impact on Ireland's metropolis is worth brief consideration. Dublin's population of 250,000 people contained a large underclass of desperately poor people, but their diet was more varied and less dependent on the Lumper potato (an inferior, tasteless variety) than that of the rural poor. Yet at the height of the famine Dublin was far from the 'brightly lit, comparatively well fed, slightly neutral country' imagined long ago by the economists Patrick Lynch and John Vaizey (1960). Several sources – burial records, census evidence, religious records, poor law registers – imply excess mortality in Dublin, and not only of unfortunate country people seeking work and relief. Moreover, all creeds were affected: burials in the Society of Friends graveyard in Cork Street rose from an average of 14 in 1841–6 to 25 in 1847–51. Yet the excess death rate in Dublin was but a fraction of that in the west coast (Ó Gráda 1999: ch. 5).

Famine and food markets

Bertolt Brecht once wrote that famines don't just happen; they are organised by the grain trade (cited in Drèze and Sen 1989: 93). In Ireland in the late 1840s many poor people doubtless believed that the determination of traders or producers to corner markets or to extract higher prices exacerbated the famine. However, an analysis of price data suggests that at least at wholesale level markets worked more or less as normal. Nor does the evidence of sales at Cork's potato markets support the belief that during the famine traders held back a higher-than-normal proportion of output earlier in the season (Ó Gráda 1999: 134–56; compare Ó Gráda 2005). That is not to say that supplies responded to price signals like clockwork. On the contrary, merchants responded cautiously to the challenge of finding substitute foods (mainly maize) for the potato, and – crucially – the government refused to step into the breach in the interim. However, as Amartya Sen (1981: 160) reminds us, 'the law stands between food availability and food entitlement. Starvation deaths can reflect legality with a vengeance'. Alas, for those stripped of subsistence by the blight, the functioning of food markets was somewhat of a red herring.

Table 1.2, based on a table in an important paper by Peter Solar, is a stark reminder of the point that markets worked slowly. Comparing the two periods, 1840–5 and 1846–50, captures the fall in production but also suggests that imports largely made up for the shortfall in production. However, this ignores the lag between the failures of the potato in 1845 and 1846 (and the accompanying reduction in grain acreage) and the arrival of large quantities of imports of Indian corn in the spring of 1847. Treating the 1846–50 period as a block muffles the grave supply problems in 1846–7 in particular (Solar 1989b; Ó Gráda 1994a: 200–1). During the famine Ireland switched from being one of

Table 1.2 **Irish food supplies, 1840–5 and 1846–50 (in 1,000 kcal/day)**

	1840–5	*1846–50*
Irish production (less seed and horses)	32.1	15.7
Less imports and non-food uses	–11.8	–3.1
Net domestic supplies	20.3	12.6
Plus exports	+0.2	+5.5
Total consumption	20.5	18.1

Source: Ó Gráda (1994a: 2000) after Solar (1989b: 123)

Britain's bread-baskets to being a net importer of food-grains. However, in the winter and spring of 1846–7 exports still exceeded imports, presumably because the poor in Ireland lacked the purchasing power to buy the wheat and oats that were being shipped out.

Post-famine adjustment

The Great Irish Famine was not just a watershed in Irish history, but also a major event in global history, with far-reaching and enduring economic and political consequences. In the 1840s the Irish cataclysm dwarfed anything occurring elsewhere in Europe. Nothing like it would happen in Ireland again. Individual memories of the famine, coupled with 'collective memory' of the event in later years, influenced the political culture of both Ireland and Irish-America, and indeed still play a role (Cullen 1997; Donnelly 2001; Ó Gráda 2001a). The blight's damage was long-lasting too: although the introduction of new potato varieties offered some respite against *Phytophthora infestans* in the post-famine decades, no reliable defence would be found against it until the 1890s.

The famine brought the era of famines in Ireland to a brutal end. Serious failures of the potato in the early 1860s and late 1870s, also due to potato blight, brought privation in the west of the country, but no significant excess mortality. Ireland thus does not lend much support to the claim advanced by Jane Menken and Susan Watkins that famines typically create a demographic vacuum that is quickly filled. Other famines, it is true, seem to fit such a model, but in Ireland in only a few remote and tiny pockets in the west did population fill the vacuum left by the 'Great Hunger', and then only very briefly (Watkins and Menken 1985; Ó Gráda 1994a: 190; Guinnane 1997).

What of the Irish famine's long-term economic impact? The relative importance of crops in agricultural output dropped sharply in its wake. Crops accounted for nearly two thirds of net output in 1840–5, but less than a quarter in 1876 and only one seventh in 1908 (Ó Gráda 1993: 57, 154). The famine resulted in higher living standards for survivors, since it increased the bargaining power of labour. Any negative impact on landlords' income from a declining population was more than compensated for by the relative increase in the prices of land-intensive output, the disappearance of thousands of uneconomic holdings, and the prompter payment of rents due. Higher emigration was another by-product of the famine, as the huge outflow of the crisis years generated its own 'friends and neighbours' dynamic. The late Raymond Crotty, an agricultural economist, claimed in a classic contribution that most of these changes would have taken place in any case, famine or no famine: the disaster only accelerated structural and demographic shifts already in train. So did the famine 'matter' in the long run? Kevin O'Rourke submitted Crotty's hypothesis to computable general equilibrium analysis in 1991, and found it wanting: the main reason being the profound impact of *Phytophthora infestans* on the pasture/tillage balance in Irish agriculture. O'Rourke's simulations suggested that had the potato remained healthy, but allowing for exogenous price shocks and an annual one per cent rise in real wages, by 1870 agricultural employment would have fallen by two per cent instead of the actual 45 per cent, and potato output would have risen marginally instead of plummeting by four fifths (Crotty 1966; O'Rourke 1991a). Thus the famine, far from being a mere catalyst, was a watershed event in nineteenth-century Irish history.

In the early 1980s, one eminent Irish historian claimed that 'even the scale of the great famine was not unique when seen in the context of contemporary European experience'. That was just before a burgeoning historiography began to reassert the cataclysmic dimensions of the Irish famine. Modern research comes closer to supporting instead Amartya Sen's surmise that '[in] no other famine in the world [was] the proportion of people killed . . . as large as in the Irish famines in the 1840s' (Boyce 1982: 170; Sen 1995a). During the 1990s research into the Irish famine, prompted in part by sesquicentennial commemorations, reached unprecedented levels. Scores of monographs and articles were published, many of them of high quality (for surveys see Ó Gráda 1996; Daly 2005). These included several excellent studies of the crisis at local level (e.g. O'Neill 1997; Eiríksson 1997a, 1998; Ó Murchadha 1998; Hickey 2002).

Several issues require further investigation, however. For instance, whether or not the famine led to the decline of certain native industries by reducing the domestic market remains a moot point (Whelan 1999). The long-run impact of the famine on the health of survivors conceived or born during or in the wake of the famine is another un-researched topic. The topic has provoked a good deal of research on better-documented and more recent famines. A study of cohorts born before, during, and after the Great Finnish famine of 1866–8 finds that apart from those aged 0–17 years, mortality was identical in the famine born cohorts and in the cohorts born before and after the crisis. However, research on other, more recent famines argues differently. Thus, it has been claimed on the basis of Dutch evidence from the Hunger Winter of 1944–5 that women whose mothers were malnourished stand a greater chance of becoming overweight in middle age, and that the children of women who were pregnant during the famine are more likely to develop late-onset diabetes. Another Dutch study finds that women exposed to hunger as children during the Hunger Winter stood a higher risk of breast cancer later in life. The authors do not know why, but speculate that the famine might have disturbed hormonal balance in young females (compare Lumey 1998). The Leningrad siege-famine of 1941–3 had a striking impact on the height of the city's surviving children (who presumably were healthier at birth than those who died). Boys aged between 10 and 13 years in 1945 were about 8 cm smaller than boys of the same age in 1939; the gap for girls was less, but still substantial. Similarly, people born in Germany in the semi-famine conditions following the Second World War are smaller than those born either before or after. One study of male Leningraders suggests that living through the siege increased the risk of high blood pressure, heart disease and strokes, while a second found no link between intrauterine malnutrition and 'glucose intolerance, hypertension, or cardiovascular disease in adulthood', but seemed to corroborate the connection between foetal starvation and obesity in later life (Kozlov and Samsonova 2005; Khoroshinina 2005; Greil 1998). Finally, modern clinical research into the impact of extreme malnutrition *in utero* and early in life on behavioural and intellectual impairment caused the medical historian Margaret Crawford (1989: 203) to speculate whether infant and child survivors of the Irish famine 'failed to fulfil their full intellectual prowess'. None of these studies addresses this extremely sensitive issue. Just as the implications of recent research into Gulf War syndrome have implications for our understanding of the consequences of survivors of earlier wars, medical-historical analysis into the long-run consequences of famine may alter our understanding of the human cost of famines – including, by implication, Ireland's Great Famine – in the past.

CHAPTER TWO

Poor and getting poorer? Living standards in Ireland before the famine

CO-AUTHORED WITH JOEL MOKYR

The definition of the 'unit' of analysis in economic history is usually deter-mined by politics. The economic history of France, for example, is written in terms of the modern political 'hexagon', and regional history in general in terms of administrative, data-producing units. By the same token, look at the 'English' or 'British' economy because it was comparatively integrated, formed a well-defined political unit, shared a legal, fiscal, and monetary structure, and produced statistical evidence which allows us to write its economic history in macro-economic terms. The advantages and difficulties of this approach are well known (see e.g. Pollard 1973). But if politics defines the unit, rates such as the standard of living debate during the industrial revolution in Britain should take into account the creation of the United Kingdom in 1800. Yet the debate lost is always written in British terms.

By 1845, about 31 per cent of the population of the United Kingdom lived in Ireland. The last tariff barriers between the two islands had been removed in 1826; the vast bulk of Irish exports went to Britain; capital and labour were free to move between the two countries and they had a common currency after 1826. Ireland shared in Britain's business cycles, and progress sectors such as transport and banking were along British lines. British industrialisation increased the demand for Irish agricultural produce and Irish labour, and at the same time prompted the decline of Irish cottage industries. Ireland's contribution to Britain was also of importance. The roles played by Irish food supplies in the British industrial revolution and Irish immigrant workers as the 'shock troops' of the factory system have been amply documented (see for instance Thomas 1985; Pollard 1973; Williamson 1986).

What happened to living standards in Ireland in the half century or so before the famine? The question should be of interest to students of the British industrial revolution simply because Ireland and Britain were part of same eco-nomy at the time. A rise in living standards in Britain alone is enough to clinch the interpretation of events. If the rise came at the expense of Ireland, for example, the optimistic conclusion might stem from the artificial division of the United Kingdom economy into a successful part (Britain) and an unsuccessful part (Ireland). Little is known about the changes in Irish living standards in this period, however. It is this issue that this essay proposes to consider.

Between 1790 and 1845, Ireland and Britain shared some of the factors likely to affect the standard of living. Both countries experienced rapid population growth: Ireland's rate of growth for the period 1750–1845 (1.3 per cent) exceeded that of Britain (1.0 per cent), although in the last two or three decades of the period Irish population growth slowed down and dipped below that in Britain (Mokyr and Ó Gráda 1984). The two economies were subject to similar weather patterns, and to the shocks to supply caused by the disruption of international trade and high taxes during the Napoleonic wars. After 1815 cereal producers in both parts benefited from the Corn Laws.

Yet the differences clearly overshadow the similarities. A few enclaves apart, Ireland experienced nothing like an industrial revolution. It remained a largely rural society, in which (with a few exceptions such as Belfast and Lisburn) towns failed to grow, performing primarily administrative and commercial functions. It was, above all, an agricultural economy catering for its own growing population and for the rapidly increasing British market. Changes in the terms of trade of agricultural to industrial goods were thus likely to affect the two economies in opposite directions. Migration from Ireland into Britain, too, affected living standards in both countries, though it is not quite clear in which direction. They do, however, complicate the question of exactly whose living standards are being discussed. Clearly, a rise in the living standards of British workers need not have implied a similar rise across the water.[1] It is even conceivable that some of the gains attained by English workers were at the expense of the Irish; or that, at least in some periods, increasing prosperity in Britain was accompanied by declining living standards in Ireland.

The source material on living standards in Ireland is even sparser than that for Britain. There is no hope of constructing an Irish real wage series similar to Lindert and Williamson's recent reconstruction of British real wages.[2] The absence of reliable real wage series is one reason to search for alternative indicators of living standards. Another is that the Irish labour force in 1845 still consisted primarily of self-employed workers in agriculture and rural industry, or workers who were paid for their labour services in allotments of small plots. Except for the urban and well-to-do, most of the Irish grew their own food, provided their own fuel, and often were close to self-sufficiency in clothing and housing. A real wage series produced by dividing a nominal wage series by some price index would capture living standards of labour markets which were highly competitive or in which, at least, the wedges between different segments remained constant. But factor markets were far from perfect; custom, ignorance and violence saw to that. Nor did the correlation between cash earnings in formal labour markets and implicit income in the quasi-subsistence sector necessarily stay constant over time. On the one hand labour markets became more efficient as labour became more mobile, which would have tended to increase the correlation. On the other hand, however, the decline of cottage industries resulting from the rise of the factory system tended to reduce it.

The alternative measures of living standards proposed in this essay are imperfect substitutes for good real wage or personal income data. If wage indices are open to the criticism that they focus too much on adult workers only, our measures, taken singly, cannot escape the charge of incomplete coverage. Thus the subjective index of impoverishment presented in section I below can be calculated for each of Ireland's 32 counties, but refers only to the poor, or the bottom half or so of the population. In section II we utilise consumption data of sugar, tea, and tobacco, which (with the possible exception of tobacco) capture trends in middle- and upper-class living standards only. In section III we use data on human capital formation and related proxies, which may have a wider coverage but still suffer from a variety of limitations. Nevertheless, taken together these measures suggest a coherent story which is that neither a Malthusian horror tale nor a rosy revisionist view regarding the Irish economy as a rapidly developing entity does justice to a complex reality. The Irish poor almost certainly grew poorer during the half century or so before the famine, but overall average incomes probably rose. This implies a sharpening of the inequality of income distribution.

I

The impressions of informed contemporaries and knowledgeable travellers such as Young, Beaumont, Kohl, Foster, Inglis, Tocqueville and Curwen usually loom large in histories of pre-famine Ireland. Though often vivid and telling, there is reason to be somewhat wary of such testimonies, even when they come from the most intelligent of men.[3] Hidden bias, lack of information, disagreements, and differences in coverage and implicit standards used in measuring economic welfare make such sources hard to use. Yet there exists at least one such source for Ireland which seems relatively free from these drawbacks. The body appointed by Parliament in 1835 to investigate the state of the Irish poor – the so-called Poor Inquiry Commissioners – sent out hundreds of copies of a questionnaire which included the following series of questions: 'Is the general condition of the poorer classes in your parish improved, deteriorated, or stationary, since the peace, in the year 1815, and in what respects? Is the population of the parish increasing or diminishing?'[4] The respondents were respected Catholic and Protestant clergymen, magistrates, land agents, and others likely to be familiar with, and report honestly on, local conditions.

In most cases the respondents replied in some detail, their answers revealing substantial variation, ranging from 'much improved' to 'much deteriorated'. Most respondents thought that the situation of the poor had deteriorated, but a determined minority took a more optimistic view and insisted that living standards had been improving. Among the pessimists, explanations of the deterioration varied wildly. Some pointed to the decline in agricultural prices, others to the crisis in weaving and spinning. A number of witnesses took a distinctly Malthusian view, claiming that the 'poorer classes have not their resources increased in proportion to the increase in numbers'.[5]

What proportion of the population of Ireland do these responses refer to? What proportion was considered 'poor'? The definition of 'poor' was not rigorously laid down by the commissioners, and they must have held differing views about where the poverty line should be drawn. A lower bound of three out of over eight million people would include those who relied almost exclusively on the potato for food, and those eventually judged by the commissioners themselves to be potential claimants for relief (Bourke, 1968). Other sources indicate a higher proportion. Take, for instance, farm size. On the eve of the famine, 55 per cent of all Irish landholders held farms of fewer than 10 acres and another 20 per cent of farms were between 10 and 20 acres (Mokyr 1985: 19). Since thousands of the rural poor held no land at all, an upper bound of 60 per cent or more could be defended. Such a figure finds support in the 1841 census division of families into those 'depending on their own manual labour', those who depended on 'the direction of labour', and those with 'vested means, professions, etc.' In the country as a whole, the first category accounted for 62.9 per cent of the total.[6] A safe middle ground would be the lower half of the income distribution.

In order to utilise the information systematically, we have converted the opinions expressed in the replies into a measure which we call the Subjective Impoverishment Index (SII). The index is derived from the unweighted scores of the opinions expressed by the respondents using the following scoring system:

much deteriorated: -2; deteriorated: -1; stationary or unchanged: 0; improved: +1; much improved: +2. The index thus measures improvement, as perceived by the respondents, directly. The higher the index, the more the countries' poor improved their condition (see also Mokyr 1985: 12). The explanations and analyses provided by some of the respondents were not used here. Nor were all responses used: some respondents, for example, stated that they had not lived in their parish long enough to make a statement about conditions 20 years before. Out of a total of 1,590 witnesses, the index utilised 1,394 responses. The average score of Ireland as a whole was negative: -0.43. A total of 752 witnesses expressed a pessimistic (deteriorated or much deteriorated) opinion, as against 324 who stated that economic conditions had improved or much improved. The index thus implies that after Waterloo, when British real wages began their alleged upward movement, the lot of the Irish was seen as having worsened.

Table 2.1 **Values of the Subjective Impoverishment Index and numbers of witnesses**

County	Number of witnesses	SII	County	Number of witnesses	SII
Antrim	79	-0.52	Carlow	27	-0.11
Armagh	46	-0.56	Dublin	32	-0.44
Cavan	33	-0.36	Kildare	30	-0.23
Donegal	65	-0.83	Kilkenny	41	-0.61
Down	109	-0.78	King's	36	-0.22
Fermanagh	28	-0.29	Longford	20	-0.85
Londonderry	48	-0.52	Louth	22	-0.91
Monaghan	36	-0.72	Meath	52	-0.15
Tyrone	55	-0.84	Queen's	38	-0.08
ULSTER	499	-0.65	Westmeath	40	-0.28
			Wexford	27	+0.22
			Wicklow	27	+0.22
Clare	29	-0.18	LEINSTER	392	-0.27
Cork	158	-0.18			
Kerry	30	-0.03	Galway	48	-0.25
Limerick	49	-0.41	Leitrim	17	-0.29
Tipperary	66	-0.27	Mayo	43	-1.02
Waterford	19	-0.32	Roscommon	29	-0.69
MUNSTER	351	-0.22	Sligo	15	-0.93
			CONNACHT	152	-0.62
IRELAND	1,394	-0.43			

Source: See text.

The geographical pattern of the scores reported in table 2.1 is also of interest. The SII scores are not equivalent to, or even strongly correlated with, poverty as such. Connacht, by general agreement the poorest province in Ireland, scores poorly, but Ulster, by all measures far less poor than Connacht or even Munster, seems to have suffered a sharper decline in its standard of living in these years. The Leinster textile counties of Louth and Longford also fared badly. The index thus reflects, as it should, the economic *changes* affecting the living standards of the poor between 1815 and 1835, and not necessarily the *levels* of poverty at the end of the period. But what were these changes? To establish the factors determining the changes in living standards, we utilise multivariate regression analysis on the county level, regressing the index on four types of exogenous variables: a variable measuring absolute living standards in about 1840; a variable measuring the importance of cottage industry; a variable measuring the proportion of small farms; and a variable measuring the type of agriculture practiced. The results are reported in table 2.2.

A number of conclusions follow from table 2.2. First, since the regressions were run to detect patterns and not to test a precise model, the specification seems adequate with F-statistics above the critical value at a 1 per cent level of significance (4.11). Second, the variables Income and Proportion Class III families (manual labourers) perform poorly, with inconsistent signs and high standard errors (low t-statistics), a reminder that on the county level being poor and immiseration were separate and distinct phenomena.[7] Third, the prevalence of cottage industry had a definite effect on changes in well-being as measured by our index. Regardless of which proxy was used, a negative relation emerged between its relative importance and the index.[8] Fourth, agricultural structure, to the extent that we could approximate it, also had a distinct effect: counties with high ratios of livestock per rural worker experienced a smaller decline in well-being, while counties which grew more potatoes (and thus, in all likelihood, had more land under arable) in 1841 experienced a sharper deterioration in the economic condition of their labouring classes. Fifth, farm size had a distinct effect: a higher proportion of small farms is clearly associated with a sharper decline. The data suggest that the critical threshold size was about twenty acres, since the effect weakens when the threshold size is reduced.[9] These results are as expected, and confirm the hypothesis that the decline of cottage industries and the proliferation of small farms were major factors in the decline in living standards in Ireland in the pre-famine decades. Attempts to find a direct nexus between population growth in the period 1821 to 1841 and the SII indicate a positive but weak relation. Here, too, simultaneous equations bias is likely to

Table 2.2 **Regression analysis of Subjective Impoverishment Index[a] (t-statistics in parentheses)**

	1	2	3	4	5	6
Constant	−.21	.73	1.24	.32	1.07	.72
	(−.41)	(1.40)	(2.07)	(.20)	(1.73)	(.95)
Income[b]	−.043		−.18		.028	
	(−.81)		(−.48)		(.71)	
Prop. Class III families[c]		.70		−.81		−1.771
		(1.15)		(−1.42)		(−2.39)
Rural textile workersd			−1.14	−1.29		
			(−2.18)	(−2.40)		
Prop. non-agr.[e]				−1.02	−1.49	
				(−1.88)	(−2.31)	
Prop. spinners[f]	−.0065	−.0053				
	(−2.13)	(−1.87)				
Prop. small farms[g]		−1.38	−1.30		−1.57	
		(−2.65)	(−2.54)		(−3.26)	
Prop. tiny farms[h]	−.43			−.87		−.93
	(−.72)			(−1.61)		(−1.68)
Livestock per capita[i]	.19			.17		.20
	(2.32)			(2.31)		(3.00)
Percentage in potatoes[j]		−2.13	−2.18		−2.04	
		(−2.04)	(−2.00)		(−1.84)	
F-statistic	4.84	5.65	6.17	5.85	5.67	5.70
d.f.	4, 27	4, 27	4, 27	4, 27	4, 27	4, 27

Notes and sources:
a SII is the dependent variable in all regressions. The estimation uses weighted least squares to correct for heteroscedasticity, with population used as the weighting factor.
b Revised income estimates, as described in Mokyr (1985)
c Percentage of all families subsisting by their own manual labour, as reported in *Census of Ireland*, 1841 (PP 1843, xxiv).
d Defined as the proportion of rural women defining themselves as 'ministering to clothing', as reported in *Census of Ireland*, 1841, p. 435.
e Defined as the proportion of families who were chiefly employed in 'Manufacturing, trade, etc' according to *Census of Ireland*, 1841, p. 433.
f Defined as the proportion of employed women whose occupation was spinning flax, wool, cotton, or unspecified material, according to *Census of Ireland*, 1841.
g Defined as the proportion of farms under 20 acres.
h Defined as the proportion of farms under 5 acres computed from the *Report from the commissioners of inquiry on the occupation of land*, pp. 280–3.
i Defined as the value of livestock per rural inhabitant, *Census of Ireland*, 1841.
j Defined as proportion of total land under cultivation under potatoes in 1845. See Mokyr (1981).

be present insofar as perceived changes in economic conditions affected demographic variables, especially emigration and the propensity to marry. By and large the behaviour of the SII seems better explained by factors related to the interaction of Ireland with the British economy than by demographic growth.

To repeat, our index captures changes in the living standards of the poorer classes, as perceived by contemporaries. The results indicate a definite perceived deterioration of the condition of the poorer classes between 1815 and 1835. This deterioration was associated with identifiable exogenous forces operating on the Irish economy such as the decline of cottage industries and the proliferation of smallholdings. In and by itself, however, the SII is not sufficient to justify conclusions about trends in living standards.

II

How do pessimistic implications of the SII square with other evidence? Another indicator of pre-famine living conditions is import data on certain goods not produced in Ireland: tea, sugar and tobacco. The idea that the consumption of these goods, properly adjusted to account for relative prices and population growth, can be used as an indirect indication of living standards is hardly new. For example, in about 1830 Daniel O'Connell wrote: 'there is not one article the consumption of which tends more to health and comfort than sugar. Every person who can afford to do so consumes as much sugar as he conveniently can . . . [its] consumption increases with wealth; its diminution is the most decisive proof of poverty'.[10] In 1854 Jonathan Pim claimed that tea consumption offered 'perhaps the very best criterion of the capability of the middle and lower classes to obtain the comforts of life . . . [offering] a striking illustration of the condition of the people' (Pim 1855–6: 23–4). Writers and historians concerned with living standards in Ireland have used data on consumption with somewhat mixed results.[11] There are serious objections against using such data, but their strengths should not be neglected either. First, because sugar and tea were available only as imports, they provide a reasonable approximation of consumption to the extent that the import statistics can be believed. The domestic cultivation of tobacco was prohibited by an act of Parliament in 1660. The prohibition was relaxed in 1779 and reimposed in 1831. In between, some quantities were grown locally, but they are likely to have been small.[12] Second, price data are available for these goods, so that some rough inferences concerning changes in real income can be made from the consumption series. The procedure requires, of course, some reasonable assumptions about the income elasticities involved. Before we can use these consumption data to assess changes in living standards, we will briefly discuss the extent to which these goods were consumed in Ireland and comment on the quality of the data.

Most authorities agree that tobacco smoking was widespread in Ireland before the famine and not limited to the upper classes alone.[13] Indeed, its use seems to have been already quite common by the mid-seventeenth century (Williams 1981: 40–1; Cullen 1981: 149–50, 175–6; MacLysaght 1950: 10, 78). Tea, on the other hand, had to wait until the second half of the nineteenth century to become a truly popular drink.[14] Consumption of legally imported tobacco in the decade 1790–9 averaged 5.057 million lb in Ireland or about 1.09 lb per caput. In England and Wales, by way of comparison, legal imports averaged 10.1 million lb or 1.15 lb per caput, which is thus quite close to the Irish figure. As late as 1840–5, Irish legal imports were 0.65 lb per caput, compared to 0.94 lb for England. On the other hand, British legal imports of sugar and tea retained for home consumption exceeded those of Ireland by a factor of about three. Consumption of tea per caput in Ireland was 0.66 lb in 1790–9, compared to 1.81 lb in Britain; the consumption of sugar per caput was 5.8 lb and 14.7 lb respectively.[15] The pre-1815 sugar import series are especially shaky, but data for a later year show a similar gap. In 1825 imports per caput were 6.7 lb in Ireland and 19.7 lb in Britain. These figures are lent some support by the occupational statistics of the 1841 census, which suggest that tea-drinking in Ireland was considerably less widespread than coking or the consumption of goods using sugar. The number of tea-dealers was small, and almost half of them were located in the cities. The entire province of Connacht, by all accounts the poorest and most backward, had none at all.

While the geographical distribution of confectioners and tobacconists was far from uniform, demand for them seems to have existed even in the remotest and least commercialised parts of Ireland. Thus, a good tobacco consumption series would contain more information about the standard of living of most Irish than would a tea series of the same quality, while the sugar series seems in that respect to be in between. Unfortunately, precisely because of its mass consumption, tobacco was heavily taxed and therefore smuggled on a large scale. Hence the unadjusted sugar and tea consumption series are a truer reflection of the situation in these decades. The import series suffer from serious weaknesses, however. The first is that completion of the customs union between Ireland and Great Britain in the late 1820s meant an end to separate import statistics.

Two exceptions to this rule are the series for tobacco and the 1835 data collected by the Drummond (or Railway) Commission.[16]

A second concern, raised by Johnson, is that some Irish imports came duty paid via England, and were thus counted as British rather than Irish consumption.[17] If these tea imports were 'a significant and rising proportion of the beverage consumed within Ireland', as he suggests, the published series would be biased in the pessimist direction. Throughout the pre-famine period most Irish tea was imported by Dublin merchants through Britain, where it was entered as re-exports to Ireland. While the duty could be paid in Britain and the tea then imported to Ireland duty paid, it is difficult to believe that this was widespread.[18] A further potential bias in the consumption data concerns changes in the quality of the goods. Imports were entered by weight, so that any improvements in quality would tend to underestimate the amount of 'effective' imports. The changes in quality present a particular difficulty with tobacco. By the middle of the nineteenth century a substantial amount of tobacco was entered dried, so as to avoid the payment of duty on water (duties were charged per pound). Moreover, the manufacturers increasingly tended to import tobacco with the stalk stripped, because the stalk was less valuable. Johnson estimates that tobacco imports in 1840 represented 13 per cent more tobacco per pound than in 1800. The first half of the century also witnessed an increase in 'adulteration' by adding sugar to the tobacco (apparently this flavouring was demanded by the Irish customers). Since sugar was far cheaper pound for pound, this meant less smoking value per pound, offsetting in part the drying and stalking processes described above. The net quality improvement may have been in the order of 8 to 10 per cent *in toto*. These changes first appear around 1808 and their impact increased gradually thereafter.[19] Thus, each pound of tobacco imported by 1850 represented more smoking material than in 1800. This quality change would introduce a downward bias, because the quality of tobacco in efficiency units was growing faster than the measured volume of imports. Improvement in the physical quality of the goods, however, should have been reflected in higher prices because the quality improvement was due not to technological change but to added foreign value. Insofar as this happened, the bias would be offset. The ensuing higher price paid for tobacco would be regarded by our procedure (which ignores quality changes) as a supply shift. An upward shift in the supply curve, *given* the quantity consumed, would then be interpreted as an increase in income. For a given quantity of imports, a rise in price implies a rise in income, and so the net bias resulting depends on the own price elasticity. If that elasticity equals unity, and quality change is fully reflected in the price, the bias is zero. If the own price elasticity is less than one the bias will be proportional to the income elasticity and the distance of the own price elasticity from minus one.[20] Without more analysis of the tobacco market, it is not possible to say how much of the improvement in quality was reflected by prices.

The size of the bias imparted to the reported import series depends on how much of it was translated into higher prices and what the elasticities were. If, for example, the income elasticity was 1.0 and the own price elasticity -0.5, the bias imparted to the upward trend is 4 to 5 per cent if the quality changes were fully reflected in prices and 8 to 10 per cent if they were not reflected in prices at all. If the income elasticity was as low as 0.5, the bias would be 8 to 10 per cent and 16 to 20 per cent respectively; a sufficiently high price elasticity could produce a bias in the other direction.

The most obvious objection against using import data as an indicator of consumption is the existence of smuggling. Tea and tobacco smuggling were widespread in the eighteenth century, when high levels of government spending were financed from custom revenues. After the tariff reform of 1784, tea smuggling largely ceased (Cullen 1968–9: 156). The history of tobacco smuggling is more complex. Tariffs were repeatedly raised during the period 1790–1845. The ratio of duty to price in bond climbed from about 3.6 in 1800 to 5.7 in 1820 and 7.9 in 1840.[21] As a result of the high duties, tobacco smuggling remained very intensive both in Ireland and in Britain until the middle of the nineteenth century. For our present purposes what matters, however, is not so much the level of smuggling as changes in the proportion of consumption entering through illicit channels. If that proportion was rising, our estimates of implied living standards would be biased towards a pessimistic conclusion.[22] Yet because tobacco is the only continuous series spanning our period, it seems worthwhile to try to correct this flaw in the data.

The rising tariff on tobacco was one factor stimulating the smuggling trade. Yet the proportion of imports smuggled in depended on other factors as well. The degree of tariff enforcement intensified with the strong naval presence after 1792, and the establishment of an effective coastguard service after 1822. The proportion of tobacco smuggled probably peaked in the early 1790s, but then levelled off for a time (Cullen 1968–9: 171–2).[23] During the height of the Napoleonic wars it picked up again, peaking in the half decade after Waterloo, but Cullen maintains that the establishment of the coastguard 'halted the upward trend' at about 1820. Other factors which affected smuggling also tended to operate in opposite directions. For instance, any increase in demand due to population growth or rising incomes tended, all other things being equal, to reduce the proportion of tobacco smuggled in. On the other hand, an increase in the world price (in bond) would tend to increase the proportion smuggled in. Finally, as the opportunities to engage in smuggling decreased after 1815, the supply price of resources devoted to smuggling could have fallen, leading to a rise in the smuggling of tobacco.

The data available for legal imports can be used to estimate the proportion of tobacco smuggled into a country.[24] Throughout the period, tobacco was imported simultaneously by smugglers and merchants using the legal channels. If we assume that the goods imported in both ways were identical and sold at the same price, and that the supply of legal tobacco was infinitely elastic at the world price plus the tariff, while the supply of smuggled goods was equal to the world price plus a mark-up reflecting the returns to the resources used in smuggling, we can estimate the amount smuggled in.

The equation which allows us to do this is that which by definition equates the total amount smuggled with the quantity demanded less the amount imported legally. If we can estimate the shifts of the demand function, changes in the amount smuggled in can be obtained by subtraction. The demand curve shifts, however, with changes in income. To check what happened to the proportion smuggled, we made a number of assumptions about the movement of income over time, and we report the upper and lower bounds.[25] The assumptions and resulting estimates show that the proportion of tobacco smuggled varied between 29 and 40 per cent in the early 1790s, fell sharply in the mid-1790s, and rose gradually until the end of the Napoleonic wars. Precisely as Cullen inferred from qualitative sources, our series indicate a rapid increase in smuggling after 1815, reaching a peak in the years 1819-21, after which the proportion smuggled in fell slowly though it remained close to one half on the eve of the famine.

Irish population grew at about 1.5 per cent per annum between 1790 and 1821, and at about 0.9 per cent between 1821 and 1841. Any growth in total consumption that differed radically from these rates should be due either to changes in relative prices, to changes in 'income' (whether money income or not), or to changes in taste. To allow for price changes the data can be transformed into a residual growth rate, which is the difference between the actual rate of growth of consumption and that predicted on the basis of population growth, changes in prices, and postulated demand elasticities.[26] The residual is calculated from the formulae:

$$R = c_i - \hat{c}_i \qquad [1]$$
$$\hat{c}_i = e(Pi/Pi - P/P) + n \qquad [2]$$

Ireland's Great Famine

where R = the residual, measured as a proportional rate of change; c_i = consumption of the good, measured as a proportional rate of change; $\hat{c}_i$ = the predicted rate of change of consumption of good i; e is the own price elasticity of the good; P_i is the money price of the good; P is the cost of living index; $\dot{P}$ and $\dot{P}i$ are the changes in P and Pi, and n is the rate of population growth.

A positive residual could be caused by a rise in the standard of living of those people who consumed the good, but it might also be due to a decline in smuggling or a change in taste (and to measurement error). In table 2.3 we present two sets of calculations of this residual for each of the three goods, computed for a lower and an upper bound own-price elasticity of demand.

Table 2.3 **Changes in adjusted consumption, expressed in quinquennial rates of growth**[a]

Elasticity of demand	Tobacco lower bound[b]		Tobacco upper bound[c]		Tea		Sugar	
	−.2	−.5	−.2	−.5	−.3	−.7	−.3	−.7
Period								
1790/4–1795/9	.686	.743	.415	.472	.272	.212	.056	.044
1795/9–1800/4	−.186	−.231	−.136	−.181	.147	.155	.196	.032
1800/4–1805/9	.002	.059	.006	.063	−.014	.074	.052	.060
1805/9–1810/14	.130	.106	.183	.159	.096	.168	−.033	.033
1810/14–1815/19	−.181	−.040	.015	.156	−.024	−.016	−.185	.129
1815/19–1820/4	−.055	.056	.140	.251	−.009	.015	−.086	.058
1820/4–1825/9	−.075	−.138	−.164	−.227	−.077[d]	.061[d]	.116	.140
1825/9–1830/4	.058	.079	.062	.083	.060[c]	.056[e]	−.217[e]	.215[e]
1830/4–1835/9	.072	.081	.044	.053				
1835/9–1840/4	.061	.085	.072	.096				
Average	.051	.080	.064	.092	.078	.096	.041	.024
Average excl. 1790–4	−.019	.006	.025	.050	.046	.077	.038	.021

Notes: a Computed from equation (1).
b Adjusted for smuggling, using lower bound of proportion of imports smuggled.
c Adjusted for smuggling, using upper bound of proportion of imports smuggled.
d Using data up to 1827 only.
e Based on Railway Commission statistics, using average prices for three years around 1825 and 1835.

Sources: See notes 16, 19, 22 and text.

The results reported in table 2.3 suggest that once we account for all other factors affecting imports, the 'residual' indicates that an overly pessimistic verdict for this period is not confirmed by the evidence. Although the residual depends, naturally, on our assumptions concerning income and price elasticities and the growth of demand, the basic finding is robust to these assumptions. For consumers of tea, sugar and tobacco, a net improvement in living standards was taking place.[27] Because we are using data of questionable quality and correction procedures which rely heavily on proxies, it would be rash to demand from these numbers a more detailed analysis of the movement of living standards within the period.

How does the result square with that derived from the SII pointing to the widespread growth in poverty? Part of the answer is that the index refers only to the poorer classes, who consumed but a small fraction of aggregate imports. Moreover, the index pertains to the years 1815–35, which also registered little growth in the consumption of these goods. Taken together, these proxies indicate that in the longer run improvement was neither ubiquitous nor steady; the positive trend in tea, sugar and tobacco consumption conceals long stretches of stagnation and decline, and growing inequality. Yet ironically, in the decade and a half before the Great Famine, still viewed by many as a Malthusian disaster, there is little evidence of severe pressure on living standards, as per caput consumption of tobacco shows an impressive recovery.

III

As stated at the outset, the standard of living in an economy is not readily captured by any single series, whether consumption or income. Other proxies can be used. In particular, the consumption of certain specific goods such as education, the standard of nutrition, or housing quality may be used as measures of the 'economic well-being' of a society. Efforts to make use of such measures have run into considerable data problems but progress has nonetheless been impressive. In what follows, we shall try to extend this work to the Irish pre-famine economy regarding two crucial variables: we first make a case for using education and schooling data; we then turn to physical-demographic measures of health and nutritional status.

The pre-famine Irish were eager for schooling and literacy. Even before the spread of public education after 1830 the country possessed an impressive network of fee-paying and charity schools. Most of these were humble one-teacher 'hedge-schools', sometimes sponsored and supervised to some extent by the local Catholic clergy, landlords, philanthropists, and a variety of evangelical proselytising societies. It was widely recognised, however, that attendance was constrained by poverty. The cost of tuition – about a penny a week on average in pay-schools at a time when a labourer's daily wage ranged between sixpence and ten pence – was the main element, but present clothes and books, and even the opportunity cost of the children's labour have been cited as factors limiting school attendance (see e.g. Akenson 1970: chs 1–2; McParlan 1802: 76–7; Daly 1980; Mokyr 1985: 183–4).

A look at schooling and literacy patterns across the country and over time should therefore provide us with another rough guide to the changes in living standards. Although more literate societies were not necessarily wealthier societies, literacy was desirable and costly, and we are thus justified in viewing it as an important component of the standard of living (compare Mitch 1982). Before discussing difficulties of interpretation, let us first examine the record. Aggregate estimates of the numbers at school span the period between the Union and the famine, but comparisons over time are quite complicated. Below are five different estimates from official sources:

Table 2.4 **School attendance before the famine**

Year	At school	Population (m.)
1808	'over 200,000'	c.5.0
1821	394,813	6.8
1824	568,964	7.1
1834	633,946	7.9
1841	502,950	8.2

Sources: Fourteenth Report of the Commissioners of the Board of Education in Ireland (PP 1813–14, v), p. 335; Abstracts of the answers and returns . . . of the 1821 Census (PP 1824, xxii), p. 817; Second Report of the Commissioners of Irish Education Inquiry (PP 1826–7, xii), p. 4; Second Report of the Commissioners of Public Instruction, Ireland (PP 1835, xxxiv), p. 13; 1841 Census, pp. 438–9.

The first entry in table 2.4 can be little more than a guess, based on a survey of school attendance in 1808 in 17 of 22 Established Church dioceses. The second, though census-based, is clearly defective: it records no scholars in many parishes in which schools existed in 1821, leaves out two baronies entirely (Salt South and Ikeathy-Oughterany in Kildare), and returns implausibly low numbers for some counties (Londonderry, Cavan). Only one small school is returned for the barony of Demifore in Westmeath, and three all-male schools for nearly 8,000 school-age children in the barony of Tyrkeeran in Londonderry.

Where numbers are produced they appear to reflect total enrolments rather than average attendances or the numbers at school during a particular day or week.[28] The 1824 returns refer to 'the number in the course of receiving education, and not merely the number who upon any particular day may be found collected in the school-room' (*1821 Census*: 24). The 1834 returns also refer to the total number of children 'on the books'. The 1841 census data, on the other hand, include only those returned by the school authorities as 'making one appearance in school during a specified week'.[29] These figures suggest very high attendance in the larger towns and cities – in Galway city, for instance, 58.4 per cent of those aged 6 to 15 were at school – but substantial variation across counties.[30]

Clearly, such comparisons are risky. Nonetheless, they are consistent with some rise in schooling during the pre-famine decades. An analysis of the data collected by the Commissioners on Public Instruction in 1834 suggests that the ratio of attendance to enrolment was about 0.7.[31] Applying this ratio to 1824 and 1834 produces the following:

Table 2.5 **School attendance**

Year	Attendance per 1,000 population	Attendance per 1,000 children aged 6 to 15
1824	5.5	228
1834	5.6	—
1841	6.0	244

Source: see text

While these numbers are rough approximations, they indicate a slight rise of school enrolments. This conclusion is corroborated by the data on the numbers of teachers: 11,823 in 1824; 14,601 in 1841.[32] The ratio of teachers to total population thus increased from 1.67 to 1.76 per thousand. The analysis of literacy data in the 1841 census provides an alternative way of searching for trends in education. The commissioners collected information by age-cohort and sex on those who could read and write, those who could read only, and those who could do neither. The returns, summarised in table 2.6, indicate that over half of the population aged over 5 years – 46.5 per cent of the males, 58.7 per cent of the females – were illiterate in the sense that they could neither write nor read.

Using age-specific illiteracy rates allows us to draw some tentative conclusions about the decades prior to the famine.

Table 2.6 **Illiteracy by age-cohort and sex, 1841 (%)**

Age	16–25	26–35	46–55	66–75
LEINSTER				
Males	26.1	27.5	34.9	40.6
Females	32.6	40.9	54.9	62.3
Total	29.5	33.5	45.3	51.8
MUNSTER				
Males	40.7	47.0	51.7	55.0
Females	55.6	66.7	75.8	80.2
Total	48.5	57.1	64.0	67.6
ULSTER				
Males	23.1	25.3	29.9	31.8
Females	31.7	39.3	47.8	49.4
Total	27.6	33.6	39.1	41.4
CONNACHT				
Males	54.2	59.2	64.9	68.1
Females	70.2	79.2	85.1	88.1
Total	62.5	67.4	73.8	77.7
IRELAND				
Males	34.6	38.5	43.1	45.8
Females	45.4	54.7	63.6	65.8
Total	40.3	46.9	53.6	55.9

Source: 1841 Census

Some warnings regarding the figures in table 2.6 are apposite. First, it must be assumed that emigrants were not disproportionately literate. If they were, the propensity of the Irish to educate their young would be more pronounced than table 2.6 suggests.[33] Second, inferring trends from cohort data may be misleading insofar as people acquired literacy in adulthood and then retained it for the rest of their lives. If many acquired literacy at a higher age, the figures would under-state the improvement. It seems, however, more likely that through lack of practice in reading and writing, some older people 'shed' their literacy, and thus the data may overstate the increase in literacy. Nonetheless, the educational improvement implied by table 2.6 is probably not entirely offset by this effect.

The proportion illiterate is one-third higher for the 66–75 age-bracket than the 16-25 bracket. The difference is consistent with a gradual improvement in literacy levels between the 1780s and the 1830s. Progress was slowest in the poor province of Connacht. The most impressive gains took place in Leinster, where those born between 1765 and 1775 were almost twice as likely to be illiterate as those born between 1815 and 1825.[34] It is also clear that the trend towards improvement was more pronounced among women than among men, indi-cating a movement toward 'catching-up', though the absolute level of illiteracy of women remained consistently higher than among men on the eve of the famine. The levels of illiteracy show marked regional variation. Leinster and Ulster were relatively literate, while throughout Connacht and Munster one of the last mainly pre-literate cultures in north-western Europe was to be found. The contrasts between the extremes of Irish society can be seen by comparing the wealthy Dublin parish of St Anne's, in which only 17.5 per cent of all males over the age of 5 could neither read nor write, to the Kerry parish of Dún Chaoin (Dunquin), Europe's most westerly point, where illiteracy reached 94.8 per cent (*1841 Census*: 17, 197). The literacy averages in Leinster and Ulster – where 74 per cent of men and 60 per cent of women aged 26–35 claimed in 1841 that they could at least read – cannot have been much below British standards. Schofield's analysis provides material for the comparison since it refers to roughly the same age group. The database, a sample of marriages in parish registers, is of a different nature. But if we use inability to sign the register as a guide, and assume that inability to sign one's own name would in most cases also mean inability to read, his data suggest illiteracy levels of about 34 per cent for young adult males and 48 per cent for females *c*.1840 (Schofield 1973). Third, other estimates of literacy suggest that Ireland was superior to both Italy and Spain in the 1840s, and about on a par with Belgium, France and the Austrian Empire. The data on teachers tell much the same story: in Ireland in 1841 there were 17 teachers per 10,000 people, to be compared with 14 in Prussia (1843), 18 or 19 in Holland, Belgium, and France (1860), and 11 in the Austrian Empire (1859) (Cipolla 1965: 12–22, 28–9, 72, 90–1).

In sum, Ireland was something of an 'impoverished sophisticate', in the sense that its literacy level was probably higher than its income level would indicate

(Sandberg 1979). The picture was very uneven regionally, and changing rather slowly in the backward west and south before the famine. Yet the data on education and literacy confirm the earlier impression of the SII and the consumption data. The poorest counties in the west and those hardest hit by the decline in cottage industries in the north and north west seem to have made the least progress, whereas the agricultural counties in Leinster and Munster, which benefited most from the union with Britain and the increase in demand for agricultural goods, show the most improvement. A very slow rate of overall improvement was accompanied by an increase in inequality and regional disparity.

Living standards can also be measured by biological indicators. Recent work in economic history has shown the possibility of measuring net nutritional status by indicators such as stature, birth-weight, and life expectancy. The study of heights has proved especially fruitful in this respect (Fogel et al. 1983; Steckel 1983; Floud and Wachter 1982). Substantial claims have been made for this source, and tolerably representative data are often readily available over long periods, though usually for males only. The connection posited by today's cliometricians was mooted by Malthus in 1798:

> The sons and daughters of peasants will not be found such rosy cherubs in real life as they are described to be in romances. It cannot fail to be remarked by those who live much in the country that the sons of labourers are very apt to be stunted in their growth, and are a long while arriving in maturity. (Malthus 1970: 93–4)

An early application of this notion to Ireland may be found in Kane, using data on third-level students in Ireland and in England, Scotland, and Belgium in the 1840s. He claimed that 'it is gratifying to have it proved, that when at all well fed, there is no race more perfectly developed, as to physical conformation, than the inhabitants of Ireland' (Kane 1845: 400). Information on height comes almost exclusively from military records which, in an age before the universal draft, drew recruits largely from the lower classes. And yet occupational breakdowns of recruitment samples show that they came from a wide range of classes, and not exclusively from the very poorest. Consequently, information on the recruits bears upon a substantial section of the population, perhaps the bottom half or two thirds of the population, comparable to those described by the Poor Inquiry Commissioners.

Since the military authorities relied heavily on Irish recruits, they figure prominently in the research carried out by Floud and his associates on the records of the British army.[35] Our own work uses the continuous service registers of the British Admiralty[36] and the recruitment registers of the East India Company.[37] The research is still in an early stage, but some preliminary results can aid us in our search for proxies for Irish living standards in this period.

At least at the beginning of the nineteenth century, the Irish were taller than the British. In a sample of 11,484 East India Company army recruits aged 20 and above who joined between 1800 and 1815, the average height of an Irish recruit was a third of an inch taller than his British counterpart, a difference which is statistically highly significant.[38] Half a century later, the difference between the Irish and the British sailors in the Admiralty sample, if anything, increased somewhat. The differences in the age groups 21–30 and 31–40 were 0.55 inches and 0.48 inches respectively, both highly significant statistically.[39]

Given that the gap between Irish and British recruits apparently not shrink in this period, it seems that, rising real wages in Britain notwithstanding, the 'backward' Irish economy did not fall behind in nutritional status and that there was no substantial difficulty in feeding a rapidly growing population in Ireland. At the same time we should note that in Britain rising real wages failed to bring any discernible increases in stature before 1850. Whether that means that the return to an optimistic view of the trend in the standard of living in Britain itself was premature remains to be seen.[40] The interpretation of the height data is not straightforward. Because younger recruits were excluded from the EIC data, we are comparing men born in about 1780 to men born in the late 1810s and early 1830s, and so these figures do not exclude the possibility of I a decline in living standards after the Napoleonic wars, as literary sources indicate. Indeed, the mean stature of men aged 21 and above was 66.7 inches, which would make them about 0.7 inches taller than the recruits of 1800–50. Yet such a rise cannot be equated with an improvement in living standards. A rise in average height may be consonant with a *fall* in living standards if changing selection biases in recruitment are not taken into account. Suppose, for example, that achieved final height reflects living standards in childhood and youth. Suppose further that only youths coming from families whose income is below a certain threshold volunteer for army service. If an across-the-board fall in incomes occurred, so that families previously above the threshold income now found themselves below it, we would observe recruits from impoverished middle-income families applying in increasing numbers. Because these men had grown up in comparative comfort, their heights would embody a higher living standard, and thus rising observed height of recruits might be associated with declining living standards. The changing geographical composition of the Irish recruits is consistent with this: in the early 1800s about 40 per cent of the recruits came from Ulster, compared with only 11 per cent in the 1840s.

Nonetheless, the seemingly paradoxical finding that the Irish were as tall as any other European nation and were possibly growing taller themselves in a period of economic decline suggests three important points to be kept in mind by those making use of physical indicators of living standards. First, the comparison is a reminder that the connection between height and per caput income should not be pushed too far. Definitions of poverty can be confounded by differences in the composition of consumption baskets: the pre-famine Irish poor, despite being branded by many other well-known hallmarks of poverty, may have been better nourished in their youth than their British or continental counterparts in this period. This does not mean that they were 'better off' in the traditional sense of economic welfare; people elsewhere may have preferred, say, a diet of toast and tea to healthier foods (for some further discussion, see Mokyr 1985: 7–10; Sandberg and Steckel 1980: 101).

Second, an apparently backward economy could still accommodate considerable population growth without revolutionary technological progress or much capital accumulation. Ireland seems to have succeeded in feeding its own population in addition to increasing food exports to Britain. The much-feared Malthusian spectre was not much visible before 1845. Prior to the Great Famine, despite seasonal scarcities and occasional temporary 'famines', starvation was rare in Ireland.[41]

Life expectancy at birth can also provide an indication of quality of life. By projecting the population reported in the Irish census of 1841 back to 1821 (making due allowance for emigration in the interim), Boyle and Ó Gráda have been able to generate an estimate of life expectancy at birth before the famine. They have suggested a figure of about 38 years, compared with about 40 years in contemporary England (Boyle and Ó Gráda 1986; Wrigley and Schofield 1981: 23, 539). Given that Irish infant mortality rates were about 50 per cent higher than in Britain, life expectancy at higher ages was very similar to that in Britain. Estimates of life expectancy at birth elsewhere in Europe are scarce, but we suspect that despite their poverty the Irish lived longer than the European norm (compare Dupâquier 1975).

IV

The Irish economy before 1845 presents its share of paradoxes. The profound difficulties that it faced, highlighted by the repeated sombre accounts of travellers, popular agitation, and ultimately the famine need no recounting. Yet the pre-famine decades also saw improvements in some respects. On some larger landholdings farming methods were transformed. Throughout the country, banking, communications, and processing industries ancillary to agriculture grew, though unevenly.[42] British innovations such as steam power and canals were introduced, their diffusion slowed primarily by the cheapness of water power and road carriage. The industrial revolution in Britain, which dealt a death blow to much Irish cottage industry, also increased demand for Irish agricultural products and thus improved the terms of trade for those Irish farmers who were involved in these markets, perhaps 25 or 30 per cent of the farming population. British-manufactured goods, from cotton to pottery, were sold in Ireland at ever lower prices made possible by the rise in productivity in Britain. The same mechanism which raised living standards in Britain – supply shifts driving down consumer prices – also affected Irish living standards, though to a lesser extent because the proportion of income spent on these goods in Ireland, especially among the rural poor, was smaller. Yet the improved terms of trade for agriculture can only have added to Irish aggregate income. At the same time, as in Britain, increasing inequality was also a factor in Ireland, if perhaps for different reasons. Industrial decline and the Corn Laws combined to hurt the landless and near-landless masses.[43]

The measures of 'poverty' used above contain a few surprises. Although every one of our indicators suffers from its own ambiguities and inaccuracies, their consistency seems to warrant some tentative conclusions. First, while economic circumstances of the Irish poor probably stagnated or even deteriorated, the population as a whole seems to have been able to hold its own and possibly even improve its lot. In the years before the famine the Irish were becoming more literate, and were probably growing taller, and they consumed somewhat larger quantities per head of desirable exotic commodities on the market. The 'opinion poll' data used in section I do not necessarily contradict this conclusion because they were intended to reflect on the poor, not on the entire population. In spite of the improvements in the economy, the bottom half of the Irish income distribution faced an increasingly harsh economic environment.[44] The response took various forms: increased emigration, a slight decline in the propensity to marry, agrarian and political unrest, and squabbling about poor relief policies. None of this was of much help when disaster struck in 1845.

In a classic statement, Ashton claimed in 1948 that Ireland's fate just a century earlier was a pointer to what might have happened in Britain in the absence of an industrial revolution (Ashton 1948: 111). Ashton's thought experiment is to some extent flawed, for two reasons. First, Ireland and Britain were already such vastly different economies in 1750 that subsequent differences cannot be attributed just to the industrial revolution. Second, Ireland's history was different from what Britain's would have been precisely because Britain was there. And yet the question remains of substantial interest: what happens in a technologically stagnant rural economy in which population more than doubles in a century? In 1845–50 Ireland suffered the Great Famine, still viewed by many as a Malthusian apocalypse. Yet the decades before the famine show clearly that increasing population pressure did not dominate the Irish economy. More was at work than just diminishing returns.

In fact, although between 1800 and 1845 the British and the Irish economies seem to have grown further and further apart, their experiences in those years were more similar than is often supposed. In both countries average incomes grew slowly, but an increasing inequality prevented the bottom half from benefiting much from this growth. In both parts of the United Kingdom these years produced clear gainers and losers, and any question about net improvement is muddled by the difficulties inherent in changes in distribution. The Irish poor were clearly the losers in the process, and it is impossible to draw cheerful conclusions about an economy in which three million people could be wiped out or displaced in five years due to a string of harvest failures. In terms of resilience to disasters, the British economy was much stronger than the Irish; yet those differences were largely in place by 1800.

To be sure, even if there was some improvement in Irish living standards, income per caput was growing more slowly than in Britain, urbanisation was negligible, and the diffusion of new technologies limited. Yet the tragic ending to this period in Irish history should not mislead us into believing that the Irish economy was inexorably steering toward a Malthusian disaster before the famine. Within limits, it was capable of progress and growth, and while the average Irish person by 1845 was still abjectly poor in the material sense, the evidence suggests that he was getting marginally less so over time. His misfortune was that whatever progress there was, was too little, too slow, and too unevenly spread.

Where do our findings fit in the standard of living debate? Data limitations preclude strong claims here. Most of our measures capture the direction of change for only a part of the industrial revolution period. The choice of the reference group is crucial to the outcome. If we simply focus on the average standard of the whole population of the United Kingdom, the Irish experience does not conflict with the overall optimistic picture. However, the direction of change in *average* British living standards has surely never been in dispute; the classic pessimist case has insisted instead on a rising inequality which prevented the living standards of the 'poor' or the 'working class' from rising much. The reintegration of Ireland into the economic history of the United Kingdom does not clinch that traditional pessimist case, but it lends it some support. Before 1850, the gains of the winners were largely, though perhaps not entirely, offset by the setbacks suffered by the losers. Even before the famine, Ireland could indeed count many losers.

CHAPTER THREE

Bankrupt landlords and the Irish famine

CO-AUTHORED WITH ANDRÉS EIRÍKSSON

Introduction

Few strata of Irish society escaped the ravages of the Great Famine of 1846–50. Owners of landed property were no exception. But how badly did Ireland's ten thousand or so landlords fare?[1] Curiously enough, specialist writings on Irish tenurial relations and landed estates offer little guidance. Well-known studies of the management of the London Companies and the Downshire estates concentrate mainly on the pre-famine period, while W. E. Vaughan's wonderful account of the Irish land tenure system begins in the 1850s; and neither R. B. MacCarthy's monograph on the massive Trinity College estates nor Lindsay Proudfoot's analysis of the Duke of Devonshire's Waterford estates, both of which straddle the whole nineteenth century, contain more than a few pages each on the famine. James S. Donnelly's researches into Cork and Kerry landed estates, and Desmond Norton's recent analysis of landlord assisted emigration, are exceptional in this respect (Robinson 1962; Maguire 1972; Vaughan 1994; MacCarthy 1993; Proudfoot 1995; Donnelly 1974–5, 1975, 1988; Norton 2005).

Impressionistic accounts of landlord hardship are plentiful. One such account described the Blake family of Renvyle in north Connemara as 'looking forward to starvation' in May 1847, another noted the relief of Hyacinth D'Arcy, former owner of a neighbouring estate and founder of Clifden, at being offered a position as a school inspector 'at a salary of £100 a year' (Lane 1972: 424; W. T .H. 1850: 92, cited in Lane 1981–2: 46). These are atypical, but there are many reports too of falling revenues and increasing outlays,[2] and the significant declines in landlords' net income in the late 1840s and in the value of their most important asset, land, tell their own stories. One way of interpreting the resort to eviction on a mass scale from 1847 on is as another signal of the pressure that the famine placed on landlords.

How many landlords lost their lands to the famine? Why did they do so? Some accounts dwell on the generosity and sense of responsibility of individual proprietors. It was claimed that one of the Martins of Ballinahinch[3]

> contracted a debt for food to support her famishing tenantry in the years of famine; a prompt payment was demanded, but, with the characteristic humanity of her family, she would not press her dependents in distress, and a sheriffs execution swept the mansion and demesne of Ballinahinch. This was the flash that disclosed the coming ruin. (Locke 1852: 30)

The impact of the Great Famine on landlordism is difficult to separate from the creation and early history of the Incumbered Estates Court, established in 1849. One of the few concrete policy recommendations of the Devon Commission, appointed by parliament to survey and recommend improvements to the Irish land system in the early 1840s, had been that 'every facility consistent with safety should be given for bringing [encumbered] estates to an early sale, rather than allowing them to remain for years the subject of expensive litigation' (cited in Lane 1972: 416). Both Whig and Tory ministries were committed to the creation of a special institution for the sale of heavily mortgaged land with the minimum of red tape. The measure introduced by Sir Robert Peel lapsed with the collapse of his Tory administration in July 1846, but the Whig ministry that followed was formulating its own version from late 1846 on. Their first measure, introduced in March 1847, produced fears of an ensuing glut in the land market and was withdrawn in July. A second bill passed in 1848 proved a dead letter, but it was a case of 'third time lucky' with the Incumbered Estates Act of 1849. Under that act a creditor could petition for a sale when encumbrances exceeded half the estate's net rent, or the annual rent less taxes and fixed charges (Lane 1972; Vaughan 1994: 133).

The decision to establish the Incumbered Estates Court was undoubtedly linked to the problems posed by the famine, and in the early years some of its business was certainly a by-product of the famine. How much is a moot point. In this essay we try to do two things. First, we establish the regional pattern of land sales through the Incumbered Estates Court (on which more below) in its early years. Second, we argue that the bulk of the encumbrances on affected sales could not have been caused by the famine alone.

Landlord bankruptcies in the wake of the famine are frequently highlighted in the literature. As the following selection from some of the best-known accounts indicates, some historians have stressed the precarious status of many

affected estates before 1845, while others imply that it was the impact of the
famine itself on landlord incomes that did the damage.

- The rise in poor-rates and the decline in rent receipts served to send many
  proprietors into the Incumbered Estates Court once its operations began in
  1849. (Black, 1960: 130)
- Under the shock of that disaster many of the old landlords had broken,
  succumbing to the crushing burden of paying vast sums in poor relief at a
  time when rents drastically diminished. Post-famine legislation, notably the
  Incumbered Estates Act of 1849, enabled numbers of them to dispose of their
  estates to a new type of owner who knew the value of money. (Lyons 1973: 26)
- To simplify this procedure and to clear away the mass of post-famine bankrupt estates the Incumbered Estates Court was set up in 1848 (Daly 1981: 34).
  While indebtedness among Irish landlords was not a new phenomenon, the
  burden of famine relief and mounting rent arrears seriously worsened the
  situation. (Daly 1986: 120)
- Some landlords, too, were ruined economically by the Famine. During the
  next thirty years about a quarter of the land of Ireland changed hands as a
  result of the working of the Incumbered Estates Act. (McCartney 1987: 173)
- [Landlords'] rents declined and their rates soared. Many (at least 10 per
  cent) went bankrupt; the Incumbered Estates Act of 1849, freeing landed
  property from legal encumbrances that prevented its sale, epitomised what
  had become of them. Irish estates worth £20,000,000 changed hands in the
  1850s. (Foster 1988: 336)
- Bankruptcies and the numerous sales of bankrupt properties through the
  mechanisms established by the Incumbered Estates Act of 1849 augmented
  the Famine's role as a Darwinian selector of the fittest among the members
  of the proprietorial community. Much of the land sold (and almost a quarter
  of the total eventually changed hands) was bought by owners who had survived the Famine in good financial shape and were able to meet the future
  with optimism and confidence. (Hoppen 1989: 87)
- The British government had to cope with the aftermath of famine . . . [I]n
  1848 the first tentative steps were forced by the bankruptcy of many landlords
  and the immediate need to sell large acreages of property (Boyce 1992: 37–8).

The overall impression given by such accounts is that much – if not most –
of the court's early business was famine-inspired. Indeed, Lindsay Proudfoot
(1995: 43) infers from K. T. Hoppen's summary that 'up to one-quarter of all

land changed hands as a result of Famine-induced bankruptcy among land-owners'. A corollary is the claim, implicit in the extract from F. S. L. Lyons above, that the landlord class was too prostrated and poor to buy land on offer at bargain prices, and that their place was taken by grasping businessmen and lawyers (see also Woodham-Smith 1962: 409–10).

It is not hard to imagine how the presence of the court might have forced an already heavily encumbered estate over the top, or tempt nervous creditors to seek their money back. But that is not at all the same thing as saying that the famine was responsible for what happened. Such was the state of landed property in Ireland that the court would have had plenty to do in any case. The circum-stances have produced a *post-famine ergo propter famine* interpretation of events.

Irish landed estates on the eve of the famine

Quite how many estate owners were in serious financial trouble before 1845 remains somewhat unclear. Data on rents due on estates managed by the Court of Chancery imply, very roughly, that one owner in twelve and one acre in twenty had become chronically insolvent before 1845 (BPP 1847–8). The embar-rassed estates were well spread throughout the island and not confined to the poorer counties. The provinces of Leinster and Munster accounted for over twice as much of the rent due as the more marginal province of Connacht in 1844, roughly the same as their proportions of the poor law valuation and esti-mated rent due (Crotty 1966: 303). Estates in Chancery represented the extremes of indebtedness; the numbers take no account of heavily indebted estates still in the control of their owners on the eve of the famine.

An estate being put into the hands of the Court of Chancery was a signal for many tenants to stop paying rent. While the Darcy estate, sold in August 1850 to the Eyre family, was in the court's hands, arrears worth eight years' rent accumulated; in the case of the Percival estate the arrears due in 1849 were 7.5 times the annual rent of £800.[4] Moreover, the numbers suggest that estates in Chancery stood little chance of proper maintenance and improvement. In 1844–7 the managers of the Courts of Chancery spent an annual average of £2,852, or 0.4 per cent of the rent due, on buildings and the land in their care – 'a state of things which', according to *Thom's Directory*, 'would necessarily require a heavy outlay by the incoming purchasers' (*Thom's Commercial Directory* 1853: 277). As a result many properties were in poor shape by the time they reached the Incumbered Estates Court. In 1852 the scene at Emo House, the former seat

of the Earl of Portarlington, resemble[d] what might be expected in the neighbourhood of some volcano', and at Sir George Goold's Shanacourt outside
Cork City the house was 'suffering from want of a moderate coat of paint and
whitewash' (Lyons 1993: 23, 25; Osborne 1850: 45–6). Naturally the owners of
such run-down estates were poorly placed to help their tenants when disaster
struck in 1846.

In this short essay we do not seek a definitive answer to the question why so
many estates were in trouble before the famine struck. However, we note that
on the basis of an analysis of a relatively small number of estates, David Large
blamed the expense of family settlements, while L. P. Curtis deemed it incor-
rect to blame 'the pressure of building mortgages alone', but claimed that 'the
cumulative cost of an aristocratic life-style drove many owners of estates to the
moneylender'.[5]

The regional pattern of sales in the Incumbered Estates Court

Estates presented for sale in the Incumbered Estates Court are described in the
so-called O'Brien Rentals, now deposited in the National Archives of Ireland.
These are named after Murrough O'Brien, who had been a long-serving Landed
Estates Commissioner until his death in 1914. Each rental contains information
on the size of the lot on offer, the annual rent payable by the tenants, the
annual head rent and tithe owned. Details of leasing arrangements are also
given (Mokyr 1985: 91–7).

The Incumbered Estates Court began its work in late 1849. It worked
smoothly, selling off land in lots of several hundred acres rather than in whole
estates in order to maximise sales revenue. The following analysis is based on a
record of its sales between then and the end of 1855. The bulk of sales forced by
the Great Famine should have been conducted by then. Certainly the character
of the court's business had evolved by the mid-1850s. An official inquiry suggested that by then its transactions were no longer mainly or even largely due to
landowners being driven to the court by pressure from their creditors, and that
petitioners tended to be owners seeking the benefit of the parliamentary title
obtainable through the court (BPP 1854–5). Including sales up to 1855 is thus
likely to provide an upper-bound measure of total sales forced by creditors in
the wake of the famine.

The results, summarised in table 3.1 and map 3.1, offer their own perspective
on the regional incidence of the famine.[6] Traces of the east–west gradient evident

Table 3.1 **Townlands with land auctioned in the Incumbered Estates Court, 1849–55**

County	Townlands with auctioned land	Total number of townlands	Townlands with auctions (%)
Galway	1,106	4,290	25.78
Leitrim	136	1,496	9.09
Mayo	709	3,251	21.81
Roscommon	239	2,016	11.86
Sligo	123	1,312	9.38
Carlow	49	597	8.21
Dublin	93	971	9.58
Kildare	58	1,221	4.75
Kilkenny	194	1,603	12.10
Laois	115	1,154	9.97
Longford	58	903	6.42
Louth	99	678	14.60
Meath	159	1628	9.77
Offaly	148	1,167	12.68
Westmeath	175	1,380	12.68
Wexford	81	2,382	3.40
Wicklow	69	1,374	5.62
Clare	202	2,215	9.12
Cork	726	5,514	13.17
Kerry	212	2,741	7.73
Limerick	303	2,065	14.67
Tipperary	607	3,245	18.71
Waterford	177	1,657	10.68
Antrim	140	1,726	8.11
Armagh	79	965	8.19
Cavan	161	1,985	8.11
Deny	47	1,246	3.77
Donegal	47	2,663	1.76
Down	103	1,284	8.02
Fermanagh	150	2,175	6.90
Monaghan	104	1,853	5.61
Tyrone	204	2,158	9.45
LEINSTER	1,298	15,058	8.62
MUNSTER	2,227	17,437	12.77
ULSTER	1,035	16,055	6.45
CONNACHT	2,313	12,365	18.71
IRELAND	6,873	60,915	11.28

Source: derived from the O'Brien Rentals (NAI)

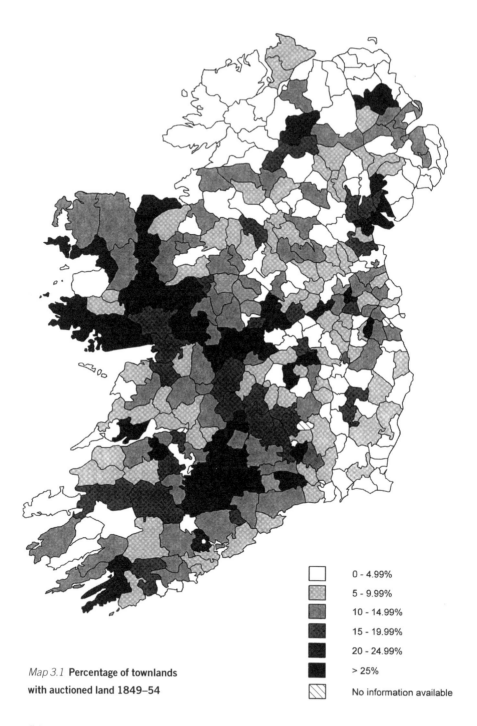

Map 3.1 **Percentage of townlands with auctioned land 1849–54**

☐	0 - 4.99%
▨	5 - 9.99%
▨	10 - 14.99%
◼	15 - 19.99%
◼	20 - 24.99%
◼	> 25%
▨	No information available

in maps in the 1841 Census and in the distribution of relief rations at the height of the crisis are also evident here (compare Ó Gráda 1993: 39, 184). Sales were disproportionately concentrated in the provinces of Munster and Connacht, west of an imaginary line from Waterford to Ballyshannon. Some baronies were barely affected (see also table 3.3). The pattern is not clear-cut, however. One interesting implication is how little of County Donegal was processed in the court. It is also significant how landed proprietors in Kerry, Leitrim, and Clare, three counties devastated by the famine, escaped relatively lightly. On the other hand, there are anomalous baronies with particularly high sales in other counties. One estate accounted for nearly all of the land sold in the Tipperary barony of Iffa and Offa West. It belonged to the Earl of Glengall, while nearly all the land sold in the baronies of Antrim Lower and Toome Lower belonged to the Earl of Mountcashel. The details are given in the appendix (p. 61 below).

The results show that landlords were by no means as badly hit by the crisis as sometimes thought. The O'Brien rentals imply that only 11 per cent of Irish townlands contained land auctioned in the Incumbered Estates Court between 1849 and 1855. More than that proportion of Irish land was seriously encumbered

Table 3.2 **Ratio of debt to rent due on encumbered estates by year of presentation**

Ratio	1849—50	1851	1852	1853	1854
0–4	3.4	4.9	6.6	6.0	11.8
5–9	20.8	20.8	20.7	19.8	29.5
10–	21.6	27.8	20.7	23.2	16.1
15–	16.8	13.7	13.8	18.8	11.8
20–	11.3	10.2	9.0	9.1	6.3
25–	7.6	7.4	4.8	4.7	2.8
30–	6.8	5.6	6.2	7.7	6.7
40–	2.9	1.8	4.5	3.4	3.1
50–	2.6	2.5	4.1	1.0	1.6
60 +	6.1	5.3	9.7	6.4	10.2
10 +	75.8	74.3	72.7	74.2	58.7
25 +	26.0	22.6	29.3	20.2	24.4
Median Ratio	15	14	15	15	12
Total	380	284	290	298	254

Source: Computed from BPP (1854–5), table 2

Table 3.3 **Percentage of townlands in a barony with auctions**

Percentage	Number of baronies
0–4	104
5–9	84
10–4	59
15–9	32
20–4	22
25–9	12
30 +	11

before the famine. On the other hand, some of the lands included here were presented to the court in 1854–5 merely for the purposes of acquiring parliamentary title.

As a check on the accuracy of the index we tested three volumes of the rentals. These volumes included 159 rentals (Dublin City excluded), totalling 781 townlands. Leinster accounted for 155, Munster 282, Ulster 100, and Connacht 284. Out of these 781 townlands 656 are marked in the index to the O'Brien Rentals, while 125 are not. This means that the index underestimates the number of townlands auctioned by about 16 per cent. Furthermore, there is a certain geographic bias as to the accuracy of the index. The percentage of townlands missing from each province is Leinster 21, Munster 17, Ulster 13, and Connacht 12.

The reason for the bias seems to be the size of the baronies, the size of the rentals, and how well the index for each county was organised. Our impression is that Counties Cork, Tipperary, Limerick, Kilkenny, Kildare, Dublin, and Meath are those most underestimated in the index to the O'Brien rentals. As for Donegal, singled out above, there is no sign of particularly poor recording in the index. We examined all Donegal rentals in sixteen of the 37 volumes and found that 14 per cent of townlands were missing in the index, a proportion similar to other counties in Ulster and Connacht.

Landlord indebtedness and the famine

The key point here is that the sheer size of the encumbrances on most estates when presented to the Incumbered Estates Court was far too great to have been caused by the famine alone. In mid-November 1849, the petitioners against the

Earl of Portarlington – whose estate was one of the first to be presented to the court – claimed debts of £700,000 against lands stated to yield only an annual £33,000 in rent. Lord Oranmore and Browne had accumulated debts of over £200,000 on an estate with a rental of less than five thousand pounds, and in the case of the Earl of Aldborough debts of £151,478 were supported by a rental of £2,629 (BPP 1854–5: 82, 83). True, these are rather spectacular examples. A more systematic analysis of the return of over 1,600 'cases pending before the commissioners, and in which anything remains to be done' shows that debts many times the declared rental were typical (see below). Those cases represent more than half the total presented to the court in that period. Does their 'residual' quality mean that they were more encumbered than the average? Clearly, the delay attaching to cases presented in the first few years and still out-standing in 1854 *could* reflect the greater encumbrances on them. However, a year-by-year analysis of the ratio of debt to rent due suggests that this cannot have been a serious bias. Between 1850 and 1853 three quarters of the estates presented had debts exceeding ten times the declared rent due on them and the median ratio of debt to rent was 14–15 years. The declared rents typically referred to pre-famine conditions; whether such rents could have been recovered in the conditions of 1850 at least is open to question. This lends a conservative bias to the ratios reported. The share of estates with debts of ten years' rent or more was down in 1854, supporting the claim that more landlords were by then using the court to gain parliamentary title. Yet the proportion of estates owing twenty-five times or more the rent due hardly fell over the period (see table 3.2). Such estates can be deemed bankrupt de facto, since few estates sold through the court fetched more than twenty-five years' purchase (compare Osborne 1850: 245).

The important point about these ratio distributions is that, even bearing the possibility of some bias in mind, they are much too large to have been caused by the famine. Even a landlord who had received only half the rents due to him during the worst famine years (say 1846–8), and who had been respon-sible for a significant share of the rates burden in his area, would not have accumulated debts anything on that scale. Even in the worst-affected poor law unions the rates very rarely exceeded three or four shillings in the pound (or, since the valuation approximated the gross rental, about one fifth of pre-famine rental incomes) at the height of the famine. So even if a landlord was respon-sible for rates on half of his land, rates would have absorbed at most about one tenth of his normal receipts. The famine, then, might have cost some landlords in the worst-affected areas as much as two or three years' rent, but that is a small fraction of the medians reported above.

When the famine was over, the pro-landlord *Mayo Constitution* conceded that the demise of ancient landed families was due to 'debts of many past generations' (11 July 1854; cited in Lane 1981–2: 50). While bad luck played a part in creating indebtedness in certain cases, poor estate management and over-spending are probably the best explanation for it. The record is full of examples of landlord extravagance. The behaviour of Cork landlords prompted Donnelly to surmise that 'although the fateful events of 1845–9 pushed the encumbered landowners of Cork over the brink of disaster, it was as clear as their best-polished silver by the early 1840s that the long-awaited day of reckoning with their creditors was close at hand' (Donnelly 1975: 72; see also d'Alton 1980: 21, 26; Ó Gráda 1994a: 29–30; Maguire 1976). In other words the famine only forced changes that were inevitable in any cases: 'the incubus of a largely bankrupt or debt-ridden landlord class was cast off by the operation of the encumbered estates court in the 1850s' (Donnelly 1975: 164).

Before the Great Famine the only way of recovering money lent on landed security was by a bill in Chancery or Exchequer. But this was a tedious and ruinously expensive route. The vast quantity of legal documents accumulating in the court's record office within a few years of its opening for business prompted the London *Times* to comment:

> What an antiquity of troubles, what a prescription of impossibility do those figures denote – 100,000 documents and muniments of title! Surely when the work is done, this mountain of spent and refuse legality will be committed to the flames like the books of the sorcerers. Let them no longer burden the earth, and crush the energies and intellect of man . . . (cited in McArthur 1854)

Complex and defective legislation allowed debts on landed property to mount, and delayed the sale of such property. 'There was no single, simple, and complete register of settlements, mortgages, and judgements. Instead, there were separate registers in different courts and in the registry office of deeds' (Donnelly 1975: 71). And yet landlords found ways of borrowing; the ability of so many to accumulate such debts offers a paradoxical reminder that Ireland before the famine was not short of idle capital.

Conclusion

British public opinion was extremely critical of the performance of Irish land-lords during the Great Famine (Donnelly 1996a). Apologists, on the other hand, pictured them as squeezed by the pincer movement of lower rents and higher outlays both on relief and taxation. The impact of the crisis on aggregate rents received can only be guessed at, but the records of individual estates suggest that landlords may have been less affected than sometimes claimed. On eight Cork estates described by Donnelly (1975: 106–7) the average gap between rents due and received between 1845 and 1853 was 16 per cent. The record on another four estates described by Vaughan (1994: 246) is even better: receipts as a per-centage of rents due hardly fell. On the Devonshire estate, rent receipts fell back by thirty per cent between 1845 and 1849, but surpassed their previous peak again in 1854 (Proudfoot 1995: 107–8). Such data suffer from a possible selection bias: the records of estates whose rents fell more drastically are less likely to have survived. Moreover, outlays on poor rates and, in many cases, on relief mounted during the famine. However, neither increased outlays nor reduced incomes can account for the staggering debts of most estates processed. Even in the worst-affected regions, poor rate outlays accounted for only a fraction of rents due.

Mass evictions are an important part of the story. Like the £4 clause, which made landowners liable for the rates formerly due on holdings of less than £4 valuation, the threat of the Incumbered Estates Court probably increased the pressure on landlords to evict tenants from small, marginal holdings from 1849 on. The number of evictions cannot be determined precisely. Vaughan (1994: 28) puts the number of families thrown out by legal process during the famine and its aftermath at 70,000, while Donnelly numbers the victims of involuntary surrenders of their holdings 'almost certainly' at more than half a million (1995: 156). Local accounts such as Tom Yager's of the Mullet peninsula give a more vivid impression of the devastation wrought by evicting landlords (Yager 1996).

The new historiography of Irish land tenure demolished the populist per-ception that evictions were common between the mid-1850s and the outbreak of the Irish Land War in 1879. The myth that the Great Famine was mainly responsible for the ruin of many Irish landlords, equally pervasive, has proved more enduring. However, the massive indebtedness of those landlords who succumbed in its wake suggests that the famine's true role was that of a catalyst: getting rid of landlords who were doomed in any case. This prompts three con-cluding speculations. First, we suspect that no landlord who was free of debt and owed no rent in 1845 succumbed during the Great Famine. Second, such landlords would have been in a good position to buy up the properties of their improvident neighbours. Transfers between landed families were probably more important than sales to grasping members of the professional and commercial classes. Third, there was a negative association between financial embarrassment and outlays on relief in the late 1840s. Debts accumulated in the years before the famine must have prevented many landlords from playing a more active part in limiting mass mortality during the famine.

Appendix to chapter three:
Notes on some high-scoring baronies

Ballinahinch, Galway. In July 1852 the estate of Arthur Gonne Bell Martin was sold, *c.*192,000 statute acres and 250 townlands, of which about 120 were in Ballinahinch (Landed Estate Commission Rentals (LEC), vol. 17/35). In the same barony another 26 townlands were sold, the land belonging to John Augustus O'Neill (LEC 15/26). These two auctions accounted for most of the townlands sold in Ballinahinch. The Martins owed the Law Life Insurance Company £160,000.

Moycullen, Galway. The sale of the Martin estate also involved over one hundred townlands in the adjoining barony of Moycullen. In June 1851 over 30 townlands were auctioned belonging to Mary Joyes and Reditia and Margaret Lynch. Half of these were in Moycullen, the other half in the barony of Galway (LEC 8/31). These two sales accounted for the bulk of townland sales in the barony of Moycullen.

Galway, Galway. The Martin and Joyes/Lynch estates account for virtually all the townlands auctioned in this barony.

Gallen, Mayor. In March 1853 lands belonging to John, Arthur, and Lawrence Knox were auctioned, a total of 57 townlands, of which 36 were in Gallen and 12 in Burrishoole (LEC, 20/57). Another sale of the Knox estate took place in November 1853, 42 townlands sold, of which two were in Gallen and forty in Tirawley (LEC 25/11). During the same month the lands of the Rev. William Jackson in Gallen accounted for another nineteen townlands (LEC5/19).

Burrishoole, Mayo. More than eighty townlands belonging to Sir Richard Annesley O'Donnell were auctioned in July 1854 (LEC 30/6). The sale of Knox estate and that of John McLaughlin in March 1850 (LEC 1/2) account for the rest.

Clanmorris, Mayo. In November 1854, about seventy townlands in Clanmorris belonging to Lord Oranmore were sold (LEC 31/13). In November 1851, 14 townlands on the Walter Blake estate were sold (LEC 12/1).

Kilmaine, Mayo. There were no large-scale auctions here, but rather a series of smaller sales. The biggest of these was the sale of lands belonging to Sir Richard Annesley O'Donnell in November 1852, 24 townlands (LEC 19/1).

Iffa and Offa West, Tipperary. Almost all of the land sold in this barony belonged to the Earl of Glengall. It was auctioned on 11 November 1853 (LEC 24/38).

Antrim Lower, Antrim Almost all the land sold in Antrim Lower and Toome Lower belonged to the Earl of Mountcashel. It was sold in November 1850 (LEC 3/34–7).

CHAPTER FOUR

Famine disease and famine mortality

CO-AUTHORED WITH JOEL MOKYR

Introduction

Today the most resonant media images of famine are of skeletal children on the verge of starvation. Such images capture the heightened vulnerability of infants and small children to famine, but they also create the misleading impression that famine deaths are starvation deaths. Now, as in the past, most famine victims die not of literal starvation, but of infectious diseases. These diseases come in various kinds, at different times, and with differing levels of intensity. Hunger and infectious disease interact in complicated ways, some of which operate through the human body and some through the fabric of human society. The causation of death during a famine turns out to be a difficult question, with the usual philosophical undertones. Here we examine these issues in the context of the Irish famine of 1846–51. This was a real famine in the old-fashioned sense, with strong Malthusian features: a catastrophic reduction of the food supply led to major demographic readjustment. Still, every famine is to some extent *sui generis*. How different were the causes of excess mortality in Ireland in the 1840s from those operating during other famines? Why were they different? Before attempting to answer these questions we must establish with as much detail as possible the causes of excess mortality in Ireland. To be sure, the Irish case is often difficult to interpret and compare with others, partly because mid nineteenth-century medical terminology and concepts are so different from our own, and partly because the statistical evidence is faulty or lacking. All the same, the available evidence can be utilised to draw some important historical conclusions.

Two broad classes of causes were responsible for augmented mortality during famines. The first is directly nutrition-related, and includes some cases of actual starvation. More often, however, victims of this class succumb to nutritionally sensitive diseases brought on by impaired immunity, or to poisoning from inferior foods that would have been discarded in normal times. The other is indirect: death is caused by the disruption of personal life and the normal operation of society resulting from famine, but was not the *immediate* result of a decline in nutritional status in the strict sense. Today an individual is deemed to have starved to death in the clinical sense only if he has died as the result of the attrition of protein and fatty deposits in the body causing gradual systemic atrophy, especially of the heart muscle. Pure starvation in this sense was relatively uncommon during the Irish famine. To what extent medical practitioners of the time meant something like this when they mentioned starvation remains to be seen. It seems likely, however, that at least three concepts in the medical literature of the day correspond roughly to what would be regarded today as pure starvation. First, there is actually a category called 'starvation'.[1] A second category is what is known today as 'oedema' or in the language of the time, 'dropsy', a swelling due to fluid accumulation often accompanying acute starvation. A third, 'marasmus', is a general term describing the death from some form of food inadequacy of infants and small children.

Yet these pre-modern terms also pertain to syndromes that are not famine-related. For instance, the 1841 Irish Census records only 17 deaths from starvation for the entire year of 1840, out of a total of over 140,000 reported deaths for that year. In 1847 slightly over 6,000 people were reported to have died of starvation, out of nearly 250,000 reported deaths for that year. On the other hand, in 1840 dropsy and marasmus accounted for over 3,000 and over 9,000 deaths, respectively, although that year was famine-free (BPP 1843: 181–3, BPP 1856b: 663).

Most of the other diseases that killed people during the Irish famine were infectious diseases. Some were opportunistic diseases that took advantage of the fall in nutritional status and the general environmental deterioration. Specialists distinguish between *individual* immuno-suppression and *social* or *collective* immuno-suppression. Individual immunity declines as the body is deprived of food, especially proteins. Recent research has questioned the widely held assumption that malnutrition *inevitably* leads to increased susceptibility to infection (Carmichael 1983: 53; Dirks 1993: 157–63). During major famines, however, there is a threshold effect whereby a switch occurs from a regime of subnutrition or even malnutrition to one of acute deprivation, in which the immune system is severely impaired. Even then the effect is uneven. Some diseases are highly sensitive to food intake, others seem to operate entirely independently of nutritional status, and still others are in-between. In Ireland the potato blight reduced food *quality* as well as its quantity. One consequence, unsuspected by contemporaries, was that the intake of Vitamin C, now recognised as an essential element in human resistance to disease, fell precipitously. Irish diets had always been rich in Vitamin C thanks to the potato; as diets changed after the onset of the blight, scurvy made an unexpected appearance in Ireland (Crawford 1988). Few people were reported to have died of scurvy, but the accompanying weakening of immune systems must have contributed to the onset of, and increased fatality from, other diseases.

Collective or communal resistance to disease during famines in the past declined for very different reasons: as famines worsened, social structures such as formal and informal support networks and medical care broke down. Moreover, the decline in human energy output reduced labour productivity throughout the economy, leading to positive feedback effects that reinforced the initial shock. Famine begot reduced agricultural productivity which led to more famine. In addition, as Fogel and Sen have pointed out, a decline in total food supply was usually accompanied by a change in its distribution, normally to the disadvantage of the poor, people at the extremes of the age distribution, the less healthy, and possibly women (Drèze and Sen 1989: 50–5; Fogel 1991: 33–71; Maharatna 1996: 9–10).

As resistance to disease declined, famine conditions greatly increased the 'insults' inflicted on the body. It is well understood today that such events produce an additional feedback effect: as disease reduces the body's ability to absorb certain foods, it creates anorexia, while by simultaneously increasing the demand for certain nutrients, it creates synergistic effects (Carmichael 1983; Taylor 1983: 285–303). These insults include:

Digestive diseases due to decline in food quality. As food supply declines in quantity, desperate people slide down the quality ladder, falling back on items that would normally not be eaten: seaweeds, diseased and spoiled foods, and wild plants. There is evidence that famished people in Ireland ate decomposing carrion as well as nettles, carrageen moss, and corn-weed. Such substances can mercilessly attack the digestive system and cause a variety of diseases which can become fatal in conjunction with the weakened immune systems.

Digestive diseases due to changes in food composition and unfamiliar emergency foods. This was particularly important in a potato-eating country such as Ireland in which what foods could be imported from overseas, especially the notorious 'Indian corn', were mostly unfamiliar and hard to prepare in those areas where the dependence on potatoes had been the most complete and the famine most acute. The reliance on potatoes had allowed much of Ireland to dispense with investment in basic food processing such as flour mills and bakeries. Specialisation increased the costs of switching to substitute food sources after the famine. Contemporary reports described the diseases suffered by people from consuming unfamiliar and improperly prepared foods from Indian meal.

Infectious diseases due to population moving around. Famine conditions frequently led panic-stricken people to quit their homes in the search for food. Mobility increases mortality in famine-stricken regions for two reasons. One is that it exposes both the famine refugees and their hosts to new disease environments and microbial regimes to which they are not immune. The other is that hygienic and sanitary needs depended on certain fixed items. As people left their homes, they left behind their laundry facilities, their cooking utensils, and sanitary arrangements, however rudimentary. The result was a decline in hygienic standards. The increase of what contemporaries referred to as 'fever' – mostly typhoid, relapsing fever, and typhus – must be in large part a consequence of this phenomenon. Indeed, the many vagrants and famine refugees on the roads produced a new term for these diseases, 'road fever'.[2]

Infectious diseases due to hygiene deterioration as people become weak and despondent. The impact of serious malnourishment is not death straightway and not even necessarily disease, but a decline in physical energy output. The first consequence of a decline in food intake may not have been a further decline in work effort and physical agricultural product (although that would follow eventually), but reduced energy spent on many of the standard household tasks such as laundry, the hauling of water, and cleaning. Fuel supplies, coming mostly from Irish peat bogs, declined as people could not muster the energy for the hard work involved. Personal care, childcare and food preparation were neglected when energy levels declined. The purely physical effects of energy imbalances were reinforced here by the psychological effects of starvation such as indifference and lethargy. The impact of reduced food intake on the effort devoted to these activities contributed to the spread of so-called 'dirt diseases'.

Outbreaks of seemingly unrelated epidemics such as cholera, influenza and other diseases. Identifying to what extent these diseases are a coincidence is always a problem. The case for opportunistic disease is strong enough, but occurrences of these epidemics in the absence of food scarcity are frequent enough to allow for some coincidence.

In this essay we first offer a critique of the main source on the causes of famine mortality in Ireland in the late 1840s, the 'Tables of Death' in the 1851 Irish Census. We then adjust the 'Tables of Death' to establish a plausible profile of the causes of death. The outcome prompts a brief look at why particular diseases were so deadly. Was it because the requisite medical technologies were lacking, or would poverty have ruled out their use in any case? Then some comparative perspectives on famine nosologies are offered and the final section is a conclusion.

The Irish nosologies: a critique

To the uninitiated, the extensive and detailed mortality tables appended to the 1851 Census of Ireland may seem like an almost inexhaustible source on the causes of death during the Great Irish Famine (BPP 1856a). Although slightly less detailed in some respects than the analogous tables in the unusually rich 1841 Census (BPP 1843), the 686-page volume of tables is probably unparalleled in the range of data included. Mortality-by-cause data are cross-tabulated county by county, year by year, disease by disease, and by gender. A distinction is made between rural and 'civic' areas, and there are separate entries for deaths in workhouses and hospitals. The nosology was the work of William Wilde, who modelled it closely on the tables of mortality he had created for the 1841 Census. It represents the best that mid nineteenth-century medical science had to offer, and while some of the diseases do not quite correspond to something a modern coroner would recognise, much of it seems to make sense.

Unfortunately, specialists have long known that the mid nineteenth-century Irish death tables leave a lot to be desired in terms of accuracy (MacArthur 1956: 308–12). Some quick calculations and comparisons confirm the serious doubts about these tables. Indeed it is easy to become so despondent about them that the best course of action would seem to be to abandon them as misleading or useless. The main reservations historians have about them are as follows.

First, the *total* numbers are clearly serious under-enumerations because most of the numbers were collected retrospectively from surviving kin. During the famine, entire families disappeared through death, migration, or a combination of the two. Hundreds of thousands of people must therefore have expired between 1841 and 1851 with no surviving household member around to report their deaths to the census enumerators in 1851. Furthermore, given the catastrophic events after 1845, it is likely that many deaths were simply forgotten by surviving relatives. There is good reason to believe that the degree of under-enumeration differed a great deal between the pre-famine years (1842–4) and the following years.

To complicate matters, the totals probably included some deaths reported by families and deaths in workhouses and hospitals, so that under-enumeration could have been offset to some extent by double-counting and in a few cases *over*-reporting cannot be ruled out, although this is the exception.[3] An added complication here is that the coverage of deaths in workhouses, hospitals, and prisons, which accounted for about one quarter of all recorded deaths, is likely to be quite reliable. Most such deaths were recorded in such institutions as they happened, and these records formed the basis of the summary data reported by the relevant authorities to Wilde in 1851.

To see the extent of under-reporting, note that the 1841 Census reported total Irish population at 8.18 million and the 1851 Census at 6.55 million. As explained in detail in Mokyr (1980), total famine mortality may be estimated by first projecting Irish population forward from 1841 to the eve of the famine in 1846. Births occurring in 1846–50 (adjusted for a famine-induced decline in fertility) are then added on and estimated out-migration during the famine years subtracted. This yields a total of 1.9 million deaths in Ireland in those five years, of which slightly over one half were due to the famine.[4] The 1851 Census tables report a total of 985,000 deaths, so for the country as a whole the reporting factor is about 52 per cent. This factor, moreover, varied substantially from county to county. The implications of under-reporting are serious for a nosological analysis: if there was a correlation between the probability of having survivors and the nature of the disease to which an individual succumbed, the distribution of diseases in the 1851 mortality tables would have been subject to a negative bias, that is, the diseases that increased the most would be systematically under-reported.

Second, some of the disease categories are rather vague. The 1851 Census distinguishes between diarrhoea and dysentery, although it would have been difficult at the time to distinguish between the modern disease of *Shigellosu* and other acute forms of diarrhoea. Indeed, the 1841 Census does not make the distinction. In the 1851 Census the ratio of reported deaths from dysentery to deaths from diarrhoea is 5.77 in County Leitrim and only 2.07 in adjacent Sligo. The largest single cause of death reported in the 1851 Census is 'fever', responsible for 222,000 (over 16 per cent of all reported deaths), mostly occurring between 1846 and 1850. The famine years thus reveal an enormous increase in mortality rates from causes which we would consider to be *symptoms* although at the time they were considered *diseases*.

Third, some respondents in 1851 seem to have projected some of their famine memories back to pre-famine days, reporting famine-related diseases as if they had occurred before 1845. This may be seen from a comparison *of* the tables for 1842 (reported in the 1851 Census) and those for 1840, the last complete year reported in the 1841 Census (see table 4.1). There is no reason why the figures for these two years should differ much, as underlying conditions were similar. Yet note, for example, in table 4.1 the implied increases in the death rates from dysentery and diarrhoea (from 0.25 per thousand in 1840 to 0.64 per thousand in 1842) and in starvation (from 0.0 per thousand in 1840 to 0.06 per thousand in 1842).[5] Some diseases that increased during the famine seem to be over-represented, others (such as marasmus) not so. How serious are these biases? A simple chi-square test using the rates per 1,000 in 1840 and 1842 fails to reject the null hypothesis of no significant differences. This suggests that the bias introduced in the 1851 Census by the disappearance of hundreds of thousands of people affected the total counts, but did not bias the distribution of pre-famine diseases unduly. Nevertheless, we use 1840 weights as our guide to 'normal' or pre-famine mortality in the calculations below. The difficulty with the famine years is more serious and will be addressed below.

Fourth, we can distinguish between categories of disease that were obviously and unambiguously associated with the famine and some opportunistic diseases (such as tuberculosis and measles) which occurred at increased frequencies as a result of the immuno-depression caused by malnutrition. All the same, this still leaves unexplained seemingly odd increases recorded in some diseases that hardly seem famine related. For example, the number of people dying of 'rheumatism' and diseases of the bones and joints was reported at 484 in 1842 and 1,145 in 1849. Diseases that should hardly be affected by the famine such as those of the 'locomotive organs' and 'diseases of uncertain seat' (tumours, phlebitis, and 'debility and old age') still show a higher level of incidence for the famine years for three of the four provinces. The exception is Leinster, where the impact of the famine was the weakest, suggesting that this effect is somehow related to the famine. As a proportion of the total number of deaths, these diseases declined, but their increased incidence remains rather puzzling.

Fifth, another case in which survivors' memories seem to have let them down relates to the question 'in what season did the deceased die?' The census tables reveal that for some reason the autumn was discriminated against. Only 14.1 per cent of all deaths were reported to have occurred in the autumn, against the 25 per cent expected in the absence of seasonal variation. While many individual diseases were of course seasonal, different patterns between diseases should

Table 4.1 **Comparing pre-famine census data.**

	1840 (from 1841 Census)		1842 (from 1851 Census)	
	(%)	(per 000, adj.)	(%)	(per 000, adj.)
Smallpox	4.35	1.04	3.99	0.96
Dysentery and diarrhoea	1.04	0.25	2.67	0.64
Cholera	0.19	0.04	0.19	0.05
Fever	12.69	3.05	10.73	2.58
Others	12.36	2.97	12.97	3.12
Total Epidemic diseases	**30.63**	**7.35**	**30.55**	**7.34**
Convulsions	5.00	1.20	4.97	1.19
Others	3.13	0.75	4.29	1.03
Total nervous system	**8.13**	**1.95**	**9.26**	**2.22**
Heart, circulatory organs	0.20	0.06	0.76	0.18
Consumption	11.39	2.73	14.40	3.46
Others	3.64	0.87	4.29	1.03
Total Respiratory	**15.03**	**3.61**	**18.69**	**4.49**
Dropsy	2.27	0.54	2.19	0.52
Imarasmus	6.37	1.53	5.21	1.25
Others	2.80	0.67	3.16	0.76
Total Digestive system	**11.44**	**2.75**	**10.56**	**2.54**
*Urin., Gen., Loc., Teg.**	**2.09**	**0.50**	**2.70**	**0.65**
Infirmity, debility, old age	19.08	4.58	11.82	2.84
Others	2.82	0.68	3.22	0.77
Total uncertain causes	**21.90**	**5.26**	**15.04**	**3.61**
Starvation	0.01	0.00	0.27	0.06
Others	3.31	0.79	3.22	0.77
Total violent and sudden	**3.32**	**0.80**	**3.49**	**0.84**
Others and unspecified	**7.21**	**1.73**	**8.96**	**2.15**
Total	100.00	24.00	100.00	24.00

* Urinary, Generative, Locomotive, Tegumentary.

have reduced the susceptibility of the total to seasonality. Moreover, some afflictions in which seasonality should not have been much of factor (for example, 'cancer and fungus', 'burns and scalds') were also subject to the same bias.

To take the 1851 Tables of Death Census at face value would thus be a grave mistake. Yet to abandon them altogether would leave us at the mercy of anecdotal titbits equally, if not more, subject to biases of memory and selectivity. The value of the Census lies first and foremost in its systematic organisation, which allows us to detect certain regional and temporal patterns that at least provide a rough reflection of the nosological nature of the famine as it appeared to those who had survived it. Rather than argue that these data are in any sense accurate and reliable, we adopt the more conservative strategy of (1) drawing inferences and making comparisons where the biases just noted do not present a problem, and (2) pinpointing and adjusting for some of their worst shortcomings on the basis of what is known about Irish population statistics in this period. What emerges is not an accurate picture, but a historian's approximation, based on assumptions and simplifications. This reconstruction can, however, be used to shed some more light on the quantitative dimensions of the causes of mortality during the famine, and through them on the microeconomics of death during catastrophic shocks inflicted upon vulnerable economies.

Adjusting the Tables of Death

As noted, the 1851 Census seriously undercounted the number of people dying both before and during the famine years. In principle there are two ways of dealing with the rate of under-enumeration across counties. The simplest ploy is to assume a constant rate. An advantage of this method is that, combined with assumptions about population growth in the absence of a famine, it generates residually calculated independent estimates of famine-induced net emigration by county after 1845. For our present purposes, however, the assumption of constant under-reporting will not do. As noted earlier, some under-enumeration was due to the emigration of survivors, some to the deaths of entire families, some to the silence of surviving kin. Assuming constant under-enumeration across counties implies, surely implausibly, that the impact of these was the same. The most serious problem with the nosologies is the possibility that certain diseases were under-reported due to the disappearance of entire families. If the degree of under-enumeration varied from disease to disease, the result might be an under-estimate of deaths due to the most murderous of them. We thus attempt adjustments that yield estimates of under-enumeration.

The under-enumeration problem presents two types of biases in the data. Let $R_i = \lambda_i D_i$ where D_i are total actual dead in county i, R_i reported dead, and λ_i is the under-reporting factor. To assume that the λ's are the same across counties would overweight the distribution of diseases in counties that under-report the least and underweight those counties where underreporting was greatest. Since under-reporting clearly was a function of the severity of the famine, this would bias the nationwide distribution of disease toward under-reporting famine-specific diseases. We call this *weighting* bias. Secondly, simply adjusting for under-reporting will not produce a correct estimate of the disease distribution because that still assumes that the distribution of diseases among those not reported *within each county* was identical to the distribution of diseases among those actually reported. This seems implausible. We call this *truncation* bias.

To solve the two problems, we need county-specific estimates of λ. We could in principle follow a procedure similar to that outlined above for Ireland as a whole, that is, arrive at total famine deaths by subtracting the population of each county in 1851 from a hypothetical population that would have been there given the population of 1846, buttyhs and migration. The trouble with such a procedure is that while there are enough data to allow a reasonably good estimate of *total* net migration, the *county-by-county* distribution of these migrants before 1850 is not known. We estimate that distribution on the basis of three alternative assumptions: the distribution of county shares in overseas migration in 1846–50 was the same as the reported one for 1851; the same as the average of 1851–5; and the same as the weighted average between 1821–41 and 1851. In addition, we had to estimate the total population between the censuses on the eve of the famine. There are two alternative ways of doing this, and we worked with both. We also adjust for internal migration, as reported in the 1851 Census. The overall estimates of the λ's are moderately sensitive to these assumptions and as there is no obvious way to choose among them, we present upper and lower bounds in table 4.2.[6]

The province-level data in table 4.2 make sense in that the λ's tend to be particularly low for the worst hit regions in Connacht, and high for the Leinster counties. We also ran simple regressions of the level of the λ's on crude measures of the severity of the famine such as the proportion 'starvation' of all deaths reported. These regressions (not reported here) show a consistent negative relation between the λ's and the *reported* incidence of starvation (though the latter itself is of course mismeasured). The nationwide nosology resulting after adjustment for the weighting bias is provided in table 4.3.

Table 4.2 **Estimates of under-reporting coefficients (λ) by province**

Assumption about emigration	Ulster	Leinster	Munster	Connacht	Ireland
Shares as in 1851	0.38	0.70	0.69	0.35	0.52
Shares as in 1851–5	0.42	0.64	0.68	0.35	0.52
Mean shares (weighted) 1821–41 and 1851	0.42	0.66	0.63	0.36	0.52

Table 4.3 **Adjusting for weighting bias**

Total deaths reported	Unadjusted	Adjusted with 1851 emigration shares	Adjusted with 1851–5 emigration shares
Dysentery	8.53	8.96	8.98
Diarrhoea	3.64	3.64	3.65
Fever	18.58	18.44	18.69
Starvation	2.02	2.31	2.35
Consumption	10.29	10.16	10.04
Dropsy	2.05	2.11	2.09
Marasmus	4.98	4.77	4.79
Cholera	3.64	3.21	3.29
Infirmity and old age	9.11	8.93	8.91
Total specified	62.83	62.52	62.79
Others	37.17	37.48	
Total	100	100	100

The adjustment, as might be expected, raises the proportion of famine-specific diseases such as 'starvation' and dysentery and reduces the shares of more traditional causes of death such as consumption and 'infirmity'. Correcting for the weighting problem by computing county-specific underreporting rates by itself is insufficient, however, because it assumes implicitly that the disease distribution for deaths unreported in the census was the same as that for those reported in a particular county. This seems unlikely, as the majority of the deceased missing from the census must have been people whose relatives had either also died or had emigrated.[7]

To correct for this truncation bias, we applied the following weighting schemes to the 'missing' dead: assume that the distribution of diseases among the missing dead was as reported in the county with highest death rate (Mayo), the counties with highest out-migration rates (Clare and Tipperary, depending on the assumptions made) or the counties with the highest overall population loss (Sligo and Roscommon). These shares are then multiplied by the estimated number of unreported dead, and added to the reported ones. The results are provided in table 4.4. Table 4.4 gives us a notion of how serious the biases in the data are. Starvation and dysentery, clearly, are most sensitive, being highest when we apply the Mayo weights and the lowest when we apply the two Munster county weights. All the same, the margins are not so large as to deny us an approximate decomposition of excess famine mortality.

The final step is to provide a breakdown of the contributions of the several diseases to excess famine mortality. This is done by comparing total mortality between 1845 and 1850 to normal mortality. Our estimate of normal mortality is that for 1840, as reported in the 1841 Census, but adjusted for under-reporting as before. Table 4.5 describes the *difference* between the 'normal' pattern so defined and a range of estimates of total disease-specific famine mortality rates during the period.

Clearly the choice of weights matters. Nevertheless table 4.5 implies that almost *every* disease listed by Wilde contributed something to excess mortality during the famine. The meaning of this finding seems clear: despite the problems of under- and mis-reporting, the famine's physiological impact on the population at large went beyond the direct and immediate effects of 'famine diseases'.

The link between malnutrition or famine and fever was controversial during the Irish famine itself (Ó Gráda 1997a: 137; Geary 1997: 101). Further examination of table 4.5 suggests that, roughly speaking, half of famine mortality was caused by diseases associated directly with bad nutrition and the other half from those resulting from the indirect effects of the famine on personal behaviour and social structure. The former status would include diarrhoea, dysentery, respiratory infections (including tuberculosis), starvation, dropsy, and a few less important diseases. Fever, cholera, and most of the diseases included in 'others' had little direct nutrition-sensitivity.

The adjusted data give us a better handle on many of the most interesting issues regarding the famine. Table 4.6 gives the estimated totals dying in Ireland's four provinces of five mainly famine-related illnesses between 1846 and 1851. These are what are described in the report as dysentery, diarrhoea, dropsy, starvation, and 'fever'. 'Fever' presumably includes deaths from typhoid, typhus and relapsing fever (MacArthur 1956: 265–8). The implication that the famine killed roughly twice as many people in proportion in Munster and in Connacht as it did in Ulster and Leinster is perhaps not too far off the mark.

Table 4.4 **Irish deaths, 1846–50, by cause of death: correcting for truncation bias**

	Mayo weights A	Mayo weights B	Clare weights A	Clare weights B	Tipperary weights A	Tipperary weights B	Roscommon weights A	Roscommon weights B	Sligo weights A	Sligo weights B
Dysentery	12.24	12.22	8.49	8.49	7.75	7.76	9.33	9.33	10.06	10.06
Diarrhoea	3.32	3.32	3.5	3.5	3.84	3.84	3.44	3.44	4.58	4.58
Fever	20.56	20.55	22.33	22.31	21.11	21.09	20.42	20.41	18.28	18.28
Starvation	4.82	4.8	2.11	2.11	1.75	1.75	3.16	3.16	2.66	2.66
Consumption	7.78	7.8	7.99	8	9.93	9.93	9.35	9.36	9.17	9.17
Dropsy	2.09	2.09	1.81	1.81	1.83	1.83	1.95	1.95	1.84	1.84
Marasmus	3.81	3.82	4.02	4.03	4.85	4.85	5	5	4.31	4.32
Cholera	3.1	3.1	4.26	4.26	3.34	3.34	2.26	2.26	3.4	3.4
Infirmity	7.1	7.11	7.17	7.18	8.88	8.88	8.54	8.55	8.44	8.44
Total specified	64.81	64.8	61.68	61.68	63.27	63.26	63.34	63.33	62.85	62.85
Others	35.19	35.2	38.32	38.32	36.73	36.74	36.66	36.67	37.15	37.15
Total	100	100	100	100	100	100	100	100	100	100

Note: Weights A use (1) the 1851 emigration shares of each county to compute the distribution of emigration rates and (2) version I of the pre-famine death rates. Weights B use the 1841 emigration share and version II of pre-famine death rates.

Two plausible nosological points emerge. First, the graver the crisis, the higher the incidence of starvation and dysentery–diarrhoea, and the more likely were these to have been the proximate cause of death. Second, the proportion of famine-related deaths due to 'fever' across provinces tended to be fairly constant across provinces although the *incidence* of fever of course increased sharply in the worst-hit provinces.

Table 4.5 **Decomposition of famine excess mortality, Ireland 1846–50**

	Mayo weights	*Clare weights*	*Tipperary weights*
Hunger sensitive:	**40.82**	**28.90**	**29.05**
Dys. and Diarrh.	28.24	21.55	20.79
Starvation	9.06	3.97	3.30
Dropsy	1.96	1.42	1.46
Marasmus	1.56	1.96	3.50
Partially sensitive	**29.48**	**35.75**	**36.40**
Consumption	4.64	5.03	8.67
Others	24.84	30.72	27.73
Not very sensitive:	**29.73**	**35.37**	**34.54**
Fever	27.51	30.84	28.53
Cholera	5.7	7.88	6.15
Infirmity, old age	-3.48	-3.35	-0.14
Total	**100**	**100**	**100**

Knowledge or income?

The Great Irish Famine killed at least one million people, but between 1846 and 1851 population declined by more than that, since the famine was also responsible for emigration on a massive scale and for hundreds of thousands of averted births (Mokyr 1980, Boyle and Ó Gráda 1986). Most of the post-colonial sub-Saharan and South Asian famines seen on our television screens seem relatively mild by comparison (Ó Gráda 1997a). In the twentieth century the *truly* murderous famines have tended to be man-made: the Soviet famine of 1932–3 and Mao's 'great leap forward' famine of 1959–62 killed many more people, although the reference populations were also much larger.

Perhaps one of the reasons why mortality was so high in Ireland is that the mechanisms linking famine to increased mortality through infectious disease were so poorly understood at the time. The problem can be laid out starkly by noting that famine kills in large part through poverty and ignorance. At one extreme, when people fall below some absolute subsistence level, they will die no matter how much they know about the causes of disease. At the other, even well-fed individuals are at risk during famine if they are not aware that they are at increased risk of infection and do not know how to avoid contagion. In between, there is a more complex reality in which people have only a partial understanding of the modes of infection, or are too poor or too weak to avoid them. Knowledge is not enough: even today in poor countries, poor water quality, overcrowding, and the prohibitive cost of medical treatment account for the continued incidence of infectious diseases, and their heightened role in time of famine. Extreme poverty is responsible for children catching deadly diseases even when their parents are familiar with the modes of transmission, simply because they cannot afford the minimal needs for prevention.[8]

All the same, ignorance, too, could be deadly. Neither the victims, nor the authorities, nor medical personnel understood how the diseases responsible for the bulk of Irish famine mortality did their work. How important was their ignorance in determining the demographic impact of past famines? How much difference would better knowledge have made? Table 4.5 suggests that more knowledge might have made a considerable difference. At least one third of all famine mortality was caused by diseases which some people might have avoided had they better understood what exactly made them ill. Typhus and relapsing fever, endemic diseases in Ireland (MacArthur 1956: 265–8), were transmitted by the human louse. The onset of famine undoubtedly made avoiding contact with lice more difficult. Yet it stands to reason that a better realisation of the dangers that lice implied would both have reduced the threat of fever in normal times and prompted efforts to slow down any epidemic during the famine itself (Geary 1996: 50). This holds particularly for less affected areas, as well as for the better off.[9] Two telling indicators of the role of 'spillover effects' from the starving rural masses to others are the excess mortality in Dublin city, and the efforts made by the authorities in Belfast to keep out famine immigrants (MacArthur 1956: 280; Ó Gráda 1999: ch. 5). Even in the case of deaths from dysentery and diarrhoea, many deaths occurring through dehydration might have been avoided had people only known basic facts such as the need to replace fluids in patients and the importance of boiling drinking water before use. Neither patients nor doctors had such knowledge in the 1840s.

Most of the worst afflicted regions of Ireland had very few trained medical personnel anyway: in 1841, Mayo, probably the worst hit county in Ireland, had

Table 4.6 **Estimated disease-specific mortality rates per 1,000, by province (1846–50)**

Total death rates Per 1,000, 1846–50	Ulster		Leinster		Munster		Connacht	
	Mayo weights	Clare weights	Mayo weights	Clare weights	Mayo weights	Clare weights	Mayo weights	Clare weights
Hunger sensitive:	**38.79**	**29.51**	**42.98**	**34.43**	**87.14**	**66.72**	**118.56**	**86.31**
Dys. and Diarrh.	22.51	17.30	21.88	17.07	54.05	42.58	71.92	53.81
Starvation	5.98	2.02	5.57	1.92	16.03	7.32	26.89	13.12
Dropsy	4.05	3.63	4.13	3.75	6.15	5.22	8.12	6.67
Marasmus	6.25	6.56	11.40	11.69	10.91	11.60	11.63	12.71
Partially sensitive:	**81.46**	**86.35**	**94.43**	**98.94**	**130.95**	**141.69**	**147.33**	**164.29**
Consumption	16.76	17.07	22.02	22.3	20.32	20.99	21.96	23.01
Others	64.70	69.28	72.41	76.64	110.63	120.70	125.37	141.28
Not very sensitive:	**48.56**	**52.95**	**63.83**	**67.70**	**98.41**	**108.08**	**120.17**	**135.44**
Fever	31.21	33.80	35.32	37.72	69.18	74.89	87.06	96.07
Cholera	3.01	4.71	8.00	9.57	10.90	14.63	11.43	17.33
Infirmity, old age	14.34	14.44	20.31	20.41	18.33	18.56	21.68	22.04
Total	**168.82**	**168.81**	**201.06**	**201.06**	**316.50**	**316.49**	**386.05**	**386.04**

one medical practitioner for every six thousand people. This compares to, say, the city of Dublin where there was a medic for every 510 people. Ireland as a whole, with one medical practitioner for every three thousand people, was relatively well endowed with doctors compared to much of the less developed world today. Whether this represented an advantage in terms of quality is dubious, however, given the low quality of mid nineteenth-century medical expertise. The inability to treat ailments that were not necessarily lethal outlasted the famine: years later, medical advice books still recommended a healthy dose of castor oil as a remedy for a child suffering from diarrhoea, without mentioning the need for rehydration. During the famine, doctors were still bleeding severely malnourished people (reportedly with 'mixed' results) and administering such medications as tartar emetic, a powerful expectorant that contributed to dehydration. Even as learned a physician as William Wilde did not really understand the basics of how to treat malnutrition and food poisoning, or how fever epidemics spread.[10]

Even without the full knowledge of what causes disease, certain measures could have been taken that would have reduced mortality. Medical practitioners and the authorities of the time to some extent realised the importance of cleanliness in the homes of the poor and of what they deemed to be pure water (Mokyr and Stein 1997, pp. 143–205). Yet this knowledge was neither specific nor accurate. For a large part of the population, moreover, resources may have been the binding constraint: cleanliness and hygiene were luxuries that the Irish poor could hardly afford even in normal times. Many, if not most, walked barefoot much of the time and were forced by poverty to rely on second-hand clothes. The poorest in Ireland shared their accommodation with pigs, poultry, and lice, and clustered settlements made the spread of disease more likely. Their cooking and food conservation skills were rudimentary. When famine struck, hunger made them cold and less likely to shed or change their clothes. It made them move in search of relief and work. The decline in energy meant poorer childcare, less effective care for the ill and the elderly, and probably less fuel and clean water, all of which relied on physical effort.

For the very poor, then, more knowledge and understanding about the causes of disease and death would have done little. Yet disease and death during Ireland's Great Famine were by no means confined to the very poor. For the better-off sections of the population, the benefits of the new science would have been more tangible. A better understanding of the causes of disease would have mattered more in preventing epidemics and deaths among those, especially in the towns but also among those sections of the rural population with enough land to hold even a cow or two. Estimating the proportion of this 'slightly better-off class' is of course arbitrary, but the 1841 Census classified no fewer than 63 per cent as 'labourers, smallholders and other persons without money, land, or acquired knowledge'. Not all of those, however, belonged to the 'poorest classes' since out of the 1.3 million houses in 1841 only 37 per cent belonged to the poorest quality ('mud cabins having only one room'). All in all, while the famine doubtlessly was above all a scourge of the poorest, its nationwide impact must be explained in terms of ignorance as well as poverty.

A comparative perspective

Medical science has advanced by leaps and bounds since the 1840s. Progress in countering infectious disease came in two distinct stages. First, in the late nineteenth century, came the identification by Robert Koch and Louis Pasteur of pathogenic agents and their mode of transmission, and the use of this knowledge for preventive care. Then, in the 1930s and 1940s, came the emergence of antibiotics. Surely one reason why some modern famines have not resulted in mortality figures on an Irish scale is the ability of modern science to prevent or contain the worst epidemics? Even the achievement of the first stage before 1846 would have made a difference in Ireland. For further insight into this issue we take a comparative look at the causes of death in some historical and modern famines.

If, as noted above, the Irish famine dwarfed most modern famines in its relative impact, how different was its nosological profile? Comparable evidence is scarce and at first sight conflicting. Wilde's data, corrected and aggregated, are compared below with cause-of-death data from some famines in nineteenth-century India and in Russia in the 1920s. The expectation of life in Ireland on the eve of the famine was higher than that in nineteenth-century India but lower than that in Russia in the 1920s (Boyle and Ó Gráda 1986; Adamets 2000). Our reworking of Stephen Wheatcroft's findings for the south Russian province of Saratov produces results uncannily similar to Wilde's (see table 4.7). The other Russian nosologies are of poorer quality, with two-fifths of the excess mortality unexplained, but they too stress the overwhelming part played by infectious diseases (Wheatcroft 1981a, 1981b, 1983). The nosologies in official sources for nineteenth- and twentieth-century India are, like the Russian, far less detailed than Wilde's, though their coverage is probably better (Dyson 1991a: table 3; Dyson 1991b: table 7; Maharatna 1996: 18–22). The comparison indicates that most of the excess mortality during the great Indian famines of the nineteenth and twentieth centuries were also due to infection (fever, diarrhoea–dysentery, cholera, malaria), not from literal starvation. This is also true in the case of Bengal in 1943–4, where malaria was the main killer. The main difference between India in the nineteenth and twentieth centuries or between Ireland in the 1840s and Bengal almost a century later is the smaller role of diarrhoea dysentery in the latter. Unfortunately the role of literal starvation in India cannot be inferred from the tables.

In the relief of famines in sub-Saharan Africa today medical supplies are deemed as important as food, and several NGOs specialise in medical assistance. Undoubtedly many lives are saved by immunisation, antibiotics and rehydration. Yet nosological data suggest that it is aggregate mortality rather than the causes of death that have changed. The major causes of death continue to be infectious diseases such as dysentery–diarrhoea, respiratory infections, malaria and measles. Aggregate cause-of-death data are lacking, but all studies carried out in feeding camps highlight the role of infection. In the mid-1980s four fifths of deaths in camps in Ethiopia and Sudan were due to diarrhoeal diseases and measles alone (Shears et al. 1987; Boss et al. 1994; Mercer 1992: 34; von Braun et al. 1998: 134).

However, a very different picture is offered by nosological evidence on a series of smaller, well-documented European famines in the 1940s. Data on the causes of death in Warsaw's Jewish ghetto before its destruction by the Nazis in July 1942 show that as the death rate there quintupled between 1940 and 1941–2, the proportion of deaths attributed to starvation rose from 1 per cent to 25 per cent. Typhus's share remained small, however: 2.4 per cent in 1940, 4.6 per cent in 1941, and 1.7 per cent in 1942. In the towns and cities of the western Netherlands famine killed about ten thousand people during the starvation-winter of 1944–5. Here also starvation accounted for a significant share of the rise, infectious diseases for relatively little. The same holds for a well-documented famine on the small island of Syros in the Aegean Sea in 1941–2, where about one tenth of the entire population succumbed. On Syros there was almost a complete absence of epidemics, and civil registration data attribute over two deaths in three to literal starvation. Livi-Bacci's account of another twentieth-century European famine – in a part of occupied north-eastern Italy in 1918 – returns a similar verdict (Burger et al. 1948; Livi-Bacci 1991: 43–6; Winnick 1994; Hionidou, 2002). Finally, a recent nosological analysis of the Soviet famines of 1933 and 1947 suggests a reduced role for epidemic and parasitical diseases. They were responsible for about one quarter of all deaths, compared to one half in 1922 (Adamets 2002).

Table 4.7 **Causes of Excess deaths in Ireland, Russia, and India**

Cause of Death	Ireland 1840s	Saratov 1918–22	Petrograd 1918–22	Moscow[c] 1918–22	Bombay 1877	Berar 1897	Berar 1900	Punjab 1900	Uttar Pradesh 1908
DDGa	24.9	19.7	10.4	16.0	9.7	30.4	37.0	3.0	−1.2
Cholera	6.8	5.1	2.0	0.7	16.5	12.1	9.6	7.6	4.6
Fever	29.2	24.1	19.3	24.6	45.9	29.0	23.9	72.2	90.9
Respiratory[b]	4.8	9.8	19.3	20.2	na	na	na	na	na
Starvation/Scurvy	10.0	5.5	12.8	na	na	na	na	na	na
Other, unknown	24.3	35.8	36.2	38.5	27.9	28.5	29.5	17.2	5.7
Total	100	100	100	100	100	100	100	100	100

Notes: a Diarrhoea, Dysentery, Gastroenteritis; b Includes normal tuberculosis and pneumonia. Defined as 'consumption' for Ireland; c Excess deaths in comparison with 1914 levels.

Sources: Ireland: Table 5, average of Clare and Mayo weights.
Saratov, Moscow, and Petrograd: derived from Wheatcroft (1983: 340; 1981b: 178) and Wheatcroft (personal communication, April 1998). The percentages are 1918–22 averages calculated for the entire five-year period.
India: Maharatna (1996: 46–7, table 2.6). We subtracted cause-specific death rates in baseline years from rates during famine years to get excess mortality by cause. We then calculated the percentages of the totals explained by the different causes. Maharatna's DDG totals are for diarrhoea and dysentery.

All of these European famines occurred before the discoveries of Pasteur and Koch had been translated into effective and widely available medical treatments or cures. The outcome underlines how an understanding of the modes of transmission of infectious disease can prompt the necessary preventive measures. Those at risk clearly knew the importance of keeping clean, of washing clothes, of disinfectants, and so on. A crucial consequence is that the infectious diseases which bulked so large during famines elsewhere were not endemic (compare Seaman et al. 1984: 50–1). However, these were all relatively advanced places in economic terms, with high literacy levels, a good supply of medical personnel, clean running water for drinking and washing, changes of clothes, housing that was easier to keep clean, less overcrowding, and adequate cooking facilities for what little food there was.

The nosologies of the famines reported in table 4.7 and of modern famines in sub-Saharan Africa have much more in common with Ireland in the 1840s than with famine-affected regions in Europe in the 1940s. Why? Part of the answer must be that while the knowledge may have spread at least as far as medical personnel and officials, behavioural patterns and consumption were subject to a great deal of inertia. It is not enough for people in some sense to 'know' what causes disease, they have to be *persuaded* to change their behaviour. More important, the associated remedies must have been difficult to put into practice in the crisis conditions obtaining. Even in 'normal' times in sub-Saharan Africa, the world's main famine-prone region, infectious and parasitic diseases alone are still responsible for nearly half of all deaths, with diarrhoeal diseases accounting for nearly one quarter of those. Another 13 per cent of deaths are due to respiratory diseases. In Asia (excluding China) the same categories account for about one third of all deaths (Murray and Lopez 1994). In other words, such diseases are endemic in these places: little wonder, then, that they still dominate during famines. Much more mortality in both Africa and Asia – both crisis and non-crisis – could be prevented by low-cost primary health care such as immunisation, prophylactics, and rehydration. In these underdeveloped areas, however, public health lags rather than leads medical science.

A final comparative point links what we know of the causes of death with the well-known gender gap in famine mortality. Famines, with few well-attested exceptions, are more likely to kill males than females. The male disadvantage, which is present throughout the life cycle except at very young ages, is usually ascribed to physiological factors. This prompts the hypothesis that the more important literal starvation as a cause of excess mortality, the greater the female advantage. A comparison of the rather scarce data on the gender gap supports the prediction. In the Irish famine the gender gap was very small. In the case of the Great Finnish Famine of 1868 there was a slight female disadvantage, while in Russia in 1892 excess death rates were practically the same for males and females across the life cycle (Adamets 2002; Mokyr and Ó Gráda 2002; Pitkänen 2002). However, in Syros in 1941–2 male deaths accounted for 59 per cent of all deaths and and in neighbouring Mykonos for 67 per cent (Hionidou 1995, 2002). Comparing famines in Russia in 1892, 1933, and 1947 is also consistent with the hypothesis; the gender gap was much greater in both 1933 and 1947 than in 1892 (Adamets 2002).

Conclusion

The dimensions of a disaster depend on the size of the impact and the vulnerability of the society upon which it is inflicted. The functional relation between outcome and the two determinants is, however, additive rather than multiplicative. Even seemingly invulnerable societies can be devastated if the impact is large enough. Conversely, weak and vulnerable societies may survive for long periods if they are lucky enough to avoid major challenges. Sadly, Ireland was not lucky. Ireland's vulnerability was in terms of its overall poverty, the physical impossibility of storing potatoes, and the thinness *of* markets in basic subsistence goods due to the prevalence of the potato. But there is a second dimension to the vulnerability which compounds the first one, and that is that all populations of the time were vulnerable to an increase in the incidence of infectious diseases in the case of outside shocks. The absence of a clear understanding of the nature of disease mean that the privations and disruptions of the famine quickly translated themselves into the horror-filled statistics of Wilde's 1851 'Tables of Death'.

A careful analysis of epidemics during past famines can help us towardS a better understanding of precisely what happened in the past. The understanding of the epidemiology and aetiology of infectious diseases and the physiology of their symptoms, and the knowledge of how to treat patients suffering from basic ailments such as fever and diarrhoea, will remain with us even if antibiotics lose some of their effectiveness with the proliferation of drug-resistant strains. Equally, an analysis of the role of epidemics in twentieth-century famines offers a better insight into famine mortality in a counterfactual mid nineteenth-century Ireland, where the potato failed but where the scientific advances following the work of Pasteur and Koch had already been absorbed. It suggests that had *Phytophthora infestans* attacked only a few decades later, a better understanding of the basic mechanisms of death would have influenced public health policy and, in particular, would have saved many middle-class lives. However, the analysis of modern third-world famines suggests that many of the poor would still have died. Economic and political progress is a precondition for modern health technologies playing their part in improving the health of the masses.

CHAPTER FIVE

Mortality in the North Dublin Union during the Great Famine

CO-AUTHORED WITH TIMOTHY W. GUINNANE

The Great Irish Famine of 1846–51 was very uneven in its incidence across class and region. Though at its peak three million people out of a total population of 8.5 million were dependent on relief, for people in comfortable circumstances life went on more or less as normal. Excess mortality ranged from one quarter of the entire population in parts of the west to negligible levels along much of the eastern coastline. Mortality varied with poverty; in econometric work, proxies for living standards on the eve of the famine account for a good deal of the variation in mortality across geographical units such as counties and baronies (Mokyr 1985: ch. 9; McGregor 1989; Ó Gráda 1999: ch. 4; Cullen 1997: 24). In local accounts of the famine, however, agents such as an indulgent landlord, an active priest or a corrupt workhouse administrator might help mitigate or exacerbate the disadvantages captured by other measures.

This study focuses on one issue often highlighted in such local accounts, the role of workhouse relief during the famine. Though designed by parliamentary legislation (1 and 2 Vict. c56) to submit the poor to the same spartan regime throughout the country, in practice the workhouse system left day-to-day management in the hands of local elites and their employees. Workhouses seem to have varied considerably in their treatment of inmates and in the competence of their management (O'Brien 1985; Guinnane and Ó Gráda 2002b). Here we provide a case study of the North Dublin Union, the administrative unit responsible for administering the Irish poor law in the northern half of Dublin city and some adjacent parishes. Interesting for its own sake as a mainly urban area where the impact of the famine on residents would have been limited but for immigration from the rest of Ireland, North Dublin Union is unusual for the quality of its surviving administrative records. Its board minutes and indoor registers, which contain considerable detail on the condition and background of each pauper admitted to the union workhouse, provide the raw material for an analysis of the union's competence in relieving its poor during the famine years.

86

This chapter is divided into four parts. The first provides background and outlines some approaches to evaluating workhouse management. The second introduces a case study of the North Dublin Union workhouse, focusing on the management of the institution before and during the famine. The third part uses statistical models to study the mortality experience of those admitted to the North Dublin Union before and during the famine. The chapter concludes with a brief appraisal of the union's management.

Background and strategy

The Irish Poor Law of 1838 was modelled closely on the 'new' English Poor Law of 1834. It divided the country into 130 new administrative units known as 'unions'. These 'unions' of civil parishes were in turn subdivided into electoral divisions upon which poor rates were levied. Each union was to have its own workhouse, funded by the poor rates, and managed by a board of guardians. Membership of these boards, part elected and part ex officio, was dominated by the landed and commercial elites. The guardians, who were unpaid, sought to protect the interests of the property owners who voted them in. A troika of poor law commissioners based in Dublin oversaw and constrained the work of the boards. By 1845 the necessary boards had been created and workhouses built, and the system was fully operational. Henceforth relief was in principle available to all those who needed it: a willingness to accept the spartan workhouse regime as laid down by the new law was deemed sufficient evidence of need. Fears that Irish poverty would make the principle of 'less eligibility' inoperable (i.e. that the workhouse regime could not be harsher than that faced by the poorest workers outside)[1] were not realised. In the event few of the workhouses had ever been full to capacity before the famine struck. From 1846 on, however, the system was subjected to challenges and strains never envisaged by its creators. Well over two hundred thousand people died in Irish workhouses and workhouse hospitals during the famine, the majority of them its victims.[2]

One of the problems facing any analysis of workhouse management is that the prospect of survival in the workhouse reflects not just conditions in the workhouses themselves but also the process which led some to enter the institution and others not to do so. Paupers who ended up in the workhouse were a group selected by events beyond their control (the specific impact of the famine on their household), by themselves (whether they decided to try to enter, say, the North Dublin workhouse), and by the workhouse officials (who carried out legislative mandates and policies dictated by guardians, but who also exercised considerable discretion themselves). Thus the population in a workhouse is a 'choice-based' sample. Two concrete examples will illustrate. A workhouse in which everyone died shortly after admittance might seem badly managed, but that would not necessarily be the case if it attracted only those in the most extreme state of need. Similarly, a workhouse where everyone survived might seem well run, but it could also be one in which the master refused admittance to anyone who might actually need assistance.

Some of those people who perished in workhouses during the famine had entered them expressly to die, while others arrived in a dying condition. Many more died of infectious diseases such as dysentery and typhoid fever contracted in workhouses. Indeed, given the high incidence of such diseases in many workhouses, it is conceivable that some poorly run workhouses did more harm than good during the famine. But how can we evaluate the performance of a workhouse or workhouses? The question is inherently relative. We can compare a union to its own pre-famine experience, or compare unions to each other. Neither of these comparisons is quite fair, since the strain caused by the famine varied from union to union. What measuring rods are available? Neither the number of deaths nor the death rate are adequate by themselves. Both were bound to rise during the famine, and both were very much functions of conditions outside the workhouses. Indeed, no measure is quite immune to outside conditions.[3]

After considering several different approaches we settled on detailed analysis of mortality rates in a single poor law union workhouse. The roads not taken are instructive and will motivate our strategy. One approach to evaluating workhouse performance would be to focus on what people died of in the workhouses. Such was the pressure on the workhouse system throughout Ireland from the autumn of 1846 on, that it sometimes risked exacerbating rather than relieving the crisis. Preserving life in the workhouse entailed not only adequate food and shelter, but protecting inmates against infectious disease. Workhouse managers were expressly forbidden from admitting diseased claimants except when they had created special quarters for them at a safe distance from other inmates. Some workhouses had an adjoining fever hospital or at least separate accommodation for fever patients, but such facilities were very limited.[4] At the height of the famine it may not have been easy to identify and refuse, or segregate, all ill and diseased claimants. Congestion also increased the likelihood of contagion, but as the crisis intensified many boards of guardians found the pressure for relief impossible to resist, even though admissions had already exceeded the accommodation provided. By early January 1847, for example, the workhouse in Fermoy in County Cork held 1,408 inmates in accommodation designed for 900, and the ratios in two other workhouses in the same county, Kanturk and Dunmanway, were even worse.[5] A relatively small number of unions pursued a very restrictive admissions policy in order to minimise their tax burden, but a combination of compassion and popular pressure biased many more towards overcrowding. The trouble was that workhouses that gained a reputation for congestion and for allowing in diseased patients presumably deterred initially healthy paupers from entering them until they too were weak and sickly. The resulting selection bias in entrants to the workhouse may help to explain why so many inmates died of infectious diseases. The point remains that admitting those afflicted with such diseases to the workhouses did them little service and risked killing others.

The prevalence of infectious disease and the pressure to admit sick people to the workhouse were greatest in the areas worst affected by the famine. So it should come as no surprise that the proportions succumbing to infectious diseases in workhouses were higher in the provinces of Connacht and Munster than those of Leinster or Ulster. More interesting are local similarities and anomalies. Thus the percentages of all deaths attributable to epidemic and contagious diseases in Kerry poor law unions did not vary much – from 67 per cent in Listowel to 78 per cent in Kenmare – but the low proportion of deaths attributed to infectious diseases in both Dublin City workhouse (30 and 33 per cent) relative to those of industrialising Belfast (48 per cent) and, to a lesser extent, Cork City (53 per cent) is significant (Guinnane and Ó Gráda 2002b: table 4).

The data on the causes of death illustrate the pressure the famine created on workhouses and explains some of the perverse outcomes we observe. But the surviving workhouse registers do not record causes of death comprehensively, making this measuring rod useful only for the union-to-union comparisons we have employed elsewhere (Guinnane and Ó Gráda 2002b). We focus instead on a second strategy. Where workhouse registers survive, we can estimate mortality rates using the time lag between admission to the workhouse and death. Because the registers record a great deal of other information – including age at admission, health status at admission, sex, and many other characteristics – we can see how mortality rates differed across different types of inmates. The level of the mortality is interesting by itself. During the famine, people who died of diseases such as dysentery and diarrhoea normally did so within days of contracting them. This implies that deaths from those diseases occurring within a workhouse several weeks and even months after admission were probably the product of contagion in the workhouse. If those who died in the workhouse did so very quickly after admission, this is an indication that they had probably caught the disease before entering. But large-scale mortality after several months in the workhouse is a fair indication of mismanagement.[6] We can also use the characteristics of those inmates with high mortality rates to tease out indications of the workhouse's management. For example, if those most likely to die are those who are brought to the workhouse very ill, the workhouse probably had little to do with their death. We discuss our approach and report an econometric model of workhouse mortality on pp. 94–104 below.

The North Dublin Union before and during the famine

We can also learn more about the pressures facing workhouses by paying close attention to their management prior to the famine and during the crisis. Dublin city's workhouses invite study because most of their records have survived. The poor law divided Dublin into two unions, with the River Liffey offering a natural dividing line. The North Dublin Union, the focus of this study, began to receive paupers in early May 1840. Its catchment area included the north city and suburbs and adjoining rural districts in the baronies of Coolock, Castleknock and Uppercross. The union contained a population of just under 100,000 people (97,065 in 1841) and rateable property valued at £265,586 10s 0d, or £2.74 per capita. The bigger South Dublin Union, which opened its workhouse a few weeks earlier, contained 135,661 people and property rated at £402,516 13s 4d, or just under £3 per capita.[7]

The North Dublin Union's workhouse had operated as the city's house of industry in North Brunswick Street until 1840. Although created as a private charity in 1772, the house of industry had long relied on government funding. Originally intended as a place where vagrants would be committed to tedious work such as picking oakum, its main function soon became 'the relief of the aged and the infirm, and of those who laboured under temporary distress from want of employment'. Vagrants could be confined there and shirkers corporally punished, but the great majority of inmates entered voluntarily and could leave as they pleased (Warburton et al. 1818: vol. 1, 618–23; Cox 1996: 1–3; Maxwell 1946: 131–2).

Refurbishment of the House of Industry left the new workhouse with accommodation for an estimated two thousand inmates. The poor law commissioners hoped that this would be more than adequate, but the closure of the Dublin

Mendicity Institution soon after the opening of the workhouses put both of Dublin's unions under pressure.[8] This crowding-out effect is reflected in a motion proposed by a member of the board of guardians, Thomas Arkins, on 5 January 1842:

> that in as much as a very great number of women and children apply to this the North Dublin Union workhouse for admission and in consequence of the crowded state of the House are rejected ... it is the duty of the Board to inform the public of this fact in order that the destitute poor may not be deprived of the assistance they formerly received from the charitable and humane under the idea that this House is all sufficient for their relief. (NAI, BG78, NDU board minutes, 5 Jan 1842)

The workhouse of the North Dublin Union was the third to open its doors under the Irish poor law.[9] Although it would rarely contain its full complement of two thousand paupers before the famine, it always contained more than a thousand people. Johann Kohl, a German traveller who visited the North Dublin Union in 1842, believed that the poor would stay there only as long as absolutely necessary, trading their 'N.D.U.W.U. slave-costume' for 'their old miserable *sans-culotte* liberty dress' (Kohl 1844: 280–1). The huge workhouse potato-boiler, which attracted Kohl's curiosity, boiled four to five hundred individual portions, separated by nets, simultaneously.

The North Dublin Union workhouse was certainly managed with a view to economy. The American travelling evangelist Asenath Nicholson noted how the straw used for bedding and suds from the laundry were recycled to produce a 'rich manure', while pigs were fattened on the house's slops. In November 1845 in the wake of the first attack of blight the house acted on a suggestion from the poor law commissioners to try converting diseased potatoes into farina, but this attempt failed.[10] The spartan regime followed in the workhouse is well reflected in the union's minutes and reflected the harshness of life outside. In June 1840 the matron complained of the lack of tables and chairs in the dining room and of inmates catching cold from sitting on the flagstones. There were complaints of inferior oatmeal and watery potatoes. On 18 November 1840 the board complied with a request for unclaimed bodies for anatomical dissection. The sectarian divisions of the day were also reflected in life in the workhouse and in recurrent controversies between guardians.[11]

Sentiments of economy and compassion alternated in board discussions about the treatment of paupers. In May 1842 a proposal in favour of better breakfasts by one guardian was met with a claim from another that his own workmen were less well fed than the adult inmates and a protest from a third that the house was not 'a board and lodging house'. In October 1846 a complaint from one guardian that workhouse women were being employed in breaking stones out of doors was met with the quip from another that but for the potato blight women like them 'would be in the open fields digging potatoes, with their sleeves tucked up'. Corporal punishment and physical labour were standard, though within limits. In March 1841 the schoolmaster was reprimanded for using 'a very severe instrument' with seven thongs on one of the boys, and a few months later for severely beating another boy.[12] The harsh routine was mitigated by treats such as the occasional visit to the zoo by the workhouse children and a meat dinner once a year, on Christmas Day.[13]

In its early years the North Dublin Union attracted considerable controversy. The death rate in the workhouse seemed excessive, with the high number of infant deaths attracting particular notice. The accusation of high infant mortality prompted an interesting and sophisticated pamphlet by Rev. Thomas Willis of St Michan's, who highlighted the poverty of the Union's catchment area. Travellers such as Kohl, Nicholson and William Makepeace Thackeray toured the workhouse on the eve of the famine. Thackeray saw old men 'in considerable numbers' and at least 400 old ladies 'sitting demurely on benches' (some of whom stood up when the visiting party entered, to Thackeray's embarrassment). He also saw lots of young, healthy females with sly 'Hogarthian faces', and 80 babies in the nursery attended by their mothers. Nicholson deemed the rooms well ventilated and floors clean. The 'open door' policy which allowed in such visitors may have been part of a public relations exercise (Willis 1844: 7–9; Kohl 1844: 276–82; Thackeray 1888 [1843]: 344–6; Nicholson 1927: 5–6).

Venality and carelessness were common accusations against poor law guardians in the early years of the Irish poor law. Attendance at meetings was correlated with the value of patronage to be dispensed or contracts negotiated. In Ballina 'the Fair of Moyne prevent[ed] a full attendance' of guardians on 24 July 1847, even though the crisis facing the union was such that the six guardians present had to sign an undertaking to pay £10 each within a month to any merchant who would advance a supply of provisions for the workhouse.[14] Corruption on the part of rate collectors and the workhouse staff was also a problem. On the other hand a strict inspection system and strong popular resistance to paying rates limited the scope for abuse.[15]

Elections to the North Dublin Union board of guardians, consisting of 33 elected and 27 ex officio members, were keenly contested along confessional or party-political lines, and there was a considerable turnover of guardians. The first meeting of a new board on 30 March 1841 attracted 39 guardians. Rarely, however, did more than half the board membership attend meetings, so that in practice the board was run by a minority of activist members. Sectarian issues provoked more controversy on the board than any other topic and voting patterns on that score were predictable. However, divisions on other union matters tended not to be on party-political or sectarian lines. On the whole the North Dublin Union guardians did not let sectarianism or politics get in the way of the management of the union. The pressure to keep down rate charges and the near-constant presence of a representative of the poor law commissioners also constrained rent-seeking. Its records and contemporary press commentary suggest that, compared to other boards, it was relatively free from scandal and corruption.

How well managed was the North Dublin Union workhouse during the famine? As noted above any answer can only be relative. It must not be forgotten that Dublin was less affected by the famine than almost any other region or county in Ireland. Dubliners were less reliant on the potato than the rural population for which it was a staple. The impact of the failure on the cost of subsistence in Dublin should not be dismissed, but the famine's indirect impact, as an externality imposed by hardship in the rest of the country, was more serious. As the crisis intensified thousands from the rural interior headed for Dublin for relief and for work, and Dublin was also the main port of embarkation for Liverpool (Ó Gráda 1999: ch. 5).

During the famine the North Dublin Union usually catered for a disproportionate share of the city's poor. In early February 1847 it accommodated 2,506 inmates against the South Dublin Union's 2,246; at the end of April the numbers were 2,838 and 2,258, respectively.[16] The north side of the city was poorer, as reflected in the lower valuation per head of land and housing north of the river Liffey. The workhouse's location also meant that infirm and disabled paupers dispatched from England or Scotland landing at the North Wall were more likely to become charges on its ratepayers. The location of the city's main night asylum on Bow Street north of the Liffey was also a factor, 'centralis[ing] in this locality a frightful mass of destitution, not alone of our own poor, but also of the distressed and starving population of country districts, flying from their wretched and famine stricken homes'.[17] The North Dublin guardians repeatedly complained that the union's taxpayers were unfairly carrying the can for those western unions which supplied a significant share of admissions to its workhouse.

Since Dublin was virtually excluded from relief under the Labour Rate Act (the measure which channelled public funds into public works throughout most of Ireland until the summer of 1847), from the outset the burden of the famine fell disproportionately on the poor law. Though admissions and departures were subject to some seasonality, before the famine the North Dublin Union was nearly always at least three-quarters full. In 1846 the number of inmates never fell below 1,700, and it already exceeded its official capacity of two thousand by early November 1846. Still the pressure for admission continued to mount, leaving the guardians no option but to convert the workhouse's dining hall into a dormitory. In late 1847 the union's capacity was doubled to four thousand places. Before the famine the weekly number of deaths in the workhouse averaged about seven. It peaked at 44 in the first week of May 1847 and fell back to single figures in mid-1848. However, the onset of cholera caused the number to rise sharply again in 1849, peaking at 39 in mid-June. Such comparisons take no account of changing numbers in the workhouse: death rates in the workhouse (ratio of deaths to inmates in any week) were highest in 1846, not in Black '47. The number of inmates in the workhouse did not fall back to pre-famine levels until 1860.[18]

Table 5.1 reports a breakdown of deaths in the North Dublin workhouse in the first four months of 1847, a period when famine mortality was at its height in Dublin. The breakdown into 'immigrants' and 'Dubliners' is rather crude; 'immigrant' refers simply to inmates born outside the union. Though the category was meant to highlight the impact of famine-induced immigration on the North Dublin Union, almost certainly some of those counted as 'immigrants' were long-standing residents of Dublin's northside. Nevertheless, the breakdown gives some sense of the famine's impact on the city. The high concentration of men and women aged sixty years and above among the dead is particularly noteworthy.

Death in the North Dublin workhouse

Our earlier discussion of workhouse conditions raised the question of whether workhouses actually helped anyone, and if so, whom. There are several possible outcome measures one might like to examine here, but the most important is the only one available to us, which is whether inmates survived their stay in the workhouse, and if so for how long. Using a one-in-ten random sample of all who entered the North Dublin Union between 1844 and 1850, we study who died in the workhouse and how long they survived before dying.

Table 5.1 **Deaths in the Dublin Union, January–April 1847**

	'Immigrants'				'Dubliners'			
Age-Group	M	%	F	%	M	%	F	%
0–9	19	22	18	19	60	52	65	50
10–19	9	10	13	14	9	8	15	12
20–29	2	2	3	3	2	2	7	5
30–39	3	3	7	8	11	10	5	4
40–59	21	24	21	23	17	15	18	14
60 +	33	38	31	33	16	14	19	15
Total	87	100	93	100	115	100	129	100

Our main tool is one of a class of statistical models that go by various names. Demographers call them 'event-history analysis' while economists are more likely to use the biometric terms 'failure analysis' or 'duration analysis'.[19] The basic idea is that we study the determinants of the duration of spells: the length of time between the beginning of a spell (in this case, entry into the workhouse) and the end of the spell (the person either dies or leaves the workhouse alive). Most of our interest is in the conditional probability that a spell ends at a particular time, that is, whether a male would survive longer than a female, or an infant longer than an adult. The Cox proportional-hazards model, which is perhaps the most popular, has two important virtues for our purposes. The model is semi-parametric, which means that we do not need to specify anything about the shape of the underlying hazard rate. The Cox model lets the data shape the hazard as its wants, and only assumes that the effect of each covariate is to produce a proportional shift in the hazard.[20] The Cox model also makes it simple to incorporate time-varying covariates. This permits us to test for the impact of things that change while an individual is in the workhouse. For example, we use a monthly proxy for non-workhouse mortality in Dublin to capture the effect of overall mortality risks. Clearly this variable changes over time and the Cox model captures this feature nicely.

The data involve some complications. There was one way to start a spell – to enter the workhouse – but two ways to end it – either to die in the workhouse or to leave. Technically we have a competing-risks model, which corresponds to a multiple-decrement life table. Someone who dies in the workhouse cannot leave the workhouse alive, and vice versa. There is some potential for complication here if there is much correlation between the two risks. In modern mortality studies, for example, the fact that smoking causes both heart disease and cancer means that these two death risks are correlated. In our situation the correlation seems low. The approach we adopt amounts to assuming that the risks are conditionally independent (in the statistical sense); once we control for our covariates, the model assumes that the risk of dying in the workhouse is independent of the risk of walking out of the workhouse. This is the most common approach, which is an over-used justification, but here it is hard to construct stories that imply strong correlation between the risk of dying in the workhouse and the risk of leaving it.[21] We have not tried to deal with a second complication, which is the problem of unobserved heterogeneity. Suppose that each inmate in the workhouse had some trait unrecorded in the data that improved their ability to survive in the workhouse. Then those still alive in the workhouse after six months would have a higher value of this trait; the weak ones would die first. In general, unobserved heterogeneity biases the estimated hazard rate in such a way as to make it decline with time (or rise less slowly with time). The estimated hazards in our model do in fact decline sharply with time. Most who die in the workhouse do so relatively quickly. (The median spell from admission to death for those who died in the workhouse was only 1.6 months. Twenty-five per cent died within a fortnight.) This effect may reflect unobserved heterogeneity in part. We have not tried to employ any of the proposed ways of dealing with unobserved heterogeneity in duration models because of reservations about the additional assumptions these models require.

The Cox model suggests two natural ways of thinking about the questions we seek to address.[22] First, one can ask whether observed covariates shift the baseline hazard function. This allows us to see whether events beyond the guardians' control raise or lower death rates. We find, for example, that food prices were positively correlated with workhouse death rates, suggesting that some mortality spikes were caused by factors we cannot lay at the feet of the guardians. On the other hand, we find that inmates who entered the workhouse alone had higher mortality rates. This finding is open to several interpretations, but one is that inmates had to fend for themselves and were not adequately supervised and aided by workhouse staff. Second, one can ask whether the famine itself altered the shape of mortality in the workhouse, making everyone more likely to die, or changing the chance of death at some months more than others. Statistically, we can allow the Cox model to have several different baseline hazards. In our application we have inmates admitted to the workhouse in each of the years from 1844 to 1850, and we allow each of these admittance years to have its own baseline hazard with its own shape. This approach amounts to asking whether the famine shaped workhouse mortality in ways that no guardian could affect, while still allowing the covariates to shift mortality both before and during the famine. The baseline risks facing inmates admitted during the famine years is quite different from those admitted prior to the famine, showing that the famine altered the basic nature of the risks facing those in the workhouse.[23]

Definitions of covariates

We measure time in the number of months since the person enters the workhouse. After some experimentation we censor all observations at 60 months. Few individuals stay longer than 60 months, and very few died after being in the workhouse that long. If we did not censor the data we would allow a very few deaths at durations of more than five years have an unwarranted effect on the final results. Our covariates are of two types: those that reflect a characteristic of the inmate that does not change over time (for example, sex or the age at which the inmate was admitted to the workhouse), and those that change over time (such as proxies for the fiscal problems facing the guardians). We have organised the information in a way that reflects a trade-off between manageable numbers of variables on the one hand, and learning as much as possible from the sample on the other. We use a dummy variable for sex, and we interact this dummy with several other covariates in a search for gender effects. Many inmates were admitted to the workhouse as part of a family group, and we employ a dummy variable for those admitted alone. We parameterise age as follows: we have dummies for infants and for children (1–4 years), and for those aged sixty and above. Those aged 5–59 have a (continuous) spline term for age and age squared.[24] Another set of covariates are dummies describing health status on admission. As noted, workhouses were not supposed to admit people who had fever or other contagious illness, though many did. Here we divide the many notations into those who appear to be healthy (the omitted category); those admitted with minor illnesses; those suffering from fever, cholera, and other more serious illnesses (many of whom were 'recovering'); and those with chronic illnesses. Many inmates are missing this information, and we use a separate dummy for those who health status on admission is not known to us. This missing information is unfortunate, but our 'Health status unknown' variable does not create any bias; it amounts to a distinct health status.

We have two sets of controls for the individual's physical condition when first admitted to the workhouse. One refers to their appearance, and contains notations such as 'dirty' or 'ragged'. We take this variable to give some indication of how far gone the person was before seeking refuge in the work-house. The omitted category here is 'clean'. Another set of covariates pertains to the inmate's place of birth. Most inmates in the North Dublin workhouse came from Dublin city and county. For the sample period as a whole Dubliners accounted for about half of all inmates. But the proportion is not constant, and in 1845 Dubliners accounted for 69 per cent of all entrants. The proportion declined as the famine intensified. Indeed, the collection of information on place of origin reflects the guardians' increasing concern with the financial burden of catering to famine immigrants from the countryside. This place of origin variable is of interest because it helps us to control for an inmate's need. Presumably someone having come from Connacht (on the west coast of Ireland) is more likely to have been in poor physical condition and dire need. We also use a set of dummies for the year the inmate was admitted to the workhouse.

Some factors that affect the risk of death in the workhouse change over time. We employ two sets of time-varying covariates to capture the effect of these risks. The first is a proxy for mortality conditions in the city at large. We use the number of burials per month in Prospect Cemetery, located north of the city in Glasnevin.[25] This burials information is the best proxy available for general mortality conditions in the city of Dublin. A second proxy attempts to capture the guardians' problem of feeding a large number of inmates on a fixed and inadequate budget. (High-frequency data on workhouse expenditure is not available.) After some experimentation with prices for oats and maize, we opted for the average price of potatoes as reported in newspapers. We know from workhouse records that the inmates were not actually eating potatoes once the potato failed.[26] During the famine the workhouse purchased oatmeal and Indian meal (maize). We use potato prices because they are strongly correlated with the prices of oats and maize throughout our period, and because they are continuously available in a way maize prices are not.[27]

To our surprise, two other sets of time-varying covariates added virtually nothing to our model's explanatory power and were dropped from the final model. First, we suspected that there were significant seasonal variations in the risk of dying in the workhouse as elsewhere; the winter months, for example, were harder on the sick and weak than others. Certainly the workhouse reports show sharp spikes in death rates in the winter months. To capture this season-ality in preliminary specifications we used time-varying dummies for months. Some months had the expected effect (March, for example, was a bad month to enter the workhouse) but the month dummies were not collectively important.[28] This finding might mean that other variables we use, such as potato prices or overall Dublin mortality, already incorporate the monthly variations in the risk of dying. Second, one would think that some measure of crowding in the workhouse would help to predict death rates. That was not the case in our data, at least not once we controlled for other factors. In preliminary specifications we introduced a variable that equalled the number of inmates in the workhouse in the second week of each month, as reported in the Union's minute books. This variable (and non-linear versions of this variable) had almost no explanatory power. We also experimented with a variable that equalled the over-all death rate in the workhouse in each month. One could worry that this second variable would have a mechanical correlation in our model; after all, if an inmate dies in the individual-level data that will be reflected in the monthly reports. This death-rate variable also had virtually no explanatory power. What is even more surprising, the correlation between the crowding variable and the death-rate variable is very low, only about 0.18. This low correlation between workhouse crowding and death rates is interesting in itself, as it suggests that in periods when the guardians allowed the inmate population to swell, they were confident of their ability to take the measures needed to keep health conditions under control.

Results

We experimented with several different specifications, the main implications of which we now mention. Table 5.2 reports our preferred model. We include all the age and sex variables, even though some are not statistically significant. Exclusion of these variables affects some of our other results and we thought it best to retain them as basic controls. Our criterion for the inclusion of other variables in the final model is that it be part of a 'block' of variables that are jointly statistically significant. Thus some of the individual place-of-birth dummies are not significantly different from zero, but the entire block of such variables is significant and was included in final model. We include the potato price variable, even though it is not significant, because its interaction with older age is significant, and an interaction without its main effect is confusing. The coefficients are relative hazard rates; so, for example, being an infant raises the risk of dying by 7.8 times the 'baseline' hazard. The t-ratios have the usual interpretation. The model reported introduces two strata by dividing two periods, with June 1846 and before considered the earlier period. The idea is to allow the baseline hazard to shift when the famine came to Dublin. Experimenting with several definitions of 'pre-famine' did not materially affect

Table 5.2 **Estimates of the risk of dying in the NDU workhouse: Cox proportional-hazards model**

	Estimate	T-ratio	Mean of covariate
Covariates that do not change over time			
Age and sex			
Female	1.121	0.98	0.491
Infant	7.769	5.70	0.027
Female*Infant	1.224	0.62	0.011
Infant admitted alone	0.231	−1.39	0.002
Child	4.870	4.60	0.078
Female*Child	1.365	0.97	0.026
Child admitted alone	1.692	1.13	0.006
Admitted alone	1.393	2.27	0.662
Age spline	1.048	2.17	14.194
Age spline squared	1.000	−1.06	426.72
Aged 60 or over	2.140	2.01	0.118
Health status (omitted category is no health problems)			
Minor problem	1.044	0.18	0.077
Cholera	1.931	4.46	0.268
Chronic disease	3.453	2.37	0.006
Fever	1.321	1.53	0.199
Unknown	1.360	1.69	0.147
Place of origin (omitted category is Dublin city)			
Britain and abroad	0.705	−0.71	0.013
Connacht	1.548	2.05	0.041
Dublin region (excluding city)	1.253	1.22	0.070
Ulster	1.137	0.59	0.049
Elsewhere in Leinster	0.939	−0.34	0.088
Munster	1.581	1.92	0.031
Place unknown	1.568	3.16	0.231
Condition when admitted (omitted category is no information given)			
Dirty	0.906	−0.60	0.116
Ragged	0.582	−2.08	0.086
Covariates that change over time			
Mortality in Dublin	1.008	2.32	381.504
Mortality in Dublin squared	0.500	−2.09	1.5770
Potato prices	1.028	0.96	7.79
Potato prices*Inmate is aged 60	1.093	2.86	0.871

Note: The log-likelihood is -2054; the Wald statistic is 205.2. The sample includes 3,328 inmates, 395 of whom died in the workhouse. There are 16,112 inmate-months of exposure in total.

the estimates for our covariates, but did dramatically improve the model's fit. The baseline survivor function during the famine is only 0.04 per cent lower in any case.

Our age results show that infants and children were at great risk in the workhouse, being almost five times as likely to die in any given month. Although striking, this outcome should be set against the high death rates of infants and children in congested cities such as Dublin at this time. Neither age splines nor the dummy for older inmates is statistically significant, although both have plausible signs. Moreover, excluding the age splines and the older inmate dummy dramatically affects the model's overall fit, which is why these variables are included here.[29] This finding suggests complicated interactions between age and the other covariates in the model.

Neither the main effect for sex nor the interaction of sex with infant and child status has any significant impact. (We also tried interacting sex with the age splines and the older-inmate dummy, with similar lack of result). The coefficient on the main effect for sex and on female infants is also greater than one, which implies that females were at greater risk. Most studies find that male mortality exceeds female during famines, and in this respect the Irish famine is no exception. We cannot claim on the basis of our results that sex made no difference to the survival of inmates in the North Dublin workhouse. Perhaps admission to the workhouse was conditioned on sex in some way, or that men were in better condition when admitted, in ways that our data do not capture. But it is noteworthy nonetheless that our extensive efforts to uncover sex impacts have come to so little.[30]

Other features of the inmate's age and characteristics upon admission also yield some surprising results. Entering the workhouse alone, as opposed to as part of a family group, raises the risk of death considerably. (Infants who entered alone actually did better, but the number of inmates in this category was tiny.) This result may reflect, again, unobserved differences in the inmate's condition. A more disturbing and probably more likely interpretation is that supervision in the workhouse did not prevent staff and inmates from taking advantage of inmates unable to fend for themselves alone. If this is the right interpretation of our finding, it is disturbing evidence that workhouse organisation was insufficient to prevent desperate inmates from preying upon one another. We also investigated two other effects with so little impact that we omit them from our preferred model. The workhouse register lists each inmate's religion and marital status. We found that neither religion nor marital status had any important impact on mortality risks. This may well be because our other covariates have already captured the essential differences between Catholics and Protestants, or between married inmates and others.

The next block of variables, describing the person's health status at entry into the workhouse, contains few surprises. People suffering from serious illness when admitted did not last long in the workhouse. The 'unknown' category here is also positively correlated with mortality risk, suggesting that when information was not recorded the inmate was ill on admission. The condition variables (Dirty, Ragged) have surprising signs, but this variable also suffers from serious under-reporting, greatly reducing their value to us. About 78 per cent of inmates have no information on their 'condition'. The place of origin dummies, we hoped, would help control for the individual's sense of desperation. Their performance is consistent with that expectation. Dublin city is the omitted category here. Compared to Dubliners, people from the hard-hit provinces of Connacht and Munster had higher risks of death. People who made it to Dublin from the west of Ireland were more likely to be in bad shape and to lack resistance to the high-density conditions obtaining in the metropolis, and their experience in the workhouse reflects their condition on entry. The same applies to those whose place of origin was not stated. Although the outcome is plausible, this category reflects current conditions in the workhouse as much as anything else. Overall about nine per cent of the sample did not state a place of origin, but in 1844 this figure was 90 per cent and, in 1849, 51 per cent. Again, by including a dummy for inmates whose birthplace was not known we avoid any bias in the other estimates, but it is unfortunate that for some years this information for so many inmates is missing.

We have two sets of time-varying covariates. The first, mortality, implies that the death rate in the city at large affected risk in the workhouse. There are probably two effects at work here. One is that the same environmental factors affected both workhouse inmates and other Dubliners. The second is that mortality crises were caused by the same factors that drove people into the workhouse. The potato-price covariate (and its interaction with the dummy for inmates aged 60 and older) shows that higher potato prices increased the risk of dying in the workhouse. The potato prices are a proxy for the cost of running the workhouse. Higher prices meant not only that each calorie in inmate diet was more expensive, but also that there was less left over for fuel, medical care, and clothing. The effect is especially strong for the elderly. This dependence of mortality on potato prices illustrates the severe problems facing the workhouse master and his staff; conditions in the workhouse were partly under his control but also reflected his limited budget and the economic crisis in the country at large.

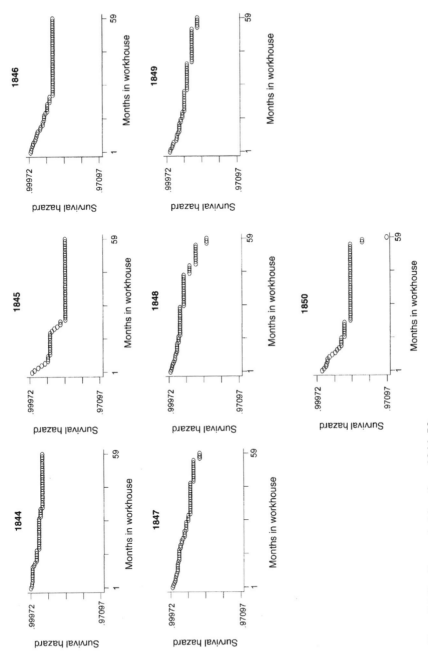

Figure 5.1 **Baseline survival functions, 1844–50**

Figure 5.1 plots the baseline survivor function for each of our seven strata. The survivor function is just an alternative representation of the mortality risks, and in this case is easier to inspect visually than the hazard rates that are actually estimated. The figure holds several lessons. First, mortality risks are surprisingly low; even in 1848, which is the worst year for the North Dublin Union workhouse, only about tw per cent of inmates die in the workhouse. Second, the figure shows the reason for allowing seven different strata. The shapes of the baseline survivor functions (which, as noted, correspond to the baseline hazards) different greatly across years. Those admitted in 1846 face good mortality risks. Those admitted in 1845, 1846 or 1850 do much worse, but once they have been in the workhouse for about two years are at little risk of death. People admitted in 1847–9 are never really out of danger, in contrast to earlier years. Finally, these graphs are powerful evidence of the famine's power. Life in the workhouse – or, more specifically, death and when it came – changed dramatically in Black '47.

Conclusions

Our study of workhouse mortality in North Dublin points to three features of inmate experience. First, contrary to expectation, males and females faced similar risks of dying in the workhouse. Second, the impact of inmate health status on arrival, and the patterns found in the place-of-birth information, show that the inmate's condition upon admission to the workhouse was a powerful predictor of mortality. The workhouse had no control over who asked for admission, and as the status of those who sought entry became more desperate, workhouse mortality increased. Third, forces entirely external to the workhouse, its inmates, and its management, including food prices and mortality conditions in the city at large, played a strong role in determining death risks inside the workhouse. All these findings must be tempered with the reminder that our information on workhouse admissions, while unusually rich for the Irish famine, is still incomplete. Although unlikely, it is possible that unobserved characteristics of the North Dublin Union's inmates affected their mortality risks in ways that are picked up by the covariates we are using to proxy for forces external to the workhouse. Yet overall our findings suggest that the poor law union and its employees performed creditably in these most trying circumstances.

The North Dublin Union, the particular focus of part of this study, was transformed by the Great Famine. A system intended to cater mainly for the elderly, the very young, and the temporarily unemployed, was confronted with a catastrophe that left some Dubliners destitute and drove thousands of others to the city in search of charity and work. In the most basic sense, the Union's managers faced the challenge competently if not brilliantly. But we should not congratulate them overmuch. The North Dublin Union never faced the challenges or the horrors witnessed and endured in the south and west of Ireland. This union also had one of the highest poor law valuations per capita in the country. On the other hand, it faced the problem of caring for a huge refugee inflow, and doing so within a system that stressed local rates even for the care of those from outside Dublin.[31] There is ample evidence of incompetence and venality in other workhouses and poor law unions during the famine. In the case of the North Dublin Union, however, most of the blame for excess mortality in its workhouse rests somewhere else.

CHAPTER SIX

The market for potatoes in Dublin in the 1840s

Introduction

Phytophthora infestans or potato blight was the proximate cause of the Great Irish Famine. Thanks to the researches of scholars such as Redcliffe Salaman, Kenneth Connell, L. M. Cullen, Austin Bourke, Joel Mokyr and Peter Solar, the chronology of the potato's diffusion in Ireland, its importance in the diet of the Irish poor on the eve of the famine, and the propagation of the blight and the extent of the damage caused by it, are by now well understood. Further afield other scholars have highlighted the problems caused by the potato's high transport and storage costs, and debated its traditional textbook role as a Giffen good. The literature has also analysed the potato's nutritional value, its varieties, its role in Ireland's peculiar version of the 'agricultural revolution', and its alternative uses as animal fodder and flour substitute.[1]

Though the potato was predominantly a subsistence crop in pre-famine Ireland, nearly every town and village had its formal or informal potato market. Over 400 towns were included in an 1846 parliamentary paper reporting the prices paid for potatoes throughout Ireland between 1840 and 1846, but this left out the smaller towns, and some of the larger towns held more than one market.[2] Such markets attracted the notice of foreign travellers, and the young William Makepeace Thackeray sketched and described several during his Irish tour of 1842. Thackeray found the busy potato market in Killarney 'a world of shrieking and gesticulating, and talk, about a pennyworth of potatoes'. In rain-soaked Galway the atmosphere was more low key, as 'bare-footed, red-petticoated women, and men in grey coats and flower-pot hats [pursued] their little bargains with utmost calmness'.[3] In their attempts to enforce the principle of 'less eligibility', the workhouses created under the Irish poor law of 1838 fed their inmates mainly on boiled potatoes. In the few years remaining before the Great Famine they relied on competition between traders in the towns to keep down the cost of potatoes.

Here I examine the market for potatoes in Dublin before and during the famine. I choose Dublin because its market is rather well documented in reports in the city's newspapers, but also because the potato was less important there, and the famine less severe, than in the rest of the island. I look first at the role of the potato in the diet of Dubliners before the famine and the competition that it faced from other foods. I then address the functioning of the market for potatoes before and during the crisis. I then focus on potato varieties and seasonality, and lastly on the impact of the blight on the market.

The potato in Dublin

A few observations on bread and baking in Dublin help to put the potato's role in the city in perspective. On the eve of the Great Famine, Dublin, a city of 230,000 people, contained well over one hundred bakeries, employing an average of between seven and eight workers.[4] Dublin's 3.2 bakery workers per thousand inhabitants exceeded Belfast's 2.9, Galway's 2.6, and Limerick's 2.4, though it fell short of Waterford's 4.8 and Drogheda's 4.2. Bakers were largely confined to the towns: compare County Mayo's 0.4 bakery workers per thousand inhabitants and even County Down's 0.9 per thousand. However, comparisons with some major European cities of the day suggest a less central role for bakers and bread in Dublin. For example, Copenhagen in 1850 (population 129,695) had 528 people working in bakeries, an average of 4.1 per thousand population; in 1851 Edinburgh (including Leith) had 1,198 bakers in a population of 191,000, an average of 6.3 per thousand. In London in 1851 it took over twelve thousand bakery workers to feed 2.3 million people, an average of 5.1 per thousand. Brussels, with a population slightly smaller than Dublin's in the 1840s, contained twice as many bakeries.[5]

Much of the difference between Dublin and these other cities is due the potato. In 1822 the physician to the Dublin Dispensary declared that the potato was 'the great barrier to the ravages of hunger, and indeed constitutes almost the only one'.[6] Yet for Dubliners potatoes never assumed the same importance in the diet as they did for Irish country people. Early in the nineteenth century 'even the working people [ate them] but once a day, and have generally substituted tea for breakfast and supper, particularly in the Liberties'. A normally reliable contemporary source put the quantity of potatoes sold weekly in Dublin in the 1810s at 56,000 stone.[7] That converts to 18,200 tons per annum; given the city's population of about 200,000 at the time, and assuming that all the potatoes sold were destined for human consumption, it would represent an average daily intake of about 0.6 lb. Given the pressures on living standards in the city between Waterloo and the Great Famine, some increase in potato consumption in the interim is likely.

Two estimates published in the wake of the second attack of potato blight in 1846 are also worth mentioning here. A report in the pro-Repeal *Freeman's Journal* in October 1846 claimed that before the blight the city's main potato market at Little Green Street had handled two hundred to three hundred sacks of potatoes 'on similar market days at the same season of the year'.⁸ A weekly average of, say, 1,200 sacks (1 sack = 21 stone) would mean annual sales of only 8,200 tons. The *Freeman's Journal* report tallies with another in the Tory *Dublin Evening Mail* two months earlier about potato traders taking £15,600 from the buying public yearly, since at the average price for potatoes this would mean about eight thousand tons.⁹ However, these estimates take no account of a smaller wholesale potato markets at St Kevin's Port and Spitalfields in the Liberties to the south-west of the city, nor of the considerable trade in potatoes off boats and ships on the quays and both canals. In this period the Royal Canal informally defined the city's northern city limits, and the busier Grand Canal its southern boundary. Nor do the estimates include the sales by hucksters who bought direct from farmers in the city's hinterland and sold direct to consumers. A little speculative political arithmetic suggests, however, that sales by hucksters may have doubled the reported totals. The 1841 census enumerated 555 male and 694 female 'hucksters and provisional dealers' in the city. Many of these, no doubt, did not deal in potatoes but let us assume that even a small fraction of the aggregate earnings of hucksters and provision dealers, say one fifth, was derived from potatoes. Then allowing them an average net income of £50 and a mark-up of fifty per cent on sales implies aggregate annual sales of about seven thousand tons.

Such numbers corroborate the point that on the eve of the famine potato consumption in Dublin was only a fraction of the estimated daily consumption of four or five pounds per head for Ireland as a whole. Still, the potato was a significant element in the diet of the poor and there was an active trade in potatoes in the city. The potato market operated throughout the year, and the potato was a regular feature of the Dublin diet except in the late spring and early summer months after the previous year's crop had run out. The seasonal rise in the price of potatoes reflected the cost of storage but also was slow enough to allow consumption to be maintained at a close to constant level for most of the year (Ó Gráda 1993: 111–21). The market at Little Green Street on Dublin's north side, where fifty factors were plying their trade in 1840,[10] was probably the biggest in the country.

This chapter describes the potato trade in Dublin during the 1840s, the famine decade. It relies largely on market reports in the contemporary press. Potatoes were sold daily at Little Green Street, but the brief account appearing on most Fridays throughout the decade in the *Dublin Evening Mail*[11] gives a good overview of prices and the market outlook in the week in question. The *Freeman's Journal* also offered a good coverage of the trade. We use these sources to describe the varieties traded, the seasonality in prices, and the impact of the famine on the working of markets. Wholesale prices were usually given per hundredweight (about fifty kilos), while retail prices at Little Green Street were reported per stone (about 6.3 kilos), and new potatoes sometimes quoted in pounds.

Potatoes, oatmeal and farina

The demand for potatoes in Ireland before and during the famine is usually characterised as both price and income inelastic.[12] In Dublin, however, the newspaper market reports imply that demand was sensitive to the price of readily available substitutes such as bread, flour and oatmeal. In early May 1840, for instance, high prices and poor quality potatoes induced less well-off consumers to opt for oatmeal 'which is not only more wholesome, but cheaper, and is used to a greater extent, from this cause, than has been known for years before'. Three years later low potato prices were attributed not only to the large supplies in the city but to 'the reduced prices of bread, oatmeal, etc.' In mid-May 1843 prices were held down by 'the very large supplies by boats and vessels at the quay' and 'the reduced prices of bread, oatmeal, etc.', while six months later reports of the potato crop were not encouraging, but 'from the low price of oatmeal [potatoes] are not likely to go high'. Some 18 months later fears that higher prices in country markets would force up Dublin prices were again tempered by the sense that 'the low price of oatmeal, as well as of flour . . . will keep prices moderate'. And not only did alternative foods exist: industrial demand for potatoes prevented their price from plummeting in years of plenty.[13]

During the famine, the high price of potatoes also reduced the demand for them. In June 1846 the prognosis for the new potato crop was already 'in favour of the grower', and the resultant speculation worried the *Mail*'s market reporter. He was reassured, however, by the sight of healthy, new potatoes arriving at

Little Green Street, and by the consolation that in the event of the 'measles' attacking the crop once again 'that coarse bread stuffs can and will be imported at one penny per lb.' In July of the following year, the same reporter noted that with good flour and oatmeal freely available 'consumers have an option to bake for themselves, if bakers will not take the hint', though soon that tune changed to a lament that the potato shortage was allowing bakers to keep up the price of bread.[14] Market reports in the *Freeman's Journal* also repeatedly alluded to these substitute foods. In September 1846 high prices meant that consumption of pot-atoes had 'sadly fallen off' and consumers 'betaken themselves to bread'. Potatoes were 'a matter of luxury than otherways, being now only in use at the tables of the opulent'. Even in hotels potatoes could not be had, or '[we]re charged as a separate dish on the bill of fare'. In May 1848, when potatoes cost between 7s and 10s per cwt, sales could be effected only 'with great difficulty . . . from the great decline in consumption, bread, flour, etc. being invariably the staple food for the higher and middle classes, as well as oatmeal and Indian meal for the poorer'.[15]

In Ireland potatoes were only very rarely used to produce alcohol, but even in Dublin they were used as animal fodder[16] and they also had a limited use as an input into starch production and farina (potato-flour).[17] The demand from starch and farina manufacturers must also have had a moderating – if minor – influence on movements in potato prices. The trade in potatoes for potato-flour or farina is first mentioned in the market reports on 9 October 1840 as an outlet for Droppers and Lumpers (inferior potatoes), 'several establishments of this kind being now at work in the city'. A second report some months later (19 March 1841) noted that 'farino' saved the baker 'from £5 to £6 for mixing'. The next reference to farina is as an outlet for potatoes tainted by the blight being sold at 1s per cwt in September 1845.[18] In the following month North Dublin Union workhouse acted on a suggestion from the poor law commissioners to try converting diseased potatoes into farina, but the attempt failed.[19] In the following weeks much of what was on offer was bought up by farina and starch manufacturers at a fraction of what clearly sound potatoes fetched. In the wake of the renewed failure of 1846 the main demand for 'tainted' and 'hazardous' potatoes again came from starch and farina manufacturers. In the wake of the failure of 1848 'from 80 to 800 tons a day' were bought for farina, and on a morning in early September 1848 one farina dealer bought fifty tons of tainted potatoes for 7d per cwt, paying £29 3s 4d for the lot. By then potatoes were being examined and graded like eggs, in two, three, or four categories; 'what, therefore, is carefully selected, and charged high for table use, is not a fair criterion to judge a crop by'.[20]

Elementary economics suggests that the less elastic the demand for a commodity the greater the impact of short-term fluctuations in supply on its price. Given factors such as the dependence of the city on coastal shipping, the pressure of other farm work on producers, and variable weather conditions, shocks to the supply of potatoes were inevitable. In the Dublin market reports such factors are mentioned, but sharp week-to-week fluctuations in prices were relatively few, even during the famine. This suggests either that other foodstuffs were usually available or else that consumers dipped into their own stocks of potatoes in weeks in which the market supplies were thin and stored up in weeks when they were plentiful.[21]

In late 1846 and again in the early summer of 1848 the price of potatoes in Dublin reached four times the pre-famine average. The rise in Belfast and elsewhere in the country was commensurate. High food prices are a frequent concomitant of famine, but the quadrupling of prices is unusual. Severe famines in England in 1556 and in Bangladesh in 1974–5 only doubled the price of the staple crop, while the increase in the price of rye in Finland at the height of the famine of 1867–8 was only about fifty per cent. In much of Scotland in 1697–8 and in Italy in the late 1640s the price of the staple food crop trebled, however, and in France during *le grand hiver* of 1709 wheat prices in several regions trebled, and quadrupled in the east and north-east. In early 2002 a severe drought increased the price of maize in Malawi fourfold, albeit for only a brief period. The huge rise in potato prices in Ireland was a reflection of how disastrous was the harvest failure and, presumably, also of the lower demand elasticity for the staple crop.[22] It is also noteworthy that the prices of substitutes such as maize, bread and oatmeal did not rise by nearly so much in the 1840s.

Porterage and retail margins

Famines are almost invariably accompanied by accusations of profiteering. On the eve of the famine the allegedly high margins demanded by potato factors at Little Green Street prompted frequent complaints in the press. In July 1840 the *Mail* called for measures to be taken against a 'combination' which obliged the purchaser to pay three pence or four pence per sack for porterage, 'whether they want to or not'. Not only was this so-called '*screech*-money' 'contrary to usage everywhere else', but it was a charge added to the four pence per sack commission that farmers as vendors were charged. Such charges – one sixth or one seventh of the price – seemed particularly onerous in seasons when potatoes were plentiful. On this issue the *Mail* and the *Freeman's* were at one; the latter also deemed the commissions charged too high since 'there is no risk – the trade is virtually ready money'.[23]

Though the Little Green Street traders may well have colluded on porterage charges, they were constrained by the growth of other less formal markets in potatoes. There are repeated references in the market reports to the influence of the coastal and canal trades in potatoes. In early June 1841 the *Mail* reported between forty and fifty boats discharging potatoes on the city's quays and selling them on the spot; in late February 1842 'the arrival of a cargo or two of pink eyes from Campbelltown'; and so on. Not that this trade was completely free of the nuisance of porterage – the *Mail* complained of 'exorbitant' charges for 'wheel out' – yet the element of competition was still there.[24] In May 1842 trade at Little Green Street had fallen off 'on account of the very large supplies by boats and vessels at the quay', and this alternative, noted the *Mail*, 'for the present, does away with gross overcharge of porterage'. In January 1845 the *Mail* claimed that the boats had got rid of 'about 8d per sack porterage, as between buyer and seller', and reduced markets at the Little Green. On the eve of the famine trade from ships or from stores by the canals or the quays bulked large.[25]

Small-scale itinerant dealers or 'hucksters', some of whom who bought directly from growers and sold direct to consumers on the streets, offered another way of bypassing the formal markets. However, they too were suspected of exploiting buyers both in terms of charging high margins and offering potatoes of dubious quality. What margins did they charge? Did their margins increase during the famine? In May 1842 the *Mail* could not help remarking 'the great difference of price charged in retail by hucksters, and more so the deficient weights they give; in fact, in and about the suburbs of the city such a thing as an examination of weights seldom takes place, and a more vigilant eye of our paid officials is absolutely necessary; a plunder of the poor in this way being a matter of course'. In October the potatoes on offer from the hucksters were 'generally mixed and unsound'. A few weeks later hucksters were the main suppliers of what potatoes there were; unlike the factors they could recoup losses on bad potatoes from their regular suppliers.[26]

On occasion the market reports distinguish between wholesale and retail prices at the city markets. The retail prices are not those charged by hucksters in the suburbs, but they reflect the price to the consumer living in the vicinity of the markets. In August 1846 the *Mail* remarked that retail prices were 'completely out of keeping with the wholesale prices being nearly double their value'. In late 1847 the *Freeman's Journal* also inferred exploitative behaviour from the margins between these same wholesale and retail prices.[27] The following mark-ups are based on such evidence. They report the average mark-up on the wholesale price before and during the famine. The numbers refer to the average wholesale and retail prices quoted. They are consistent with some 'exploitation', but the higher margins during the famine might also be a reflection of the reduction in trade.

Table 6.1 **Margins in the potato trade in the 1840s**

Year	Mean mark-up (%)	Standard deviation	Obs.
1842–4	10.8	8.7	12
1845–6	34.6	23.9	26
1847	22.4	15.4	17
1848	15.0	9.4	8

Such gaps between retail and wholesale levels leave little scope for heightened profiteering during the famine. In the 1840s monopolistic margins were most likely constrained by the fact that the potato trade was one requiring little capital to enter and characterised by repeat transactions with the same customers.

A well-known drawback of the potato in the nineteenth century was that it was costly to transport by road: Elizabeth Hoffman and Joel Mokyr[28] reckon that before the famine one quarter of its value 'evaporated' with every ten miles it travelled. Much of Dublin's potato supply accordingly came from market gardens around the city. Carriage by canal or coastwise was not so expensive, however, and considerable quantities also arrived by canal or coastwise. In 1842–5 the inward traffic in potatoes on the Grand Canal, mostly Dublin-bound, averaged 1,600 tons.[29] High priced new potatoes and seed potatoes travelled from Britain, Spain and even the Azores. Bulk movements of potatoes both influenced and responded to prices and supplies on the market. In May 1844 high prices were attributed to a reported outward shipment of two thousand tons or more. Three months later 'large quantities' were arriving by steamer from British ports. In October 1844 the *Mail* noted that 'large quantities' were being sent from Liverpool to America.[30]

The coastwise and canal trades in potatoes were much more important than the import–export trade with the ports of Liverpool, Glasgow and Bristol. Market reports are replete with references to the presence of boats on the city's quays. While sales in Green Street were by the hundredweight, the boats typically quoted by the ton. Boats at the canals and quays were credited with keeping down prices in January 1845, but amid the gloom and panic of autumn 1845 in the wake of the first attack of *Phytophthora infestans*, the *Mail* predicted more than once that 'large exports towards spring' would result in higher prices. In October 1845 markets would have been better supplied but for vessels arriving with other provisions 'taking out return cargoes of potatoes'. In December 1845 the arrival of large supplies by canal and coastwise were expected to relieve pressure on the city markets. In January the *Mail* reported the import into England of seed potatoes from the Channel Islands and Spain, and anticipated imports from the same quarters into Dublin as well as from the Azores. Again throughout the spring the canals and harbour contained 'a good many boat loads' of potatoes, including some from Scotland and England, and in March there were supplies from Kildare. In early January 1847 thirty tons of imported potatoes were sold at auction for seed, at from £10 to £14s 10d per ton. On 14 February 1849 the *Freeman's* noted the 'considerable' importation of 115 tons of potatoes from Spain. Organised wholesale markets virtually ceased to function for some months in early 1847, 'yet we find considerable quantities in the hands of hucksters, either had from vessels or from persons now digging them out'. On 9 July 1847 the *Mail's* correspondent gleefully reported the arrival of large supplies of early potatoes from areas hitherto too costly and time-consuming to ship from:

> we, therefore, cannot but congratulate our readers and the public on the immense advantages the several railways will bestow upon the city. These supplies are furnished by the Cashel and Drogheda lines from some 30 and 40 miles distant in a couple of hours; prices therefore have lessened and at 2d they can be had throughout the streets.

Potato varieties

A potato is not a potato is not a potato. In mid nineteenth-century Ireland as today, potatoes were far from being a homogeneous crop. They differed according to shape and colour, season, durability, starch content, and taste. The hierarchy of varieties shifted as old varieties degenerated and new ones were introduced. The standard story is of all other potato varieties losing ground to the high-yielding but watery Lumper in the pre-famine decades. The shift was a symptom of the increasing impoverishment of the rural masses. A sense of the Lumper's inferior status is well captured by William Cobbett's report from Waterford in 1834 that 'when men and women are employed, at six-pence a day and their board, to dig *minions* or *apple-potatoes*, they are not suffered to *taste them*, but are sent to another field to dig *lumpers* to eat'.[31] That the evidence from the Dublin market does not give the Lumper pride of place most likely reflects the higher living standards of Dubliners. A report in October 1840 that large quantities of coarse potatoes will be required by 'the cow feeders', is followed by price data on 'lumpers and coarse potatoes'.[32]

Table 6.2 refers to the number of times a price was given for eight varieties in the *Mail*'s weekly market report. By far the most traded varieties were the Cup and the Apple. The Apple, which had been grown in Ireland for about a century, was important for its keeping quality, while the Cup seems to have been the staple of the Dublin poor. Before the blight struck the Apple usually commanded a premium of 8*d* to 12*d* per cwt over the Cup. The Lumper features too, at the lower end of the market. The variety called 'White' was not the Lumper, since its main feature was that it was an early potato. Typically the Cup cost less than the Apple. Note too the implication that the Apple lasted longer than the Cup; indeed, old Apples were still traded in July, even after the arrival of new potatoes. The Apple, once 'the aristocrat of potatoes', was no longer as reliable or high yielding in the 1840s as it had been in its late eighteenth-century

Table 6.2 **Varieties available on the Dublin potato market 1840–8**

Month	Pinks	Cups	Bangors	Whites	Apples	'New'	Kemps	Lumpers
January	7	24	1	0	24	0	0	9
February	4	21	1	0	20	0	0	6
March	3	27	1	1	30	0	0	14
April	4	26	0	1	26	2	0	8
May	0	29	0	1	30	2	0	1
June	0	25	0	1	23	18	0	5
July	8	10	6	2	21	21	1	1
August	19	2	10	6	1	3	2	3
September	14	13	3	3	1	0	1	4
October	21	24	0	1	4	0	2	9
November	14	13	0	0	13	0	3	7
December	9	18	0	0	16	0	2	5
Total	103	232	22	16	209	46	11	72

Source: Dublin Evening Mail

heyday.[33] Also occasionally mentioned is the Bangor; its early appearance on the market and the premium that it commanded suggest that this may be the Wicklow Banger described by Austin Bourke. There are also occasional references to the Black, a 'coarse' variety. It was claimed that a new variety, the Kemp, was more blight resistant than the rest.[34] Also mentioned several times in 1840–2 were coarse potatoes dubbed 'Droppers', which fetched prices at the lower end of the range, though often above Lumpers.[35] Table 6.2 offers an overview of the seasonality of supply of the main varieties in the 1840–8 period.

The market reports in the newspapers were very much alive to seasonal regularities and deviations in potato prices. The prices obtaining in March 1841 indicated that 'we shall have smart prices the whole summer', while those reached in early July 1842 were deemed to be 'probably the highest of the year', and 4*d* to 4.5*d* per stone retail in November 1844 was declared 'equivalent to 6*d* to 7*d* per stone next Easter'.[36] The drop in prices in May 1845 was noted as an 'unusual thing' and its persistence into June prompted the declaration that prices thereafter would be 'moderate'.[37] In this section we describe seasonality as reflected in the prices of the two main varieties traded, the Cup and the Apple.

The seasonal pattern was interrupted by fluctuations caused by the impact of bad weather or sowing and harvest work on market supplies. The 1844–5 season was 'one of the few . . . wherein the potato markets have fallen in the months of May and June'.[38] The panic in autumn 1845 about the nature and extent of the potato blight had a very unsettling effect, as traders sought to dispose of potatoes which they feared might rot later. The *Mail* duly noted the glutted markets and counselled purchasers not to be fooled by the low prices. In November uncertainty still reigned, with 'every one . . . hurrying to market and selling, fearing further damage'. However, by early December farmers had allegedly discovered that pitted potatoes were safe, and were 'consequently holding over for extreme prices'.[39]

Figures 6.1 and 6.2 describe the week-by-week changes in the minimum and maximum quoted prices for Cups and Apples between 1840 and 1848. On the whole the outcome reflects the seasonality movements described above. A pattern of gradual price rises from autumn to late spring or early summer is detectable, as are the weeks when the supplies of one or other variety has been exhausted. Before the famine the only steep rise in these years occurred in May 1842. As figure 6.1 shows, Apples disappeared from the Dublin market after the first attack of blight. Note, however, the steep rise in their price in 1845/6, much greater than in any earlier season. Figure 6.2 indicates that Cups continued to be traded though in much reduced quantities in 1845–6, 1846–7, and 1847–8.

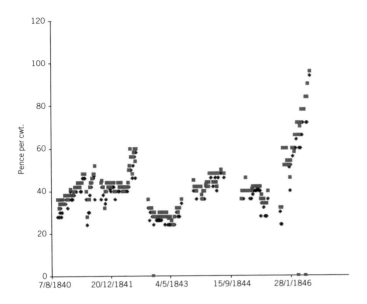

Figure 6.1 **Apple prices, 1840–6**

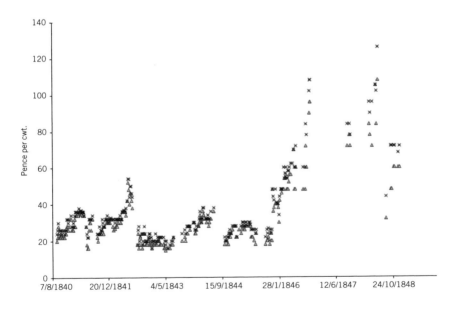

Figure 6.2 **Cup prices, 1841–8**

In this case too, the trough-to-peak rises were bigger during the crisis. As I have argued elsewhere, these patterns render unlikely the hoarding on a significant scale of potatoes destined for the Dublin market.[40]

The impact of the potato blight

The acreage under potatoes in Ireland almost certainly reached its all-time high in 1845.[41] The *Dublin Evening Mail* struck a very cheerful note about potato supplies during the summer of 1845, noting that in late July large supplies of good quality Apples were still on offer, and new potatoes 'coming in freely'. During August the accounts continued of large supplies and low prices, and on 5 September the reporter could not remember having seen larger markets of potatoes, 'not only good in quality but cheap'. A week later he sounded a sombre note for the first time, though 'from the most minute inquiry none of this kind has yet been offered for sale in the Dublin markets'. Panic struck the markets on the following week. Suppliers glutted the markets with potatoes, 'all attempting to sell as fast as they can'. For some weeks uncertainty about the state of the harvest and the keeping quality of even sound potatoes reigned. On 31 October the reporter remarked that prices were not much higher than the seasonal norm, partly because suppliers were still keen to sell, 'fearing the worst'. On 4 November the *Freeman's* reporter noted 'the anxiety to get rid of the decaying potatoes'. The pressure on the market was 'of the seller, not the buyer', and with the result that 'where most damage has been done, the price of potatoes is low'. By early December, however, such fears were at an end; 'the farmers have discovered that the potatoes will keep and are consequently holding over for extreme prices'. Prices rose thereafter, though not extravagantly so. Yet on 10 July 1846 old Apples were fetching 7s 10d to 8s per cwt, more than double their price a year earlier.

The Tory *Mail* reacted cautiously to news of the 1846 harvest. Though by late July its market reporter feared that the blight was more general than in 1845, editorials deemed alarm 'premature at least', in the belief that the disease was confined to the early crop. On 21 August the *Mail's* editor still clung to the hope that reports of the blight had been exaggerated by vested interests. A week later the unprecedented nature of the calamity 'with which it has pleased Providence to visit our country' was finally recognised. Reports in the *Freeman's Journal* were also initially cautious, though by late August it was predicting that in a few months there would be no potatoes, and 'probably in the following years they will be known only as a garden vegetable'. Tragically that prediction would prove close to the truth. By October supplies in Little Green Street were only one tenth of their pre-blight norm, and by January the market hardly functioned, with prices being reported only intermittently in the press. On 12 February 1847 the *Mail* reported the closure of the market at Little Green Street, and it seems to have remained shut until early April, though hucksters kept up a limited retail trade. Cups seemed to have resisted the blight best in 1846.[42] The closure of the market did not represent 'market failure' in the sense that the increasingly poor quality of potatoes coming to market deterred buyers:[43] the problem was almost certainly that supplies had dried up.

The failures of 1845 and 1846 reduced the aggregate acreage under potatoes in 1847 from about two million acres to less than 0.3 million acres. The *Mail*'s reports about the 1847 harvest began on a cheerful note, countering scattered reports of the appearance of blight with the [unfounded] assertion that the crop was strong enough 'to be able to recover where only partially attacked'. This time the optimism was largely borne out to the extent that supplies were mainly free of taint, and that the prices of substitute foods were much lower than in the 1846–7 season. In early September the *Mail* was happy to refute a panic that 'ha[d] been attempted to be got up' through false reports that the crop was rotting everywhere. Yields per acre would turn out to be not far short of the pre-famine norm. However, the reduced acreage under potatoes in 1847 – 0.27 million acres (or slightly over 0.1 million hectares) against the pre-famine norm of over two million acres (or about 0.8 million hectares) ensured that prices continued high during the 1847–8 season.

In 1848 the press was also circumspect about confirming the blight at first. The *Southern Reporter* accused some interested parties of spreading rumours of blight about as early as mid-July, but 'in our own county, and in every other in Ireland, if we may believe the local journals, the potato disease of 1846 has not yet made its appearance' (*Southern Reporter*, 13 July 1848). On 14 July, the *Mail*'s reporter hoped that fears of a new outbreak would not be realised. On 17 July the *Freeman's*, citing the *Southern Reporter*, mentioned 'isolated cases' of blight. On 19 July it pronounced the markets 'decidedly favourable', with less in the press about the prevalence of the disease than in 1847. On 21 July, however, full markets and the sudden lowering of prices offered tell-tale signs of a realization that the crop had failed. Whites and Cups were being sold for 3s to 4s 6d per cwt, and Pinks for 4s to 5s. Still, the *Freeman's* tried not to sound an alarmist note, declaring on 26 July that 'the disease has been stayed', reprinting an attack in the *London Morning Advertiser* on 'the speculators and the alarmists' on 1 August, and expressing the hope the following day that a change in the weather might yet save most of the crop. The markets on the previous days were crowded all the same, and while there had been a 'remarkable decline in prices', sacks of disease-free potatoes commanded a considerable premium. Lumpers could be had for 1*s* 6*d* to 2*s* 6*d* per cwt but 'very picked' sacks cost 3*s* 6*d* to 4*s* per cwt. On 9 August the prevalence of blight was 'unmistakable' and both sellers and buyers were transacting their exchanges accordingly. By the third week of August the potato fields around the city had 'the appearance of November', with farmers busily pulling up the stalks in the hope of salvaging some of the crop. In the following days hundreds of tons of contaminated potatoes sold for farina, and most offered for sale were small and unripe. On 6 September the *Freeman's* reported that potatoes were being examined and classified like eggs 'in two, three, or four kinds'. Three days later 'picked' samples were selling at a shilling a stone retail, infected potatoes at tuppence a stone. With quality now so variable – some infected, some prematurely harvested, some safe – market prices conveyed far less information than before. Again the impact of the blight across varieties seems to have been uneven: only Kemps and Lumpers seemed blight free, with Pinks and Cups being the hardest hit.[44] In the following weeks the market was sustained by shipments from abroad and coastwise. But the failure of 1848 was a turning point, since it convinced farmers that the blight was now endemic and the potato accordingly no longer a dependable crop.

Conclusion

In the apocalypse that unfolded in Ireland from the autumn of 1846 on, the city of Dublin escaped lightly. Yet the performance of its potato market traces the contours of the crisis quite well. In normal times the Dublin market, like other potato markets, was characterised by the range of potato varieties on display, and a rather regular seasonal movement in prices. Once the blight struck, the Dublin market experienced a rush of supplies from nervous growers and merchants, just as markets throughout the country did. And from early 1847 until the following summer other markets also basically ceased to function, just as Dublin's did. Two other features of the market for potatoes bear emphasis. First, the seasonal tempo of supplies during the famine rules out hoarding on the part of sellers or panic buying on the part of consumers. Second, the tell-tale symptoms of *Phytophthora infestans* enabled buyers and sellers to distinguish healthy from blighted potatoes, so that prices adjusted to quality, ruling out the creation of what economists call a market for 'lemons'.

CHAPTER SEVEN

Mass migration as disaster relief

CO-AUTHORED WITH KEVIN H. O'ROURKE

Introduction

Mass long-distance emigration from Ireland did not begin with the Great Irish Famine. Yet the outflow was greatly swollen by that famine, and this distinguishes the Irish crisis from most historical and modern Third World famines. The migration was the product of the United States' open door policy and Ireland's being part of the United Kingdom. No similar prospect is open to modern famine-threatened economies. The distinction raises many questions about the character and scope of the famine migration and its effectiveness as a complement to, or substitute for, the lack of other forms of famine relief.

All famines induce people to move temporarily in search of food and in order to escape disease. Much of the movement is from rural areas into the towns, and when the worst is over most of the migrants usually return home (Sen 1981: 98, 205; Watkins and Menken 1985: 652; Findley 1994). Some of the migration during the Great Irish Famine followed this pattern, as cities and bigger towns were swollen by the arrival of thousands of largely unwelcome famine migrants seeking relief or work. The huge increase between 1841 and 1851 in the percentage of Dubliners born outside Dublin (from 27 to 39 per cent) was largely the result of the Great Famine. The inflow into the cities provoked its own problems and responses.

However, a distinction must be made between such 'local', largely temporary, movements and permanent long-distance migration. A crucial difference between the Great Irish Famine and most other famines is that for many of the Irish poor in the 1840s, mass emigration provided a welcome safety valve. As explained in more detail later, estimates of Irish famine-induced emigration can be only approximate, but famine emigrants certainly numbered more than half of the one and a half million or so who left Ireland for good between the mid-1840s and the early 1850s. The number of Irish-born persons living abroad more than doubled in that period, and the number in the United States and Canada probably increased by more than that.

The famine migration occurred just before steamships won out over sail on the north Atlantic route. A great deal has been written about the terrible conditions and high mortality endured by Ireland's 'economic refugees' on the long crossing (e.g. Scally 1995: ch. 10), but what such accounts hide is the reality that most Irish emigrants made it safely to the other side during the famine years. Raymond Cohn (1984, 1987) has inferred migrant mortality on the passage between Europe and New York between 1836 and 1853 from a sample of contemporary passenger lists. What is most remarkable about his findings is that neither the Irish as a group nor the famine years stand out; the record of German ships in 1847 and 1848 was much worse, and curiously 1849, not 1847, produced the highest mortality overall. Cholera was presumably responsible for the high mortality in 1849. In table 7.1 Irish ports and Liverpool represent Irish emigrants. While the death rate out of Liverpool was higher in 1847–8 than in 1845–6, the mean mortality rate was still less than two per cent. Whether the high mortality out of Irish ports in 1852 reflects a 'rogue' small sample (two ships) deserves further checking. Other data, it is true, highlight Black 1847, and mortality among poorer passengers who chose ships bound for Maritime and Canadian destinations (who accounted for nearly half of the Irish who crossed the Atlantic in Black '47, but only 10–15 per cent thereafter) was much higher than

Table 7.1 **Mortality on New-York bound ships, 1847–53**

	(a) Irish ports		(b) Liverpool		(c) France		(d) Germany		(e) London	
Year	MR	N	MR	N	MR	N	MR	N	MR	N
1845	—	—	0.76	13	0.61	8	0.96	5	3.57	1
1846	—	—	0.91	18	1.18	11	1.07	13	1.28	5
1847	1.33	5	1.73	17	0.83	6	3.77	5	1.09	3
1848	2.74	5	1.36	34	1.35	11	3.36	2	1.04	2
1849	3.36	14	3.33	47	1.74	7	1.51	8	0.56	1
1850	1.16	7	1.54	50	0.55	3	4.41	3	1.89	2
1851	0.67	16	1.28	78	0.79	12	1.05	8	0.52	8
1852	3.59	2	0.88	67	0.74	16	0.55	5	0.96	12
1853	0.62	5	1.73	54	1.30	18	1.01	27	1.23	10

MR = Mortality rate (%)
N = Number of ships
Source: Ó Gráda (1999: 107), based on data supplied by Raymond Cohn.

those bound for New York. Cohn's numbers exclude ships that sank or turned back and unrecorded deaths on board. Nor do they include deaths in the wake of arrival. Still, his results suggest that Mokyr's assessment of the overall death rate on the north Atlantic passage – 'five per cent of the total overseas migration at the most' – is not far from the truth (Mokyr 1985: 267–8). In the sometimes chaotic circumstances, the outcome is an impressive achievement.

On arrival, the prospects facing the typical Irish immigrant were unskilled labour and slum accommodation in the big cities. Yet surely the fundamental comparative point to make here is that most migrants survived the passage and that many of today's famine victims would welcome such prospects in North America, Japan or western Europe.

The power of migration to reduce famine mortality depended in part on the extent to which a poverty trap operated: the really poor, who were most vulnerable during the famine, and who most needed to emigrate, were less likely to be able to afford the voyage than their better-off neighbours. In fact, several considerations suggest that emigration may have provided a more effective safety valve than would be possible today. First, it occurred during that 'liberal interlude' when the international movement of labour was freer than ever before or since. Second, it occurred at a time when long-distance travel by sea was relatively cheap. A steerage passage from Ireland to Britain could be had for a few shillings and to one of the Canadian maritime ports – the least expensive transatlantic route – for a few pounds. True, £3 or £4 still amounted to one third or one half of an unskilled worker's yearly wages or a similar fraction of pre-famine income per capita (compare Mokyr 1985: 10), and this must have ruled out long-distance migration for the most destitute; but long-distance travel for the poorest of the poor is relatively more expensive today. Even the cheapest one-way fares from Addis Ababa, Mogadishu or Khartoum to London or New York are multiples of income per capita in Ethiopia, Somalia or Sudan, rather than fractions, as was true in the Irish case. Nonetheless, and in particular despite the possibility of very cheap fares to Britain, a poverty trap probably did prevent emigration from being an efficient form of famine relief. We try to verify this intuition using the available cross-county data, and speculate on the contribution which emigration *did* make to reducing excess mortality during the famine (see pp. 133–6 below).

Long-distance emigration differs from famine relief in another crucial respect: it may well be irreversible. In modern famines, food is shipped to the hungry, and when famine retreats, outside food shipments cease. In the Irish case, the hungry went to where the food was, and they never returned. The famine thus had a permanent impact on the Irish economy, whereas other famines leave a more transitory imprint on the societies which they afflict. On pp. 135–41 we deal at length with the long run demographic and economic consequences of the Irish famine emigration.

Poverty and population on the eve of the famine

A few remarks first on the Great Famine's context. How did Irish incomes in the early 1840s compare with those in the Third World today? Only the crudest answer is possible. However, Irish economic historians believe that average income in Ireland just before the famine was somewhat less than half of that in Great Britain, and British economic historians estimate that incomes in Britain have increased eight- or tenfold between then and now. In the late 1980s, moreover, the average purchasing power of incomes in Ethiopia was about 2.8 per cent of Great Britain's, and in Somalia about 6.6 per cent (Summers and Heston 1991: table 2). Taken together, these numbers indicate that Irish living standards on the eve of the Great Famine lay somewhere between those of Ethiopia and of Somalia a few years ago, though closer to Somalia's (Ó Gráda 1995a).

Much of the recent discussion about the Irish economy before the famine seeks to answer the question, 'Was Malthus right?' In 1817, Malthus wrote, in a letter to Ricardo, that 'the land in Ireland is infinitely more peopled than in England; and to give full effect to the natural resources of the country a great part of the population should be swept away from the soil'.[1] In subsequent decades the notion that Ireland's poverty was a result of overpopulation took a firm hold in British policy-making circles.[2] Politically, the Irish famine and Irish emigration have to be viewed in the context of this debate, and when the famine struck many intellectuals regarded it as an inevitable consequence of Ireland's failure to adopt preventive checks (such as emigration, or a lowering of the fertility rate). This belief clearly influenced the British government's attitude towards famine relief during the crisis. Nonetheless, whether ecological disasters such as the havoc wreaked by the potato blight in Ireland in the 1840s or the volcanic eruption which resulted in the deaths of one third of Iceland's population in the 1780s should be regarded as Malthusian checks is a moot point. The mini-famines which affected Ireland before 1845 are much more plausible candidates.

Mokyr's classic analysis of Irish poverty on the eve of the famine (1985) exploited the county-level data offered by a range of pre-famine social and statistical surveys. The 32 counties provided a convenient cross-section for econometric analysis, just large enough for conventional statistical inference. To his surprise Mokyr failed to find any strong connection between land hunger and living standards on the eve of the famine. That result, and the rather weak association between excess mortality during the famine and variables such as the land–labour ratio and potato consumption, suggested, controversially, a rejection of traditional Malthusian interpretations of Irish poverty before the famine. Analysis of excess mortality during the famine found roles for variables such as illiteracy and income, though other variables such as farm size and urbanisation failed to yield the predicted effects (Mokyr 1985: 270–4).

A finer grid, previously unexploited, is provided by baronial data.[3] The barony is an obsolete administrative unit introduced in Elizabethan times; at the time of the famine Ireland was divided into 327 of them. The following correlation matrix and regression estimates are based on a subset of 305 baronies, for whom good data are available. The descriptive statistics in table 7.2, grouped below by province, show Leinster to have been the richest province in 1841, followed by Ulster, Munster and Connacht. Living standards are captured by indices of housing quality (the proportion of households not living in fourth-class accommodation) and literacy (the proportion of people who could at least read) in the 1841 census, and by the poor law valuation, as reported in the 1851 census, divided by the 1841 population. The poor law valuation was an official valuation of fixed property carried out for the purpose of levying rates under the Irish Poor Law of 1838. Since land dominated the poor law valuation, the last of these proxies amounts to a measure of quality-adjusted land per head.

The human cost of the famine, measured by population loss between 1841 and 1851, was greatest in Connacht and least in Ulster.[4] Table 7.3 correlates this measure with living standards indicators. The results suggest

1   A positive association between our different measures of living standards in 1841 and population change in 1841–51; in other words, the better-off a barony on the eve of the famine, the smaller the demographic impact of the famine.
2   A negative association between improvements in living standards in 1841–51 and population change in the same decade; that is, where population decline was greatest is, broadly speaking, where the rise in literacy and housing quality was greatest.
3   A negative association between population growth before the famine (1821–41) and living standards on the eve of the famine.
4   Some sign of a convergence in living standards across counties. The negative correlations between our proxies for living standards in 1841 and changes in

living standards during the famine decade indicate that initially poorer counties saw greater improvements in their standard of living.

Only one of the measures of living standards on the eve of the famine (the poor law valuation per head) comes close to capturing Mokyr's land-based proxies for population pressure. Still, the findings reported in table 7.3 imply

Table 7.2 **Descriptive statistics by province**
(means and standard errors; standard error in parentheses)

Variable	Ireland	Leinster	Munster	Ulster	Connacht
DPOP4151	−0.219	−0.199	−0.253	−0.173	−0.285
	(0.115)	(0.118)	(0.107)	(0.102)	(0.089)
DPOP2141	0.202	0.144	0.259	0.183	0.292
	(0.166)	(0.155)	(0.199)	(0.103)	(0.154)
GOODH41	0.642	0.724	0.543	0.697	0.504
	(0.150)	(0.091)	(0.149)	(0.095)	(0.155)
DGOODH	0.206	0.127	0.251	0.230	0.307
	(0.116)	(0.092)	(0.100)	(0.077)	(0.114)
LIT41	0.541	0.585	0.456	0.663	0.376
	(0.139)	(0.074)	(0.088)	(0.142)	(0.082)
DLIT	0.028	0.033	0.024	0.029	0.022
	(0.037)	(0.041)	(0.036)	(0.037)	(0.027)
AVPLV	1.576	2.131	1.288	1.425	0.822
	(0.878)	(0.990)	(0.641)	(0.487)	(0.285)
SEA	0.236	0.127	0.356	0.290	0.244
	(0.425)	(0.335)	(0.482)	(0.457)	(0.435)

Source: Ó Gráda (1995a).
Notes:
– DPOP4151 = POP51–POP41
– DPOP2141 = POP41–POP21
– POP21, POP41, POP51: population in 1821, 1841 and 1851
– GOODH41 and GOODH51: the proportion of families not relying on fourth-class housing in 1841 and 1851
– DGOODH = GOODH51–GOOD41
– LIT41 and LIT51: the proportion of the population which could at least read in 1841
– DLIT = LIT51–LIT41
– AVPLV, poor law valuation per capita divided by population in 1841
– SEA, a dummy variable set equal to one for coastal baronies

Table 7.3 **Population and living standards**
(correlation coefficients)

	DPOP4151	DPOP2141	AVPLV	GOODH	LIT41	DGOODH	DLIT
DPOP4151	1.000						
DPOP2141	0.072	1.000					
AVPLV	0.365	−0.201	1.000				
GOODH41	0.414	−0.281	0.430	1.000			
LIT41	0.405	−0.262	0.429	0.638	1.000		
DGOODH	−0.285	0.242	−0.518	−0.786	−0.391	1.000	
DLIT	−0.240	−0.082	0.077	−0.028	−0.127	−0.036	1.000

Source: see text.

that the famine struck hardest in the poorest baronies, and that the increase in living standards that followed was greatest where population loss was greatest. Moreover, population growth before the famine was associated with poverty in 1841. Unfortunately, we lack data at the baronial level on changes in living standards in the decades before 1841, and so cannot test whether pre-famine population growth was associated with impoverishment across baronies.

Regression analysis of population change during the famine refines these findings somewhat. Our focus is on the effect of living standards on the eve of the famine on the gravity of the famine at baronial level. Table 7.4 reports the results; the dependent variable throughout is DPOP4151. Regressions [1]–[3] describe the explanatory power of GOODH, AVPLV, and LIT on DPOP4151, controlling for coastal location. These proxies are not perfect correlates, and including two of them in [4] increases explanatory power. It is interesting to note that adding DPOP2141 fails to support the belief that counties with higher population growth before the famine had higher population declines during the 1840s. By and large, high population growth before the famine meant high population growth in its wake. In general, baronies with a sea boundary fared better, after controlling for poverty on the eve of the famine, suggesting that access to fish, seashells, seaweed and sea-borne relief mattered during the crisis.

The key point to take from the table is, however, that the poorest baronies were the worst hit during the famine. Indeed, one does not need to delve into the baronial records to reach this conclusion. Regressing famine-induced or excess mortality rates (by county) (*LDEATH*) against the log of wages in 1836 (*LWAGE*) yields the following result (both variables are in log form):[5]

$$LDEATH = 2.84 - 2.24LWAGE \qquad\qquad R^2 = 0.69 \qquad\qquad (1)$$
$$(4.45)\ (-7.98) \qquad\qquad\qquad F(1,29) = 63.62$$

Pre-famine poverty was clearly associated with suffering during the famine. But did emigration provide a safety valve, in the sense that death rates were lower where emigration rates were higher? And to what extent did poverty traps prevent emigration from reducing death rates in the poorest counties? Was emigration higher from poor counties, as standard migration models suggest, or was it the rich who managed to escape to the New World? We turn to these questions in the next section.

Table 7.4 **Accounting for population change during the famine**

(t-statistics in parentheses)

	[1]	[2]	[3]	[4]	[5]	[6]
CONSTANT	−0.430	−0.450	−0.313	−0.235	−0.451	−0.484
	(−17.66)	(−17.06)	(−23.84)	(−22.49)	(−17.63)	(−16.77)
LIT41	0.363					
	(8.57)					
GOODH41		0.338			0.258	0.291
		(8.63)			(6.17)	(6.95)
AVPLV			0.051		0.032	0.035
			(7.42)		(4.53)	(4.92)
DPOP2141				0.029		0.132
				(0.72)		(3.77)
SEA	0.065	0.061	0.059	0.045	0.065	0.057
	(4.65)	(4.43)	(4.15)	(2.87)	(4.87)	(4.33)
F	42.5	43.1	33.1	4.9	37.4	32.8
Rsq	.220	.222	.180	.032	.272	.304

Source: see text.
Note: the dependent variable throughout is DPOP4151

Poverty, emigration and death

Welfare assessments of Irish emigration have often dwelt on the human capital characteristics of those who left relative to those who stayed behind (Mokyr and Ó Gráda 1982; Nicholas and Shergold 1987). It is certainly true that emigration in normal times was age-selective: young single adults had the most to gain from emigrating, and they were disproportionately represented in the flow. This implied a 'life cycle' loss for Ireland, and a 'life cycle' gain for the New World and Great Britain, as Ireland lost the productive capacity of children she had reared, and the New World and Great Britain gained 'instant adults'.

Was emigration selective in other ways as well? Both theory and the available evidence are inconclusive. If poor countries have a higher ratio of unskilled labour to skilled labour than rich countries, then standard Heckscher-Ohlin logic suggests that the unskilled should have the greater incentive to migrate. Taking into account the fixed cost of migration makes the outcome uncertain, however, as skilled emigrants may gain more in *absolute* terms. If emigrants' skills are initially unobservable to foreign employers, or there are segmented labour markets in the host country, with immigrants consigned to low-level jobs, then unskilled workers may again have a greater incentive to migrate (Katz and Stark 1989). The evidence on the skill composition of Irish emigrants is ambiguous.

What about the quality of emigrants within given skill categories? *A priori* reasoning suggests that, in normal times, workers with 'drive' are more likely to emigrate than the more risk-averse, or the more leisure-prone (O'Rourke 1992). Of course, this intuition is impossible to test, although there is no shortage of anecdotal evidence. During the famine, when emigration was largely determined by push factors, a lower quality of emigrant might be expected as it was the more vulnerable who fled the crisis. There is some direct evidence that this was in fact the case. In March 1847, in a frequently cited passage (e.g. Handlin 1941: 55), the *Cork Examiner* noted that 'the emigrants of this year are not like those of former ones; they are now actually *running away* from fever and disease and hunger, with money scarcely sufficient to pay passage for and find food for the voyage'. The analysis of lists of New York-bound Irish emigrants offers some clues here (Glazier et al. 1989; Ó Gráda 1983). First, it suggests a sharp drop in the share of unaccompanied passengers during the famine. This and the accompanying shift in the age composition of the migration reflect the more family-oriented character of famine migration. The share of females in the migrant outflow was largely unaffected by the famine, however.[6] Occupational data suggest little change either: both before and during the famine unskilled categories such as labourers and servants accounted for over three fifths of the total. But another important difference is that the shares of the worst-hit provinces of Connacht and Munster rose significantly (compare Handlin 1941: 56).

The increase in the proportion of children and older people means a lower 'life-cycle' gain from immigration to host countries. The occupational spread suggests no deterioration, however. Other clues about the relative 'quality' of the famine migrants are scarce. We may examine the numeracy, or what Mokyr (1985: 244) has called the 'quantitative sophistication', of the migrants by calculating the degree of age-heaping in the passenger lists. Age-heaping refers to the tendency for responses to questions about age to concentrate on rounded estimates, and in particular on the nearest zero (20, 30, and so on). Table 7.5 reports the outcome of an analysis of age-heaping in Boston passenger lists in 1822–39, and in New York passenger lists just before and during the famine. It relies on the simplest index of age-heaping: the ratio of migrants reporting their ages at 20, 30 and 40 to those reporting ages of 20–24, 30–34, and 40–44 years, respectively. The value of this index can range from 0.20 (no age-heaping) to 1.00 (complete age-heaping). The trends in each category in table 7.5 show little difference between 1820–39 and 1846–50 except in the 20–24 year category, where a deterioration is indicated. Yet there is little sign in the passenger lists of a drop in emigrant quality during the famine period.

Table 7.5 **Age-heaping indices 1820–49**

	1820–39	*1846*[*]	*1847*[**]	*1848*[^]	*1849*[***]
Index					
20–24	.27	.50	.33	.40	.47
30–34	.67	.69	.62	.63	.78
40–44	.83	.78	.79	.82	.87

Source: the 1822–39 estimates are from Ó Gráda (1983: 128); those for 1846–8 are derived from data in Glazier (1984).
(*) January–March, (**) July, (^) January, (***)1–20 January

The evidence above suggests that the famine emigration was qualitatively different from emigration in normal times: it was less age-selective and the migrants were lower skilled. However, the migrants were not the very poorest or the worst affected by the potato failure. Most of them relied on their own resources in funding their emigration; perhaps 50,000 of nearly a million were

assisted by landlords or the state (MacDonagh 1956: 335; Fitzpatrick 1984: 20).
This implies that the very poorest, those with no savings or goodwill to capi-
talise on, could not travel. The implication is that the receiving countries were
not getting the paupers.

Though data on the socio-economic backgrounds of those who died and
those who emigrated are lacking, it seems fair to assume that the latter were
mostly people of some modest means. For most of the landless poor, with no
savings or compensation for eviction to fall back on, the cost of a passage
to America would have been too high (compare the account of would-be
Roscommon emigrants in chapter 13). Turning yet again to the cross-section
evidence, we first try to compute emigration rates across counties. Easier said
than done! True, we have censal estimates of population in 1831, 1841 and 1851,
and we have Cousens's (1960) estimates of excess mortality by county. The
latter are problematic, alas. Cousens gave a national total for excess mortality of
only 800,000, whereas more recent estimates have opted for a higher figure of
one million. But not only is Cousens's aggregate too low; his strategy of com-
bining recorded deaths in institutions and deaths in households as retrospectively recorded in 1851 lends an unknown bias to the cross-county variation in
his data. On the one hand, emigrant families were not around in 1851 to report
earlier deaths in their households. On the other, under-reporting is likely to
have been greater in poorer counties. Nevertheless, the exercise which follows
relies on Cousens's county estimates of excess mortality scaled up uniformly
by 25 per cent.

To derive an estimate of emigration between 1841 and 1851, it is necessary to
guess what the 1851 population would have been in the absence of the famine. A
reasonable guess might be that the national population would have grown at
0.5 per cent per annum between 1841 and 1851, had the potato blight not
intervened.[7] However, population growth would not have been uniform across
counties. Between 1831 and 1841, population growth per annum ranged from a
high of 1.1 per cent in Kerry to a low of 0 per cent in Derry. This excludes
Dublin where, remarkably, the official figures show population *shrinking* at
0.1 per cent per annum! Because Dublin's unusual demographic experience – it
experienced substantial immigration during the famine years – make it a substantial outlier, it is not included in the correlation exercises which follow.

We therefore adopt the expedient approach of first assuming that county
populations would have continued to grow between 1841 and 1851 at the same
rate as they had between 1831 and 1841. This implied a counterfactual national
population in 1851 of just over 8.6 million. We then scaled down each county

population estimate for 1851, so that the national total was just *under* 8.6 million, as would have been the case if the national population growth rate was 0.5 per cent per annum.

This procedure gave county estimates of counterfactual, 'no-famine' populations in 1851. From these totals we subtracted the actual 1851 population figures. The difference was taken to be due to either emigration or excess mortality. Subtracting the adjusted excess mortality figures thus gave an estimate of excess emigration by county during the decade, i.e. of emigration above pre-famine rates. The implied provincial emigration and death rates are given in table 7.6. The numbers are consistent with qualitative accounts: Connacht was most severely affected by the potato blight, followed closely by Munster, with Leinster and Ulster being the least affected. Interestingly, the data show Leinster's death rate being higher than Ulster's (as expected), but Ulster's emigration rates being higher than Leinster's. Otherwise, the ranking of provinces by death rates is the same as that by emigration rates.

However, the correlation between emigration and death rates is not strong across counties, just 0.147. Consequently, counties such as Clare and Galway, with high death rates, also tended to have a low ratio of emigration to deaths (figure 7.1). There is a strong negative correlation between these variables (–0.605), consistent with the notion that it was not the poorest who emigrated. To explore this possibility further, county-level emigration and death rates are correlated with a number of variables indicating living standards and vulnerability on the eve of the famine.

Table 7.7 gives the results. Not surprisingly, counties with low wages, a high dependency on the potato (as measured by 1841 acres per capita) and a large drop in the potato acreage, had higher death and emigration rates (figure 7.2).

Table 7.6 **Provincial excess mortality and emigration rates, 1841–51**

	Population	Emigration	Deaths	Emigration rate (%)	Death rate (%)
Ulster	2,386,373	290,970	184,123	12.2	7.7
Munster	2,396,161	332,936	382,951	13.9	16.0
Leinster	1,973,731	171,287	193,397	8.7	9.8
Connaught	1,418,859	245,624	239,529	17.3	16.9
Ireland	8,175,124	1,040,816	1,000,000	12.7	12.2

Source: see text.

Table 7.7 **Deaths, emigration, wages and potatoes**
(correlation coefficients)

	Death rates	Emigration rates	Emigration/Deaths
Wages	−0.820	−0.353	0.383
Potato dependency	0.333	0.038	−0.215
Decline in potato acreage 1845–7	0.374	0.423	−0.038
Decline in potato acreage 1845–8	0.456	0.442	−0.055

Note: the wage data are for 1836, and were obtained from Líam Kennedy. Potato dependency was defined as the potato acreage per capita in 1845. Potato data are from Mokyr (1981) and the *Agricultural Statistics*.

However, the relationship between potato dependency and emigration was almost non-existent. Interestingly, the relationship between wages and death rates was far stronger than the link between death rates and any of the potato variables.[8] Once again, in richer counties, the ratio of emigration to deaths was higher than in poor counties, again supporting the intuition that the poorest died rather than emigrated (figure 7.3).[9]

Emigration was thus an inefficient form of famine relief: it did not help those most at risk. Nonetheless, without the emigration option, famine mortality

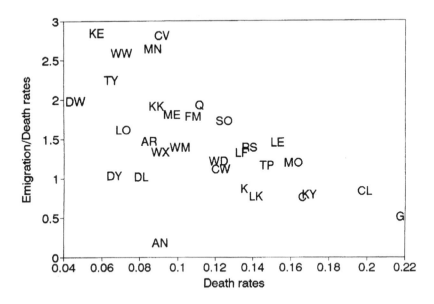

Figure 7.1 **Famine deaths and emigration**

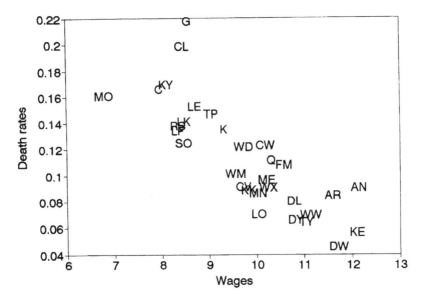

Figure 7.2 **Wages and death rates**

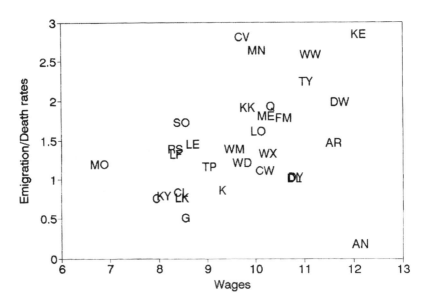

Figure 7.3 **Emigration, deaths and wages**

County	Symbol	County	Symbol	County	Symbol
LEINSTER		MUNSTER		ULSTER	
Carlow	CW	Clare	CL	Antrim	AN
Kildare	KE	Cork	C	Armagh	AR
Kilkenny	KK	Kerry	KY	Cavan	CV
King's County	K	Limerick	LK	Derry	DY
Longford	LF	Tipperary	TP	Donegal	DL
Louth	LO	Waterford	WD	Down	DW
Meath	ME			Fermanagh	FM
Queen's County	Q	CONNACHT		Monaghan	MN
Westmeath	WM	Galway	G	Tyrone	TY
Wexford	WX	Leitrim	LE		
Wicklow	WW	Mayo	MO		
		Roscommon	RS		
		Sligo	SO		

KEY TO FIGURES 7.1–7.3

would surely have been higher, with more people competing for scarce food supplies. Unfortunately, it is impossible to quantify the magnitude of this effect.[10] It is unlikely, though not inconceivable, that the absence of distant outlets for emigration would have increased mortality by more than the number of frustrated would-be emigrants. A more plausible outcome would have been the death of a fraction of those forced to remain. In addition, some migration would have been diverted to the already crowded cities of Ireland and Great Britain. The negative externalities through the spread of disease and misery resulting from such migration are impossible to calculate, but should be borne in mind.[11]

The permanent impact of the famine emigration

Malthusian theory traditionally assigned an important role to famines in helping to regulate population. In the absence of the preventive check, population would grow to the point where positive checks such as higher infant mortality or disease became inevitable. If these failed, famine provided the ultimate sanction. As mentioned earlier, this attitude informed much contemporary British opinion regarding nineteenth-century Ireland. Ireland's poverty was due to overpopulation; famine, while regrettable, was inevitable.

In an important paper, Susan Watkins and Jane Menken (1985) argue that, contrary to Malthusian doctrine, famines have only limited long run demographic effects. Surveying historical and contemporary famines, they conclude that mortality does not rise by as much, and fertility does not fall by as much, during famines as is commonly thought; moreover, severe famines have been relatively infrequent. The heart of their paper is a simulation of the long run demographic consequences of famine using demographic parameters typical of Asian society ('high mortality, early and virtually universal marriage, and relatively moderate fertility', p. 658). The authors allow for excess mortality rates during famines which vary by age cohort, and trace out the implications for the long run evolution of a population. The striking finding is that even severe famines do not reduce population size in the long run (except in a counterfactual sense). For example, in a population with an initial growth rate of 0.5 per cent per annum, which experiences a famine involving mortality rates 110 per cent higher than normal, and birth rates one-third lower than normal, for a period of two years, population returns to its original level less than twelve years after the crisis (p. 660). However, if mortality rates are 150 per cent above average for five years, it takes fifty years for the population to regain its original level.

The point can be illustrated by the 'no emigration' line in figure 7.4, which takes the Irish population on the eve of the famine as 8.5 million. Excess mortality was one million, and was largely over by 1851. Imagine that birth rates declined enough during the crisis to reduce population growth, net of excess mortality, to zero during the six years; and imagine a world without emigration. Assume further (and implausibly) that excess mortality would have remained the same in the absence of emigration. Population would then have been 7.5 million in 1851. *If* excess mortality had affected all age cohorts equally, population growth would simply have resumed at its pre-1845 rate in 1851. At this rate, population would have recovered by 1877, 32 years after the onset of the crisis.

Moreover, if one allows for excess mortality to vary by age cohort, as Watkins and Menken do, and as was surely the case, then it would have taken even less time for the Irish population to recover. The reason is simple, and is highlighted by Watkins's and Menken's simulations. During famines, the old and the young are more likely to die than adults of childbearing age: the share of the latter group in the total population thus increases. In reality, therefore, after famines have passed, given age-specific fertility rates translate into higher birth rates for the population as a whole; and this implies a higher population growth rate post-famine than pre-famine. This age cohort effect alone can make a big difference to the time to recovery. In the four experiments presented in their table 3, not allowing for excess mortality to vary by age group increases the time to recovery by 5 per cent, 50 per cent, 66 per cent and 69 per cent.

Furthermore, these simulations assume that age-specific fertility and mortality rates return to normal after the famine; whereas unless famine forces a shift in preferences, mortality rates should decline and fertility rates increase as

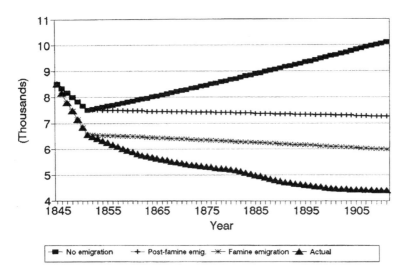

Figure 7.4 **Actual and hypothetical population 1845–1911 (thousands)**

Malthusian pressures ease. (There should have been greater scope for this in post-famine Ireland than in the Watkins–Menken simulations, which assume that everyone was already married before the crisis.) Again, allowing for these typical responses to famines would speed up post-famine population growth rates, and lower the time to recovery; as would relaxing the assumption that the population growth rate, net of excess mortality, fell to zero during the crisis. Taking all these factors into account, Ireland's population might have recovered in 15 or 20 years, rather than the 32 years suggested by figure 7.4, had it behaved in a 'normal' fashion. The one important consideration which works in the opposite direction is the assumption in this no-emigration counterfactual that excess mortality would have been the same in the absence of famine emigration. Presumably excess mortality would in fact have exceeded one million in this case, as the previous section suggested.

In any event, the general point is clear enough. In economies without labour market links to the rest of the world, famines do not generally result in long-lasting population declines. Figure 7.4 tells us immediately that Ireland was a very different case indeed. Far from returning gradually to pre-famine levels, Ireland's population actually entered into a steady decline, which in the 26 counties of the present-day Republic of Ireland persisted until 1961. The Great Famine's effects on Ireland's population were clearly permanent, rather than transitory, and emigration holds the key to understanding this.[12]

Clearly the emigration which took place during the famine – about one million people left – contributed directly to long run population loss; but it is the sustained emigration which followed that explains the perverse Irish population decline. However, this post-famine emigration was intimately linked to the famine exodus, for at least two reasons.

First, by increasing land-labour ratios the famine and its associated emigration eliminated the poverty trap which had prevented people from the poorer parts of Ireland from emigrating before 1845. This argument is consistent with the general view of European emigration presented by Hatton and Williamson (1994). They note that emigration rates rise during the course of development, before falling again, despite the fact that the initial development should have made emigration less attractive. The explanation is straightforward: initially potential migrants were too poor to afford the costs of migration. With growth, this poverty trap was overcome; path dependence ensured that an initial burst of emigration would lead to ever-increasing levels of emigration; only eventually would rising wages choke off the demand for emigration.

In Ireland, many victims of this poverty trap died during the famine, while many of those who were slightly better off were forced to emigrate. These developments of course implied higher wages post-famine; furthermore, relatives and friends in the USA or elsewhere could now make information and money available to potential emigrants. Emigration became available to all, and Irish living standards began to increase rapidly. Boyer et al. (1994) estimate that real agricultural wages doubled between 1860 and 1913; moreover Irish wages converged on their British counterparts. Williamson (1995) estimates that unskilled building wages were 51 per cent as high in Ireland as in Britain in 1852, but 93 per cent as high in 1904, a finding echoed by Boyer et al.

To check the notion that the famine helped overcome the poverty traps which had constrained pre-famine emigration, we examined the inter-county variation in net migration rates before and after the famine. Since reliable net migration statistics are lacking, we proxied migration by age-cohort depletion: we chose the reduction in the 5–15 year-old age cohort between 1821 and 1841, 1851 and 1871, and 1871 and 1891. We then correlated the loss across counties with estimates of the unskilled wage, and also calculated the elasticity of the migration rate with respect to the wage. The outcome, seen in table 7.8 below, suggests a significant difference between pre- and post-famine patterns. Before the famine, emigration was only weakly correlated with wages, and the wage-emigration elasticity was low, suggesting that it was not necessarily the poorest who were emigrating. After the famine, wages and emigration were strongly and

Table 7.8 **Wages and emigration before and after the famine**

Year	Mean wage (pence)	Wage-emigration correlation	Elasticity of emigration w.r.t. wages
1829	61.09	−0.049	−0.08
1835	54.09	−0.023	−0.03
1836a	9.88	−0.202	−0.14
1836b	6.80	0.194	0.10
1850	57.69	−0.547	−0.66
1860	84.25	−0.397	−0.48
1860a	83.25	−0.613	−0.95
1870	94.38	−0.216	−0.42
1880	108.09	−0.489	−0.63

Source: the data are mostly taken from Bowley (1899). 1860a replaces the Bowley numbers for Waterford and Roscommon by more plausible estimates (i.e. 72*d* in each case). 1836a is a weighted estimate of a male labourer's daily summer wage, without food, derived from evidence to the Poor Inquiry; 1836b excludes diet. We are grateful to Líam Kennedy for these last estimates.

negatively correlated, and wage-emigration elasticities were high.[13] Convergence on living standards overseas was accompanied by internal convergence: the coefficient of variation across counties of wages was 0.175 in 1835, 0.154 in 1836, 0.156 in 1850, 0.121 in 1860, 0.109 in 1870, 0.166 in 1880, 0.116 in 1893, and 0.075 in 1911. The 1880 figure may be an aberration; that observation apart, the picture is one of steady convergence after the famine.[14]

The second way in which the famine exodus contributed to subsequent emigration is that emigration directly begets further emigration: there is a powerful path dependency at work here. This point is illustrated by the econometric work of Hatton and Williamson (1993), who estimate a time series model of Irish emigration over the period 1877–1913. The microfoundations of the model assume utility-maximisation and risk-aversion on the part of migrants. Thus, while relative wages are key for long-run migration, the timing of migration will be largely influenced by unemployment rates. Moreover, risk aversion implies that unemployment rates and relative wages should be entered separately into the equation, in contrast to the expected wage approach of Todaro (1969) and others. Finally, the model includes a migrant stock term, to capture the 'friends and relatives' effect: prior migration makes current migration less costly (in terms of places to stay, flows of information, and remittances) and thus more common. This of course implies path dependence. The model estimated is:

$$M/P_t = \alpha_0 + \alpha_1\Delta\log(EF)_t + \alpha_2\Delta\log(EH)_t + \alpha_3\Delta\log(W)_t + \alpha_4\log(EF)_{t-1} + \\ \alpha_5\log(EH)_{t-1} + \alpha_6\log(W)_{t-1} + \alpha_7(MS/P)_t + \alpha_8(M/P)_{t-1} \qquad (2)$$

where M/P is the emigration rate (emigrants divided by population), EF and EH are the foreign and home employment rates, W is the ratio of foreign to domestic wages, and MS is the stock of previous migrants.

Hatton and Williamson find that emigration responded strongly to relative wages, and to the foreign unemployment rate. More importantly for this chapter, they also find strong evidence of path-dependence: after controlling for the influence of wages and employment, for every thousand previous migrants, an extra 41 were attracted overseas each year. Of course, these results were derived for a much later time period, but they are useful for illustrative purposes in thinking about the long run impact of the famine emigration.

The famine directly led to at least one million people emigrating. The Hatton–Williamson results imply that this shock alone might have implied as many as 41,000 extra migrants per annum. The Irish population was roughly 6.5 million in 1851; the path dependence effect alone might have boosted the emigration rate by 6 (i.e. 41,000 divided by 6,500) per thousand per annum, which is in fact the amount by which average post-famine emigration rates (13) exceeded pre-famine rates (7).[15] The famine was crucial to subsequent high emigration rates.

This extra post-famine emigration is by itself sufficient, in an accounting sense, to explain the failure of Ireland's population to revert to its original level (in fact low birth rates worked in the same direction). The 'post-famine emigration' line in figure 7.4 assumes, as does the 'no emigration' line, that birth and death rates on their own (combined with 'normal', pre-famine emigration rates) would have led to the population growing at 0.5 per cent per annum. However, it now lets excess emigration take place at the rate of 41,000 per year, the figure suggested by the Hatton–Williamson exercise. This emigration places a sufficient drag on the overall population to ensure that population continues to decline after 1851, rather than increase to its original level. Allowing both for this level of post-famine emigration, and the famine emigration itself (the 'famine emigration' line in figure 7.4) brings us a lot closer to what actually happened to the Irish population. Once you take account of the famine exodus, and the subsequent emigration which it spawned, the long run evolution of Ireland's population, so different from the Watkins–Menken norm, no longer seems perverse.

Furthermore, the assumption of Watkins and Menken that birth rates would revert to their pre-famine norm, or even increase, after the crisis, did not apply in Ireland. The lack of civil registration and the likely underenumeration of very young children in the census rule out firm estimates of post-famine birth rates. However, the drop in the proportion of children aged 0–4 years in the total population from 12.6 per cent in 1841, to 12.0 per cent in 1861, and 11.1 per cent in 1881 is indicative of a *decline* in birth rates. The rise in the percentage of never-married Irishwomen aged 45–54 years from 12.5 per cent in 1841 to 14.3 per cent in 1861 and 17.1 per cent in 1881 is corroborative.[16] And this helps further to explain the drop in Ireland's population. One might imagine a fifth line on figure 7.4, somewhere in between the lower 2, which incorporates the fact that the 'no-emigration' natural population growth rate was lower than it would otherwise be.

In conclusion, the famine does appear to have put an end to Irish 'over-population', in the sense that most survivors experienced higher and increasing living standards. However, this is in large part due to the mass emigration associated with the famine and its aftermath: Boyer et al. (1994) conclude that perhaps half of the Irish convergence on Britain can be explained by Irish emigration, while O'Rourke and Williamson (1997) argue that the *entire* Irish convergence on Britain and America can be explained by mass migration, a dubious distinction Ireland shares with Italy. Watkins and Menken's work is a reminder that in the absence of emigration, Ireland's population might well have recovered from the crisis, however slowly, as has been the experience elsewhere.[17]

Conclusions

Emigration was by no means an ideal substitute for other forms of famine relief in the 1840s. A million people still perished. Because only a tiny fraction of the emigration was state assisted or landlord assisted, those who could afford to emigrate were not those at greatest immediate risk from starvation. The timing of the migration – heavier after than during Black '47 – also suggests that it was not ideally tailored to relieve the worst hit. In the words of Robert Murray, general manager of the Provincial Bank of Ireland, in 1847, 'the best go, the worst remain' (cited in Black 1960: 229). He might have added, to die!

Still, emigration reduced famine mortality. Moreover, few of the emigrants returned when the crisis had passed, suggesting an asymmetry with other forms of disaster relief. While emigration did not target the poor as effectively as soup-kitchens or the public works, unlike them its effect went well beyond mere crisis-management. The famine emigration has often been seen as one of the great tragedies in Irish history, and in human terms this is of course correct. Nonetheless, in the long run this emigration played an important role in increasing the living standards of those who stayed behind.

CHAPTER EIGHT

The New York Irish in the 1850s

Two hundred years ago New York City was still a relatively small city, less than one third of the size of Dublin and less than one fifteenth that of London. Europe contained more than three dozen cities with bigger populations, and within the USA Philadelphia still rivalled New York in terms of numbers. On the eve of the Civil War, however, New York had swollen twelve-fold to a city of over 800,000 people. The populations of New York and Brooklyn combined then exceeded one million, almost double that of Philadelphia. New York had left its other northeastern rivals far behind and become one of the world's great cities.[1] Its rapid growth, spurred on by industrialisation and better communications with the interior, and fuelled by immigration from Europe, was largely a function of its longstanding position as a seaport. Luck played its part too. Before 1815 both Boston and Philadelphia rivalled New York in terms of ship tonnages cleared, but when north Atlantic trade routes were reopened in 1815, the preference of British traders for New York allowed it to forge ahead of its rivals. By 1860 36 per cent of US exports and 69 per cent of imports passed through the port of New York (Albion 1939: 390–1).

In mid-century New York was still a compact urban space. About two New Yorkers in three lived in the densely populated area south of Fourteenth Street, and the bulk of economic activity was conducted there. The area to the north of Fourteenth Street was fully settled as far as about Thirtieth Street. Though the familiar gridiron street landscape of Manhattan had been planned as long ago as 1807, further north much of Manhattan, particularly its east side, remained unsettled and semi-rural: only nine per cent of the population lived north of Forty Second Street. In lower Manhattan the streetscape, then as now, was mostly one of irregular rectangles. The almost complete lack of open spaces and gardens meant that population density was very high. The five or so square miles below Fourteenth Street contained about 200 people per hectare in the mid-1850s, making them much more congested than either Dublin (about 160 people per hectare) or London (135 people per hectare).

New York City was the main port of entry into North America for mid nineteenth-century immigrants from Ireland and elsewhere in Europe. Between 1820 and 1860 about two thirds of all US immigrants landed there (Albion 1939: 337). Though more prone to fluctuation in the short run, New York's trade in people grew even faster than its trade in goods. And though most of those who arrived did not stay in the city for long, New York became a city of immigrants. By mid-century half its residents were foreign born. As its population grew rapidly, so did its numbers of Irish-born, rising from 70,000–80,000 in 1845 to 175,735 in 1855 and 203,740 in 1860. The Irish were by far the biggest immigrant group in the antebellum city. In the New York state census of 1855 they made up 28.2 per cent of the city's entire population; the Germans came next with 15.7 per cent and the English with 3.6 per cent. In the same year the population of the neighbouring borough of Brooklyn had reached 205,250, of whom 56,753 had been born in Ireland. Greater New York thus contained almost as many Irish-born people as Dublin. Moreover, because of their high labour force participation and their age structure, the Irish formed a much bigger proportion of the labour force than of the population. In 1860 Irishmen and Irishwomen in their twenties, thirties, and forties easily outnumbered native New Yorkers of the same ages.

This immigration was in part a product of the Great Irish Famine. As explained in chapter 1, that famine had a catastrophic impact on Ireland's poor. It is often described as having exacted a toll of one million lives and one million emigrants. The departure and the crossing were probably the most traumatic events in the lives of most of these who emigrated. Accounts of coffin ships and of exploitation and high death rates in the wake of arrival in America emphasise this aspect. In one sense they paint too dark a picture of the historiography of the famine migration. It bears remembering that among famine victims the emigrants – or at least those among them who sailed for the United States – were the fortunate ones. Compared to the Canadian routes, mortality on the better regulated New York crossing was low (Ó Gráda 1999: 106–7). Most of the emigrants who chose New York had to be people of some modest means, because the cost of the passage required some accumulated savings or other assets that could be converted into ready cash. The cost was not trivial: for an unskilled labourer contemplating emigration the fare alone (about £5) was equivalent to several months' wages.

During the winter of 1846–7 the head of the Board of Works in Dublin referred to the 'great delusion' about emigration. It was not the poorest who were about to leave, he complained, but 'all the small farmers [who are] hoarding all the money they can procure in order to make a stock for the spring, when they intend to bolt, leaving the landlords in the lurch'. Indeed, many contemporary accounts refer to small farmers leaving or planning their departure. Around Skibbereen in County Cork, for example, 'a good many' were giving up their land and preparing for departure; these were the 'substantial farmers, who still have a little means left'. In west Kerry farmers swapped their holdings with their more prosperous neighbours for passage to America. In the words of the inimitable Kerry storyteller Peig Sayers, 'nach shin é a thug na feirmeacha móra do dhaoine mar éinne go mbíodh tógaint cinn aige agus aon phingin airgid thiocfadh fear des na comharsain chuige agus thabharfadh sé dó a chuid talmhan ar chostas Mheiriceá [isn't that how the people got the big farms around here, since all those who had any standing left would find neighbours willing to trade their land in return for a passage to America]'. Such claims were commonplace (Ó Gráda 1999: 107–8; *FJ*, 12 Mar. 1847; Póirtéir 1996: 241–2, 243).

Among Irish famine emigrants, those who took the more expensive route to New York were mostly better off than those who opted for (or were given) the Canadian route. New York offered a safer passage and better prospects of employment on arrival (Schrier 1958: 17). For the majority who ventured beyond the city, it also offered easier access to the interior. By mid-century New York was already connected by railway to the Great Lakes, New England, Philadelphia and south towards Baltimore.

The relatively privileged status of those in a position to leave Ireland for America in the 1840s was not replicated in America itself. As immigrants the Irish were less skilled and poorer than their German or British counterparts, and as a result the vast majority of them were confined to the most menial occupations and the poorest housing. This was particularly so for those who remained in the big cities on the east coast. Compounding their greater poverty on arrival was the non-transferability of skills acquired in Ireland and discrimination in the markets for skilled labour (Ferrie 1994: 6; 1997: 108–9; Mooney 1850: 83–4).

Recent research confirms the accuracy of contemporary advice to would-be immigrants not to stay long in New York and, indeed, most of the new arrivals seem not to have stayed in the city for long. Nonetheless, contemporary accounts suggest that many Irish immigrants lacked the means to proceed any further than New York. This sense that impoverished immigrants were flooding New York with cheap labour is made in a letter home in 1850 from one recent immigrant:

But there is one thing thats Ruining this place Especially the Frontirs towns and Cities where the Flow of Emmigration is most the Emmigrants has not money Enough to Take them to the Interior of the Country which oblidges them to Remain here in New York and the like places for which Reason Causes the less demand for Labour and also the great Reduction in wages and for this Reason I would advise no one to Come to America that would not have Some Money after landing here that [would] Enable them to go west in case they would get no work here (Ellis 1960: 360).

Yet ghettoisation or concentration in the poorer neighbourhoods of a city has always been a key feature of immigrant life. The long-run advantages of the ethnic ghetto are debatable. They hinge on the quality of public goods it generates and on whether the more talented and successful in the relevant ethnic group remain or not. But in the short run the ethnic neighbourhood confers several advantages on the recent immigrant. It reduces the costs of adjusting to life in a setting very different from home by providing less expensive lodging, friendship and recreation, better opportunities of finding work quickly, and a modicum of security (Borjas 1995; Wegge 1998; Cutler and Glaeser 1997; Cutler et al. 1999; Bertrand et al. 2000). Surviving emigrant letters give a flavour of how networks eased the immigrant's lot in antebellum New York. Take John Burke, who on landing in 1839 went to the lodgings of a friend's kinsman and 'time flew fast and friends & Conversation made us forget the parties we have left perched on their Boxes and Baggage at Peck Slip'. Or Margaret McCarthy from Kingwilliamstown, who made the journey in 1848, and who had an offer from a friend 'Saying that if I wished to go up the Country that he would send me money but I declined so doing untill you Come'. And when Eliza quen [Quinn] reached New York in 1847 she had 'good frinds here befor me when I had my cussen Edward And his wife'. In 1858 Mary Brown was met 'with all sorts of kindness' by friends. Examples of this kind are typical and could be multiplied.[2]

Quite apart from the impact of nativist racism, such contacts made it much more likely that the New York Irish would congregate in particular areas. Not only that: there were ghettos within ghettos so that immigrants from particular counties and even parishes tended to gravitate toward particular corners and particular employments. A recent micro-study of Irish immigrants in the Five Points area of the Sixth Ward (on which more later) in the 1850s illustrates the point. It shows that five out of every six immigrants from County Kerry lived in just two of the neighbourhood's twenty blocks. These blocks – Orange Street between Anthony and Leonard Streets and Anthony Street between Centre and Orange Streets – were among the most squalid and crime-ridden in the whole city. Almost two-thirds of the Irish-born inhabitants of these two blocks had been born in Kerry. Moreover, most of these immigrants hailed from same two or three impoverished parishes in the south of the county. At ward level, Kerrymen and Kerrywomen were more likely to be found in the Fourth, Cork people in the Seventh, and so on. Moreover, as we shall see, male immigrants tended to marry women from their own home regions (Lyne 2001: 102 (citing Tyler Anbinder); Ridge 1996: 276; Ó Gráda 1999: 114–21).

The Roman Catholic Church played an important role in the Irish immigrant community. It was its most valuable 'social capital'. Its priests were mainly Irish-born or the sons of Irish-born parents. Besides creating a sense of belonging in an alien, intimidating environment, the church encouraged and focused volunteering activity. Both the Irish Immigrant Society and the Emigrant Industrial Savings Bank, the subject of chapter 9, were largely church creations. The church also marshalled and unified the different strata in the immigrant community and increased their political clout. It was in this period, under the leadership of Bishop (later Archbishop) John Hughes, that it began to accumulate physical capital in a significant fashion. Between 1842, when Hughes took over from an elderly John Du Bois, and the 1860s the number of Catholic churches in New York rose from eight to 31. The number of Catholic schools rose in tandem. Work on Hughes's most ambitious project, the new St Patrick's Cathedral on Fifth Avenue, began in 1858 (though it would not be completed until 1879) (Ernst 1949: 136; Dolan 1983: 22).

At first sight at least, this image of a vibrant and powerful church is contradicted by the low attendance rates suggested by the 1855 New York State Census. That census, like other nineteenth-century censuses, was hardly perfect; nonetheless social historians have long deemed it adequate for inferences like those drawn here. Well-known studies relying on the census include those by Ernst (1949); Groneman Pernicone (1973); Glasco (1980). The census puts the 'usual' attendance at mass in the city's 24 Catholic churches at 100,500. Given that the Catholic Church was by no means exclusively Irish and that most of the Irish community was nominally Catholic, this implies that about half the Irish attended regularly. The census figure included 78,488 communicants. The data need to be placed in context, however. Firstly, church attendance in Ireland itself on the eve of the famine was probably no higher than this. David Miller's recent reappraisal suggests that north-west of an imaginary line linking Killarney and Dundalk only 20–40 per cent of the Catholic population attended mass regularly in the mid-1830s. Elsewhere attendance averaged about one in two, being highest in the towns and cities (Kerr 1982: 45–7, 1994: 318–21; Miller 2000). Secondly, at this time Easter communion was still a better measure of loyalty or belonging than weekly mass attendance. And lest these numbers give the impression that New York's Catholics were a lax minority in a pious city, it bears noting that they were far more observant than members of the other major denominations. In a city where the great majority of those born in the USA belonged, at least nominally, to the main reformed churches, the 'usual' attendance in 1855 included only 12,140 Baptists, 17,675 Presbyterians, and 21,850 Episcopalians. This suggests that in New York Catholic church-goers were almost as numerous as all other churchgoers put together. Given the size and poverty of the recent influx, it is hardly surprising that the Catholic Church in New York was still under-resourced both in manpower and buildings in the mid-1850s. Its priest-to-people ratio was lower than in Ireland and its ratio of mass-goers to church seats was three-to-one. In this respect it was the poorest of all listed denominations, large and small: the main Baptist churches had 2.1 seats per 'usual' worshipper, the Presbyterian church 1.7 seats, and the Protestant Episcopal church also 1.7 seats (Hough 1857: 447, 464, 468, 472; Dolan 1983: 57; Miller 1985: 331–2; Stott 1990: 240–2; Burrows and Wallace 1999: 629–31, 749–51).

The 1855 New York Census (Hough 1857) also offers some insight into the character of ethnic segregation. Like all censuses of the period it is far from perfect, but it is adequate for present purposes. The city at that time was divided into 22 municipal wards. I report the correlations between the population pro-portions of the four main immigrant groups across 22 wards in 1855 below. Note first how English- and Scottish-born immigrants tended to settle in the same wards, while neither showed a preference for settling in wards with a big Irish presence. Though their high overall shares make a negative correlation between Irish and German immigrant shares less surprising, nevertheless the outcome suggests that the Irish and the Germans concentrated in separate neighbourhoods. Note too how, by and large, the Irish and black populations shunned each other.

The picture in the neighbouring borough of Brooklyn was also one of the Irish and the Germans tending to live apart, though in this case wards with heavy concentrations of Irish were also likely to contain disproportionate numbers of English and Scottish. The Irish and Afro-Americans also tended to be concentrated in different wards in Brooklyn, while the positive correlation between black and German shares is largely explained by the high proportions

The New York Irish in the 1850s

Table 8.1 **Correlations across wards between ethnic population shares, 1860**

	New York	*Brooklyn*
English and Irish	+0.095	+0.259
English and Scottish	+0.765	+0.330
Scottish and Irish	−0.131	+0.423
Irish and German	−0.538	−0.533
English and German	+0.143	−0.659
Scottish and German	−0.041	−0.619
Irish and Black	−0.224	−0.359
German and Black	−0.146	+0.413

Source: derived from Hough, *1855 Census of New York*.

of both in Brooklyn's Sixteenth Ward. The 1855 census is also a reminder that despite their association with particular wards such as New York's Fourth and Sixth or Brooklyn's Twelfth the Irish were well scattered throughout both cities. Perhaps partly for language reasons, German immigrants were much more concentrated. In 1855 the coefficient of variation in the percentage Irish-born across New York's 22 wards was 0.308, against 0.602 for the percentage German-born. In Brooklyn the coefficients of variation were 0.444 and 1.204, respectively.

In 1845 the New York census did not list the Irish separately, but they undoubtedly accounted for the bulk of those labelled 'British'. The dominance of the Irish in the 'British' population in 1845 is suggested by the very high correlation across wards (+0.948) between the percentage British-born in 1845 and Irish-born in 1855. This correlation is striking, given that Irish and British workers tended to live in different parts of the city in 1855. German immigrants also clung to wards where their compatriots were already relatively numerous, the correlation across wards between the percentages German-born in 1845 and 1855 being 0.865. The coefficients of variation in shares across wards in 1845 also anticipated those found in 1855: 0.280 for British-born and 0.589 for German-born.

Together, the Irish and the Germans accounted for about four fifths of the immigrant labour force. Robert Ernst's useful cross-tabulations of the 1855 manuscript data confirm the Irish concentrations in unskilled occupations such as labouring, domestic service, and laundering (see table 8.2). The Irish also dominated on the docks, in construction work, and in transport. They consti-tuted nearly nine out of every ten immigrant labourers, and 86.8 per cent of

Table 8.2 **Percentage shares of certain occupations by nationality**

	Irish	*German*	*English*	*Scottish*	*Other foreign*
All Foreign-born workers	56.8	29.3	6.2	2.7	5.0
(i) *Disproportionately Irish*					
Labourers	*88.1*	9.5	1.2	0.5	0.7
Laundresses	*86.8*	8.2	1.8	1.4	1.8
Hostlers, grooms	*84.8*	11.7	1.3	0.6	1.6
Drivers	*82.8*	5.9	7.1	1.4	2.8
Boilermakers	*82.8*	6.7	4.7	2.0	3.8
Stevedores	*82.0*	3.0	9.5	0.0	6.5
Domestic servants	*79.4*	15.2	2.7	1.3	1.4
Cartmen	*78.6*	11.9	4.4	2.0	3.1
Masons, bricklayers, plasterers	*76.8*	11.7	7.1	2.9	1.5
Policemen[1]	*74.3*	11.7	7.6	3.3	3.1
(ii) *Disproportionately German*					
Organ-grinders, scavengers	5.2	*89.0*	1.1	0.3	4.4
Tobacconists	6.5	*79.9*	4.8	0.5	8.3
Cabinet makers	14.0	*73.8*	3.7	1.9	6.6
Barbers	8.0	*71.2*	6.7	2.2	11.9
Paper box makers	24.2	*67.5*	1.5	1.0	5.8
Locksmiths	17.8	*65.1*	10.4	2.7	4.0
Turners, gilders	17.6	*63.2*	7.7	2.6	8.9
Musical instrument makers	11.0	*58.6*	12.7	3.4	14.3
(iii) *Disproportionately British*					
Lawyers	34.8	15.7	*20.9*	7.0	21.6
Riggers, sailmakers	41.3	16.8	*20.9*	6.8	14.2
Merchants	16.3	36.8	*19.1*	7.4	20.4
Artists	12.9	35.8	*17.0*	5.6	28.7
Physicians and surgeons	20.0	40.3	*16.6*	4.6	18.5
Ship carpenters	54.6	9.8	*14.8*	7.8	23.0

Source: derived from Ernst 1949: Appendix 7.

1   In early 1855 chief of police George Matsell reported to the city's aldermen that 718 of his men had been born in the United States, and 417 abroad. Of the latter, Matsell found, 305 were born in Ireland. The aldermen conducted their own count, which put the number of foreign-born at six hundred, mostly Irish. Of the 246 policemen appointed in 1855 143 had Irish names. See Richardson 1970: 70, 72, 89.

immigrant washerwomen. German immigrants were more likely to be found in semi-skilled occupations. They accounted for the bulk of immigrant tobacconists, organ-grinders, cabinet-makers, and barbers. British immigrants were over-represented in the higher professions (law, medicine) and in a few niche occupations such as acting, and sail-making and rigging (Stott 1990: 91–3).

Aggregating Ernst's long list of occupations into four broad categories – [1] well-off, [2] professional and business, [3] artisanal, and [4] unskilled – also highlights the low status of the New York Irish on the occupational ladder. In some cases the allocation is necessarily rather arbitrary; in others a seemingly unskilled occupation may conceal both skill and responsibility. Our categorisation is given below in table 8.3. It turns out that in New York in 1855 62.9 per cent of the immigrant Irish were in the category 4, against 19.3 per cent of German immigrants, and 21.2 per cent of the British-born. Only 0.6 per cent of the Irish immigrants worked at occupations in category 1, against 2.1 per cent for the Germans, and 5.0 per cent for the British. The modal occupation for Irish workers was in category 4, for German and British in category 3.

Table 8.3 **Occupational status and nationality, 1855**

Occupational Code	Irish (%)	German (%)	British (%)	All Foreign (%)
1	530 (0.6)	936 (2.1)	682 (5.0)	2,672 (1.7)
2	7,155 (8.1)	8,070 (17.7)	2,667 (19.4)	19,631 (12.6)
3	25,053 (28.4)	27,709 (60.9)	7,480 (54.4)	64,068 (41.2)
4	55,551 (62.9)	8,809 (19.3)	2,912 (21.2)	68,972 (44.4)
Total	88,289 (100.0)	45,544 (100.0)	13,741 (100.0)	155,343 (100.0)

Source: derived from Ernst 1949: Appendix B.
Key:
1   financiers, merchants, architects, authors, physicians and surgeons, lawyers, clergy
2   brewers and distillers, clerks, engineers, government employees, actors and performers, artists, musicians, teachers, other professional, hoteliers, restaurant owners, superintendents, clothiers, dry goods dealers, food dealers, retail shop-owners, wine and liquor dealers, speculators, students
3   dressmakers and seamstresses, cooks, domestic servants, housekeepers and janitors, laundresses, nurses, waiters, labourers, porters, boatmen, cartmen, drivers, hostlers and grooms, stevedores
4   all other occupations

The Integrated Public Use Manuscript Sample (IPUMS) of the 1860 US Census provides an alternative profile of the skill composition of the labour force on the eve of the Civil War. In the sample each worker's occupation is assigned two measures of skill, *OCCSCORE* and *SEI*. *OCCSCORE* is an

IPUMS-constructed variable that assigns occupational income scores to each occupation representing the median total income (in hundreds of 1,950 dollars) of all persons with that particular occupation in 1950. *SEI* (for Socioeconomic Index) is also an IPUMS-constructed index of occupational status, based upon the income level and educational attainment associated with each occupation in 1950. Applying measures that relate to mid twentieth-century conditions to 1860 data is clearly rather crude and ahistorical, since skill premia and the relative ranking of occupations are unlikely to have stood still in the interim.[3] Still, for what it is worth, a comparison of immigrant and New York-born workers produced the following result (table 8.4):

Table 8.4 **Occupational status and nationality in 1860**

Place of birth	OCCSCORE	SEI
New York		
Ireland	18	18
New York	25	37
Germany	24	23
Great Britain	26	33
Boston		
Ireland	20	15
Boston	23	26
Great Britain	24	21
Philadelphia		
Ireland	20	19
Germany	22	19
Philadelphia	21	26

Source: derived from IPUMS

The outcome confirms the lowly status of Irish male labour in New York. It is also worth noting here that while skill levels as measured by *OCCSCORE* among the Irish declined somewhat with age, among the Germans they rose and among the New Yorkers they did not change.[4] The Irish pattern probably reflects the 'residual' status of the older workers, an aspect to which we now turn.

Table 8.5 **Wealth and nationality in the USA in 1860**

	Irish	German	British	US-born
% of population	0.09	0.09	0.04	0.74
Avg. wealth	1,021	1,247	1,822	3,027
Avg. wealth (north only)	965	1,209	1,555	2,435
Gini coefficient	0.897	0.807	0.834	0.816
% owning property	24	37	41	47
% owning any wealth	42	57	59	66
% owning any wealth in urban areas	36	—	—	57

Source: Soltow 1975: 44 (referring to the US as a whole in 1860)

A residual population

Their numbers in mid nineteenth-century New York suggest that the city acted as a kind of irresistible magnet for Irish immigrants. Contemporary commentary cited the lure of friends and community, but also counselled immigrants against clinging to the east coast cities. Throughout the 1850s, but particularly at times of high unemployment such as in 1854–5 and in the wake of the Panic of 1857, philanthropists, labour and ethnic activists, and the local press urged the westward movement of labour. In June 1855 the *New York Times* even called on the city to finance such movement. Irish newspapers such as the *Citizen* and the *Irish-American* also advised people to move. In the wake of the financial panic of October 1857 Irish philanthropist Vere Foster prevailed on the Women's Protective Emigration Society to pay for the westward journey of about 700 unemployed Irishwomen (Anbinder 2002). During the decade the New York State Commissioners for Emigration helped about thirty thousand indigent immigrants to move west, and for a time operated a labour exchange on Canal Street linking prospective employers with recent arrivals in the city. Yet the sense that too many Irish failed to grasp the opportunities awaiting them in the interior by remaining close to their ports of arrival pervades the historiography. That 'failure' was put down in part to fecklessness, in part to a poverty trap which prevented settlers in the east coast ghettos from proceeding further (Maguire, 1868: 214–15; see also Ernst 1949: 62; Miller 1985: 315; Stott 1990: 71).

The claim that the famine and post-famine Irish failed to take their chances like other immigrant groups needs qualification. First, it bears emphasis that throughout the 1840s and 1850s only a small fraction of those who arrived in the city stayed there (Purcell 1938: 593; Ernst 1949: 61). Between 1847 and 1860 1.1 million Irish immigrants landed in New York port. The rise in the Irish-born population of New York – from nearly 0.1 million on the eve of the Famine to just over 0.2 million in 1860 – was far from commensurate.[5] Moreover, comparing the increases in the numbers of Irish, Germans and British in the city between 1850 and 1860 with gross immigrant flows implies that the Irish were hardly any more inclined to remain than the Germans. An immigration of 841,000 from Ireland fuelled a population increase of only 70,000, while a German inflow of 761,000 helped boost the number of German-born by 64,000. In this respect the British were very different. Despite a gross inflow of over 300,000 the number of New Yorkers born in Britain rose by only six thousand (Albion 1939: 353). The implication of these numbers must be tempered the fact that they include both travellers and immigrants and the likelihood that a much higher proportion of the British arrivals returned to Europe.[6]

Corroboration for the outward mobility of the New York Irish at a more micro level is found in Jay Dolan's well-known study of Irish and German Catholics in two Manhattan parishes in the 1850s. Dolan found that nearly two-fifths of a sample of Irish families present in the Transfiguration of Our Lord parish in the heavily Irish Sixth Ward in 1850 had left before 1860. Over the same period, a slightly higher proportion of German families living in Holy Redeemer parish in the Seventeenth Ward in 1850 had moved. Life expectation in the Sixth Ward was much lower, however; taking deaths into account, the German percentage remaining in New York exceeded the Irish by 57 to 41 per cent (Dolan 1983: 38).[7]

Comparing the stock of Irish-born in New York in 1860 with the age-structure and gender of the inflow into the city during the 1840s and 1850s is also interesting in this respect. Table 8.6 describes the age structure of the New York Irish as reflected in the IPUMS sample and that of a sample of over three thousand immigrants who arrived in ten shiploads in 1851. Note that while men dominated the immigration, women dominated the population of New York in 1860. Note too, judging from the sample, that the 1860 stock was rather 'old' – with one third of the men aged over forty (compared with only 22 per cent of the women) – while the migrant inflow tended to be very young. The passenger lists suggest that well over two thirds of the inflow were aged under 25 years and that – in common with migrant flows in other times and other places – women tended to leave home sooner than men.

Although nothing specific is known about the mortality patterns of immigrants, the bulk of those arriving in 1851 would have been still alive in 1860 (Herscovici 1998: 932 n15). A plausible if hardly rigorous reading of table 8.6 would therefore be that a disproportionate proportion of New York's Irishmen had arrived before 1850, and that younger women were much more likely to remain on than men. Our discussion of the prospects facing women immigrants below implies that this was a 'rational' outcome in the economic sense.

Table 8.6 **Age-distributions of Irish arrivals and residents**

	1860 sample		Immigrant flow	
Age	M	F	M	F
0–9	1.7	3.3	12.4	13.2
10–14	3.7	3.1	8.6	8.8
15–19	9.4	10.3	12.7	19.2
20–24	13.8	17.9	32.7	28.2
25–29	13.8	22.3	13.8	10.3
30–34	13.8	13.4	8.9	8.0
35–39	11.1	7.4	3.3	3.1
40–44	11.1	8.5	4.6	4.7
45–49	8.4	4.5	1.5	1.9
50–54	6.7	5.4	1.4	2.0
55–59	2.7	1.3	0.6	0.5
60+	4.0	2.7	0.2	0.2
Total	298	448	1773	1431

Note: immigrant flows based on [a] *Epimandias* (dep. 2 Apr. 1851), *Infanta* (dep. 3 Apr. 1851, *State-Rights* (dep. 3 Apr. 1851), *Liberty* (5 Apr. 1851), *Manhattan* (5 Apr. 1851); [b] *Perseverance* (27 Dec. 1851), *Constitution* (27 Dec. 1851), *Panola* (29 Dec. 1851), *Siddons* (29 Dec. 1851), *James Fagan* (31 Dec. 1851).

The Irish who left the city fared better than those who remained, but the selection bias aspect of the onward migration must not be forgotten. It was widely understood that the 'pith and marrow' of Irish immigrants – those with skills and capital – were most inclined to move on. Bishop Hughes, who was in a good position to know, commented:[8]

Most move on across the country – those who have some means, those who have industrious habits. . . . on the other hand, the destitute, the disabled, the broken down, the very young, and the very old, having reached New York, stay. Those who stay are predominantly the scattered debris of the Irish nation.

Clearly, concentrating only on those who stayed in New York and other eastern cities is likely to produce an overly gloomy picture of the fate of Irish immigrants. Overlooking the likelihood that those who moved on were better resourced than those who remained will bias any assessment of their relative progress. Moreover, taking account of their gender breakdown influences the assessment of those who stayed. Whatever may be said about the men, it is far from obvious that the women who remained – and they represented the majority of the New York Irish – would have fared better elsewhere.

A female immigration

The popular historiography of mid nineteenth-century New York, with its focus on topics such as Tammany Hall, the Bowery Bhoys, gang rivalries, prostitution, and the draft riots of July 1863, highlights its 'maleness'. Yet insofar as early adulthood was concerned New York was very much a 'city of women'. In 1855 56 per cent of New Yorkers aged 15–29 years were women (Stansell 1987: 83–4; Hough 1857: 38–9). The very female character of ante-bellum New York's Irish population is sometimes lost sight of. The female share of New York's Irish-born population in the 1860 IPUMS sample was 60.9 per cent, compared to 41.4 per cent of the German-born, and 52 per cent of the New York-born. In Philadelphia too the female share of the Irish-born population was very high (58.4 per cent). In Boston Irishwomen also outnumbered Irishmen, though by less (51.1 to 48.9 per cent). The age-by-gender distribution of the New York Irish-born population is striking. Both Irishmen and Irishwomen were less likely to be part of a family group than either German- or New York-born. 'Other non-relatives', nearly all single and childless, bulked large in the Irish immigrant population, accounting accounted for 20.5 per cent of all the males and 30.7 per cent of the females. By comparison 'other non-relatives' represented 15.5 per cent of German-born males and 13.9 per cent of German-born females, and 11 and 6.5 per cent, respectively, of the New York-born.

Ernst's cross-tabulations of the 1855 census do not disaggregate by gender, but their clear implication is that the proportion of women in the Irish immigrant labour force was relatively high. Exclusively female occupations such as domestic servant (23,386), dressmaker and seamstress (4,559), and laundress (1,758) accounted for a much higher proportion of the Irish labour force than of other immigrant groups. Moreover, the labour force participation rate of Irishwomen was much higher than that of German women. In the 1860 IPUMS census sampl,e women accounted for 45 per cent of Irish-born labour force, but only ten per cent of the German.

Irishwomen in New York held low-status, low pay jobs with an average *OCCSCORE* of 8.7 and an average Duncan *SEI* of 12. These low scores reflect the fact that more than two employed women in three were domestic servants. Several points need stressing here. First, domestic service as an occupation was held in low esteem in the USA in the nineteenth century. Yankee women rarely worked as servants, and the same went for second generation Irish-American women.[9] Servants were often prey to boorish treatment by their female employers, and to sexual harassment and worse from male household heads. The hours were long and the work dull. Yet socioeconomic measures such as *OCCSCORE* and *SEI*, which are based on mid twentieth-century relativities, probably undervalue the attractiveness of domestic service in the mid nineteenth century relative to alternatives such as sewing, laundering, and factory work. Though comparisons are made difficult by the big in-kind component in the wage, domestics seem to have been relatively well paid. One of the earliest detailed studies of women's wages in the USA refers to Massachusetts in 1872. A study by that state's Bureau of Statistics of Labor, based on a survey of over 20,000 women including 1,220 domestic servants, suggests that the annual earnings of servants exceeded those of most other women workers, without even taking into consideration that servants got their board free. Other studies from the late nineteenth century confirm this pattern. The historian David Katzman concludes: 'the overall pattern, then, suggested that women in unskilled and semiskilled work received no higher earnings than domestics, and when widespread unemployment occurred during hard times, probably they earned significantly less.' A contemporary Stephen Byrne suggested an average wage of about $10 a month with board for female servants, while Stott states that in antebellum New York servants were better paid than other working women (Byrne 1874: 160; Stott 1990: 62–3; Katzman 1978: 314). Note that New York's Irishmen were more likely to be found in wards like the First, Fourth and Sixth, and Irishwomen in the wards north of Fourteenth Street. The high proportion of Irish in the more middle-class Fifteenth Ward was a reflection of the high number of Irish servants resident there (Ernst 1949: 193; Hough 1857: 8; Stott 1990: 62, 204).

Thus it may not be correct to see these Irishwomen as 'locked in' to the city and domestic service by poverty. Though it is true that domestic service was widely frowned upon by others, it may well have been the occupation of choice of many Irish immigrant women. The stigma which deterred both Yankee women and first generation Irish-American women from service did not apply. Irishwomen therefore paid a lower psychic price for the higher wages and safer work environment that domestic service conferred. Domestic service held out several advantages. It offered a healthier lifestyle than factory or needlework, and also steadier employment. It involved living in private dwellings on middle-class streets rather than in tenements.[10] It facilitated saving and remitting funds home, and evidence discussed in chapter 4 suggests that servants did indeed save.[11] It was an occupation in which most immigrant Irishwomen had a comparative advantage by virtue of being English-speaking. The high proportion of the Irish among domestics was a function of the high share of young unmarried females in Irish immigration. For most, domestic service was a temporary avocation. New York, populous and rich, offered more opportunities for this kind of work than virtually anywhere else.

The Sixth Ward

In 1855 three of New York's wards – the First, the Fourth and the Sixth – contained more people born in Ireland than born in the United States. Though the First and the Fourth contained slightly higher proportions of Irish-born, the Sixth was considered the quintessentially Irish ward. More than three quarters of its voters were naturalised immigrants, a higher proportion than anywhere else in the city. It was also the ward with the highest proportion of self-declared illiterates: about one in five of those aged 21 and above (Hough 1857: 8). This tiny triangular space of about sixty acres in lower Manhattan, wedged between Broadway and Chatham Street, and bordered on its north side by Walker Street, contained over 25,000 people in 1855 – more than two fifths of them born in Ireland. With about four hundred souls per acre the 'Bloody Old Sixth' easily matched Dublin's Liberties or London's East End for congestion.

Sensational accounts from the pens of Charles Dickens, New York journalist George Foster, and many others helped create an image of the mainly working-class Sixth Ward as a virtual no-go slum area. Particularly infamous was its core at the Five Points, a junction of cramped tenement streets. To the evangelical missionaries who sought to reform its inhabitants in the 1850s, the Five Points was 'a synonym for ignorance the most entire, for misery the most abject, for crime of the darkest dye, for degradation so deep that human nature cannot sink below it'.[12] Even the modern historiography of New York still conveys the impression of an area populated largely by prostitutes, vagrants, thieves, and juvenile delinquents. The Sixth Ward's reputation for crime and debauchery was no by no means undeserved. In the early 1860s it contained 406 'drinking shops' and 26 brothels.[13] Yet it is also true that most of its inhabitants in mid-century were poor people trying to make a living. A mid-1860s survey by the Citizens Association divided the population into two thirds 'composed of the labouring poor, and of vicious classes', and a third 'made up of better classes of people who live upon wages'. The same survey described many of the Irish as trading in strong drink, groceries, or junk. Carol Groneman in particular has contrasted the gap between the negative assessments of Charles Dickens and others and the picture gained from an investigation of contemporary census and other quantitative data. She cites the local evangelist Samuel Halliday, who surveyed the Five Points area in 1860 and concluded that the number of 'abandoned women' was much smaller than implied in such assessments. Moreover (Groneman Pernicone 1973: 201): 'To me it is a matter of surprise that there is so much that is decent, even respectable, for a very large proportion of these families, though poor, are virtuous and comparatively cleanly. Some of them are models of neatness.' Groneman's corroboration relies mainly on scrutiny of the manuscript New York Census of 1855, which suggested the presence of strong family ties among the Sixth Ward's Irish immigrants, as reflected in the high percentage of co-resident teenage children. It also indicated the dominance of nuclear family households, augmented, perhaps, by a boarder or two. Boarding houses containing large numbers of unattached Irishmen or Irishwomen were the exception. In the Sixth Ward one in four of German-born males aged under forty lived in boarding houses, and nearly one in three of US-born, but only five per cent of Irishmen under forty did so. Groneman interprets this as evidence of the closeness of Irish family and kinship ties, though she concedes that economic factors may also have played a role: lodging with a family cost less than staying in a boarding house. For Groneman these findings imply that most of the Irish Sixth Warders were conventional working-class people forced by poverty to live in rough surroundings, very different from the traditional image of New York's slum-dwellers as a rootless, unemployed, and corrupted *demi-monde*. Finally the census shows that although pre-famine immigrants were more skilled than recent arrivals, there was a negative association between skill levels and age (see table 8.7). This curious finding is presumably a reflection of selection bias in migration out of the Sixth Ward in this period.[14]

Table 8.7 **Age and male skills in the Sixth Ward**

Age	15–19	20–29	30–39	40–49	50+
Unskilled (%)					
Pre-famine	31.4	25.8	40.2	43.9	51.6
Post-famine	39.5	56.6	54.6	64.3	73.4
Skilled (%)					
Pre-famine	55.7	51	37	29.7	28.3
Post-famine	52.3	33.7	33.6	23.1	16
Other (%)					
Pre-famine	12.9	23.2	22.8	26.4	20.1
Post-famine	8.2	9.6	11.7	12.5	10.6

Source: derived from Groneman Pernicone, 'Bloody Old Sixth', 116, table iv-13.

The census also confirmed the unskilled character of the Irish labour force in the Sixth Ward (see table 8.8). In 1855 Sixth Ward Irishwomen specialised in the sewing and dressmaking trades (25.7 per cent of the total), in domestic service (36.3 per cent), and in taking boarders (31.9 per cent). The relative importance of sewing and dressmaking is a sign of the ward's poverty: in the city as a whole, Irish-born servants outnumbered dressmakers and seamstresses by four to one (Groneman Pernicone 1973: 155, table v-2; Groneman 1978; Ernst 1949: 215). Groneman's findings offer a useful corrective to earlier accounts, though they are probably coloured somewhat by an undue reliance on the 1855 census. As noted earlier, this was an imperfect enumeration which was most likely to miss the more marginal and unattached elements in the population. An even more revisionist gloss on the Sixth Ward Irish is offered by a 1996 archaeological survey of one of its most impoverished corners near the Five Points. In this federally funded exercise in 'the archaeology of domestic trash', the Irish struggle for stability and even a modicum of respectability is revealed in the 'pretty things' – pieces of cutlery, commemorative vases, and the like – that they left behind. This study goes much further than Groneman Pernicone in its critique of the earlier sensationalist literature, and even exaggeratedly refers to the Five Points as a 'mythic slum' (Yamin 1997).

The church registers of the Transfiguration of Our Lord parish report the ages and addresses of most brides and grooms married there in the 1850s, and their place of birth. The records highlight not only a tendency for Irishmen to marry Irishwomen, but also the remarkable strength of regional or local networks within the Irish community. Most marriages involved couples from the same or neighbouring counties in Ireland, particularly so for well-represented counties such as Sligo and Kerry. More than two thirds of men reported as born in those counties married women from the same county, and most of those marriages involved couples from the same corner of the same county.[15]

Remarkably, in about one marriage in every four grooms and brides-to-be gave the same address to the church clerk. This does not necessarily mean 'living in sin', however; even if practised, cohabitation would certainly have been concealed from the local clergy.[16] A more plausible explanation is that it reflected the tendency of immigrants from the same region in Ireland to live cheek by jowl in tenement housing. Certain addresses recur again and again in the records. For instance, 13 men, mostly with different surnames and mostly from County Cork, married out of 5 Mulberry Street in the 1850s. The twelve men who married out of 22 Mulberry Street had come from a range of Irish counties but those living in 20 Mulberry Street were mainly Sligo people, while between 1853 and 1856 three men with different surnames, but all from Ahamlish in County Sligo, married out of 10 Franklin Street. 31 Baxter Street supplied eight grooms, all from Kerry or west Cork, and five of them married women giving the same address.

The fertility of these marriages is unknown but the fertility of women in the Sixth Ward as a whole in the 1850s may be gauged, albeit only roughly, from the 1855 Census report. The census gives the number of children aged less than one, and the ages of women at five yearly intervals (15 to 19 years, 20 to 24 years, and so on). Such data provide the raw data for a lower-bound estimate of I_f, a standard measure of total fertility which corrects for the impact of the age-distribution of women on child-bearing capacity. Like the census, I_f does not distinguish between married and unmarried women or between legitimate and illegitimate offspring. The numerator used here, the number of children less than one, is a fallible measure of births for two reasons. First, it takes no account of infant mortality, bound to have been high in a crowded city such as New York. Second, it does not allow for under-enumeration, a universal feature of censuses in the nineteenth century. Bearing both factors in mind, the estimate for New York city as a whole – 0.271, uncorrected for mortality and under-enumeration – suggests that fertility there exceeded that of Paris (0.265) and probably London (0.293) in 1851. By this reckoning, fertility in the Sixth Ward (0.277, uncorrected) was marginally higher than in the city at large and, assuming that infant mortality was higher in urban than in rural areas, also higher than in the state as a whole.[17]

In Ireland many of the residents of the 'Bloody Old Sixth' had been residents on the estates of landlords who had paid their passages for them. Most of those from Kerry living in the Sixth Ward had been born on the estate of the third marquess of Lansdowne in the south of that county, while the majority of the Sligo immigrants had lived on or near that county's north-west coast on the estates of Lord Palmerston and Sir Robert Gore-Booth. The Kerry scheme was the work of William Steuart Trench, agent of the Lansdowne estate, though his employer may have provided the spur, being an intimate of prominent supporters of subsidised emigration such as the economist Nassau Senior and the Whig landlord Lord Monteagle. That the Kerry emigrants arrived in New York in a destitute state is borne out by several contemporary press accounts. One described tenants and their families 'without a penny of money . . . mak[ing] their way on foot from Kenmare to Cork . . . from whence their passages were paid to Liverpool, and thence to New York'. Another stated that the US Commissioners of Immigration had charged the carrier of one shipload of Kenmare emigrants $25 per head, the cost of their maintenance out of public funds in New York. Later accounts by the journalist John Francis Maguire and the parish priest of Kenmare, Fr John O'Sullivan, painted an unduly bleak picture of Trench's scheme, however. Within a few years some of the immigrants were earning enough to save substantial sums of money in New York, and 'it was to Trench that they owed their newfound economic opportunity' (Lyne 1992: 104–5, 2001: ch 2; Anbinder 2002).

The Irish economist R. D. C. Black has shown that publicly funded emigration schemes had commanded the support of a majority of British economists since the 1820s (Black 1960: ch. 7). Only a few such schemes had come to fruition, however, and before the famine landlord-assisted schemes were also few. The total number of paupers 'shovelled out' by Lansdowne, Palmerston and Gore-Booth in the wake of the famine, though not known with precision, did not exceed more than a few thousand.[18] Yet from a landlord perspective the 'shovelling out' of pauper tenants made perfect sense. It meant a lower tax burden and more scope for estate rationalisation. As Steuart Trench noted, proprietors who rendered no assistance retained their paupers and lost their 'respectable' tenants, while on the Kenmare estate 'none but abject Paupers' left. Trench's control of the local poor law union gave him the power to exclude any potential 'free riding' proprietors. His scheme cut drastically both the numbers in the workhouse (3,350 on the eve of his scheme, about 260 a decade later) and in surrounding parishes. Paranoid that improvident marriages and the growth of begging would fill the demographic vacuum left on the Lansdowne estate, he fined or evicted without mercy tenants who sublet farms or offered hospitality to travelling beggars (Lyne 1992: 86).

Migrants either formally transplanted by their landlords through emigration schemes or assisted by rent rebates accounted for only a small minority of famine emigrants, perhaps forty or fifty thousand of the half million or so who crossed the Atlantic because of the famine.[19] Schemes such as Trench's, which specifically targeted workhouse inmates, many of them presumably landless, rather than small tenants unable to pay rent, were very much the exception. But suppose more of the really poor had been helped in the same way? How different would the character of the flow have been? Our profiles of the Lower Manhattan Irish in the 1850s provide one answer, and prompt a few comments on the role of assisted migration during the famine. The large numbers of men and women from Kerry and Sligo mentioned in the EISB and Transfiguration Church records indicate that many of those who emigrated stayed there in the 1850s. Nor does the 1855 census data leave much scope for success stories then in terms of skills acquisition. Taken together these bits of information suggest that an increase in the share of more emigrants like those sent by Trench would have reduced the geographical and occupational mobility of the Irish as a group. Further assisted emigration would have made the record of the Irish seem even worse relative to other immigrants in this period (Ferrie 1997: 203–4).

A comprehensive history of assisted emigration during the famine remains to be written. Some schemes, such as that funded by Major Denis Mahon in Strokestown, ended in disaster and earned lasting notoriety. Others were efficiently managed. The crown-financed emigration from Ballykilcline, next to Strokestown, seems to have been a model of its kind.[20] The assisted emigration of over three thousand people from the Lansdowne estate in south Kerry in 1850–1 or so was the most ambitious scheme of all. By economising on maintenance and concentrating the emigration on the low season, the organiser of the Lansdowne scheme, William Steuart Trench, kept its cost down to a modest £10,000 or so. Trench and his employer were criticised at the time, not unfairly, for their stinginess (Lyne 1992).

Yet surely the broader implication of the profiles painted by the statistical sources described above is that further schemes, properly timed and more humanely managed, would have been a viable form of famine relief. The possibilities must be kept in proportion. Firstly, none of these statistical sources captures conditions in the New York Irish slums at their worst. Very few of the individuals recorded in the marriage registers were included in the censuses of 1855 or 1860, highlighting 'the necessity for using other primary sources to supplement census data'.[21] The 'Ladies of the Mission' exaggerated the depravity and violence of the slum-dwellers, but the census commissioners almost certainly erred in the other direction by failing to include the most marginal inhabitants. For instance, the 1855 census of New York state did not list the number of prostitutes separately, but the 122 foreign-born and ten black prostitutes counted by Robert Ernst in its manuscript folios must be set against the five thousand or so women 'on the town' estimated by the chief of police George Matsell a year later.[22]

Secondly, assisting people to emigrate in 1847–8 would not have eliminated the need for other kinds of public relief during the winter and spring of 1846 and 1847. Nor, thirdly, could the very young and the very old have travelled; neither could heavily pregnant women or the mothers of very young children. Fourthly, the absorptive capacity of New World and particularly its cities was limited; in the late 1840s the total population of north America was not much more than twenty million, and only ten per cent of the total lived in towns and cities. Fifthly, the capacity of the passenger trade in 1847 was already sorely stretched and probably subject to rising costs at the margin. Moreover, a significant increase in immigration from Ireland would undoubtedly have prompted increases in mortality in US cities, as they did in Liverpool and Glasgow. Further immigration would have intensified anti-Irish feeling, already at an all-time high. In the New York mayoral election of 1854 the candidate of the rabidly anti-immigrant Know Nothing Party, James Barker, obtained about 31 per cent of the popular vote and came second in a four-way race. In the same year Know Nothing candidates won the mayoralties of Boston, Philadelphia, Chicago and San Francisco. Electoral support for the Know Nothings did not last, but at its peak it far exceeded that for even the most successful anti-immigrant movements in Europe today. Such considerations mean that mass migration was no panacea. Nevertheless, the assisted migration of even, say, a further 100,000 Irish famine victims in 1847–8 would have almost certainly have saved many more lives in Ireland itself. An outlay of public money of, say, £1 million (about 0.2 per cent of UK national income or 2 per cent of annual public spending) would have easily covered the cost of such a scheme (Ó Gráda 1999: 120–1).

Human capital

One of the benefits of immigration to the receiving country is that it saves on the cost of bringing up and educating part of the labour force. The age-structure of immigrant flows means that immigrants typically arrive as 'instant adults'. Irish immigration was no exception. In terms of skills and education, however, Irish labour was inferior to American. Moreover, the disadvantage persisted into the next generation. This was partly because in antebellum America poverty and religion militated against the Irish sending their children to school. David Galenson has shown how in Boston in 1860 Irish attendance lagged behind in an elementary school system still controlled by a native Yankee elite, while Dennis Clark has described the rapid growth of a parochial school system in Philadelphia in response to nativist bigotry. New York was also the locus of a protracted struggle between church and state about schooling. After fighting and losing the battle for state funding for Catholic schools in the 1840s the church embarked on a programme of private school building. Within a decade there were 28 Catholic schools catering for ten thousand pupils, but teachers were in short supply. In 1860 about three fifths of Irish-born children aged between six and fifteen were attending school, better than for German-born children (38 per cent) but far behind New York-born children (77 per cent). However, 79 per cent of children with two Irish-born parents had attended school in the previous year (Galenson 1998; Herscovici 1994; Clark 2005: 93–9; Ernst 1949: 140–1; Lannie 1968).

The literacy data in the 1855 census provided no breakdown by nationality, but the correlation across wards between Irishness and adult illiteracy is a striking +0.674. In the city as a whole the illiteracy rate was about seven per cent, but in the heavily Irish Sixth Ward it reached nearly one-fifth. The information on literacy and age-heaping in the 1860 IPUMS confirms that the New York Irish were relatively poor in human capital. The question on literacy in the census referred to those aged twenty years and above only. Not surprisingly, the New York Irish emerged as less literate than either the German-born or native New Yorkers. Eight per cent of Irishmen and 14 per cent of Irishwomen were illiterate, compared to rates of zero and three per cent for German immigrants, and zero and one per cent for the New York-born. Yet significantly, too, illiteracy rates among the New York Irish were much lower than in Ireland itself in 1861. In the 1861 Irish census 28 per cent of males and 31 per cent of females aged 16 to 25 years were unable to either read or write, and for the 46 to 55 year age cohort the ratios were 35 and 51 per cent, respectively.

It is well known that people with low literacy and numeracy rates are prone to age-heaping (i.e. are more likely to record their ages in years ending with zero or five, or with even rather than odd numbers) in official documents. Sometimes age-heaping may reflect mainly the carelessness of those charged with taking down the information. Too busy or lazy to ascertain exact ages, they may have resorted to rounding. Between-group differences within a given area, however, presumably reflect genuine gaps in educational levels among those being counted (e.g. Mokyr and Ó Gráda 1982). One very simple measure of age-heaping is the proportion of people aged 20–4, 30–4, etc. who reported their ages as 20, 30, etc. The higher this ratio, the greater was the degree of age-heaping. Figure 8.2 shows that by this measure in 1860 the New York Irish were much more likely to age-heap than the German or the New York born.[23]

Table 8.8 **Age–heaping in New York by place of birth**

	Ireland		Germany		New York	
	M	*F*	*M*	*F*	*M*	*F*
20 to 24	0.24	0.25	0.25	0.16	0.28	0.20
30 to 34	0.51	0.53	0.32	0.45	0.33	0.50
40 to 44	0.73	0.79	0.43	0.43	0.57	0.58

Note: the entries show the percentage in each age-group reporting an age ending in zero. See appendix, pp. 173–4 for underlying data.

The arrival of the mid nineteenth-century Irish cannot have made New York a healthier place. How the Irish fared health-wise is unknown, however. In mid-century admissions into the city's Bellevue Hospital, a long-established public institution located on the northern outskirts of the city at Twenty-fourth Street and First Avenue, were predominantly Irish. Between 1846 and 1858 the Irish-born accounted for 71 per cent of all admissions to Bellevue, and for 84 per cent of foreign-born admissions (Ernst 1949: 200). But comprehensive, reliable data on mortality and morbidity in antebellum New York are lacking.

However, the city was not quite as unhealthy as might be expected from congestion and poor housing conditions. Rejection rates of men drafted by the Union Army were greater in mainly rural upstate New York than in the city in 1863–4. Hardly surprisingly, draftees were more likely to be rejected for tuberculosis and heart ailments in the city, but general debility and digestive ailments were much more common in rural areas (Stott 1990: 184). Mean adult height, a common measure of nutritional status during childhood and adolescence, was greater in New York (at nearly 67 inches or 170 cm) than anywhere in western Europe in mid-century. Stott also notes that physicians 'were impressed with the health of city residents' (Stott 1990: 185).

Crime

Antebellum New York had a reputation for lawlessness. The reputation was exaggerated by sensationalist contemporaneous reports, and by many accounts in history and in fiction since then. The preposterous claim that a single notorious building in the Sixth Ward had 'averaged a homicide a night for fifteen years' tells its own story. The true murder rate (an annual 2.5 per 100,000 inhabitants in the late 1840s, rising to 4.4 per thousand in the 1850s and 1860s) was considerably lower, but still higher than that obtaining in pre-famine Ireland (2.4 per thousand in 1836–40, including manslaughter but not justifiable homicide or infanticide; much lower in the 1850s) or in England and Wales (1.7 per thousand in 1834–50, also including manslaughter).[24]

Nativists blamed immigrants for the high crime rates in American cities – in the same way that Irish people today often blame immigrants for a disproportionate share of Irish crime. The raw correlation between immigration and crime has long been a key component of anti-immigrant rhetoric. There is no denying the over-representation of immigrants, and especially Irish immigrants, in New York's law courts and prisons. In the 1850s most of those committed to prison in New York were foreign born, and the bulk of the foreign born were Irish. The children of Irish-born parents who had arrived before the post-1846 influx constituted the bulk of juvenile delinquents in the city. In one well-documented year, 1858, over half the city's 35,172 prison commitments were Irish-born, with women accounting for nearly half the Irish total. Most Irish crime was directed at Irish people, however, not native New Yorkers; assaults of women by men of the same name were common.[25]

In mitigation poverty often breeds crime and, as we have seen, the Irish were the most marginal group in New York in these decades. The high crime rate was also in part a reflection of the demographics of the immigrant population and of how the authorities defined 'crime'. Those who commit crime are always more likely to be young, and the New York Irish were disproportionately young and unmarried. The historian Eric Monkkonen estimates that 'demography alone' would have doubled the homicide rate for the Irish relative to native born whites. The young were a particular target of George Matsell, the city's chief of police in the 1850s, and Christine Stansell has suggested that the doubling in the number of juvenile commitments in that decade sprung in part from 'the tendency of the police to see a child on the streets as inherently criminal'. More of the 'crime' was simply the product of the rowdy, boisterous culture of the immigrant poor, and would have gone unpunished at home. It bears noting that most Irish 'criminals' were committed for no more than being drunk and disorderly or for vagrancy. For example, 57.8 per cent of arrests in the first half of 1854 were for 'intoxication', 'disorderly conduct' or both; another eight per cent were for 'vagrancy'. Between 1850 and 1858 87 per cent of all those committed were 'intemperate', and more than half were unmarried. In Ireland such 'crimes' were not treated as such, and there was more sympathy for the drunk and the beggar. Nonetheless, it seems that in New York the Irish played a disproportionate part in more serious crimes too.[26]

The high crime rate was also a reflection of the rapid growth of the city and the parlous state of law and order. In the mid-1850s New York was seriously under-policed, having about 1.2 policemen per thousand inhabitants compared to London's 4.6 per thousand in 1851 and Dublin's 3.3 per thousand in 1841. Moreover, New York's police force was much more subject to political influence. Rates of pay were high, and connections mattered. Matsell, a supporter of pro-immigrant Mayor Fernando Wood, encouraged the hiring of Irishmen as constables, forging a link between the Irish and the NYPD that would last for generations. The city's nativist board of aldermen sought to frustrate Wood's policy. New York's police force was also less well trained than, say, the Royal Irish Constabulary or the British bobby.[27]

Wages and wealth

Systematic, continuous data on the trend in real wages in antebellum New York are lacking. Scattered evidence from contemporary sources suggests that in the 1850s Irish tradesmen and artisans in the city might earn $10 to $12 a week, but the great majority of male immigrants were unskilled and therefore earned on average no more than $6 to $7 weekly. Robert Ernst gives female servants' wages as averaging $6 a month in the mid-1840s, in addition to free bed and board. Chambermaids and house-workers received from $5 to $6 a month, and slop-women $4. Cooks, ladies' maids, nurses, and waiters were better paid, enjoyed more comfortable living quarters, and earned extra compensation if they cared for children. In the depressed mid-1850s a tailor might earn $25 to $35 per month, or the equivalent of $6 to $9 a week. Dockers and unskilled building workers earned $1.00–$1.25 a day, bricklayers and painters $1.50–$1.60 a day. Building work was more regular than work on the docks, but impossible in severe weather.[28]

These are averages of wage *levels*: what of movements during the 1850s? First, real wages fell for most of the decade. Robert Margo's real wage index for the Northeast, which includes New York, falls from 119.5 in 1848 and 104.0 in 1849 to a trough of 82.2 in 1858, before rising to 96.7 in 1859 and 100.0 in 1860. The fall in real wages between 1848 and 1858 was unprecedented in antebellum history.[29] Second, the decade was punctuated by two severe cyclical downturns. According to the *New York Tribune* the winter of 1854–5, 'unlike any of the fifteen preceding it', reduced thousands of workers to beggary. Admissions into the city's almshouse were 26 per cent higher in 1854–5 than in 1852–3, and the resources of the New York Association for the Improvement of the Condition of the Poor (AICP), which also targeted the destitute, were stretched to the limit. The panic of October 1857 was even more severe in the short run. On 21 October *Herald* highlighted its dire impact on the clothing trades with the claim that half of those employed in the city's rag trade were out of work (Ernst 1949: 201; Stott 1990: 108–10; Anbinder 2001). Without huge declines in foreign immigration into the city – from 327,000 in 1854 to 161,000 in 1855 and from 204,000 in 1857 to 101,000 in 1858 (Margo 1999: table 3A.11)[30] – the impact of these crises on wages and unemployment would have been much worse.

Several studies have shown that real wages were higher in the western United States on the eve of the Civil War than in the east. Economic historians attribute the significant westward drift of labour and population in the antebellum decades to this gap. Yet systematic real wage data are still lacking for antebellum New York City in particular. Presumably wages were higher in New York than in its rural hinterland, but the cost of living is also likely to have been higher (Long 1960; Coelho and Shepherd 1976; Margo 1999: ch. 5). Robert Margo has found that the gap in wages between east and west was greater for skilled workers than for labourers. In the 1850s the real wages of artisans were 24 per cent higher in the Midwest than in the Northeast, whereas the real wages of common labourers were only 11 per cent higher (Margo 1999: 139). Perhaps this helps explain why those who remained on in New York were more likely to have been the unskilled.

The enumerators of the 1860 US census were instructed to ascertain the dollar value of the real and personal estate of each person. The value of real estate was to be obtained from the household head, and any encumbrance on the property was to be ignored. Personal estate was to include money, livestock, slaves, bonds, and household furniture and jewellery. Absolute accuracy was unlikely 'but all persons should be encouraged to give a near and prompt estimate'. Since the 1960s these data have been quarried in systematic fashion by several US economic historians in addressing a broad range of issues.[31]

One of the most interesting revelations of the economic historian Lee Soltow's pioneering study of a large samples of males aged twenty years or more in the 1860 census was the high proportion of people with no wealth whatsoever. Soltow showed that the Irish were considerably poorer than the native born and immigrants from Great Britain, and also poorer than German immigrants. Note that while the American-born living in the North were poorer than those living elsewhere, for the Irish the reverse was true. Note too that the distribution of wealth among the Irish was very uneven even by the standards of the time. Moreover, further disaggregation showed that the English did better in the northeast than in the northwest, while for the Irish it was the other way around. For the Germans it was much of a muchness (Soltow 1975: 61, 149, 156). Table 8.9 describes wealth holding by place of birth and age. The big apparent difference here is the relative failure of the older Irish to accumulate wealth. This is probably linked to their residual status, as explained earlier.

Table 8.9 **Wealth by nationality and age**

Age-group	20–29	30–39	40–49
% owning property			
All	21	45	63
Native	22	50	68
Foreign	16	35	46
% owning property (Non-farmers)			
All	14	33	45
Native	16	39	51
Foreign	11	24	31
% owning property (IPUMS sample)			
New York Irish	23	39	31
New York Germans	30	66	63
New York British	26	56	50
New York born	23	37	67

Over two thirds of the Irish household heads in New York in 1860 reported no personal wealth at all, and over four fifths of them owned less than $200. In Boston the proportion of Irish adult males declaring no personal wealth at all in the same year – 54 per cent – was significantly lower, but in the (admittedly small) Philadelphia IPUMS sample an even higher proportion of Irish-born male household heads – 84 per cent – reported no personal wealth (Herscovici 1993; IPUMS sample). The proportion of Irish immigrants holding real estate in 1860 was also lower than that of other immigrant groups, or of native New Yorkers, and, as implied by the median value reported in table 8.10, the small minority declaring some real estate were very modest property owners indeed relative to the other groups.

Table 8.10 **The distribution of wealth of adult males in New York City by place of birth, 1860**

A. PERSONAL WEALTH

Wealth ($)	Ireland	GB	Germany	New York
Zero	68	52	51	56
1–199	17	10	14	4
200–499	8	10	18	11
500–999	3	11	9	3
1,000–4,999	4	11	6	14
5,000+	1	5	1	7
Total				
Percentage owned by				
Wealthiest 1%	56	78	38	28
Wealthiest 10%	91	95	67	80
Average wealth	252	1571	281	1013

B. REAL ESTATE

Wealth ($)	Ireland	Germany	GB	New York
Zero	97	89	85	83
1–1,999	2	5	5	4
2,000–4,999	0	2	1	5
5,000–9,999	0	2	3	4
10,000 +	0	1	5	5
Median holding (when > 0)	1,100	2,000	5,000	4,500

Source: IPUMS (males aged 20 and above)

Finally, it would seem that the Irish in New York in 1860 were disadvantaged relative to the Irish in other cities. In New York the proportions reporting real estate and personal estate in that year were 2.9 and 23.5 per cent, respectively. In Chicago the proportions were 21.9 and 33.6 per cent, in San Francisco 15.8 and 36.3 per cent, and in Indianapolis 24.4 and 71.5 per cent.[32]

Conclusion

The 'popular' understanding of Irish New York on the eve of the Civil War, given a new lease of life by Martin Scorsese's gory and violent *The Gangs of New York*, stresses the hostility that met them, their *macho* image, their alienation, their lowly economic status, and their criminality. That understanding is obviously true in part. Yet it is based more on inferences from specific events and locales than on a comparative survey of the city's immigrants as a whole. Such a survey, based largely on statistical evidence, tells a more mundane story. It confirms the poverty of the New York immigrants, but in also highlighting their residual and female character, it is less condescending about their 'failure' to achieve and to be successful. If there was more to Irish America on the eve of the Civil War than Irish New York, it is also true that there was more to Irish New York than the Sixth Ward or the Five Points.

Appendix to chapter eight:

Age-heaping

Age	Ireland M	Ireland F	Germany M	Germany F	New York M	New York F
14	4	5	3	1	19	20
15	7	9	3	3	17	15
16	8	6	2	1	12	19
17	4	8	1	3	18	11
18	5	11	4	3	19	21
19	4	12	2	4	12	16
20	10	20	8	3	11	10
21	5	10	10	3	11	11
22	10	20	3	3	9	9
23	8	11	6	4	5	9
24	8	19	5	6	3	10
25	10	28	14	6	11	9
26	9	19	6	6	6	13
27	7	17	5	6	8	8
28	12	28	11	5	8	8
29	6	8	5	7	9	4
30	21	32	12	10	11	17
31	1	8	5	4	4	3
32	8	9	10	2	7	9
33	6	8	3	4	4	3
34	5	3	8	2	7	2
35	12	10	4	4	7	4
36	4	11	7	6	7	9
37	3	2	3	1	6	2
38	3	8	4	2	6	4
39	1	2	2	2	4	3

	Ireland		Germany		New York	
Age	M	F	M	F	M	F
40	24	30	3	3	8	11
41	2	4	2	0	0	2
42	2	1	1	1	3	2
43	3	1	1	1	1	2
44	2	2	0	2	2	2
45	9	7	4	3	6	4
46	4	4	1	0	2	5
47	4	4	0	2	3	1
48	4	3	2	1	4	3
49	4	2	4	5	1	1

Source: IPUMS sample

CHAPTER NINE

The Famine, the New York Irish, and their bank

Introduction

Economists and economic historians sometimes assume that the poor don't save, or don't save much.[1] Controversies about the trade-off between economic 'justice' and economic growth turn, in part at least, on this assumption. Social reformers, though, have long sought to make the poor save. The early savings bank movement is an important part of the story. That movement can be traced back to the bank set up by the Rev. Henry Duncan in the Scottish village of Ruthwell in Dumfriesshire in 1810. In the following decades hundreds of savings banks were established throughout the United Kingdom. Ireland's first savings bank dates from just a few years later, and by 1830 there were 81. Still, the charitable savings bank movement was far more successful in Britain than in Ireland, where the famine and a series of highly publicised frauds impeded its progress (Pratt 1845; Porter 1849; Black 1960: 152–3; O'Shea 1989).[2]

The savings bank idea spread quickly to the United States, where both Boston's Provident Institution for Savings and Philadelphia's Saving Fund Society were founded in 1816. New York obtained its mutual savings bank first three years later. The Emigrant Industrial Savings Bank, the focus of this paper, was one of a score of such banks set up in New York State before the civil war. Most authorities agree that these banks were founded and operated for a time on a strong philanthropic motive. Banks usually began by operating on a part-time basis with volunteer help, but gradually became more professionalised. They were managed by trustees seeking to encourage the habit of saving and industry among the poor: hence the common appellation, 'trustee savings bank'. Trustees were prohibited from using depositors' money personally other than to defray expenses, and were strictly limited in the range of assets they could invest in. Lending was constrained to government, state, or city securities, incorporated banks, and mortgages on real estate valued at twice the amount of the loan. Savings banks were also obliged to keep their books open for inspection by the relevant public officials and to produce an annual report to the relevant legislature. Yet by operating on a very tight margin between borrowing and lending rates, the banks managed to offer both high interest and liquidity to their customers.

Their relatively high interest payments attracted many depositors who were by no means poor, however, whom the banks sometimes sought to discourage by paying better rates on smaller deposits, by imposing maximum deposits and even by scrutinising accounts from time to time and ordering money to be returned to wealthier depositors. In the United Kingdom, in the early decades savings banks restricted individual savers to £30 annually and £150 in total. Yet although savers with deposits of less than £20 accounted for half of all United Kingdom savings bank accounts in the early decades, they made up only 10–12 per cent of the total deposited. In pre-famine Ireland, savings banks catered disproportionately for the artisan and the lower middle class. Thus in Thurles, County Tipperary, in the 1840s farmers accounted for 56 per cent of all depositors reporting an occupation and labourers (a more numerous group in the community) only 29 per cent. In Ireland as a whole in November 1846 accounts holding over £20 – or more than twice a farm labourer's annual income – accounted for 56 per cent of all accounts and 88 per cent of all deposits (Pratt 1845; Kniffin 1918: 12; Payne and Davis 1956: 32–5; Fishlow 1961; O'Shea 1989: 102; *Thom* 1849: 194).

In New York by 1860 there was one savings bank account per four people (Olmstead 1976: 4). At the outset these banks were allowed to invest only in government and local state bonds, but that stipulation was gradually relaxed (Sherman 1934: 70–5). In 1831–2 the Poughkeepsie Savings Bank and the Brooklyn Savings Bank were the first to be granted legal permission to lend on bond and property mortgages. Such lending would dominate later. For good economic histories of the early savings banks see Payne and Davis (1956) on Baltimore and Olmstead (1976) on New York City.

This chapter is about the Emigrant Industrial Savings Bank, which was established in New York City in 1850 to serve that city's Irish community. The bank's early history is described, followed by an analysis of the savings behaviour of its early account-holders, with particular attention being paid to savers in the city's impoverished Sixth Ward.

The Emigrant Industrial Savings Bank

The Emigrant Industrial Savings Bank was chartered in April 1850. It began to accept deposits in a rented two-storey, iron-fronted premises on Chambers Street[3] on 30 September 1850. Most of its customers were Irish immigrants. Much of the credit for its creation must go to John Hughes, the able and energetic Catholic bishop (later archbishop) of New York. It was Hughes who prevailed on a group of 18 merchants and other prominent citizens, most of them Irish-born, to organise a safe deposit institution for immigrants, and to encourage the saving habit among them. For a community mostly new to urban life and to savings institutions, Hughes's leading role probably gave the new institution much-needed credibility. Chambers Street was a central location; the bank's opening hours in its early years – 5 p.m. to 7 p.m. Monday to Saturday – reflected both client needs and demands on trustees' time. The founding board included Fanning C. Tucker, who was president of the Leather Manufacturers Bank, which held the Emigrant Savings Bank's cash; Gregory Dillon, an ex officio Commissioner of Emigration since 1847, and first president of the Bank; and the prominent merchants Joseph Stuart, Andrew Carrigan, and Felix Ingoldsby. Becoming the trustee of a savings bank was a fashionable form of philanthropy at the time (compare Orcutt 1934: 20–1). Unlike many savings banks in nineteenth-century Ireland and Britain the Emigrant Industrial Savings Bank (EISB) was never threatened by corruption or mismanagement.

The EISB was an outgrowth of the Irish Emigrant Society, which had been founded by Irish immigrants in 1840, also at the behest of Bishop Hughes, and which had built up a considerable bill business in sending emigrant remittances back to Ireland during the 1840s (Murphy 1983). Until 1865 the Bank's chief officers – president, vice-presidents, and secretary – were unpaid. At the outset its depositors were mainly Irish, but as it expanded it became a more cosmopolitan institution. By the mid-1850s German immigrants and Irish-Americans accounted for about one tenth of the accounts. By the early twentieth century 'every nation on earth [was] represented among its depositors', and some of the bank's clerks, tellers, and guards were chosen for their linguistic as well as their other skills (Manning 1917: 181). Tables 9.1 and 9.2 give a sense of the bank's expansion. Growth in the twentieth century was more significant than in the nineteenth (again compare Payne and Davis 1956: 139), and the EISB did not open its second banking office until 1925. The early records reflect the legal constraints faced by the savings banks movement. The Bank was prohibited by

Table 9.1 **The growth of the Emigrant Savings Bank**

Year	Deposited $	Withdrawn $	Due depositors $	Dividends	Accounts Open
1850	39,665	4,766	34,899	35	265
1855	703,481	548,003	977,932	44,088	4,291
1865	4,038,134	3,413,994	4,876,941	215,721	16,076
1875	4,750,156	4,659,492	13,784,399	726,842	28,551
1885	9,871,608	8,809,468	30,124,245	943,011	57,161
1895	15,206,832	12,831,344	49,649,731	1,767,479	80,562
1905	25,977,716	18,819,473	85,096,972	3,028,826	109,785
1915	33,205,884	29,247,777	148,557,398	5,468,276	165,572

Source: Manning, 1917: 187

Table 9.2 **The bank's first ten years**

Year	Accounts	Deposited $
1851	265	34,899
1852	1,098	186,313
1853	2,183	455,310
1854	3,661	813,996
1855	3,691	822,453
1856	4,291	1,001,233
1857	5,461	1,302,791
1858	5,698	1,348,730
1859	6,686	1,628,755
1860	8,487	2,172,873
1861	10,096	2,627,542

Source: Olmstead, 1976: 159

charter from investing its money other than in bonds or in mortgages worth double the amount lent. At a meeting on 19 January 1851 the board protested:

> In consequence of the great abundance of capital and the very limited amount of those stocks for sale and their consequently increased price in the market, it has been found quite impossible to realize an interest exceeding four per cent

per annum. It is believed that a much wider range of investment can be safely confided to savings banks. The Bank for Savings is authorized to invest in the stocks of any of the states of the Union (Act of 29 March 1830) and are in the practice of loaning money on it and upon property worth one third more than the amount of the mortgage – no loss, it is stated, has ever occurred from the use of these powers and this board is desirous that the same powers be confided to them. They are also of opinion that perfectly safe investments can be made in a certain class of the bonds of rail road companies of this state – they are readily taken up by the most cautious private capitalists.

The EISB's predicament is reflected in its first investment – a loan returnable on demand to W. & J. O'Brien at the modest rate of four per cent on the security of United States and New York State stock. This loan was called in on 8 February and replaced by one made to De Launay, Iselin and Clark on demand at five per cent. At the end of February 1851 the EISB's assets were as follows:

Account	Sum $
De Launay *et al.*	20,000.00
Jacob Little @ 4%	10,000.00
New York City stock 7%	1,804.68
Two loans on bond and mortgage at 6%	10,000.00
Two loans on bond and mortgage at 7%	4,500.00
Cash deposited in Leather Manufacturers Bank	2,909.69
Total	50,414.37

Soon most of the bank's assets would realise about seven per cent, allowing it to pay savers six per cent.

The amateurish ethos of the bank in its early years is reflected in a letter to board members in May 1858 pleading with them to attend, as business was increasing, and some meetings had to be abandoned for the want of a quorum. As the bank grew, professionalisation was inevitable, and at a meeting in January 1865 it was resolved that in fixing salary levels, 'each one of the officers, with the exception of the porter, shall immediately devote their leisure time to become accomplished accountants, by taking lessons and instructions from competent persons, with the view of enabling them to fulfil the duties of others in case of temporary absence, and to be entitled to promotion in case of vacancy'.

The high interest offered by the savings banks inevitably attracted customers who had little in common with the 'industrious poor' envisaged by the founders. Some banks sought to discriminate against such depositors, but in the case of the EISB such discrimination was never a feature. In August and September 1852 substantial depositors included American-born John Charles Cooley, an apprentice who deposited $1,150; Catherine Lyons, no occupation, $700; Rev. James Mackay of Ogdensburgh, $1,200; Rev. Patrick Prendergast of Carbondale, Pennsylvania, $1,400; William Caffrey, a Long Island boarding-house owner, $772; Sarah Lehman, London-born wife of Israel Lehman, $2,200. These were substantial sums, and it should be noted that some of the addresses were quite a distance from Chamber Street.[4]

However, the records of the EISB show that such depositors were atypical of EISB account-holders in its early years. Those records offer rich pickings for both historians of Irish-America and historians of banking and saving behaviour. Our focus here will be on the EISB in its early years. A preliminary canvass suggests that people with proletarian, blue-collar occupations were very much to the fore among both male and female account-holders (see table 9.3). One quarter (51) of the first 200 or so (204) men to open accounts declared themselves to be in unskilled labouring jobs. Many more were in jobs requiring little skill or literacy. On the other hand, literate occupations such as clerk and clergyman, and self-employed or capitalist occupations also featured strongly. Among women the proportion in menial jobs was greater: 48 out of 94 were in domestic service and other 19 in clothes-making jobs. As the number of accounts grew, the savers became more representative of the community. By 1860 the EISB had 10,000 depositors, or about one in twenty of an Irish-born population of over 200,000 in New York and Brooklyn, but a much higher proportion of those in the age-groups supplying most of the savers.

The riches of the EISB archive are only now being tapped. A limitless quarry for genealogists, it probably also constitutes the single most important source available anywhere on the socio-economic history of the New York Irish after the famine. Test Book No. 1 shows, for example, that Bridget White, the bank's first depositor, was the wife of a tailor living on Henry Street in New York's Seventh Ward. Born near Mountmellick in Queen's County (Laois), she had arrived from Ireland nine years earlier on the *Fairfield* out of Liverpool. Her father still lived in Ireland, but her mother was no longer living. She had four brothers (whose names are given), three of them living in the United States, and three sisters. This is typical. The deposit account ledgers give individual savings histories. From the late 1850s on the age of the account-holder is also recorded.

Table 9.3 **Occupations of the early Irish account-holders**

1 Women

Domestic, cook, chambermaid	48
Dressmaker, seamstress, milliner, tailoress, vest maker	19
Nurse	4
Farmer's wife	1
Lady, no occupation	3
Washerwoman, ironer	7
Dealer, pedlar	5
Store worker	1
Factory worker	1
Porter house owner, boarding house keeper	2
Furniture store owner	1
Gaiter fitter	1
Waiter	1

2 Men

Labourer, porter	51
Book-keeper, clerk	17
Dealer, grocer, pedlar	16
Carpenter, cabinet maker	19
Publican, cookhouse or hotel keeper	14
Plasterer, mason, bricklayer	10
Shoemaker	9
Clergyman	8
Gardener, clothing business, farmer	4 of each
Machinist, morocco dresser, smith	3 of each

Two each of the following:
Combmaker, cooper, cigarmaker, bookseller, hatter, sexton, carriage-maker

One each of the following:
Teacher, founder, pressman, ropemaker, parasol maker, sailmaker, marble sawyer, 'in telegraph office', barber, money collector, miller, rectifier, perfumer, moulding business, coffee roaster, musical instrument maker, cook, chandler, upholsterer, weaver, printer, print cutter, spinner/carder, policeman

One issue on which the records throw interesting light is the regional pattern of emigration before and after the Great Irish Famine. The famine is likely to have produced a radical shift in the county and provincial origins of Irish emigrants to the United States. *Hard* data on this are lacking, though. Official emigration statistics begin only in 1849, and in any case they are an unreliable guide for a few decades after then. Passenger lists provide only very partial data on county origin. The issue of origin is an important one, however, because the variation in the roles of excess mortality and emigration across counties and provinces has a big bearing on our understanding of the famine. The estimates of net county outflows during the 1840s derived by Ó Gráda and O'Rourke (1997) hinge on admittedly debatable assumptions about the degree of under-reporting of deaths in the 1851 census; alternatively, estimates of regional variation in excess mortality hinge on estimates of emigration during the 1840s. Hence the importance of other sources which shed some light on regional origins. One such source is the records of the EISB. As already noted, in the early 1850s most of the bank's depositors were Irish, and most were recent immigrants. However, a considerable number of those attracted by the new bank were older Irish people who had been in the USA for a decade or more, and they also included a sprinkling of German, British and French immigrants, and of native Americans. Test Book No. 1 provides the name and date (sometimes only the year, but usually the precise date and name of the ship) of arrival of many thousands of Irish-born account-holders. Table 9.4, based on an analysis of over four thousand names, highlights the difference in the origins of those arriving and staying in New York before the famine and those arriving from 1846 on. Before the famine Ulster and Leinster were over-represented and Munster and Connacht (particularly Galway, Roscommon and Mayo) under-represented. The numbers imply that the New York Irish were disproportionately from the east and north of Ireland before the famine. Pre-famine Sligo and Leitrim had also provided a higher number of account-holders than might have been suspected: if Sligo is excluded from the reckoning, the number of account-holders from the rest of Connacht more than trebled during the famine, though admittedly from a very small base. The poor contributions before 1846 of counties like Clare, Kerry and Mayo, which were devastated by the famine, are also noteworthy. Table 9.4 thus corroborates the claim that before the famine wealthier counties in the north and east of Ireland supplied most of the transatlantic emigration from Ireland (compare Adams 1932: 158–60).

Finally, some features of the shifting distribution are worth noting. Munster which, though relatively poorer, had been greatly under-represented relative to their population before the famine, was over-represented during the famine. The same could not be said for Connacht, though the increased representation of four west-coast counties – Mayo, Galway, Clare, Kerry – is also noteworthy. For emigration to have been a truly effective solution during the famine, however, even more out-migration from the poorer counties would have been needed.

Table 9.4 **Emigrants and population by region**

	Percentage of emigrants		Percentage of
	pre-1846	1846–52	Population, 1841
Leinster	30	29	24
Munster	20	37	29
Ulster	35	20	29
Connacht	15	14	17
Mayo–Galway–Clare–Kerry	7	15	15

Source: New York Public Library, Emigrant Savings Bank Archive, II.1. Based on all those emigrating before the end of 1852 who had opened an account by the end of June 1854.

The marriage registers of the Church of the Transfiguration of Our Lord, located in the part of Lower Manhattan as the EISB, offer corroborative evidence on regional origins. Table 9.5 compares the regional origins of Irish-born brides and grooms for the 1853–60 period with those of EISB account-holders living in New York's Sixth Ward (on which more below) in the 1850s. The province-by-province match is quite good.

Table 9.5 **The provincial origins of parishioners and EISB depositors**

Province	Transfiguration Church (%)	EISB (%)
Leinster	235 (16.1)	72 (15.3)
Munster	606 (41.6)	238 (50.5)
Ulster	149 (10.2)	35 (7.4)
Connacht	467 (32.1)	126 (26.7)
Total	1,457	471

Profiling the bank's early savers

Banking archives containing information on customer accounts are few.[5] Exceptionally, the EISB deposit account ledgers contain complete details of all customer transactions in the early decades. Our focus here is on the 1850s. Movements in the numbers of accounts opened and closed between 1851 and 1863, the number of deposits and drafts, and the sums involved are described in figures 9.1 to 9.3. Besides highlighting the early growth of the EISB and the panics that beset it (in 1854, 1857, and at the beginning of the civil war), they suggest the strong seasonality also apparent in figure 9.4, where indexes of deposits and drafts by month (adjusting for month length) for the 1851–3 period are shown. Drafts were subject to much more seasonality than deposits, with two major peaks in January and July. Deposits also peaked in July, though much less spectacularly. The number of accounts opened and closed also varied somewhat seasonally (figure 9.5). We still lack a full understanding of these patterns, but the striking bi-annual peaks in withdrawals are a reflection of a form of 'coupon-clipping': a significant number of depositors regularly withdrew interest payments due without touching the principal. It is worth noting that the seasonal pattern of withdrawals from the Philadelphia Saving Fund Society studied by George Alter, Claudia Goldin, and Elyse Rotella (henceforth Alter et al. 1994: 761) was quite different (see figure 9.6).

How different EISB savers were in other respects remains to be seen. Meanwhile, a preliminary look at the savings habits of depositors in a particularly poor part of New York, the Sixth Ward, suggests some interesting features that should repay further study. In the mid-nineteenth century the heavily Irish 'Bloody Old Sixth' had an unenviable reputation for crime, destitution and depravity. It may thus seem an unlikely source of savers in the new bank. While account-holders indeed represented only a small fraction of the district's population, nevertheless they turn out to have been an interesting and by no means entirely atypical cross-section of that population.

First, most EISB customers living in the Sixth Ward seem not to have used the bank to accumulate substantial savings. In 34 of 100 accounts opened in the bank's early years (1850–5) the last withdrawal was smaller than the original deposit, while in another twelve the sum withdrawn was the same as that deposited. In a further ten cases the advantage was ten dollars or less. Thus the image of account-holders accumulating nest eggs which they then withdrew as they made an investment in situ or as they moved to another place is not typical in this case. One hundred and ninety-eight of a broader sample (i.e. not confined to Sixth Ward account-holders) of nearly six hundred accounts opened between 1850 and 1854 and still open towards the end of 1854 had accumulated negative sums between opening and December 1854, 158 had added $0–$9.99, 133 had added $10–$49.99, 78 had added $50–$99.99, 65 had added $100–199.99, and only 57 sums of $200 or more. Only two savers, a German-born essence maker and an Irish-born bread-seller, had accumulated savings of over one thousand dollars when they closed their accounts. Nor, in contrast with the Philadelphia Saving Fund Society, does our preliminary canvas reveal that women savers were more likely to accumulate nest eggs than men. Further analysis of the same 599 accounts produced the following result (table 9.6):

Table 9.6 **Sums accumulated in accounts opened 1851–4**

Sum Accumulated ($)	Women (%)	Men (%)
Negative	30 (17)	76 (18)
0–9.99	54 (31)	106 (25)
10–49.99	52 (30)	81 (19)
50–99.99	18 (10)	60 (14)
100–199.99	14 (8)	51 (12)
200 +	4 (2)	53 (12)
Total	172	427

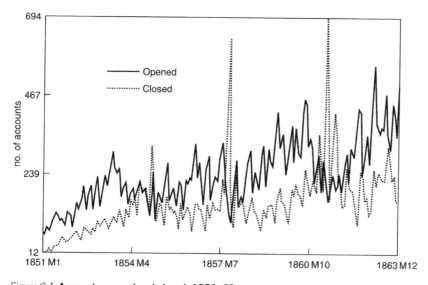

Figure 9.1 **Accounts opened and closed, 1851–63**

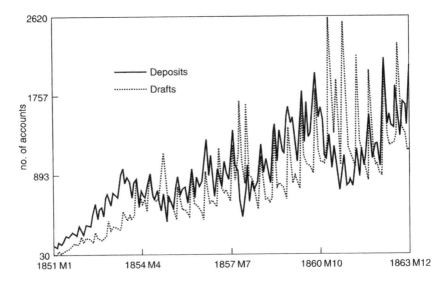

Figure 9.2 **Deposits and withdrawals, 1851–63**

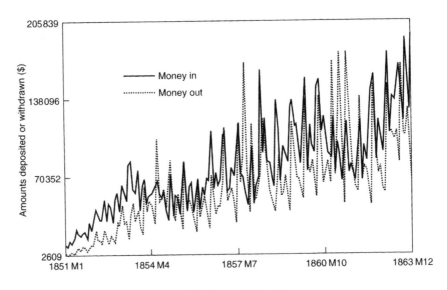

Figure 9.3 **Amounts ($) deposited and withdrawn, 1851–63**

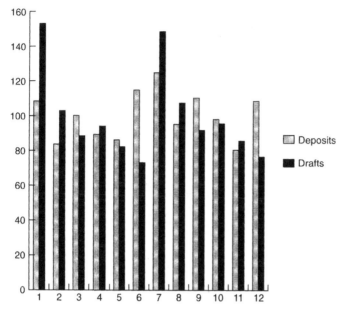

Figure 9.4 **Emigrant Savings Bank, deposits and withdrawals per month**
Note: Based on monthly data for years, 1851–63

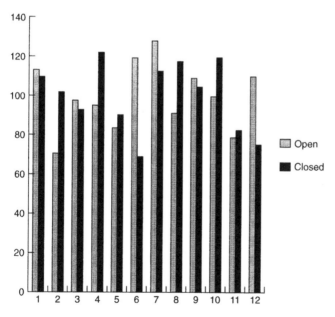

Figure 9.5 **Emigrant Savings Bank, accounts opened and closed per month**
Note: Based on monthly data for years, 1851–63

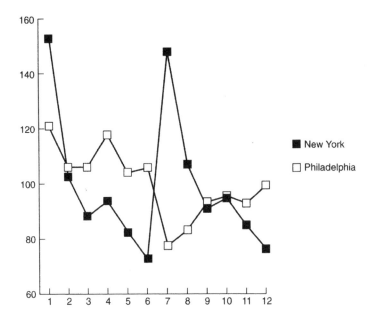

Figure 9.6 **Monthly withdrawals, New York and Philadelphia**
Note: Based on monthly data for years, 1851–63

Should the EISB be characterised as a true, typical 'savings bank', or did other savings banks at the time also serve more of a 'current account' function than previously suspected? Further analysis and comparisons should provide a better understanding of why and how the poor saved.

Table 9.7 **Opening deposits**

First Deposit ($)	Women (%)	Men (%)
0–9.9	7 (4)	7 (2)
10–49.9	66 (38)	107 (25)
50–99.9	49 (29)	109 (25)
100–199.9	26 (15)	98 (23)
200–499.9	21 (12)	80 (19)
500 +	3 (2)	24 (5)
Total	172	425
Average	92.3	149.4

Table 9.7 describes the sizes of opening deposits in the early years. On average women deposited less than men; 71 per cent of women's opening deposits were less than $100, but only 52 per cent of men's. The averages by origin were: Ulster $131, Munster $123, Leinster $118, Connacht $91, non-Irish $141, though these averages were subject to wide variation. Most accounts were held for a year or two, though a preliminary canvas suggests that many customers who closed their accounts reopened them later. Some account-holders behaved in true Smilesian fashion, making small and frequent deposits, and allowing them to accumulate. Others made substantial and frequent deposits and withdrawals, never allowing more than a small balance to remain at Chambers Street. Compare the case of Ann Murphy who, inexplicably, withdrew the $85 she had deposited on 9 August 1854 a day later, and that of Mary Kelly, a washerwoman, who deposited $140 in February 1855 and withdrew $500 in May 1869, after making many withdrawals and deposits in the bank. Overall, though, our preliminary analysis replicates Alter et al.'s finding for Philadelphia in 1850 of accounts opened as 'relatively large in size, brief in duration, and inactive' (Alter et al. 1994: 764).

An analysis of the sums deposited by a more broadly based sample of those opening accounts implies that several had already acquired the saving habit before the creation of the EISB. Table 9.8 summarises the situation for women among the first thousand account-holders. Women savers accounted for about one saver in five. The median sum deposited was just short of $50, not an insignificant sum (about one third of a male labourer's annual income in 1850). About one third of the deposits were under $30 (compare Alter et al. 1994: 738), and the highest was $600. Table 9.9 describes the age distribution of first-time depositors in 1862, and shows that first-time depositors were most likely to have been in

Table 9.8 **Opening deposits by Irish women savers, 1850–1**

Amount ($)	No.	Amount ($)	No.
0–10	40	101–200	45
11–20	48	201–300	13
21–30	56	301–400	8
31–50	78	401–500	12
51–75	44	501–600	6
76–100	55		
		Number	415

Note: these accounts were among the first two thousand opened at the Emigrant Savings Bank.

Table 9.9 **Ages of first-time depositors, 1862**

Age	Number	Age	Number
Less than 20	17	40–44	60
20–24	25	45–49	34
25–29	57	50–54	32
30–34	91	55–59	18
35–39	63	60 +	10

their thirties (the median here was 35 years). Only one in ten was under 25, and about two thirds of first time depositors were aged between their mid-20s and their mid-40s. In Philadelphia account-holders were considerably younger: well over a quarter of recently opened accounts in 1850 were held by people under 25 (compare Alter et al. 1994: 745–6). The predominance of immigrants in the Emigrant Savings Bank probably accounts for the difference.

Fleeing from famine: the New York Irish[6]

The interaction between the EISB and those living in its immediate neighbourhood is of particular interest. The bank was located next to the greatest concentration of poor Irish immigrants in North America. Moreover, during the bank's early years, emigration out of Ireland reached an all-time high. That emigration was in large part a product of the Great Famine; indeed the Irish famine is often described as having exacted a toll of one million lives and one million emigrants. Yet describing the cost of the famine in such terms risks hiding the sense in which, paradoxically perhaps, the migrants – or at least those among them who sailed for the United States – were the fortunate ones. They were certainly victims of the famine, but most of them were also people of some means, because the cost of the passage required some accumulated savings or other assets that could be converted into ready cash. During the winter of 1846–7 the head of the Board of Works in Dublin referred to the 'great delusion' about emigration. It was not the poorest who were about to leave, he complained, but 'all the small farmers [who are] hoarding all the money they can procure in order to make a stock for the spring, when they intend to bolt, leaving the landlords in the lurch'. Such claims were common.[7] Reliable data on net migration flows by region during the famine are lacking, but modern estimates of the variation in excess mortality and migration rates across counties are consistent with such impressionistic evidence. In the hierarchy of suffering the poorest of the poor emigrated to the next world; those who emigrated to the New World had the resources to escape (Ó Gráda 1999, ch. 3).

Because emigration failed to target those at greatest risk of death, it was an inefficient form of disaster relief. Yet without the emigration option, famine mortality would surely have been even higher. It is unlikely, though not inconceivable, that the absence of distant outlets for emigration would have increased mortality by more than the number of frustrated would-be emigrants. A more plausible outcome would be the deaths of a fraction of those forced to remain. In addition, some migration would have been diverted to the already crowded cities of the United Kingdom. As matters stood, famine immigration placed considerable strains on the cities of Dublin and Liverpool, for example, and much of the excess mortality in Dublin was due to it. Most of the huge increase between 1841 and 1851 in the number of Irish-born living in Britain – from 417,000 to 727,000 – happened in the wake of the potato failure. Many of the Irish who fled from famine died in Britain in 1847, prompting middle-class sympathy at first and, soon, widespread fear and resentment. English vital statistics are consistent with a 'famine effect' in the late 1840s (Neal 1995, 1996). In sum, the impact of the Irish migration to Great Britain was bad as matters stood; in the absence of the safety valve of emigration to North America, it would have been much worse.

New York was the main port of entry into North America for Irish famine emigrants. As the city's population grew rapidly during the 1850s, so did its number of Irish-born. By the mid-1850s greater New York contained almost as many Irish-born people as Dublin. Most of those who entered there during or just after the famine did so on their own money. The New York route cost more than the Canadian alternative, but it was safer and offered better prospects of employment on arrival. Ferrie's research confirms the accuracy of contemporary advice to would-be immigrants not to stay long in New York and, indeed, most of the new arrivals seem not to have stayed in New York for long (Ferrie 1997: 108–9; Mooney 1851: 83–4, 93–4). One guide to would-be immigrants painted the following picture of employment prospects in New York (Mooney 1851: 84–5):

[T]hey are generally employed in buildings, either as masons, bricklayers, plasterers, carpenters, or as helpers and hodmen; they are found portering on the quays, repairing, cleaning, and watching the city; sawing wood, carrying packages; serving as waiters, hostlers, barkeepers in the hotels and boarding-houses, eating-houses, and provision shops; owning or driving carts, cabs, hackney coaches or omnibuses; working as hostlers, trafficking in the vegetable and fruit markets; carrying newspapers, dealing in paper, owning small fishing or ferry boats; at work in the tailoring 'sweating shops', in the printing offices, foundries; digging foundations or blasting rocks up town, mending the streets, digging sewers, and laying water or gas pipes for the corporation or other companies; plying on the river as firemen or boatmen, in the thousand canal and steam boats that flit too and fro on the Hudson and 'East River'; attending the merchants' auctions in Pearl Street, and buying an odd damaged bargain in a small way, which is peddled at a good retail profit in the suburban districts of the city; having a fruit and temperance stand in the summer season in a recess of the street, &c. &c.

Given such lowly employment prospects it may seem ironical that, as noted above, most of those who travelled to New York needed to be people of *some* means. Presumably the poorest of them were people whose passage from Ireland to America had been financed or subsidised by landed proprietors and by the government, most of whom had occupied smallholdings no longer viable after the failure of the potato. From a landlord perspective their removal meant a lower tax burden and estate rationalisation. As the architect of the most ambitious of these schemes reported that on other estates, 'where no assistance is given, *retain their paupers* whilst *all the respectable Tenants are moving off*', while his own scheme resulted in the departure of 'none but abject Paupers' (Lyne 1992: 86). Migrants either formally transplanted by their landlords through emigration schemes or assisted by rent rebates accounted for only a small minority of famine emigrants, perhaps forty or fifty thousand of the half million or so who crossed the Atlantic because of the famine (Fitzpatrick 1989). But suppose more of the really poor had been helped in the same way? How different would the character of the flow have been?

A partial answer is offered by an analysis of the Irish community of New York's Sixth Ward in the 1850s. Many of the Irish living in the 'Bloody Old Sixth', located in lower Manhattan, east of Broadway and north of City Hall, in these years had formerly been smallholders on the estates of the third marquess of Lansdowne in south Kerry or of Lord Palmerston and Sir Robert Gore-Booth in Sligo. These landlords had paid their passages for them. As a result most of the Kerrymen and Kerrywomen who settled in the Sixth Ward had been born in a small, impoverished Irish-speaking area in south Kerry, while the majority of the Sligo immigrants had lived on or near that county's north-west coast. That the Kerry emigrants arrived in a destitute state is borne out by several contemporary press accounts. One described tenants and their families 'without a penny of money . . . mak[ing] their way on foot from Kenmare to Cork . . . from whence their passages were paid to Liverpool, and thence to New York'. Another stated that the US Commissioners of Immigration had charged the carrier of one shipload of Kenmare emigrants $25 per head, the cost of their maintenance out of public funds in New York (Lyne 1992: 104–5).

Arriving in New York together was likely to induce former neighbours to stick together initially in the USA. Perhaps it also reduced their mobility later: to argue that the poverty trap which prevented more of their compatriots from leaving Ireland prevented some of these inhabitants of the Sixth Ward from moving beyond it seems plausible enough. The Irish immigrants who remained in New York were numerous and some met with considerable success, yet they were a residual population. In Joseph Ferrie's sample of antebellum immigrants, which links passenger lists and manuscript census data, less than one fifth of the Irish who arrived in the port of New York between 1840 and 1850 remained there on census day in 1850 (Ferrie 1997: 44–5).

Charles Dickens's *American Notes for General Circulation* (1842), local journalist George Foster's *New York By Gas Light* (1850), and other reports in a similar vein conjured up an image of the mainly working-class Sixth Ward as a virtual no-go slum area. To the evangelical missionaries who sought to reform its inhabitants in the 1850s, the Five Points was 'a synonym for ignorance the most entire, for misery the most abject, for crime of the darkest dye, for degradation so deep that human nature cannot sink below it' ('Ladies of the Mission' 1854: 34). But the 'new social history' has generated a revisionist response on the Sixth Ward. Carol Groneman Pernicone's University of Rochester dissertation contrasts the gap between the negative contemporary assessments of Dickens and others and the picture gained from an investigation of contemporary census data.

It is interesting in this context to compare the socio-economic profile captured in the 1855 census with that reflected in the EISB records. It turns out that although only a small minority of Sixth Ward inhabitants held accounts in the EISB, the occupational profile of Sixth Ward account-holders in the 1850s reflected the social mix of the population rather well. Comparing the profile of Sixth Ward Irish male account-holders with the results of Groneman Pernicone's analysis of the Sixth Ward Irish as a whole implies some bias among the account-holders towards a residual 'other' category containing sales and clerical workers, petty entrepreneurs, storekeepers, and white collar workers. This is to be expected. Still, the Sixth Ward savers were mainly unskilled workers and petty traders. Included among 563 savers identified as Sixth Ward addressees were 89 labourers, 36 domestic servants, 24 washerwomen, 19 porters, 13 fruit dealers, 12 seamstresses, 12 pedlars, 18 tailors, nine junk dealers, and one teacher. Martin Hogan from Limerick described himself as a 'fireman in Sweeny's saloon', while John O'Donoghue from Longford was a 'barkeeper at John Dempsey's'. John Shea of Tuosist distributed handbills, Jeremiah Daly of the same parish sold matches, and Bridget Gilmartin from Ahamlish picked hair. It is interesting to find such people using the Emigrant Savings Bank.[8]

Conclusion

At the outset we noted that the savings bank movement had made only limited progress in Ireland before the Great Famine. Nevertheless, in the early stages of the famine editorials in *The Times* and *Morning Chronicle* linked the savings banks and the developing disaster, highlighting reports from Ireland of increases in savings banks deposits as evidence of 'successful swindling' or welfare fraud on the part of the Irish people. In Killarney rumours that the local savings bank was about to fail allegedly induced workhouse inmates to escape in hopes of reclaiming their deposits (O'Rourke 1902: 214–15; Smyth 1844–9: III, 29). Such depictions of Irish 'character' fed on the kind of anti-social behaviour that invariably accompanies catastrophes such as the Great Famine. But they hide two more important truths. First, though the savings banks had managed to harness substantial savings in Ireland – their trustees had nearly £3 million invested in the national debt in 1846 – most of those at greatest risk during the famine are unlikely to have held accounts in them. Most account-holders in savings banks lived in the towns and the cities; the province of Connacht, poorest, least urbanised, and worst affected by the famine, accounted for 17 per cent of the population but only five per cent of savings in savings banks. Second, both aggregate data and individual case studies suggest that the economic shock caused by the famine dealt a serious blow to Ireland's savings banks. Between 1845 and 1849 aggregate deposits fell from nearly £2.9 million to £1.2 million, and the number of depositors from 95,348 to 44,919. On the eve of the famine, Great Britain contained nearly eight times as many savings banks as Ireland, yet of the 44 savings banks in the United Kingdom that ceased business between 1844 and 1852, 24 were Irish (O'Shea 1989; Ó Gráda 1999: ch. 4; *Thom* 1850: 195; *Thom* 1851: 264; BPP 1852a, 1852b).

The famine that halved Ireland's savings banking sector also contributed to the rapid growth of the Emigrant Industrial Savings Bank. Indeed, some of those who opened accounts in Chambers Street in the 1850s had almost certainly closed their accounts in some Irish savings bank before travelling. Such connections should not be pressed too far: as noted, most of the Emigrant's early account-holders were recent immigrants from the rural, less commercialised regions of Ireland. Yet the early history of the Emigrant offers testimony of the adaptability of emigrant Irish, even the very poorest among them, and their eagerness to better themselves.

CHAPTER TEN

The Great Famine and other famines

An unbroken link?

Much has been made over the last few years of the link between Irish folk memory of the Great Famine and Irish generosity towards the Third World. Sometimes the link has a prescriptive aspect, as when President Mary Robinson tells us that 'we can honour the profound dignity of human survival best . . . by taking our folk memory of this catastrophe [the Great Famine] into the present world with us, and allowing it to strengthen and deepen our identity with those who are still suffering' Robinson (1994). That aspect is one stressed by the various charity agencies. But the link is also given a historical gloss. Again President Robinson: 'the past gave Ireland a moral viewpoint and an historically informed compassion on some of the events happening now'.[1]

In truth, the ties are less strong that some us might like to think. Since I am not going to prove this rigorously, I hope I can get away with a few cameos. I was struck by the reaction of Raymond McClean, a volunteer doctor from Derry and for a time mayor of that city, when first accosted by the horrors of famine in Harbu in the province of Wollo, Ethiopia, in 1984.

'Suddenly', he remarked, 'the thought struck me, right between my eyes – my God, I am walking through the Irish famine'. In Dr McClean's case the Irish famine, then, far from being the motivating force for his time in Africa, was an afterthought (McClean 1988). Again, I think the remarks of Bob Geldof are relevant here.[2] In his autobiographical *Is That It?* Geldof says that his 'point of light' was an image from Michael Buerk's news report [on the BBC]. 'Buerk had used the word biblical. A famine of biblical proportions. To expiate yourself truly of any complicity in this evil meant you had to give something of yourself. I was stood against the wall'. Nothing about the Irish famine in Geldof's reaction either.

Again, thinking of the impact of the famine on recent Irish literature in English, it is the sequence of poems by Séamus Heaney in *Death of a Naturalist* (1968) and Thomas Murphy's *Famine* (1977) which most readily spring to mind, but it turns out that the inspiration for both was not folk memory but Cecil Woodham-Smith's bestselling *The Great Hunger*, published in 1962. And I think that most of what many Irish people today know about the famine stems not from what they heard by the fireside but from the likes of Woodham-Smith and Robert Kee. How could it be otherwise in a country where most of the population is now urban and lives in areas least affected by the famine?

I have argued elsewhere that a much more important influence on Third World giving is the Irish tradition of missionary activity far afield, particularly in sub-Saharan Africa. With the growing self-confidence of the Irish Catholic Church after the famine, whole generations of Irish people became missionaries, literally or vicariously. The link is direct in the case of Concern Worldwide, a reincarnation of Africa Concern, established by Holy Ghost missionaries in west Africa in the late 1960s (Farmar 2002), while Trócaire, another major charity agency, was created by the Irish Catholic hierarchy.

Yet here, too, the story is not quite that simple. Until relatively recently, the emphasis in Irish missionary endeavour was more on souls than on bodies. In the widely sold *Far East*, for example, in the mid-1940s there was very little about economic development or the relief of poverty, and money was sought to support personnel and church buildings. Nor, despite articles about Christ's poor in Nancheng City or how tribesmen in Upper Burma subsisted on a diet of rice, was there a single mention of the Great Irish Famine between 1945 and 1947. When precisely Irish missionaries began to take up Third World causes is an interesting topic: but it was probably in the 1960s, with the changes augured in by Pope John XXIII.

Third World charities, then, have re-discovered the famine. Perhaps the credit for being first should go to Gorta, which proclaimed in the first issue of its *Gorta News* in 1970: 'Gorta is the Irish word for famine, which word itself will always stir emotive responses in Irish hearts.' However, this was to be the only mention of the Irish famine in *Gorta News*, which ceased publication in 1973.

History never quite repeats itself, and the contexts of Ireland's famine and modern, mainly African, famines are quite different. Superficially, of course, all famines are alike. But the differences are worth reflecting on. Before turning to comparison, two important caveats are necessary. First, my own research has focused much more on Ireland than on modern famine-stricken regions.

Second, because comparison is often part of the rhetoric of condescension, it should be stressed that all famines, whatever their cause and their scope, are horrible and a scandal.

Excess mortality

In New York City in May 1995 I heard the great Indian, Harvard-based economist Amartya Sen – on whom more later – declare that the Great Irish Famine may well have been the greatest ever in a relative sense. This is surely somewhat of an exaggeration. But it turns out that, by comparison, the numbers perishing in many highly publicised Third World famines in the recent past are modest. There is no ready-made list, but I have gathered together some numbers from here and there.

For example, the official death toll in Bangladesh in 1974 was 26,000; the Sahel famine of 1973–4 killed perhaps 100,000; the famine in Darfur, western Sudan in the mid-1980s killed somewhat fewer than 100,000. All three occurred in countries with a far bigger population than Ireland in 1845. One guess at mortality in the famine-affected areas of Ethiopia in 1973 puts it at 40,000; another puts excess deaths in Ethiopia as a whole in 1972–4 at about 200,000. In Malawi (then Nyasaland), official sources estimated that the famine of 1949–50 was responsible for the deaths of 100–200 people.

Moreover, few famines on record in western Europe matched the Great Famine in intensity: one such may have been *bliain an áir* (the year of carnage), 1740–1, again in Ireland, but the evidence for this is sketchy (see Dickson 1997). But neither the *années de misère* towards the end of Louis XIV's reign nor the famines affecting England before the reign of Elizabeth I were in the same league.

Now, two recent African famines are exceptional in this respect. The death tolls from war and famine in Biafra in 1968–70 may have reached a million people. Reliable estimates of famine deaths in Ethiopia in 1982–5 are lacking. In 1987 Gopalkrishna Kumar argued for a toll of at least one million, but the information reported by John Seaman suggests a smaller number. One has to reach back for other disasters on the Irish scale. The Soviet famine of 1921–2, Stalin's famine of the early 1930s, the Great Bengali Famine of 1942–3 killed many more people than the Great Irish Famine, while the Chinese Great Leap Forward Famine of 1959–62 is in a league of its own (Seaman 1993; Kumar 1987; Davies and Wheatcroft 2003; compare the data in Devereux 2000).

The high mortality that followed from the Great Famine raises another related issue. In his *Why Ireland Starved* (1983), Joel Mokyr proposed a definition of poverty in terms of the likelihood of 'a random individual at a random point in time dropping below subsistence'. A plausible implication of this definition, which stresses that poverty is not just about averages but fluctuations around averages, is the expectation that famines become gradually less lethal as the proportion of the population at risk declines. It follows that, considered historically, the last peacetime famines to affect a particular region should be whimpers rather than bangs.

The historian John Iliffe's claim that between 1927 and the end of the colonial era, Africa (Ethiopia apart) saw very few 'famines that kill' fits this scenario. Iliffe points to 'effective government, good transport, wider markets and some increases in average wealth' as the main reasons for this. The trouble is that in many parts of Africa, alas, wars and political stability brought a return to famine after independence (Iliffe 1987). We have good information on the years of 'crisis' mortality in England between the 1540s and the 1860s, and this suggests that both the size and the duration of famines also declined gradually over time.

Ireland's pre-famine famines fit such a neo-malthusian pattern. Mortality from famine had been considerable in 1800–1 and 1817–19 (perhaps 40,000–60,000 in each case). The famines of 1822 and 1831 also produced excess mortality, but on a far smaller scale (O'Neill 1996; Royle 1984). Had the potato failed only in 1845 we would be saying the same of 1845. But that was not to be, and the Great Famine brought the age of famines in Ireland to a dramatic, apocalyptic, end. This underlines the ecological shock aspect of the Great Famine.

The Great Famine was also the true 'last great subsistence crisis of the western world' – unless one includes the Great Finnish Famine of 1868 (Pitkänen 1993). What of the eastern world? In recent decades famines seem to have been eradicated in China and India. It would be nice to think that just as the Irish famine marked the virtual end of famine in western Europe, the modern famines listed above reflect the last whimpers of what John Iliffe (1987: 6) had dubbed 'conjunctural poverty' in Africa.

Mortality by age and gender

Estimating excess mortality during the Irish famine is a tricky business. Estimating the relative impact on men and women and on different age groups is more difficult still. Any such exercise for the country as a whole hinges on necessarily debatable assumptions about normal mortality rates, deficiencies in the 1841 census, and emigration before and during the famine period (Boyle and Ó Gráda 1986). For what they are worth, the gender ratios implied in the 1851 census are given in table 10.1. Since deaths in rural areas accounted for the bulk of the total, the outcome is consistent with a slight male edge in mortality during the famine years. The relative advantage of women must be seen against their relative deprivation, marked in nineteenth-century Ireland, in normal times.

Table 10.1 **Gender ratios of reported deaths in the 1851 census**

Year	Rural areas M/F	'Civic' areas M/F	Public institutions M/F
1843	1.16	1.15	1.14
1844	1.15	1.14	1.10
1845	1.13	1.10	1.05
1846	1.17	1.07	1.09
1847	1.25	1.13	1.11
1848	1.20	1.11	1.14
1849	1.22	1.07	1.09

What of microdata? Catholic parish registers are of little use here, since even the best of them lack detailed burial data. Protestant registers can add some insight, however. Some were destroyed in the Four Courts fire of 1922, but those that survive contain the names and ages of most of the people buried. As part of a larger study of the famine in Dublin, I have looked at the evidence on burials in several Dublin city registers. In the 1840s about one quarter of the people of Dublin were Protestants, and the city still contained a large working-class Protestant population, as likely to be affected by the crisis as their Catholic neighbours. An analysis of the registers of three southside parishes suggests: (a) that Dublin indeed experienced some excess mortality during the famine years, and (b) that male mortality exceeded female.[3]

Table 10.2 summarises the data in the burial registers of two neighbouring parishes in the south of Ireland, those of Ballymodan and Kilbrogan in County Cork. These were then largely urban parishes: almost two thirds of their people lived in the (economically depressed) town of Bandon. About one in four of the combined population of the two parishes was Protestant at the time. Bandon was very badly hit by the famine. A Yorkshire newspaper proprietor noted soon afterwards (Anon. 1854: 34):

Bandon is a clean town, and has a rather prosperous appearance. But it suffered severely during the Famine, and one street was pointed out to us in which not a single inhabitant was left. Those who escaped death fled to distant lands, and when we saw it, every house was desolate; the garden fences were broken down; the doors and windows were partially in a state of visible decay; and the rank grass was growing about the thresholds. Altogether, it was one of the most saddening sights we ever looked upon.

Two broad impressions follow from Bandon's Protestant registers. First, the burials evidence confirms that the famine did not kill Catholics only; among Bandon's Protestants mortality was almost sixty per cent above its immediate pre-famine level during 1846–8. Second, the crisis seems to have increased male mortality more than female, but there were no striking changes in the incidence by age.

Table 10.2 **Burials in Ballymodan and Kilbrogan by age and gender, 1843–51 (Percentages in parentheses)**

	Males			Females		
Age	1843–5	1846–8	1849–51	1843–5	1846–8	1849–51
0–9	34 (36)	51 (30)	24 (25)	27 (28)	40 (29)	21 (23)
10–19	18 (19)	29 (17)	19 (20)	13 (13)	21 (15)	15 (16)
20–49	8 (9)	19 (11)	11 (11)	17 (17)	13 (10)	12 (13)
50–69	13 (14)	29 (17)	24 (25)	20 (20)	27 (20)	19 (21)
70 +	12 (13)	43 (25)	18 (19)	21 (21)	35 (26)	25 (27)
Total	94	171	96	99	141	92

What of modern famines? Several studies find that male mortality rates rise more during famines. One reason for this may be the reduction in female fertility – a universal phenomenon – and an associated fall in maternal mortality. Another reason mentioned is that healthy females store more body fat than males, and therefore can withstand deprivation longer. A Trinity College, Dublin colleague suggests that it may have had something to do with female control of the purse strings, but I have my doubts about that one.

The evidence on mortality by age is less clear-cut. Some studies report a relative pro-child bias in intra-familial allocations during crises. In south Asia in the nineteenth and early twentieth centuries, contrary to what might be expected, the biggest increases in mortality occurred in age-groups where normal mortality was light – among older children and adults. In a recent study of excess mortality in Darfur, western Sudan in the mid-1980s, Alex de Waal found that child deaths rose more than infant and child deaths. Overall, there are no universal patterns in the age- istribution of famine deaths.[4]

Medicine and nosology

Relatively few died of literal starvation during the Great Famine: dysentery, typhus, typhoid fever, and other hunger-related infectious diseases did most of the damage. Many of those contracting fever recovered from it, but it is important to remember that when the disease struck there was little that medical knowledge *per se* could contribute. Isolation in fever hospitals was the main institutional remedy for fever. In an era when cupping and leeching, mercury, opium, and a variety of powders or concoctions were the order of the day, medical 'remedies' were likely to have done more harm than good. Of course, the fact that the relevant aspects of scientific medicine were still far in the future did not prevent doctors from having a very high opinion of themselves in the 1840s. The importance of cleanliness in the homes and yards of the poor was understood, and the link between contaminated food, water and dysentery stressed, but it was not so easy to do much about it.

Doctors hadn't a clue. Many believed that 'the epidemic, like the ague, owes its origin to terrestrial miasms'. And there were controversies between medics. In an attack on other medical men who held that famine conditions caused fever, the editor of the *Dublin Medical Press* thought that 'it could easily be shown that famine and destitution are more frequently the effect than the cause of fever' (Ó Gráda 1999: 96). Medical historians have lauded the commitment and heroism of medical personnel, but results are another matter.

How much difference would better medical knowledge have made? Would the famished simply not have died of something else? These are difficult questions, awaiting considered answers. But the evidence of Third World famines may tell us something. Since the 1840s medical technology has made massive strides both in diagnosis and treatment.

First, antibiotics and anti-bacterials can relieve typhus, typhoid fever and dysentery, and anti-malarials have also been available since the 1940s. Second, disinfectants and insecticides that help control or eradicate flies, fleas, lice, and ticks that cause these fevers, have been in widespread use since the 1940s. Third, mass vaccination campaigns reduce the incidence of meningitis and measles, which are more likely to be lethal in famine conditions. Finally, although therapeutic drugs are of little help against dysentery, a major killer, ways of providing clean water are well understood.

Morbidity and mortality surveys have highlighted the vital role of rehydration together with nutrition in the recovery from dysentery. However, it has to be said that in recent famines resistance to commonly used drugs against bacillary dysentery has been reported. And although vitamin supplements are more easily distributed than food, the right kind of food is the main defence against xerophthalmia, scurvy and pellagra, common occurrences in Ireland during the 1840s. The evidence of modern famines suggests that medical technology alone is not enough to eliminate mass mortality. Almost invariably, there are time lags between detection and action, and red tape brings its own delays and conflicts. Famine-induced anaemia makes it difficult for people to absorb oral medicines. Ignorance on the part of those at risk is also a problem. Thus one suspects that in Ireland in the 1840s, as in modern Africa, modern medicine alone would have been a poor substitute for plenty of healthy food, clean clothes, proper housing, and sanitation. But given food, medicine can achieve much.

Another aspect of the medical issue is that medicine has probably shifted the class tructure of famine mortality somewhat since the nineteenth century. In Ireland, the poor were the main targets of disease such as mild typhoid fever in normal times, but during the Great Famine 'when fever attacked the higher classes it was universally of a much more fatal character than amongst the poor'. Its better off victims included the Rosminian preacher Luigi Gentili, who died in Dublin in 1848 of a fever caught while hearing confessions.

At greatest risk were those who came into contact with the disease in the course of their work. Among doctors an eminent example is the anatomist Valentine Flood, who had been working for the Board of Health in Tipperary, and who was 'among the many voluntary victims offered by the profession to the Moloch of typhus contagion' (Ó Gráda 1999: 94–5). With the clergy it was similar story. It is occasionally claimed that 'no priest died during the Famine', but that is ignorant cant. In fact, many priests died of fever during the famine, as did many clergymen of other denominations.

By implication, then, another important difference between the Irish famine and today's famines is that modern elites are largely immune from the externalities once caused by famine. Modern Irish aid workers are similar enough to the priests and the medical personnel of the famine era to carry the point. Of the hundreds of volunteers who have worked in Africa since the 1980s, one was murdered in Somalia and several were attacked by famine fevers, but it seems that none so far has died of famine-related illnesses (McClean 1988: 22, 34–8).

The difference may have a broader implication. The American evangelist Asenath Nicholson, one of the most perceptive and humane outside observers of the Irish famine, wrote of the 'comfortable classes' of Dublin, that 'whatever the hospitality they might manifest towards guests and visitors, [they] had never troubled themselves by looking into the real wants of the suffering poor' (Ó Gráda 1999: 175). Nonetheless, the danger of contracting famine fever through contact with the poor or through inhaling infected air was a major preoccupation of those 'comfortable classes' during the Great Famine. Long before the famine, those seeking to help the poor had found that appealing to the self-interest of the better-off in towns and cities was a good way of pro-ducing results. During the famine it prompted the creation of fever hospitals, the financing of the Board of Health, and the control of begging in Dublin and Belfast. One suspects that such enlightened self-interest on the part of elites counts for less in parts of the Third World today.

War and peace

The poem that begins 'Ní cogadh ná carragail fhada idir ard righthibh (it is not war or enduring strife between high kings)' by the Jacobite Séamus Mac Coitir is about another great Irish famine, that of 1740–1. Earlier famines had been the products of invasion and civil strife, but Ireland was tranquil in 1740. Mac Coitir's first lines lines have a modern ring. 'In much of Africa', writes Alex de Waal, 'war has become synonymous with famine' de Waal 1993: 33). War increases the vulnerability to famine in obvious ways such as by destroying crops, deflecting economic activity, frustrating relief, and dampening democracy and protest.

However, as in the 1740s, Ireland faced no civil war or major unrest in the 1840s. Indeed some contemporary observers spoke of a delusive calm in Ireland on the eve of the famine. Faction fighting and rural strife, so common in the 1820s and 1830s, had been quelled by an alliance of police and priests. Ordinary crime was also in decline. The inoffensive 'rising' of 1848 lasted only a matter of hours and in any case took place when the worst of the famine was over. Therefore disrupted communications and military distractions were not a factor in Ireland during the famine.

This was all quite unlike the situation in so many African countries in recent decades. The horrors of Biafra, Ethiopia or Somalia immediately spring to mind. Discussing Mozambique in the 1980s, Alex de Waal writes that some 'analysis' of famine there amounts to 'little more than a catalogue of Renamo vandalism' (de Waal 1993: 33). The risk of famine in Angola today is increased by the land mines (an estimated 10–15 million) left behind by the warring parties. In war-torn parts of the Sudan mines are more likely to kill cattle than people, but with potentially grave consequences too for pastoral farmers. Civil conflict also produces its IDPs (internally displaced persons) and refugees. Modern famines have less to do with Malthus than with Mars.

Rich neighbours, poor neighbours

Another difference is that today's famine-stricken areas are located in the most economically backward regions of the regions of the world, where neighbouring regions seem to be nearly as poor as the region directly affected. We need consider only famine-afflicted Ethiopia or southern Sudan. But one of the striking things about the Irish famine of the 1840s is its geographical setting: it occurred in the back yard of a relatively prosperous region. However, economic history suggests the need for perspective here. We should not overlook the harsh conditions faced by the British poor at the time, and the poverty of even smug, mid-Victorian Britain by our own late-twentieth century standards.

How poor was Ireland in the early 1840s compared with, say, Ethiopia or Somalia today? Only the crudest answer is possible. I reckon that Irish living standards on the eve of the famine lay somewhere between those of Ethiopia and Somalia a few years ago, though closer to Somalia's. The comparison also suggests that the rich world today has a much greater margin to spare than Britain did in the 1840s. According to the kind of political arithmetic just described, living standards in Britain in the 1840s paralleled those of Indonesia or Egypt today. Without seeking to absolve those in power in Westminster of responsibility for not have tried harder, does this not make the persistence of famine in the Third World in the 1980s or 1990s a greater scandal than its presence in Ireland in the 1840s?

Ideology and bureaucracy

Nor is the philosophical context the same today as in the 1840s. This is an important point, but one well rehearsed elsewhere. Peter Gray has argued – and I agree – that 'the charge of culpable neglect of the consequences of policies leading to mass starvation is indisputable' (Gray 1995). That a conscious choice to pursue moral or economic objectives at the expense of human life was made by several ministers is also demonstrable. So there is some truth in John Mitchel's claim that 'Ireland died of political economy'. Now, this is not to argue that a native government would have done a better job. Its heart might have been in a better place, but it would not have had the wherewithal. Daniel O'Connell's plea to fellow MPs in Westminster is apposite here: 'Ireland was in their hands', he said, 'if they did not save her, she could not save herself.' (Hansard, 3rd ser., vol. 89, p. 945)

No modern government or international agency would argue that offering unstinting relief to famine victims somewhere now would only make things worse down the road – or that famines are a divine plan to teach people a lesson. Such heartless claptrap is not much heard today. Ideology may still exacerbate crises or the risk of crises. I have given a few examples elsewhere. But history also suggests that 'good' government can help avert famines. Prompt and enlightened action in Kenya, in Botswana, and in Bangladesh in the 1970s and the 1980s provide good case studies, but the ambitious public works programme set up in the Indian province of Maharashtra (population fifty million) in the early 1970s is the best-known case in point. Indians are proud of the success of policy there, and rightly so, because the threat to a large area in a poor country was very real. In Maharashtra the output of foodgrain and pulses was 19 per cent less than normal in 1970–1, 27 per cent less in 1971–2, and 53 per cent less in 1972–3. Nevertheless, there is no evidence of a significant rise in mortality, and the birth rate fell off only slightly in these years. Now, in Maharashtra, though poor, the institutional infrastructure was there to begin with: 'fair price shops' which distributed rations of grain at slightly subsidised prices were already widely established, and the public works though which most relief was administered were set up very early on. Moreover, anybody who wanted work on the works got it.

The civil servants with responsibility for Ireland in the 1840s were certainly less corrupt and more sophisticated than most Third World bureaucrats today. So were those handling the poor law on the ground – inspectors, clerks, and guardians. The same goes for the police, unloved perhaps, but pretty straight. I cannot remember a case of one of them being arrested for fraud. Ireland then is not Somalia or Zaire now. Moreover, Ireland's vibrant and relatively free press offered an adequate 'early warning system' of looming disaster and detailed information on where needs were greatest, and communications were quite good.

But was it that simple? There is the issue of the efficient transmission of aid from the centre to those at risk, or what is called 'agency'. Agency has become one of the disputatious issues in famine studies. The claim here is a double one. First, supporters of the agency view argue that the areas with most 'voice' or influence tended to be those less affected by famine. And so, Connacht had fewest priests to plead the poor's case. Skibbereen had no relief organisations, and the Society of Friends helped Munster more than Connacht. Second, the argument goes, corruption and favouritism at local level may have meant that the allocation of funds, not their provision, was the fundamental problem. And of course, it is easy to pinpoint cases of landlords supporting their own pet projects and their own tenants, and of labourers cheating on the public works.

Against the objection that the clergy were there to speak up for the most needy, the 'agency' interpretation sees the priests supporting the landlord sympathetic to the Church over the landlord who refused a site for a new church. Or it mentions that some priests seemed more preoccupied by church-building than by relief. Against the objection that labouring on the public works in the winter and spring of 1847 was no picnic, it objects that there were riots when the works ceased. Again Mary Daly, a cogent and persuasive proponent of the 'agency' view, writes of 'undeserving large farmers' being employed at the expense of neighbours on the works and of resentment against farmers being paid for horses supplied. Such 'agency' theorising implies that ideology was no real constraint, because throwing more money at the problem would simply have lined the pockets of the wrong people – gombeen men, farmers, landlords, and so on. I still believe that in Ireland the problem was less institutional than ideological. The way was there in the 1840s, but not the will. Today, very often, where there is a will there is no way.

To argue that spending more would have made no difference in Ireland in the 1840s is to argue that what was spent saved no lives either – or else that Whitehall had managed to 'fine tune' relief to a degree that seems quite implausible. Given its (so far) slender evidential base, the new emphasis on agency smacks just a little of apologetics. Yet this is a controversy about which we will hear much more and which only detailed research will resolve. This is a reminder of how much research remains to be done.[5]

Food shortages and entitlements

It is often said of modern famines that they are less the product of food shortages or poor harvests *per se* than a lack of purchasing power. In particular, the economist Amartya Sen has pointed to famines in his native Bengal and in

Ethiopia as products of a drop in what he dubs the 'entitlements' of the land-less. In Ethiopia in 1973, he says, 'famine took place with no abnormal reduction in food output, and consumption of food per head at the height of the famine was fairly normal for Ethiopia as a whole' (Sen 1981: 111). Not everybody agrees, of course, but Sen's approach has the cardinal advantage of stressing the role of maldistribution or inequality, which is a key feature of every famine.

How does the cap fit Ireland? One of the most evocative images of the Irish famine is of a people being left to starve while their corn was being shipped off under police and military protection to pay rents. Jean Drèze and Amartya Sen (1989: 22) write of 'English consumers attract[ing] food away, through the market mechanism, from famine-stricken Ireland to rich England, with ship after ship sailing down the river Shannon with various types of food'. Not all the food left. Even in Skibbereen in December 1846 'notwithstanding all this distress, there was a market plentifully supplied with meat, bread, fish, in short every-thing' (Ó Gráda 1999: 122). What Woodham-Smith called this 'extraordinary contradiction' – images of poverty in the midst of plenty – has inspired modern artists from playwright Thomas Murphy to pop-singer Sinéad O'Connor.

However, this enduring, populist image of the famine as starvation when there was enough food to feed everybody oversimplifies. It is somewhat ahistor-ical in that it ignores the inequalities at the root of Irish society in normal times: few of those who died around Skibbereen would ever have been able to afford the meat, bread and fish referred to above. And dwelling on the exported grain masks the reality that at the height of the famine grain exports were dwarfed by imports of cheaper grain, mainly maize (see table 10.3) (Bourke 1993a: ch. 10).

Table 10.3 **The Irish grain trade, 1843–8 (in 1,000 tons)**

Year	Exports	Imports	(Maize)
1843	480	15	1
1844	424	30	1
1845	513	28	7
1846	284	197	122
1847	146	889	632
1848	314	439	306

In the history of the Great Irish Famine the issue of grain exports has more symbolic than real importance. In order to see this, let us suppose that the transfer of all the exported grain from farmers to the starving masses had been costless in terms of resources spent on collection and future output foregone. Alas, the ensuing increased supply of food would have made only a small dent in the gap left by the blight. On the eve of the famine the potato harvest yielded about 12–15 million tons annually, half of which went to human consumption. Thus the 430,000 tons of grain exported in 1846 and 1847 must be set against a shortfall of about 20 million tons of potatoes in those same years. Allowing the exported grain four times the calorific value of potatoes, and ignoring animal feed requirements, the exported grain would still have filled only about one seventh of the gap left by the potatoes in these two crucial years.

Thus, although official neglect and endemic injustice played their part in Ireland in 1846 and 1847, there is no denying that the Irish famine was also, at least in those years, also a classic case of food shortage. Only by adopting an all-UK perspective to the problem in those years might an interpretation stressing entitlements instead of food availability be defended: but that would run against two strong historiographical traditions.

A further difficulty is the long-drawn-out character of the Irish famine. The transfer implicit in the entitlements approach, instead of being a once-off surprise, would have become a kind of repeated game. The consequences for the farmers' output reaction could not have been good.

In support of the entitlements approach, deaths from starvation continued during 1848–9. Those deaths, confined largely to the west of Ireland and occurring after Whitehall had washed its hands of the famine, might well fit an entitlements approach better. The issue requires further analysis.

Mass emigration

All famines induce people to move in search of food and in order to escape disease; there is much movement from rural areas into the towns. But a distinction must be made between such local movements, disproportionately by adult males from more to less afflicted areas, and permanent long-distance migration. Mass long-distance emigration is another legacy of the Irish famine that distinguishes it from modern famines. For many of the Irish poor in the 1840s, unlike the Somali or Sudanese poor today, mass emigration provided a welcome safety valve.

Though data on the socio-economic backgrounds of those who died and those who emigrated are lacking, it seems fair to assume that the latter were mostly people of some modest means. For most of the landless poor, with no savings or compensation for eviction to fall back on, the cost of a passage would have been too high. The pathetic story of Anne Nowlan, a Roscommon woman who had sought refuge for herself and six children in a night asylum on Dublin's Bow Street, is telling in this respect. Nowlan had been placed in custody by the keeper for failing to account for a large sum of money in her possession. The magistrate evinced surprise at the family's condition, 'while she had so much money about her'. The following is Ann Nowlan's account (*Freeman's Journal*, 8 May 1847):

> She lived in the county Roscommon, and her husband held about ten acres of land, but he died last Shrovetide; she had no means of sowing a crop, and she gave up the place to a collector of poor rate, who gave her £15 for it; she got £5 for a mare, and £4 for a cow, 10s for a cart and harrow, and more money for other things, and this made up all she had; she was about going to America, but she would not be taken with her children for less than £27.

When her eldest boy, a thirteen year old, corroborated her story, the magistrate deemed it 'evidently true', and discharged her.

Much has been written about the terrible conditions endured by these 'economic refugees' and the high mortality on 'coffin ships'. But it was not quite so simple. The American historian Raymond Cohn has inferred migrant mortality on the passage between Europe and New York between 1836 and 1853 from a sample of contemporary passenger lists. What is most remarkable about his findings is that neither the Irish as a group nor the famine years stand out: the record of German ships in 1847 and 1848 was much worse, and curiously 1849, not 1847, produced the highest mortality overall. In table 10.4 Irish ports and Liverpool were higher in 1847–8 than in 1845–6, but the mean mortality rate was still less than 2 per cent (Cohn 1987; see also chapter 7 above).

Other data, it is true, highlight 1847, and mortality among passengers who chose ships bound for Maritime and Canadian destinations (nearly half of the Irish who crossed the Atlantic in Black '47 but only 10–15 per cent thereafter) was much higher than those bound for New York. Cohn's numbers exclude ships that sank or turned back and unrecorded deaths on board. Still, his results suggest that Joel Mokyr's assessment of the overall death rate on the north Atlantic passage – 'five per cent of the total overseas migration at the most' – errs on the high side.

In the circumstances, the outcome is a rather impressive achievement. Crucially, most of Ireland's 'boat people' eventually reached their destinations in America or Britain. None of this is to deny that conditions on the passage were harsh, or that there was exploitation of emigrants. But the fundamental comparative point to make here is that surely many of today's famine-stricken poor would give everything up in return for manual jobs and poor housing in North America, Japan, or western Europe. Reflecting on the alternative offered by Third World experience tells us that the Irish were relatively 'lucky' to emigrate and to be allowed in, and that many more would have died in Ireland had this safety-valve not existed.

Traders and famines

As Jean Drèze and Amartya Sen remind us, this is a topic 'that is not always approached dispassionately' (1989: 89). Part of the problem is that the empirical evidence for and against the traders is mixed. Traders make their money by moving goods from low to high price areas and by speculating correctly on price movements over time. Markets have a poor reputation in the context of Third World hunger, and I thought therefore that some musings about them in the context of the famine would be of interest.

If markets help even out scarcities, regional or temporal, that would seem 'a good thing'. Modern evidence also points to the disastrous consequences of governments paralysing private trade. Drèze and Sen compare policies pursued in Botswana and neighbouring Kenya during the droughts of the 1980s. In Botswana, where trade was free, a competitive food market kept price differentials across regions to a minimum. In Kenya grain movements were strictly controlled: as a result huge price differentials between regions emerged, reaching a ration of ten to one between the highest and the lowest for a short time (Drèze and Sen 1989: 138–58). This suggests the need for the free movement of goods. However, when there are few traders government intervention may be needed.

In Ireland in the 1840s, as in India later, officialdom had learnt its Adam Smith and Edmund Burke well: allowing private traders full freedom was a major preoccupation. But what about the situation on the ground? This is a topic where accounts rarely go beyond anecdote or assertion. It is easy to find contemporary criticisms of rapacious traders. The huge rise in grain prices in late 1846 prompted one of the Treasury Under-Secretary, Charles Trevelyan's informants to tell him in late December 1846 that '£40,000 to £80,000 were spoken of as being made by merchants' in Cork, and to hope that government would intervene to check 'the extortionate prices'. Bessborough, the Lord

Lieutenant, informed the Prime Minister Lord John Russell a few weeks later that 'there was no great doubt that the merchants in the great towns have taken advantage . . . and in some places are keeping up the prices by the most unfair means' (Woodham-Smith 1962: 167; Black 1960: 118–19).

Such exploitation is the stuff of fiction and oral history too. Neither William Carleton's *The Black Prophet* nor Liam O'Flaherty's *House of Gold* is directly about the famine, but Carleton's was prompted by the famine and both are full of famine resonances. For Carleton (referring to the Clogher Valley in the early nineteenth century) and O'Flaherty (referring to south Connemara in the late nineteenth century) the case against the exploiting mealmonger or gombeen man was an open and shut one. Yet (and maybe for that reason) hard evidence on how they behaved in crisis times is lacking. The notion that either collusion on the part of greedy merchants or extortion by remote monopoly traders exacerbated an already serious crisis is often echoed elsewhere. For example, many accounts of the greed of Malawi's maize traders in 1949 survive.

Did the traders and the moneylenders make the killings that such accounts imply? Here all I can offer are some preliminary, tentative clues. Before doing so, three simple points based on the kind of elementary price theory we teach first years in University College Dublin are worth bearing in mind. First, supply shocks would have caused monopolies to increase their prices less than firms in a competitive industry. Second, higher prices induced by supply shocks would have reduced the profits of monopolists. Third, the drastic fall in the purchasing power of their customers would have induced mealmongers – other things remaining the same – to reduce, not increase, their prices. These theoretical points suggest that some contemporary observers may have mistaken adverse supply shocks for monopoly power. On the other hand, some of the criticism may have referred to trades (such as that in Indian corn) that were unfamiliar, and therefore more amenable to exploitation.

There are several ways to interpret the claim that markets worked poorly during the famine. The failure could have been temporary (e.g. early on, as in late 1846, when the trade in Indian corn was new); it could have been partial (for example, restricted to remote areas); or it could have been intertemporal (perhaps agents hoarded, or held on to their stocks for too long). The business accounts of famine traders that might shed light on these possibilities have not survived, but food price data from the period are plentiful. My tentative verdict, based on recent research into this subject, is that markets worked fairly well. The analysis is quite technical so the best I can do here is try to give an intuition (for a fuller account see Ó Gráda 1999: ch. 4).

In a well-integrated market, persistent price differences between regions stem largely from transport costs. Therefore if markets continue to work well during a harvest failure, a reduction in the price variation across regions such as counties or provinces should follow, since the fixed transactions cost element should decline as a fraction of the whole. However, if markets become more segmented, a bigger gap between regions or counties might be expected. An analysis of potato prices in hundreds of Irish towns between 1800 and 1846 suggests that the market for potatoes worked tolerably well till then. These numbers are not ideal for our purpose: they extend only as far as the harvest of 1845, the first to be affected by the blight.

Data on grain prices also survive, and are probably of higher quality in that a grain crop such as wheat or oats was more homogeneous than the potatoes underlying the information above. To summarise simply, my strategy here was to look for persistent gaps between grain and oatmeal prices in the main Irish cities and between such cities and London. On the whole the trends do not incriminate Irish grain merchants. There is one tentative exception. The outcome seems to point a finger of suspicion at Cork grain merchants, since the ratio of mean Cork to Liverpool price in late 1846 and early 1847 was considerably (10–15 per cent) higher than in the following months. But whether the outcome reflects a conspiracy on the part of Cork's grain factors or merely delays in maize reaching Cork remains unresolved (Ó Gráda 1999: 143–6).

What of remoter rural areas? That is a question for future research; a priori reasoning is not enough. In late 1846, when the famine was really beginning to bite, one senior poor law official alerted Trevelyan to how hard it was to procure retail supplies in 'remote' districts, and about the lack of small retail outlets for corn. The result was that the poor were forced to 'travel considerable distances from their homes to purchase food'. Given that most poor people moved about on foot, knowledge about prices was hardly perfect.

Hoarding and speculation are also part of the story. Modern evidence suggests that speculation can be destabilising in famine situations. Sen (1981: 76) blames the situation in Bengal in 1943 largely on 'speculative withdrawal and panic purchase of rice stocks encouraged by administrative chaos'. Speculative withdrawals of foodgrains were also important in Bangladesh in 1974. As a crude test in my own *Ireland Before and After the Famine* (1993: 112–21) I analysed the seasonal movements in potato prices before and during the famine. The test, inspired by work on late medieval corn prices, was to compare the seasonal rise in prices from autumn trough to summer peak before and during the famine. If prices rose more from trough to peak than before, then traders were hoarding.

The outcome of this admittedly limited test did not support the hypothesis that speculation made a bad situation worse.

Before leaving traders, I shall make a few comments on the provision of credit to the poor during the famine, limiting the discussion here to pawnbrokers. In Ireland pawnbrokers operated under relatively liberal laws, which allowed them to charge higher effective rates than their English counterparts. The result was a thriving Irish legal pawnbroking sector. Some sense of the extent of the business before and during the famine is captured in table 10.4 (see also Ó Gráda 1999: 149–56).

Table 10.4 **Pawnbroking during the famine**

Year	Tickets issued	Sums lent (nearest £)	Average (pence)
1843	10,517,022	1,458,839	33.3
1844	11,501,108	1,603,789	34.2
1845	13,039,882	1,849,758	34.0
1846	14,161,152	1,922,343	32.6
1847	11,081,865	1,293,332	28.0

Though pawnbrokers could be found throughout most of the island, there were still few in some of the most backward areas in the 1840s. In Erris (which I think of as Ireland's Ultima Thule) 'the trade [was] unknown' (Ó Gráda 1999: 150). Nevertheless, pawnbrokers had made inroads into much of the west and south before the famine, and their humble clients were from the strata most likely to be hurt by the famine. The typical pledge was in clothing and for the equivalent of a few days' wages. Pawnbrokers' surviving records therefore allow some insight into how moneylenders fared during the crisis.

Did pawnbroking thrive during the famine? The answer is a pretty emphatic no. In late 1848 pawnbrokers' premises in Tralee were 'filled with wearing apparel of every description, homemade clothing materials, feather-beds, bedding, and tradesmen's tools of every kind'. A 'most respectable' pawnbroker in Fermoy related the increase in pledges in 1846 to 'the destitution which commenced in that year', and the subsequent fall-off in business to the lack of suitable articles to pledge. And there is much more of that kind (Ó Grada 1999: 51).

The aggregate number of legal pawn tickets fell by over one fifth between 1846 and 1847 and the total lent by almost one third. Neither those numbers nor individual accounts support the notion that the famine was golden opportunity for pawnbrokers. Surely the most plausible interpretation of them is that as creditworthiness dropped, business fell back in tandem.

Overall our findings are not robust enough to reject outright the hypothesis that the greed of millers, mealmongers, and the like exacerbated the famine.

A long drawn-out affair

Another important feature of the Irish famine, which of course makes it difficult to fit into any neat commemorative schedule, is that it was very long-drawn-out affair. If the second and near-total failure of the potato crop in 1846 marks the real beginning of the Great Famine, in Whitehall Russell's Whigs were already in effect declaring it over in the summer of 1847. The lion's share of the responsibility for relieving those affected was then turned over to Ireland.

The crisis did not end in the summer of 1847. Famine conditions lasted for a long time after, particularly in western counties such as Clare and Mayo. In January 1849 a thoroughly disillusioned Edward Twistleton wrote to Trevelyan that 'others might say that we are slowly murdering the peasantry by the scantiness of relief'. At the level of macroeconomic indicators such as banknote circulation or company profits, the recovery took a long time to occur. The number of inmates in Ireland's bleak workhouses, a more immediate proxy for deprivation, remained high long after 1847.

Mortality did not end in 1847 either. The Great Famine had therefore more in common with the seven lean years of the Old Testament than the better-known famines of the 1980s and 1990s. One likely result is that 'compassion fatigue' was more of a problem in Ireland's case. The Society of Friends threw in the towel quite early on, believing that it was the government's responsibility to do more. Compassion fatigue also constrained the more modest efforts of local charities such as the Society of Sick and Indigent Roomkeepers, the Mendicity Institution, and the Dublin Parochial Association.

By contrast, the Finnish famine of the 1860s, another major catastrophe, lasted just one awful year. The latest verdict on the better-known Soviet famine of 1932–3, based on newly available data, suggests that it too lasted a year. Even in the case of the Great Bengali Famine, which according to Amartya Sen yielded excess deaths for several years after 1943, a recent reassessment confines excess mortality to 1943–4 (Dyson 1991b; Maharatna 1996). And the modern famines I have mentioned typically did not last nearly as long as the Irish famine.

In sum, then, there are similarities between the Great Famine and modern famines, just as there are similarities between the Great Famine and famines throughout history. I have tried to show that the differences are at least as interesting as the similarities, and how we can learn from both.

CHAPTER ELEVEN

Famine, trauma and memory

A key theme of the sesquicentennial commemorations of the Great Irish Famine in the mid-1990s was that Irish people everywhere shared a collective or communal memory of that catastrophe. In speeches to the Oireachtas (the Irish Houses of Parliament), at Grosse Isle in Quebec (where thousands of famine emigrants died in 1847), at the opening of the Irish famine museum at Strokestown, and elsewhere, President Mary Robinson led the way, arguing that the Famine had defined Irish people's 'will to survive' and their 'sense of human vulnerability'. For Robinson, commemoration was a 'moral act', a means of strengthening bonds between present-day Ireland and its 'diaspora', and of increasing good will towards, and concern for, Third World famines.[1] There was also a flip side to this collective memory. For some at least, the trauma caused by the famine had long been repressed, hence the need to 'recover' the memory of what had been 'forgotten' since the 1840s. Much of the commentary by politicians, journalists and poets embodied an understanding of the famine which bears comparison with the historical record, as understood by historians.

Historical scholarship suggests that the impact of the Irish famine was unequal and divisive. A disaster that struck the poor more than the rich and that pitted neighbour against neighbour is hardly promising material for a communal, collective memory. But surely folklore or the oral tradition represents such a collective memory? Such may well have been the belief of the Irish Folklore Commission, which began to assemble material on the famine and on much else in the 1930s (Ó Ciosáin 2000; Ó Giolláin 2000: ch. 3). Here I will try to show, however, that some specific features of famine suffering which might be expected to leave their mark on the oral tradition – such as personal reminiscences of the workhouse or employment on the public works – are reflected only faintly or at a safe distance in the Commission's archive. I then turn to collective memory as articulated in the commemorations, and show the tension between the historical and folklore records, on the one hand, and 'memory' and 'trauma', as reflected in speeches and publications, on the other. I find that as famine history the 'collective memory' voiced in the commemoration is in large part artefact or myth. This conclusion is influenced by a reading of some the recent literature on psychotherapy and the historiography of collective memory.

A catastrophe unequally shared

The Great Irish Famine brought the era of major famines in Ireland to a brutal end.[2] In terms of the proportion of the population killed, though not in absolute terms, this was a big famine by world-historical standards. The human cost of the famine is often captured in two numbers: a million died and a million emigrated. When set against a population of about 8.5 million, the resonance of these numbers is very powerful. The numbers who received relief of one kind or another also underline the scope of the disaster: nearly one in twelve of the population on the public works at their peak in the spring of 1847; more than one in three on daily soup rations at their peak in July 1847; and over 140,000 in the workhouses and another 800,000 on outdoor relief a year later. The sheer scale of these numbers would seem to suggest a disaster that affected the entire population. However, the famine's impact was very uneven: poverty and death were closely correlated, both at local level and in cross-section. In some areas, particularly along the east coast, mortality was low and mainly confined to the first half of Black '47; in others the famine removed one-quarter or one-third of the entire population and normality had still not been restored by 1851. In considering collective memory of the Irish famine, a crucial aspect is that, like all famines, it produced a hierarchy of suffering.

As is usually the case when famine strikes, the first to succumb were elderly beggars and vagrants (Ó Gráda 1999: 9; see also Lachiver 1991: 82–8). However, the one third or so of the population which was made up of farm labourers and mini-farmers and their dependants accounted for most of the famine's dead. These were overwhelmingly the people forced on to the public works and the soup kitchens and into the workhouses by the failure of the potato.

As noted above, there is a tendency to aggregate as victims those who perished and those who emigrated. Such 'adding up' must not be allowed to obscure the point that dying was a much worse fate than emigrating – unless, as on the so-called 'coffin ships' plying the Canadian route in 1847, a significant proportion of those who left died en route. Considering famine emigration as a whole, the striking point is how, despite the evidence of overcrowding and malnutrition, so relatively few perished en route or on arrival. Nor did the migrants fare worse after arrival than those more numerous survivors who remained at home. Moreover, far from being a disaster, emigration relieved what would have been a much worse disaster in its absence. Without the safety valve of North America, far more would have been forced either to remain at home or to move to Great Britain. The consequences may be imagined (Ó Gráda and O'Rourke 1997).

Most emigrants relied on their own savings or on other assets, such as a tenancy or livestock, which could be readily transferred into liquid funds. This implies that only people with some land or capital could afford the move. So, while not denying for a moment that emigrants were also famine casualties, it is also clear that they were more fortunate than the hundreds of thousands locked in by poverty. And yet it is the emigrant rather than the labourer who died at home who has become 'the archetypal figure of the famine' (Boyce 1990: 120).

Those who perished and those who emigrated were the most obvious victims of the famine. For the rest, landlords fared badly, though not as badly as implied by the historiography. Farmers faced reduced rent bills, but most were hurt by the failure of the potato and the increase in the efficiency wage or effective cost of farm labour. Outside of agriculture, workers' suffering varied according to their dependence on the potato for their food and on the rural market for their output. In sum, in rural Ireland there were few 'winners' in the late 1840s. It is more difficult to gauge the impact of the famine on small traders, village usurers, and the like. In famines everywhere such people always incur the resentment and wrath of the people most at risk. An analysis of the Great Famine's impact on pawnbroking, one activity perhaps representative of such people, suggests that the famine produced an initial rush of business, soon followed, however, by an increasing burden of unredeemed pledges and forced sales (Ó Gráda 1999: ch. 4). The main winners are likely to have been those with ready access to credit who had the foresight and the toughness to buy up the assets of the vulnerable.

Because they apply broadly similar occupational categories, the population census reports of 1841 and 1851 offer an indication of how different occupations and occupational groups were affected. Given that population is likely to have grown somewhat between 1841 and 1846 the true impact of the famine is not fully captured by the data. Some of the main features are summarised in table 11.1. The overall decline in the labour force in the island as a whole was 19.1 per cent. There were 14.4 per cent fewer farmers, and 24.2 per cent fewer farm labourers. The shift in the diet forced by the potato is reflected in the increase

Table 11.1 **Occupational change, Ireland 1841–51**

Occupation	1841	1851	% Change
Farmers	471,398	403,638	–14.4
Farm labourers, herds, ploughmen, gardeners	1,362,756	1,032,845	–24.2
Domestic servants	328,889	260,522	–20.8
Millers, bakers	11,007	14,490	+31.6
Tavern-keepers, vintners, wine and spirit merchants	7,484	6,070	–18.9
Huxters, provision dealers, tobacconists	6,515	5,425	–16.7
Butchers, poulterers, victuallers	9,169	9,115	–0.6
Dealers (unspecified)	15,347	15,920	+3.7
Shopkeepers (unspecified)	10,732	12,176	+13.5
Merchants (unspecified)	3,257	2,133	–34.5
Bailiffs	1,398	1,902	+36.1
Rate collectors	182	587	+222.5
Ministering to charity	253	1,898	+650.2
Coffin makers	8	23	+187.5
Barristers, attorneys	3,326	3,268	–1.7
Physicians, surgeons	2,850	2,439	–14.4
Spinners	516,424	112,275	–78.3
Weavers	122,631	118,559	–3.3
Shoemakers	55,728	42,742	–23.3
Sailors, boatmen, pilots	8,756	23,724	+170.9
Paupers, beggars	36,137	41,808	+15.7
All others	537,613	730,064	+35.8
Total	3,511,860	2,841,623	–19.1

Source: 1841 and 1851 Census reports

in the number of millers and bakers, one group of possible 'winners'. The figures suggest that most trading categories were affected, though the number of traders overall may have held its own. The number of servants dropped by one fifth. Not surprisingly, given their exposure to infectious disease, there were also fewer medical practitioners in 1851. The fate of doctors offers a reminder that though famine mortality was quite class specific, it was less so than in modern famines. Not only medical personnel but also workhouse officials and clergymen of all denominations succumbed, mainly from typhoid fever. The impact on the legal profession is less expected. The decline in spinning was part exogenous shock, part consequence of the famine. The small number of coffin makers (eight in 1841, 22 in 1851) is a reminder that during the famine most coffins were not made by coffin makers. The mass evictions of the period probably explain why there were more bailiffs in 1851, and the demands made on the poor law why there were more rate-collectors. The increase in the paupers and beggars group is as expected, that in sailors and boatmen less so. Note the significant increase in the 'all other' category, consisting mainly of non-agricultural and more urban occupations.

Table 11.2 replicates table 11.1 for Connacht, the worst affected of Ireland's four provinces. Broadly speaking the pattern is the same, but magnified. The number of farm labourers fell by one third over the decade, and the huge drop in the number of spinners is also noteworthy. In Connacht, the 'all other' category also increased, but only by eight per cent.

These census tables corroborate the point that while it is not easy to identify any significant group of winners in the famine, the suffering was by no means evenly shared. Some historians would go further. W. E. Vaughan insists 'for many life went on normally' during the famine, and that 'any local study of the famine should, therefore, keep an eye on that large section of the population who were unaffected by starvation'. Vaughan instances 'not only those who went to the Curragh races in 1847 but those who consumed six million gallons of whiskey in the same year and the hundreds of thousands of farmers who reorganised their farming to cope with the permanent loss of over two-thirds of their potato crop' (Vaughan 1995: 7–8). He also points to the big increase in the number of second-class houses between 1841 and 1851 ('more than in any subsequent decade of the nineteenth century'), the rise in the number of children at national schools from 456,410 in 1846 to 507,469 in 1848, and the 'slight' decline in the number of horses between 1847 and 1851 (558,000 to 522,000). The point about housing is well taken, even if the increase was greatest in Ulster and in urban areas where the impact of the famine was least. But the rise in the number of schoolchildren, which was greatest in the south and west, 'may be ascribed, to a considerable degree, to the fact of food having been distributed by the British Relief Association, to the children attending a large number of the National Schools, especially in the south and west of Ireland'.[3] Perversely, that reflects the gravity of the famine, not its 'invisibility'.

Vaughan's revisionism was supported by L. M. Cullen in a bravura address to the Douglas Hyde Summer School in 1996 (Cullen 1998: 181):

Table 11.2 **Occupational change, Connacht 1841–51**

Occupation	1841	1851	% Change
Farmers	80,278	69,212	–13.8
Farm labourers, herds, ploughmen, gardeners	288,206	193,798	–32.8
Domestic servants	35,484	27,882	–21.4
Millers, bakers	1,090	1,514	+38.9
Tavern-keepers, vintners, wine and spirit merchants	564	527	–6.6
Huxters, provision dealers, tobacconists	630	594	–5.7
Butchers, poulterers, victuallers	1,131	1,027	–9.2
Dealers (unspecified)	2,558	1,211	–52.7
Shopkeepers (unspecified)	1,103	1,022	–7.3
Merchants (unspecified)	231	168	–27.3
Bailiffs	255	311	+22.0
Rate collectors	1	101	+10,100
Ministering to charity	10	372	+3,620
Coffin makers	0	0	—
Barristers, attorneys	83	184	+121.7
Physicians, surgeons	245	183	–25.3
Spinners	113,998	25,433	–77.7
Weavers	8,982	3,285	–63.4
Shoemakers	5,800	3,927	–32.3
Sailors, boatmen, pilots	1,019	1,404	+37.8
Paupers, beggars	8,183	11,825	+44.5
All other	55,276	58,394	+5.6
Total	605,127	402,374	–33.5

Source: 1841 and 1851 Census reports

There was no central menace to existence at large. Comfortable people lived their normal lives . . . Church building . . . reflected the perspective that life remained quite normal for many and for institutions . . . The 1847 general election was conducted normally and on the basis of normal political issues. One Waterford paper reported in relation to the conditions in one area that 'we since had not room, owing to the press of parliamentary and other reports, to return to the subject as promised'. The priorities were clear.

This may exaggerate the degree to which people were fully insulated from the disaster, but it is a reminder that for some the famine did not last long and was not life threatening.

Not only are famines uneven: they are also, always and everywhere, deeply *divisive* tragedies. The charity and solidarity that bind communities together are strengthened for a while, but break as the crisis worsens: hospitality declines, crime and cruelty increase, as do child abandonment and infanticide. Examples abound in the literature of appalling inhumanity and heartlessness. A chronicler wrote of a famine in the Russian city of Novgorod in 1230: 'There was no kindness among us, but misery and unhappiness; in the streets unkindness to one another, at home anguish, seeing children crying for bread and others dying'. At the height of the French famine of 1693–4 Louis Jacquelin, a haberdasher on his way to a fair, was killed in a forest near Poitiers by a gang of soldiers, 'who stole his trunk and his money and beat him to death'. In Lyons in 1709 a note attached to an abandoned infant read 'This girl is called Claudine, aged three years. Necessity obliges me to expose her. I hope when the times change to get her back'. A survivor of the Great Finnish Famine of 1868 reminisced how 'the flow of beggars was so great that the farmers became quite tired of them' and how they have 'only scraps of food' themselves. On the streets of Leningrad in 1941–2, 'deadly criminals attacked people for their ration cards'. In Somalia in the early 1990s the notorious 'technicals', heavily armed thugs in trucks, terrorised the poor. In Burgessbeg, near Nenagh in County Tipperary, on the night of 19 January 1848, farmer Denis Gorman bludgeoned to death one Mary Ryan, a destitute woman, for stealing 'a few sheaves of wheat' from his haggard. There is much more in the same vein from Ireland in the 1840s. All too often hospitality was abandoned, and private charity dwindled as the crisis was prolonged. Instead of *ar scáth a chéile a mhaireann na daoine* (people rely on each other in order to survive), it became a question of everyone for himself (Christiansen 1997: 10; Lachiver 1991: 53; Monahan 1993: 90; Häkkinen 1992: 156; Salisbury 1969: 482; *FJ*, 24 Jan. 1848; Ó Gráda 1994b, 1999: ch. 6).

Folklore and memory

The Great Famine centennial prompted the Irish Folklore Commission to circulate a questionnaire on famine folklore, the responses to which provided the raw material for Roger McHugh's pioneering study (McHugh 1956). Asking folklore or oral tradition to bridge a gap of a century or more and generate reliable evidence on the famine was asking a lot. The long gap between the event and the collection of the evidence allowed ample time for confusion, forgetting and obfuscation. It also virtually guaranteed contamination by extraneous data. The variable quality of this source and some of its pitfalls have recently been noted (Ó Gráda 1994a; Ó Ciosáin 2000). And just as the questions posed of the archive by modern scholarship are shaped by current intellectual and ideological concerns, the material on the famine collected by the Irish Folklore Commission (IFC) in its heyday in the 1930s and 1940s reveals as much about the concerns of the 1940s as it does about the 1840s. Such considerations inform American historian Peter Novick's advice to place 'greater reliance on contemporary sources than on recollections produced years later, after memory has been reprocessed and re-figured' (Novick 1999: 83–4, 274–5). An added consideration, given the subject matter, is the memory loss possibly caused by the famine itself. Psychiatric research suggests that adult survivors of catastrophes such as earthquakes 'often show considerable memory impairment'. Memories of more protracted catastrophes such as war or famine may be weighted towards their early phases. Moreover, some traumatised victims may be reluctant to talk, while more may be silenced by the reluctance of non-victims to listen (Kotre 1996: 137). These are serious problems. And yet the folklore record at its best is vivid, harrowing, telling and, sometimes, intriguing and puzzling. Rejecting what it has on offer would be going too far (compare Ó Gráda 1994b; Beiner 1999).

Half a century after the material was collected, a number of scholars revisited the IFC archive for new insights. It provided the raw material for Patricia Lysaght's articles on the impact of the famine on women and Carmel Quinlan's re-analysis of the famine questionnaire organised by the IFC (Lysaght 1996, 1996–7; Quinlan 1996). Lysaght's strategy was to draw from the archive at large in order to flesh out a storyline or a generalisation. Inevitably, perhaps, the outcome was a somewhat clichéd collage of Irishwomen as models of compassion and 'heroic self-sacrifice', with the twist that they were also 'women of power' who cursed evildoers such as evicting landlords and land-grabbers (Lysaght 1996–7: 43–4). But given the unequal and divisive character of the famine, should the archive be expected to yield an 'identikit' famine woman? And if it did so, would this not be a worrying weakness? Or is it that the quest for such an identikit has conditioned the reading of the evidence? While Lysaght's focus on a sub-group rather than on the nation is a step in the right direction,[4] the implicit double assumption in her approach that Irishwomen were similarly affected in the 1840s and similarly remembered a century or so later is questionable. The same tendency to generalise is present in Carmel Quinlan's recent analysis of the archive (Quinlan 1996: 84):

> The inability of a society to bury its dead obviously leaves a deep scar on the imagination of the people . . . The testimony is an echo from an earlier generation. It seems to have an air of detachment about it which perhaps comes from the inability of survivors to confront the sheer horror of the famine; instead they accepted it in a fatalistic way as the will of God.

It was not 'society', however, but the very poor in that society who were unable to bury their dead. Nor were the better off forced to confront 'the sheer horror of the famine' first-hand like the poor. Nor had they the same need for fatalism.

Both of these studies *impose* a collective framework on Great Famine folklore. An alternative approach is to seek out the *range* or *kaleidoscope* of memories or evidence on particular topics. I deal here with how three aspects of the famine are represented in the folklore archive. I rely mainly on a simple analysis of Cathal Póirtéir's two compendia of IFC famine material (Póirtéir 1995b, 1996).

(i) The public works
As noted earlier, at their peak the public works employed nearly 700,000 people, or one twelfth of the entire population. In the poorer parts of the island, over-represented in the IFC archive, they employed a higher proportion, and of course a higher proportion still of the adult male population. Over forty accounts (19 in Irish, 24 in English) in Póirtéir's compendia refer to the public works. Some of them are striking and rich in detail; most are critical of the authorities. Only *three* narrators in Póirtéir's compendia refer to an ancestor who participated in the works, however. One, Martin Manning from Carrowholly near Westport in Mayo was the son of a ganger or foreman on the local works. The other two refer to labourers. Mick Kelly's father worked on a relief scheme near Castletowngeoghegan in Westmeath, while John Doyle's grandfather worked for four pence a day building the ditch at 'the straight mile' near Aughrim in south Wicklow (Póirtéir: 1995b: 151, 155). A Béara woman's father-in-law also worked on the works as a young man, but somebody complained that he did not need relief – '*go bhféadfadh sé sin mairiúint sa bhaile*' (he could live at home) – so he lost his place (Verling 1999: 50). In all other instances, 'memory' of the public works as reflected in these accounts is not only distanced in time, but also vicarious in the sense that the memory was not autobiographical even a few

generations back. I don't know why this was so. Perhaps 'silence' or 'denial' had something to do with it. Hidden selection bias in the narrators chosen by the IFC's collectors in the 1930s and 1940s is another possible reason: in selecting the most articulate in the local community they may have also inadvertently missed the descendants of those worst affected by the disaster.

(ii) Thieves and their victims

Taken as a whole, the material on thieves and thieving in the archive is less distanced. Here several accounts are given by the descendants of perpetrators, victims or potential victims. The narrators include a Wicklow woman whose grandfather stole a leg of mutton from the pot of a well-to-do farmer in Slievenamoe and a Roscommon woman whose father stole some oatmeal. Representing the victims, an old man from Tullaghan, County Leitrim, lamented the theft of his parents' potatoes, a 'cruel wrong', while Colm Ó Caoidheáin related how his grand-uncle was robbed of oatmeal in the city of Galway by a woman who cut a hole in the sack he was carrying. We learn how Galwayman Pádraig Ó Discín's grandfather let a thief away with meal, while a Wicklowman's grandfather who drove a horse and car for the local landlord was protected by guards. Mairéad Ní Mhionacháin's mother, then only a little girl, spent many nights guarding the family potato plot in Béara against thieves (Póirtéir 1995b: 68–9, 71, 72, 78–9, 82; 1996: 97; Verling 1999: 49). A striking, if understandable, feature is that the descendants' victims never name the perpetrators. The accounts are divided in their perspectives on the morality of the theft, with a majority showing some sympathy for the thief.

(iii) The workhouse

Memories of the workhouse have the same vicarious quality as those describing the public works. This may come as a surprise, given how large the workhouse looms in both contemporary commentary and the historiography of the Irish famine. And so it should loom large: over one in five of those who perished from the famine died in a workhouse or in a workhouse hospital (Guinnane and Ó Gráda 2002b). Moreover, workhouse deaths represented only a fraction of those admitted, and workhouse survivors were unlikely to have had the resources to emigrate afterwards. Therefore a significant number of the famine's survivors in Ireland must have had personal experience of the workhouse. It is curious to find, then, how distanced are the Irish Folklore Commission's accounts of the workhouse. The following clips are representative (see Póirtéir 1995b: 116–31; 1996: 157–62):

> Patrick Reilly, Culleagh, tells of people found along the roads weak with hunger, grass on their mouths and who were brought to the poorhouse (Belturbet, County Cavan).

> Auld Mrs Corcoran, the wife of Peter Corcoran, went into Granard workhouse and took three children out of it (County Longford).

> *Ní babhta nó dhó a d'airigh mé m'athair críonna, a chónaigh anseo thíos i Maigh Adhair agus a bhí ina fhear phósta le linn an Ghorta, dhá rá go raibh oiread sin ag tarraingt ar na poorhousaí seo nárbh fhéidir óstas a thabhairt dá leath* [More than once I heard my grandfather, who lived down here in Magh Adhair and who was a married man during the Famine, say that there were so many making for the poorhouses that there wasn't accommodation for half of them] (Luogh, County Clare).

> *Bhí seanchapall ag . . . Beait, agus nuair a fhaigheadh é an seans, na daoine a bhíodh ag dul go dtí an* workhouse *(na mBeathach), capall Bheait Rua a chuireadh ann iad* [Bat had an old horse, and when the opportunity arose, it was Foxy Bat's horse that would convey people to the Beathach workhouse] (Cahirdaniel, County Kerry).

> Anthony O'Dwyer's father told him that he saw people dead, dying and staggering about at a rest house at Knockroe, a short distance on the Cashel side of Golden (County Tipperary).

> To be buried in a workhouse coffin was regarded as a slur on the friend and on the deceased (Ballymoe, County Galway).

> '*Tá* brand *an Union ort*', adéarfaí le duine ['You have the brand of the Union on you', is what people would be told] (Cahirdaniel, County Kerry).

Literally *none* of these accounts conveys a real sense of 'having been there'. There is virtually nothing about living conditions inside the workhouse walls. Even when the account is specific, it is always about somebody outside the narrator's family. Not a single informant refers to an ancestor who had been a pauper inmate during the famine, the closest being one Johnny Callaghan, whose father worked as a baker in Castlerea workhouse during the famine (Póirtéir 1995b: 128). This 'silence' may in part reflect the enduring shame associated with the workhouse. Once again, however, an unintended bias in the selection of informants may also be responsible. For whatever reason the memories of those who suffered most are simply not represented in these folklore accounts.

A collective famine memory?

The material collected by the Irish Folklore Commission in the 1930s and 1940s – distanced and fractious and individual – is quite distinct in theme from 'memory' as represented in much of the famine commemoration of the 1990s. The theme of a collective memory of the famine was a key feature of the commemorations. Popularised by President Mary Robinson, it was echoed repeatedly by (then) Minister of State Avril Doyle, by academics such as Kevin Whelan and David Lloyd, and by representatives of the Third World charities. *The Irish Times* journalist John Waters, California state senator Tom Hayden, pop singer Sinéad O'Connor, and others identified with a bleaker version of the same theme, stressing repressed memory and communal trauma.

When asked by a CBS reporter in Somalia in 1992 'why there were so many Irish aid workers on the ground, and such an Irish interest in Somalia', Mary Robinson replied with 'the story of the Choctaw Indians: how they as a poor dispossessed people had raised over seven hundred dollars for the relief of Irish famine victims in the 1840s, and how Irish people had a folk memory of famine which helped us identify with countries like Somalia' (Robinson 1994: 23). Elsewhere President Robinson proclaimed that the famine more than any other event 'shaped us as a people. It defined our will to survive. It defined our sense of human vulnerability. It remains one of the strongest, most poignant links of memory and feeling that connects us to our diaspora. It involves us still in an act of remembrance which increasingly, is neither tribal nor narrow' (Robinson 1995). Fr Aengus Finucane of Concern saw the anniversary as 'provid[ing] us with an opportunity to reach across the centuries and, in the name of our own Famine dead, try to heal the hurts of history' (Concern Worldwide 1995: 2).

'We are a First World country with a Third World memory of famine, dislocation, and exile . . . Our own Famine echoes are constantly with us', proclaimed Minister of State Avril Doyle in 1996. Indeed the phrase 'a First World country with a Third World memory' became one of Minister of State Doyle's key phrases. Elsewhere she talked of the famine as 'an event which traumatised this country', echoing Kevin Whelan's claim that 'the famine experience burned itself into the Irish character'. And again Kevin Whelan:[5]

> The frail Famine voices now reach us across an aching void. We need to amplify that acoustic; in hearing them attentively, we might reclaim our Famine ghosts from their enforced silence and invisibility. In doing so, we can rescue them from the enormous condescension of posterity, paying them the respect which their lonely deaths so signally lacked. That very gesture of reconnection may alleviate a cultural loneliness we do not even know we have and liberate us into a fuller and more honest sense of ourselves, showing us how we got to be where we are, even as we leave it behind.

In 1997 Tom Hayden dedicated a collection of commemorative essays on the Irish famine 'to all those who have had to live with their deepest story denied'. One of his contributors, literary critic David Lloyd, referred to 'our memory of hunger' and 'its psychic and corporeal costs'. Another, Irish language poet Nuala Ní Dhomhnaill, referred to 'our recovery from the collective trauma of the Famine', while novelist Seán Kenny wrote of 'restoring our memory of the Famine' (Hayden 1997: 9, 46, 69, 190). Elsewhere historian Christine Kinealy (1999: 244, 252) has referred approvingly to ongoing work on the 'healing process' and 'post-colonial traumatic stress' by Irish-Californian psychotherapist, Dr Garrett O'Connor. Sinéad O'Connor's 1995 rap poem offers an extreme case of this approach to collective famine memory. For O'Connor 'all the old men in the pubs' and 'all our young people on drugs' were the product of the famine and the resultant post-traumatic stress disorder. The Irish were like 'a child that got itself bashed in the face' and 'if there ever is gonna [*sic*] be healing there has to be remembering'.

I have quoted these statements to give the flavour of the discourse on collective memory. Note throughout the collective rhetoric of 'we', 'us', 'all those', 'ourselves', 'Irish character', 'Irish people', 'this country', 'a country with a memory', 'our own', 'our memory'. This is collective or communal memory with a vengeance. But such inclusive, collective language occludes the uneven and divisive character of the famine.

The view that their shared famine suffering sensitised Irish people taken as a whole to suffering in the Third World or, more prescriptively, should spur them to greater generosity was also a constant echo during the sesquicentennial commemoration. 'Inherited values trigger our sympathy for anyone, anywhere facing starvation', according to Michael Callopy of the Cobh Heritage Centre.

A Dublin nurse told a Boston physician that 'she came to Rwanda because her grandmother never let her forget'. David Andrews, Irish foreign minister in the mid-1990s, has described the 'Irish people's . . . generosity of thought and action' as 'one of the few positive legacies we gained from our terrible experiences during the Great Famine last century'. In the same vein Stephen Jackson, director of University College Cork's International Famine Centre, claims that Ireland's bond with famine-afflicted places stems from 'the sense that we were as they are'.[6]

In Avril Doyle's rendition, 'As such, we as a people have contributed significantly on both a personal and national level to relieving global hunger'. On a more prescriptive note Minister of State Doyle urged in the rather excessive style typical of her commemorative speeches that 'commemoration of the Famine should equally sensitise us to current social inequality and injustice, notably our travellers and urban underclass, whose marginalised positions so eerily replicate that of the rural underclass of pre-famine Ireland'. A year later, no longer junior minister, Doyle would say: 'We are now giving back what we received during our own darkest hour . . . The migration of families to relief centres in Korea and other areas of famine is similar to our people's emigration to the workhouses'.[7] In more sober tones a 1993 Department of Foreign Affairs policy document states that 'our historical experience, the absence of colonial or exploitative interest, the fact that we experienced famine within the relatively recent past . . . have made us especially aware of and sensitive to the economic and social needs of developing countries'. Such rhetoric had a clearly prescriptive role, but whether the famine commemorations spurred the public at large into greater generosity towards Third World NGOs remains a moot point.[8] Moreover, it bears noting, given all the claims to the contrary, that the supposed link between famine memory and generosity in the face of Third World hunger is really for the most part a tradition invented in the comparatively recent past (in the 1970s and 1980s).[9] If a historical link is required, a century-long tradition of Irish missionary activity far afield, particularly in sub-Saharan Africa, has a stronger claim. However, such a 'collective memory' would be out of place in a modern, outward-looking Ireland (Ó Gráda 1997a: 129–31.).

The rhetoric of famine memory today, such as it is (or was a few years ago), is all-inclusive. It is as if virtually all those living in Ireland during the famine were forced to die or emigrate, with knock-on effects on their traumatised descendants. But how could the memory of such an uneven and divisive disaster as the Irish famine be truly collective? How could such a range of experiences have spawned a common memory? Surely, only by glossing over and filtering out much of the history of the famine?

Nor is the correlation between the intensity of memory of the famine and the injury suffered by any means straightforward. As argued earlier, those who managed to emigrate to America were *relatively* fortunate, yet it is their 'descendants' – real or vicarious – who 'remember' the most. But this is as much a reflection of modern American culture as it is of the sufferings of these people's ancestors in Black '47. In their campaigns for compulsory Irish famine studies some American-Irish activists are now competing with Black and Jewish activists in a sordid victimhood stakes (Donnelly 1996b; Novick 1999: 9–10; compare http://www.irishholocaust.org/).

When the French sociologist Maurice Halbwachs coined the term 'collective memory' in the 1920s he was interested in how the present conditions a community's understanding of its past. Modern historians' fascination with memory and tradition owes much to his insights (see e.g. Nora 1979; Hobsbawm and Ranger 1983; Fentress and Wickham 1992; Gillis 1994; O'Carroll 2000; Roth and Salas 2000). For Halbwachs, there was something inherently ahistorical about shared group memories. They lasted only insofar as they adapted to what the American psychologist John Kotre calls 'the needs of changing times'. Typically, such shared memories gloss over complexities and awkward evidence, they are prone to being highly partisan, and they make events in the distant past seem as if they had happened just yesterday. Collective memory, informed by a simplistic understanding of the past, always tells us more about the present than the past. Historical scholarship, by contrast, is complex and multifaceted and ambiguous, though hardly value-free either (Kotre 1996: 238–9; Novick 1999: 4–5). One has only to compare collective memories in the two Irelands of, say, William of Orange and Oliver Cromwell with the ambivalent verdicts of historians.

'Collective trauma' is a concept of more recent vintage. In the hands of John Waters, Tom Hayden, and others cited earlier, it acquired a particular meaning: the transfer of the early Freudian notion of repressed memory from a micro to a macro context. John Waters justified this transfer by declaring that when he had asked psychoanalysts whether the trauma and repression that affected individual people 'might also be true of peoples, of societies, of nations . . . [t]he answer . . . ha[d] invariably been yes' (cited in Hayden 1997: 27). This understanding of collective trauma misses an important aspect emphasised elsewhere in the literature: that is, communal trauma as a blow 'that damages the bonds attaching people together and impairs the prevailing sense of community' (Erickson 1994: 23; cited in www.aaets.org/arts/art55.htm). Analyses of recent natural disasters such as Chernobyl, the civil war in Mozambique, or the

Exxon Valdez oil spill focus on the resultant disarticulation of the cultural systems of the affected communities.

But these are all recent disasters; so perhaps it comes as no surprise that in the Irish case the focus is on the 'repressed' memory of an event that took place long ago. Nobody doubts the psychic scars inflicted by an event like Chernobyl or the Great Famine on those who had to live through them, or even on the following generation. Arguing that Ireland in the mid-1990s was in need of 'recovered memory therapy' (RMT) because of the famine is quite another matter, however. What, one may wonder, is the life span of a collective trauma? How does one measure its intensity? Were Irishmen and Irishwomen in the mid-1840s still emotionally affected by the massive famine that struck the country in 1740–1? When did the French stop suffering the trauma of the massive famines of 1693–4 and 1709?

But the argument suffers from several other weaknesses. First, it forgets that RMT has been subjected to a vigorous critique over the past decade or so. In the course of the high profile 'memory wars' critics have cast serious doubt on the empirical underpinnings of both the original Josef Breuer/Sigmund Freud version and its more recent reincarnation (as represented in, say, the bestselling *The Courage to Heal* by Ellen Bass and Laura Davis). Critics have also accused the RMT approach of simply ignoring the organic or biological component of mental illness. Instead of taking account of what UCLA sociologist and psycho-analyst Jeffrey Prager (a sympathetic critic) dubs 'the extraordinary complexity of individual subjectivity', trauma therapy 'tend[ed] to reduce all understanding of the human psyche to external material conditions that impinge on the person'. Prager deems trauma diagnosis and RMT clumsy tools against the complexity of the individual character. They over-emphasise 'the effects of the external world . . . and dispute memory's subjectivity' (Showalter 1997: 155–8; Prager 1998: 131–3; Crews 1998; Borch-Jacobsen 2000).

Another, more fundamental problem is the transfer from the individual to some national or communal psyche. When a whole group is subject to precisely the same shock this might make sense, though it is not easy to think of examples. In a recent contribution urban sociologist and historian Richard Sennett offers a microstudy of a group of white-collar workers dismissed by IBM in upstate New York, treating them as 'people who have shared common injuries at the hands of the modern economy and are seeking to interpret them' when they meet for coffee (Sennett 1998: 15, 22). Fair enough, perhaps. But one of the points at issue here is that the famine did *not* inflict 'common injuries' at the time, never mind across the generations. And even supposing for the sake of argument that the famine inflicted the same shock on everybody, we are still left with the problem that the concept of communal trauma leaves no room for the subjectivity of the individual psyche. Some of those who encountered and experienced the horrors of Irish famine were emotionally scarred for life; others, perhaps less sensitive or more resilient, coped better. But in the 'common injuries' approach, a given shock is supposed to influence everybody, and thus be remembered by everybody, in the essentially same way.

Conclusion

Peter Novick's reminder that collective memory is subject to 'memory spasms' that coincide with anniversaries certainly rings a bell regarding the Irish famine sesquicentennial commemorations of the mid-1990s. Equally apposite is his denial that 'the flurry of commemorations on such occasions doesn't signify that we're in the presence of important collective memory' (Novick 1999: 4). The famine commemorations and the collective memory they articulated even got the chronology of the famine wrong. They began too soon, in 1995, and came to an abrupt end in 1997, glossing over the awkward historical reality that people were still dying of famine-related causes in some parts of Ireland into 1850 and even 1851. As a friend put it at the time, a new form of famine fever in 1995 gave way to new form of famine fatigue a year or two later. Then it was on to the next collective memory. Now collective memory of the Irish famine has presumably gone into hibernation for a few more decades. If it re-awakens in 2045 or so, its concerns will be different and so will its interpretation of the past.

CHAPTER TWELVE

Making famine history in Ireland in the 1940s and 1950s

Foillsitear gach ni le haimsir
(Everything gets published in due course)

Shortly before presenting their typescript to the publisher, one of the editors of *The Great Famine: Studies in Irish History* (Edwards and Williams 1956) mused that explaining its long gestation 'in even one paragraph [would] not be easy'.[1] The brief preface to the book gives little hint of the delay. The story is worth disentangling and retelling for the light it sheds on Irish history-writing in the 1940s and 1950s. In the preface, the editors thanked J. H. Delargy (Séamus Ó Duillearga), Director of the Irish Folklore Commission, for first proposing a history of the Great Famine. What they failed to mention is that the idea for such a history had stemmed from a conversation between the Taoiseach, Eamon de Valera, and Delargy in late 1943 or early 1944. The ensuing contacts between civil servants and historians are chronicled in a recently released official file. The file suggests that de Valera kept up an interest in the idea, and indeed after publication one of the editors remembered that 'it was the Taoiseach, he thought, who first proposed a book on the great famine'. De Valera wanted a study to mark the centenary of the Famine 'for publication, if possible, in 1945'.[2] The director of the National Library of Ireland, Dr Richard Hayes, was consulted in the quest for 'a trained historian whose name is already favourably known', and who would be a specialist in the period. Hayes brought the proposal to the notice of the recently constituted Irish Committee of Historical Sciences. The ICHS at first hoped to subsume the project under a broader scheme of monographs in Irish history to be published by Faber and Faber, but that plan was rejected by the government. An author's fee plus a subsidy towards publication by Irish publishers was thought to constitute the best arrangement.

However, another aspect of the ICHS's proposal – history-writing by committee – survived. The ICHS proposed a volume based largely on essays by graduate students, who would be supervised by members of the ICHS. These essays would comprise the results of new masters' dissertations on various aspects of the Famine, and part of the government grant would be passed on to the students involved. According to Hayes, Professor Theodore W. Moody (Trinity College, Dublin), Professor Robin Dudley Edwards (University College Dublin) and Dr David B. Quinn (Queen's University, Belfast), who would act as joint editors, believed the work would take three to four years. Nothing seems to have happened for six months, when Muiris Ó Muimhneacháin (Maurice Moynihan), secretary of de Valera's department, issued the first of many reminders and queries to the historians. Edwards (who happened to be a close friend and neighbour of Moynihan) replied by phone, saying that 'the arrangements he would propose for the production of the book formed part . . . of a general scheme for the production of historical works'[3]. Moynihan's request for an outline in writing produced the following letter in September 1944 from Edwards acting in his capacity as secretary of the ICHS:

'The great famine, 1845–52'

> It is proposed to issue a book of approximately 1000 pages under this title to be edited by T. W. Moody and R. Dudley Edwards. (Dr Quinn whom it had been intended to include is leaving Belfast for Swansea.) The work will include *separate contributions* dealing with the events, medical history, relief (including poor law amendment), emigration, population, agriculture, the people, political implications, the place of the famine in Irish history. A few of the contributors will be paid some fee and the total under this head should not exceed £250. Cost of printing 1000 pages should not exceed £1250. It is proposed to ask the government of Eire for a grant of £1500 the expenditure to be supervised by this committee. Contributors are already at work. The book should be in print in 1946.

In 1944 none of the three intended editors could have claimed an expertise in the famine or even in the nineteenth century, though Moody was beginning to concentrate his researches on that century. Edwards thus based his list of topics on the suggestions of Thomas P. O'Neill, then a graduate student in history at UCD. The proposed publication date would have been appropriate, since 1846 marked the true beginning of the Great Famine. In February 1945 Maurice Moynihan passed the project on to the Department of Education, who already had some experience in dealing with the ICHS and with publishing. A few weeks later Proinsias Ó Dubhthaigh of Education sought approval from the Department of Finance for a grant to the ICHS, adding that the money would be refunded to the government if sales of the book warranted it. The figure envisaged was the £1,500 mentioned in Edwards's letter, a considerable sum in those days. The plan was announced in the *Irish Press* on 28 April 1945. Five of the authors eventually included in the published volume were recruited around this time. In addition to O'Neill, they were Oliver MacDonagh (a graduate history student at UCD), Roger McHugh (a lecturer in English at UCD), Rodney Green (then completing his study of the industrial revolution in the Lagan Valley at Trinity College, Dublin), R. B. McDowell (about to return to Trinity as a member of the Department of Modern History), and the noted medical historian Sir William MacArthur. Green and McDowell, besides being competent scholars, were Belfastmen and gave the project the ecumenical, all-Ireland character sought by the ICHS.[3] The original choice for the medical chapter, Sean Moloney, was replaced by Belfast-born MacArthur (1884–1964), after a visit by the latter to Dublin to address the Irish Historical Society.[5] Folklore was not included in the original list of topics: McHugh, a friend of Edwards and author of a series of articles in *Studies* on pre-famine Irish authors (see McHugh 1938a, 1938b, 1938c), was the radical of the group. The seventh contributor, Kevin B. Nowlan, was recruited somewhat later.

The Irish Folklore Commission, through Delargy, also made a considerable contribution at this stage to what was described in its minutes as 'an scéim a bhí bunaithe ag an Rialtas chun staidéar mór údarasach a chur ar fáil don phobal ar an mór-imtheacht san (the government scheme to provide the public with a large authoritative study on that important event)'. The Commission first submitted its standard questionnaire to most of its correspondents and this produced 908 pages of reports. A larger questionnaire (devised by T. P. O'Neill) followed, accompanied by special notebooks, and these were sent to collectors and to other potential contributors. This produced almost four thousand pages of accounts, which were lent to the ICHS.[6] The accounts inevitably are very uneven in quality, yet non-historian Roger McHugh's chapter on this material – again largely completed in 1945–6 – turned out to be the most evocative contribution in the book.

The next item in the Department of the Taoiseach's file is a request from the ICHS, through a letter from Moody in August 1946, that the agreed money be paid over. This prompted Proinsias Ó Dubhthaigh to seek information on the project's progress. In reply Edwards claimed that 'substantial portions of this work have already been submitted to the editors, and that Messrs Cahill & Co., Dublin, have agreed to print and publish it in 1947'.[7] Edwards added that the ICHS had agreed to pay the publishers £600 towards the cost of printing, give £600 to contributors, and 'the remaining £300, it is hoped, will cover typing, secretarial and supplementary expenses'.

Edwards's reply caused some consternation in the Department of Education. Indeed an official had noted on the margin of his original letter, 'What about receipts from sales?', and Ó Dubhthaigh wondered why 'it [was] not proposed to adhere closely to the arrangements already made'. Further equivocation from Edwards (29 September 1946) led to a sterner response from the Department of Education. Had the Committee sought estimates from other publishers? Was there a contract? If so, what were the details? The Department was justifiably concerned about complaints from rival publishers. The big increase in payments to contributors elicited a request for details about their distribution. Finally, had contributors not sent in their material ready for the printers? If so, why the provision for typing costs? While such questions were aimed at eliciting a less cavalier attitude about public moneys from the historians, at the same time the Department of Education tried to rectify matters with the Department of Finance.

After a promising start, the sources suggest that the project was put into cold storage for three years or so. However, on 10 May 1950, the Secretary at the Taoiseach's Department asked for an update. The reply from Tarlach Ó Raifeartaigh (or Terry Rafferty), Deputy Secretary of the Department of Education, a historian himself, friend and neighbour of Edwards, and also a friend of Sir William MacArthur (and later president of the Irish Historical Society), provided chapter outlines. The ICHS promised nine chapters, plus an epilogue:[8]

Section	(1)	Ireland in 1845 – R.B. McDowell	(Complete in first draft)
"	(2)	Course of the Famine – Kevin B. Nowlan	"
"	(3)	Relief – T. P. O'Neill	"
"	(4)	Emigration – Oliver MacDonagh	"
"	(5)	Economics – J. F. Meenan	"
"	(6)	Agriculture – E. R. R. Green	(In 2nd draft)
"	(7)	Medical Aspects – Sir William MacArthur	"
"	(8)	English Public Opinion – Brian Osborne	(Complete in first draft)
"	(9)	Folklore – R. J. McHugh	(In 2nd draft)
"	(10)	Epilogue – the Famine in history.	(Must await revision of Sections 1 to 9 inclusive)

Moody had resigned from the project in 1946, focusing his efforts for the ICHS on the Faber & Faber 'Studies in Irish History'.[9] In January 1947 Moody's place was taken by John Francis O'Doherty, until recently professor of ecclesiastical history at St Patrick's College, Maynooth. The choice of O'Doherty (a medieval specialist and an active member of the Irish Historical Society), who had resigned from Maynooth in rather difficult circumstances to become a curate in Omagh, was a curious one. He was charged 'with full responsibility for the final revision of the work'. In an era long before xeroxes and faxes, O'Doherty's location in Tyrone would have made progress difficult, but other distractions ensured that the project would mark time in 1946–8. They included the Foyle Fishery court case, which involved several historians as expert witnesses, and academic intrigues in connection with the plan to create a School of Irish Historical Research within the Dublin Institute of Advanced Studies. The last-mentioned was the brainchild of Moody and Edwards, and its collapse in 1948 was a crushing blow for Edwards in particular.[10] O'Doherty was replaced by Desmond Williams in 1949, after the latter's return to University College Dublin, as professor of modern history.[11]

When work on the book resumed in 1950, efforts at enticing Moody back as a third editor failed, and R. B. McDowell also refused to join the editorial team, which Williams put down to the influence of Moody who 'wished to be out of this long-delayed project'.[12] Edwards and Williams also briefly hoped that Kenneth Connell (whose classic *Population of Ireland* had recently been published) would join them on the editorial team, and later that he would contribute 'a statistical section' to the volume. Such hopes were not to be realised, but Connell did comment astutely on several chapters for the editors. Connell's suggestions had little impact on the final product, however. He had considered Green's work below par, but there is no evidence that the editors forced Green to make any substantial amendments.[13]

The ICHS hoped – rashly, as events proved – to have revised versions of Sections 1 to 9 completed by the end of 1950, 'when they will be in a position to arrange for the preparation of the final Section'. The Committee had received the grant in three instalments of £500, in 1946–7, 1947–8, and 1948–9. But little had been achieved in that period, and the Committee now anticipated that it might require another grant.

Only seven of the nine 'sections' [sections (1), (2), (3), (4), (6), (7), and (9) in the contents list on p. 237 above] ever saw the light of day, though Kevin Nowlan was to contribute an excellent chapter on the high politics of the period. Osborne's contribution was soon excluded on Moody's 'implied condemnation', a decision later regretted by Edwards.[14] The promised epilogue never appeared. Edwards's academic diary, full of astute comments and asides and disappointments, captures the fitful progress of the project after 1951. Late in 1951 the editors promised the Department of Education the finished product before the end of the financial year. Edwards deemed the chapters by McDowell, MacArthur, McHugh and Green 'virtually finished', but 'Nowlan, MacDonagh, and O'Neill will have to revise within 20,000 words or their sections will not go in'. The original plan of a thousand-page book would have encompassed the master's theses of the last-mentioned three without much pruning, but the scaled-down work now contemplated required considerable rewriting. For O'Neill, this entailed omitting a great deal of useful material on privately funded relief.[15] Edwards still hoped for an epilogue, though he added – presumably with Desmond Williams in mind – that 'future collaborative work must only be undertaken in circumstances in which every associate's control of his own time can be assured'. Later Edwards was to complain about 'TDW pursuing his own Cambridge London and Berlin interests while assuring me that he had drafted his Famine contribution'.[16] There were to be several other setbacks. Economist James Meenan, whom Edwards had known since their days together at the Catholic University School, had been recruited at the outset of the project, and attended some meetings in connection with it, but 'flopped' on his promised contribution.[17] Edwards and Williams hoped for a time that Kenneth Connell (then external examiner to the National University of Ireland) would fill in for Meenan, and also hoped for a co-authored chapter from graduate student Joseph Maher and Dr R. C. Geary of the Central Statistical Office on the land question on the eve of the famine. Other names mentioned around this time included George Duncan of Trinity College and R. D. C. Black of Queen's University.[18] The annual reports of the ICHS, published in *Irish Historical Studies*, reflect the painfully slow progress of the project. They also capture the editors' diminishing expectations as regards the scope of the final product. At the outset the book was referred to as 'The History of the Great Famine', but from the 14th report onward (that for 1951–2) there was an ominous shift to 'Studies in the History of the Irish Famine'.[18]

Edwards's diary in 1951–3 reflects a recurring concern with bringing the project to a conclusion. Another look at MacArthur's medical chapter in February 1952 proved reassuring, and a query from Kenneth Connell about the book's progress in June was optimistically interpreted as a willingness to co-operate. Maurice Moynihan (presumably egged on by de Valera) kept up the pressure from Merrion Street, with repeated inquiries about the project's progress. In October 1953 Tarlach Ó Raifeartaigh, very much the historians' advocate throughout, relayed word that the publishing company of Browne & Nolan Ltd had agreed to produce the book on condition that they kept all the proceeds from sales. Michael Tierney, president of University College Dublin, was a director of Browne & Nolan, and provided the link between the company and the ICHS. Browne & Nolan had a very cosy relationship with University College Dublin, and held the contract for the UCD Calendar. Ó Raifeartaigh added (on behalf of the historians) that the State should keep its distance from publishing 'ós rud fíor-achrannach cursaí staire (as history is a complicated business)', and that his own reading of the proposed book revealed that 'cé go bhfuil a leagan amach féin ag gach údar nach bhfuil éinní ann go bhféadfaí claon-stair a thabhairt air ná go bhféadfaí ceann a thógáil de ó thaobh polaitíochta ná eile (though each author had his own approach, there was nothing which could be termed biased history or which might cause political controversy)'. The Taoiseach's Department's reaction was that other Irish publishers should be given a chance to bid before Browne & Nolan were handed the contract. This put Edwards and Williams, anxious not to appear ungrateful to Tierney, in somewhat of a dilemma. A further communication elicited a reply from Tarlach Ó Raifeartaigh, who enclosed the following letter from Desmond Williams to Ó Raifeartaigh dated 30 March 1954:

Dear Mr Ó Raifeartaigh
In reference to my letter of 28 July, 1953 concerning the 'Studies in the history of the famine', and in reply to your letters of August 10 and October 24, 1 have been directed by the Irish Committee of Historical Sciences and by the editorial sub-committee, to express our view that we are satisfied that no other Irish pub-lisher would be prepared to publish suitably, as an academic production, 2,000 copies of the proposed work on the conditions which you mention in your letter of October 24

It is true that publishers could be found to produce some copies of the work, under some of the conditions you mention, but Dr Edwards and I, as editors, are entirely satisfied with the proposals put forward by Messrs. Browne and Nolan Ltd. In these circumstances we would point out that a rejection of our views on this matter would be considered by us as representing a lack of confidence in the performance of our duties, and that we would have to take the logical steps arising out of such a decision.

Furthermore, we would stress the desirability for the publishers, for the public interested in the history of the famine, as well as for ourselves as

University people with other duties to attend to, of a decision being taken as soon as possible in this matter. We would also point out that our services in connection with the production of the work have taken a considerable amount of time, and that (a fact that perhaps does not need to be stressed) they have been entirely of an honorary nature.

Other public servants might have been upset by the tone of Williams's letter, but Ó Raifeartaigh (who may well have seen a draft of the letter before receiving it in the Department of Education) merely passed on a copy in a reply to Merrion Street, where Williams's request for a quick decision elicited an irate marginal note from Nioclas Ó Nunáin (Nicholas Noonan): 'After taking over 5 months to reply to Mr Ó Raifeartaigh's letter!' The departmental file reveals that de Valera was not 'ro-shásta' ('too pleased') either with Williams's reply. Nevertheless, the plan was agreed. In the end the publication of the book was largely due to the commitment of Dr Kevin Nowlan (then a junior lecturer), Joyce Padbury (Secretary to the History Department), and the late Maureen Wall (*née* Maureen McGeehin) (then a part-time lecturer).[20]

It was Kevin Nowlan, quite late in the day, who 'ghosted' the introduction at the request of Desmond Williams. Edwards and Williams appended their initials to Nowlan's essay without changing a word; only the crisp writing style (reminiscent of Nowlan's earlier contributions to *The Leader*) and the references to 'the Baltic lands' and 'Lettish peasants' (hints of Nowlan's year-long stay at Marburg in 1953–4) provided clues to the *cognoscenti*.[21] It was left to Joyce Padbury to prepare the index: that it contained only references to names and places was the editors' decision, not hers. Padbury, Nowlan and Wall helped with tidying the material that had lain for several years in UCD's history department, and organising the more recent contributions. The end product contained not a single word from the pen of Desmond Williams; Edwards was responsible for the brief acknowledgements section. The illustrations, with one exception, were suggested by T. P. O'Neill. Browne & Nolan were probably responsible for the only unattributed illustration, that facing the title page: though purporting to show paupers outside a Dutch-gabled workhouse in New Ross in 1846, it seems to have been first published in 1887 in an illustrated golden jubilee biography of Queen Victoria.[22]

The typescript of the book was finally deposited with Browne & Nolan on 29 December 1954, with some misgivings. Edwards hoped that 'the individual impression of the contributors [would] emerge without any formalising in the name of academic sameness'.[23] The book appeared just too late for the Christmas market in 1956, well over twelve years after the idea had first been mooted. On receiving advance copies, Edwards expressed satisfaction in his diary, but with the following sobering caveat:

> The overall impression is that the team can stand up to it. But would they do so in a Butterfield sense? Hardly. If it is studies in the history of the Famine, it is because they are not sure all questions are answered. There are still the fundamental matters whether its occurrence was not due to the failure of the sophisticated to be alert.

The end product, though a substantial volume, contained slightly over one half of the thousand pages promised earlier by the ICHS in 1944. For all its good points, the book showed several signs of lackadaisical editing. First and foremost, lacking a narrative structure or even an overall narrative chapter, *The Great Famine* was far from being the comprehensive history of the famine commissioned in 1944. Rather, it reads more like an *administrative* history of the period, with the core chapters (those by Nowlan, O'Neill, MacDonagh, and MacArthur) dwelling on the tragedy mainly from the standpoint of the politician, the poor law administrator, those who controlled passenger movements, and the medical practitioner. But there were less serious shortcomings too. While there is little overlap between the individual contributions, there is little sense either of this being a collaborative venture, and cross-references from chapter to chapter are lacking. On the crucial matter of excess mortality, the lack of co-ordination produces a ludicrous outcome. In its foreword the book eschewed discussion of the tragedy's demographic toll – 'what is certain is that many, many died' – but this did not deter several contributors from producing their own (conflicting) guesses.[24] None of the surviving contributors remembers a single joint meeting of the entire group.

Few of the contributors relied on the wealth of manuscript sources available even then on the famine years. Moreover, while paying lip service to the need for context, the book lacked any proper analysis of economic conditions during the famine period. Sir William MacArthur's frequently cited chapter on the medical history of the famine appeared virtually without references, because one of the editors (Desmond Williams) had mislaid the author's notes, allegedly in a London taxi-cab; Williams attempted to placate the aggrieved MacArthur by noting that the text of a historian of his reputation stood on its own ground – which turned out to be true![25] For all this the blame ultimately rested with the editors, who were not properly geared to the task. Edwards had a fine intuition and an astute mind, but found great difficulty in expressing himself on paper.[26] He was a great originator of ideas and schemes: the Irish Historical Society, the Irish Catholic Historical Committee, the Inter-varsity History Students Congress, the Irish Society for Archives, and the Archives Department of University College, Dublin, all owe their beginnings in large part to Edwards. But Edwards was no great organiser. Neither was Desmond Williams, who in any case was preoccupied with other things (notably with editing *The Leader* and with academic politics in Dublin and Cambridge) in the period discussed here. It was rather late in the day in January 1955 for Edwards's self-criticism that 'the Famine book could be more justifiable if the editors had first sat down and assessed O'Rourke and O'Brien and on that basis planned the whole'.[27] And yet, despite all this, *The Great Famine* contained some excellent material that is of enduring value.

Edwards and his colleagues in University College Dublin were reasonably happy in the end, and duly celebrated the book's completion. The book was widely, and favourably, reviewed.[28] The publishers too had every reason to be satisfied. The volume sold well, and in late 1958 only 100 of the print run of 2,000 remained, while another 1,500 unbound copies had been sold to an American co-publisher, New York University Press. These excellent sales, one of the contributors opined, had been achieved 'despite mismanagement in regard to the publicity'.[29] However, one publicity ruse on Browne & Nolan's part produced some hard feelings. On the eve of publication excerpts from the book had appeared in *The Sunday Independent* without the permission or prior knowledge of contributors. With some reluctance, Browne & Nolan eventually made ex gratia payments to the long-suffering contributors. The book was reprinted in 1962, and an American firm specialising in reproducing classic works produced a new printing in 1976. Second-hand copies of *The Great Famine* grew quite scarce. This, and the enduring value of several chapters, justified the decision of the Irish publisher, Lilliput Press, to produce a new paperback version in 1992. The editors sent de Valera (then in opposition) a complimentary copy of their book. He thanked them graciously enough, though he also felt it necessary to remind them in his reply of the conditions endured by 'ordinary people' in Bruree (the Limerick village where he had spent his childhood) during the famine. Later he expressed unhappiness with the book, presumably because it seemed to downplay those aspects of the tragedy that had been etched in his own memory.[30] That he much preferred Cecil Woodham-Smith's *The Great Hunger* tells its own story. *The Great Hunger* was published in 1962, and immediately became a runaway success.[31] Late in

1963, when Woodham-Smith gave a public lecture in Trinity College about her experiences in writing the book, de Valera paid her the honour of attending[32] and when some months later, the National University of Ireland awarded her an honorary doctorate, de Valera, as Chancellor of NUI, may well have been responsible. On that occasion he organised a lunch in her honour at Áras an Uachtaráin, to which he also invited his old-time comrades Jim Ryan, Frank Aiken, Sean T. O'Kelly, and their wives. T. P. O'Neill – then at work on de Valera's biography – was also present, the only link with the Edwards–Williams volume. Curiously, the introductory address by Michael Tierney, the then Vice-Chancellor of NUI (and President of UCD), at the conferring ceremony struck a note that anticipates some later criticisms of Irish famine historiography:

> The lady whom I have the honour to introduce today has proved that while remaining a science, [history] can be a great deal more; and what in her case above all has contributed to this enlargement is not merely her mastery of a vivid, subtle and delicate style. It is above all the quality of sympathy with her subject, a sympathy that shines so brightly from every page she has written . . . The Great Hunger, which by reason of the thorough research on which it is based, the vividness of its style and the sympathy with which the terrible subject is treated, has received the praise of the world. By this book . . . Mrs Woodham-Smith has shown herself not only a great historian and a great writer, but also a great benefactor to Ireland.

To some readers, Tierney's address may sound like an appeal for history as melodrama. Indeed, *The Great Hunger* has been accused of being just that. Nevertheless, its immense popular success was, in part at least, a measure of the opportunity lost by Edwards and Williams. After all, had the ICHS performed its task properly and on schedule, Woodham-Smith might never have embarked on her own book in the mid-1950s. There was thus undoubtedly an element of sour grapes in the Irish historians' reaction to Woodham-Smith. Her work has rarely been out of print since publication, and probably still ranks as the all-time bestseller among Irish history books.[33]

Yet Edwards never treated Woodham-Smith as a rival. He had befriended her when she first broached the topic of her planned book with him in January 1954, and that friendship endured. She publicly acknowledged his help and that of T. P. O'Neill and R. B. McDowell in due course. Years later she was to travel to Dublin at Edwards'ss request to attend the inauguration of the Irish

Archives Council.[34] For his own part, Edwards was alive from the outset to one of the real weaknesses in Woodham-Smith's approach to the subject:

> How will Cecil Woodham-Smith tackle the Famine? It seems a safe bet that she will tie it to a few personalities – administrators, landlords, gombeenmen. There will also be a chance to enliven the generalisation that Ireland has in consequence bedevilled the good relations of Britain and America.

> In the last resort this is in danger of not being history. The pouncing upon the conspicuous personality and the vivisecting of him may create a charicature [*sic*] and impose upon him a type which is only partly illustrative (could one get 2 or 3 of each type in each of say three areas). There is also the danger of accepting some contemporary thesis such as that of the *Economist* that the landlords were to blame. [35]

This showed remarkable prescience, because several critics were to fault Woodham-Smith for organising her narrative around 'key' personalities, and the demonisation of Prime Minister Lord John Russell and Treasury under-secretary Charles Trevelyan. While Woodham-Smith's was a highly effective rhetorical device, it overemphasised the importance of those individuals in the tragedy. Moreover, Edwards correctly noted Woodham-Smith's propensity to oversimplify issues such as culpability and international relations.[36]

The Great Hunger had many other flaws. It was weak on the economic context, and underestimated the difficulties entailed in avoiding mass mortality.[37] Yet Irish academic historians have been less than fair to Woodham-Smith. Roy Foster's memorable but cutting depiction of her as a 'zealous convert' captures the condescending professional consensus. But since I have made the point before,[38] let me add just one further, comparative illustration here. It concerns F. S. L. Lyons, whose remarkably indulgent review of Edwards and Williams bears comparison with his delayed, rather snide reaction to Woodham-Smith. Lyons's only criticism of Edwards and Williams concerned the limitations of the index! His belated review of *The Great Hunger* in *Irish Historical Studies* made several valid points, but there was also a great deal of nit picking, and in one important respect at least, Lyons stands accused of double standards. Thus, in 1957 he wrote of the Edwards and Williams volume: 'We can see now that the Great Famine was a logical consequence of a vicious system of land-holding, a pitifully backward agriculture, and a social structure which invited disaster'. Historians today might question Lyons's undue emphasis on land tenure and the underlying determinism, but as an argument against facile populist notions, this was fair enough. Yet when Woodham-Smith reasoned in *The Great Hunger* that 'all this wretchedness and misery could, without exception, be traced to a single source' – the land system – Lyons pounced: 'that phrase "a single source" betrays an attitude of mind which is not, in the deepest sense, historical'.[39] Woodham-Smith's book has many weaknesses but, to its lasting credit, it laid bare anew the horrors of the tragedy glossed over in *The Great Famine*. That Irish historians in the 1950s should have sought to rid Irish history of its undue emphasis on the tragic is understandable; but the appalling catastrophe of the 1840s was an unhappy choice for that campaign. In defence of those involved in *The Great Famine,* the raw state of Irish historiography in the 1940s must be not be forgotten. In May 1943 Moody had addressed fellow-members of the Irish Historical Society on 'things to be done in [nineteenth-century] Irish history'. The lecture survives only in summary form, but reading that summary nearly half a century later, it is striking how little scholarly dispassionate research had been produced in the field by that date. Moody noted the lack of even a satisfactory general historical outline, and referred those interested to the *Oxford History of England.* For a general bibliography, he recommended appendices to the *Cambridge Modern History.* The few specialist works on Irish history that Moody considered worth mentioning – George O'Brien's *Economic History of Ireland from the Union to the Famine* (1921), John O'Donovan's *Economic History of Live Stock in Ireland* (1940), Nicholas Mansergh's *Ireland in the Age of Reform and Revolution* (1940), and the works on land tenure by Elizabeth Hooker (1938) and N. D. Palmer (1940) – would be considered dated or unimpressive today.[40]

Individual contributors to *The Great Famine* faced other obstacles easily forgotten today. In the 1940s the National Library of Ireland's collection of catalogued manuscripts barely exceeded a thousand, compared to well over 20,000 now; while the authors were doing their research, thousands of potentially useful documents lay in large wooden boxes with their lids screwed on. The National Library had yet to appoint a permanent keeper of manuscripts. No list of land estate materials had been compiled, and Irish parish registers had not been microfilmed.[41] The records of Workhouse Boards of Guardians lay scattered around hospitals and county council offices, and no location list of them existed.[42] In the mid-1940s, the hundred-year rule still applied to famine-related material in the State Papers Office.[43]

In such circumstances, that *The Great Famine* might 'not claim to be a definitive history of the Great Famine but rather a contribution towards such a history'[44] is more understandable. Yet if the cream of Irish historians could not organise such a history in twelve years, then who could? Almost three decades later, that 'definitive history' remains to be written, though a great deal of work has been done in the interim. In the end, the ICHS failed to provide de Valera with what he had sought – and offered good money for – in 1944, a comprehensive account of the Great Famine. I suspect that the kind of collective history writing instituted in 1944 could not have provided that. Overall, the episode does not reflect well on the professionalism of the Irish historical establishment of the 1940s and the 1950s. At a more parochial level, while 'history in UCD [may have] had a special air of excitement and innovation'[45] about it during the period discussed here, its strengths lay in teaching and postgraduate research. Publishing was another matter, and the delays and the nature of the final product point to serious organisational shortcomings too.

That Eamon de Valera, nurtured on stories of perceived wrongs from his grandmother in a cottage in Bruree, should have sought a book on the Great Famine is almost predictable; that the Irish historical establishment should have denied him the kind of reassurance that he sought is almost equally predictable. Yet, ironically, Edwards clearly anticipated the kind of criticism that would be made of Irish famine historiography later, though he could not bring himself to do anything about it. Reading E. C. Large's brilliant *Advance of the Fungi* early in 1952 turned his mind 'rather uneasily' to the famine work. With some foreboding, he noted:[46]

> I begin to feel that there is real danger that the sections of the specialists will fail to convey the unity of what was clearly a cataclysm in the Butterfield sense. The modern Irish of the countryside are largely predestinarian. Was the famine inevitable? and was the belief in its inevitability a factor which has tended to strengthen a tendency which one can well believe was always an Irish belief? I doubt if I can answer either but the need to ensure that at least in the final result the Famine book will contain some attempt to see the explosion as a whole, mark its beginnings and indicate its short and long term limits. Neither politics, relief, agriculture, emigration (not to say history or folklore) can bring this out. It requires a careful assessment of the cumulative factors and a demarcation of how they became explosive. This will also answer the question of responsibility, so unhesitatingly laid at England's door by John Mitchel.[46]

Such thoughts lay behind Edwards's plan, alas never acted upon, to produce a volume of documents to accompany the book. This would not only allow people 'to see the truth of what is written down, [but] enable the historians [to] control interpretation, and see how one another behave in their work of reconstruction'.[47] Edwards returned to the alleged shortcomings of the contributions again on 9 September 1952:

> I feel a little depressed at the dulling effects of academic discipline . . . In our anxiety to bring out this book we must not be satisfied with pretty academic studies which fall dead from the press: Carleton and Liam O'Flaherty have at least an equal right to be taken for history as such. McHale and Mitchel are the prophets and must be treated as such. The logic of all this – and TDW agrees – is that the historiography of the famine (and a brief introduction) will have to state the real (as opposed to the administrative) position.[48]

There Edwards put his finger on a real weakness of the contributions to the project, taken together. That was their largely administrative focus. Further doubts were recorded a few days later:

> *The Famine: danger of dehydrated history.* [emphasis in the original].

> The more one thinks of the Famine the more the approach of contributors makes it necessary to take effective action. An integration could be attempted in the introduction and the stage set with some vivid contemporary extracts such as the Catholic hierarchy's address to the LL of 21 October 1847. The historiography is crucial when one recollects how the Mitchel–McHale story is as effective on the next generation as the depositions story on the post-1641 world. It had probably more effect on the writing of Irish history than the Young Ireland nationalism which really acted as a medium for translating Irish ideas (often wrongly) for foreigners.[49]

The preoccupation persisted:

> The essential weakness of the Famine studies came to me very clearly after reading Dr T. O'Herlihy's booklet published seven years ago with its obvious analogies to Mrs. Woodham-Smith's ability to be on fire. The circumlocution office was not exactly the same as Dublin Castle, but the fact remains that we have failed to include anything on the Castle and KBN [i.e. Kevin Nowlan] admits they were a sorry lot. In the light of what we see today of a Kenya such a factor should get some proper treatment.[50]

Again, re-reading Roger McHugh's chapter on the famine in folk memory convinced Edwards that something was lacking in the other chapters: 'Mitchel's popularity is explainable not because he was merely defiant. It was because he correctly interpreted the feeling of the people. The attitude to relief, to the soup kitchen comes well out of McHugh.'[51] I do not believe that Edwards should be interpreted here as claiming that the resentment of the starving provides a full or coherent explanation of the famine, merely that Mitchel was articulating widely held views. Indeed a thorough analysis of the contents of the replies to the questionnaire would return a more equivocal verdict on popular feeling (or folk memory), and McHugh's contribution let slip the opportunity to weigh folklore and literary evidence against other sources. Still, Edwards's comment about folklore and Mitchel captures something that is lacking in the book, read whole. It also begs the question why Irish historians since – with a few exceptions such as Kenneth Connell – have been so reluctant to invoke or confront folklore evidence.[52] Roger McHugh's essay is so much out of tune with the other contributions that one may well wonder whether the chapter on folklore 'was a sop to Séamus Ó Duilearga because of his involvement in the early idea of the book'.[53]

A final comment on Edwards's reservations about the project and famine historiography. The relevant passages in his diary – and his remarks on Woodham-Smith – suggest a healthy scepticism towards nationalist 'genocide' interpretations of the Great Famine. Yet Edwards worried that in their eagerness to produce an antidote to the 'ochone, ochone' emphasis of Irish nationalist historiography and what the introduction deemed its undue reliance on 'the political commentator, the ballad singer and the unknown maker of folk-tales', some of the contributors might come across as too unfeeling about what was, after all, an immense human tragedy. To this extent, *The Great Famine* might be seen as contributing to 'a version of Irish history which downplayed the tragic dimension of Ireland's historical experience'.[54] Edwards anticipated such a reaction, and indeed sympathised with it.

Completion of *The Great Famine: Studies in Irish History* provided a morale boost to historians in Earlsfort Terrace and led to a resolution to beef up nineteenth-century studies there.[55] Maureen Wall and Kevin Nowlan would soon supervise a batch of master's dissertations on the pre-famine famines of 1816–17, 1822, and 1831.[55] But in nearby Merrion Street, the departmental file on *The Great Famine* closed on a further request for funds from the ICHS, this time for a subvention towards a book on the Fenian era. The government denied that request. Once bitten, twice shy?

Postscript (2006)

Readers may now wish to refer back to remarks about this chapter in the Introduction.

CHAPTER THIRTEEN

Making famine history in Ireland in 1995

O half-potato on my plate
It is too soon to celebrate the centenary of '48
Or even '47

Patrick Kavanagh, 'Restaurant reverie'

Introduction

In 1995 the Irish – and others – commemorated the sesquicentennial of their Great Famine. The commemorations were multifaceted. They included a museum opening, a government-funded research project, an international conference, a series of special television and radio programmes, new music and paintings, summer schools, exhibitions, and many books and articles. Ireland's president, Mary Robinson, lent the commemorations her prestige by visiting the famine graves at Grosse Isle in Quebec, by attending several commemorative functions, and by being patron of the Famine Museum at Strokestown. Most events attracted large audiences.[1] Some journalistic and literary-ideological rumblings apart, the commemorations passed without much rancour.

The commemorations jumped the gun, however, because there was no famine in 1845. The first visitation of *Phytophthora infestans*, or potato blight, killed nobody in Ireland that year, nor did many perish before the autumn of 1846. The damage to the 1845 crop was partial, and occurred late in the growing season. This is not to deny hardship; but a combination of timely relief and the poor's resilience in the face of harvest shortfalls kept them going. Nor, as they planted their seed potatoes in the spring of 1846, did the people expect a recurrence. Had the blight chosen then to wander off somewhere else, that year's potatoes would have been safe and there would have been no major catastrophe. Then the 'famine' of 1845 would have been like the minor famines of 1822 or 1831, the stuff of specialist histories.

Still, though nobody at the time could have anticipated it, the die was cast as soon as the leaves and stalks began to blacken in the autumn of 1845. This offers some rationale for launching the sesquicentennial commemoration of the Great Famine in 1995. Such was the rush that even for those academics – like this one – who argued on historical grounds that opting for 1995 was 'jumping the gun', there could be no holding back.

The main trouble with focusing on 1995 was revealed by some signs of a new kind of 'famine fatigue' by year's end. In November one Irish journalist claimed that 'it's hard not feel that, really, it's all been said by now', and another in December that 'the arguments had been thrashed to death'.[2] Even among Irish-Americans there was talk of being 'famined-out'. The sentiment is understandable, but doubly unfortunate. First, as Patrick Kavanagh's lines above remind us, the true sesquicentennial of the famine still lay ahead. It is unfortunate, but a fact of life, that historical events lasting several years risk being straitjacketed and distorted in standard commemorative schedules. Second, the journalists are wrong. Despite all the activity and the publicity, much about the Great Famine remains hidden, waiting to be discovered and studied.

This chapter takes stock of some of the new findings in publications that coincided with, or anticipated, the year's commemorations. Some of these had been in the works for a long time previously (e.g. Kinealy 1994; Kerr 1994; Scally 1995; Morash 1995a). Others were produced speedily, and capitalised on the buoyant market for famine books (e.g. Póirtéir 1995a, 1995b, 1996; Litton 1994; Gray 1995b; Percival 1995; Killen 1995).[3] I also refer to some related works published in the previous year or two. Though they leave plenty of room for debate and disagreement, most of these new contributions have certain points in common. First, they re-establish the centrality of the famine in Irish and European history. Next, they give due scope to its catastrophic dimension. Third, they emphasise the unfriendly ideological and awkward economic contexts in which it happened. We have come a long way from 'revisionist' claims that the famine was just a regional crisis blown out of proportion by nationalist propagandists, a mere catalyst of long-term changes already in train or inevitable, or a tragedy which no government could have done more to alleviate. The 'new' history of the famine restores its tragic and world-historical significance and does not shy away from the political-economic aspects. It is therefore closer in spirit to economist Amartya Sen's surmise that '[in] no other famine in the world [was] the proportion of people killed . . . as large as in the Irish famines in the 1840s' than D. G. Boyce's complacent and indefensible assertion that 'even the scale of the great famine was not unique when seen in the context of contemporary European experience'.[4]

I begin this survey of the new famine historiography with work that seeks to set the famine in an historical and spatial context. This involves a brief review of research on Irish agriculture before the famine, and an account of some comparative analyses of the famine. Subsequent sections are concerned with how the famine affected different sections of the Irish population. They review in turn the impact on landlords, on emigrants, and on the medical profession and the clergy. The impact of the famine on these groups raises the question of whether the famine yielded any winners. Then I consider a previously neglected aspect: representations of the famine in folklore, in literature, and in art. Next I summarise current understanding on the issue of ideology, followed by the controversial issue of responsibility. The final section offers some concluding remarks.

The potato and agriculture

The Irish famine is often described as the 'potato famine'. Giving it a more contextual focus implies paying more attention to the potato and agriculture. In a pioneering work written mainly in the 1960s but widely available only since 1993, the late Austin Bourke showed how the diffusion of the potato was earlier and more extensive in Ireland than anywhere else in Europe. Bourke also added new insight into the role of potato varieties, and the diagnosis of the potato blight in the 1840s (Bourke 1993a; see also Bourke and Lamb 1993; Daly 1997; Solar 1996; Denecke 1976; Mokyr 1981).[5] Several studies published since complement and build on Bourke's researches: David Dickson has worked on the chronology of diffusion, Peter Solar on yield variability, and Kevin Whelan and Mary Daly on the potato's role in the pre-famine farming regime. Analysis by Kevin O'Rourke, Michael Turner, and others of the impact of the potato's failure on the structure of post-famine agriculture also gives some indication of its centrality before 1845. Other issues require further analysis. One such issue is the connection between the potato and Irish population growth during several decades of the eighteenth and early nineteenth centuries – did the potato prompt or merely accommodate that growth? Other questions include: Why did the Irish place more trust in the potato than the Scots, the French or the Scandinavians? Was it simply because they were poorer, or did Ireland's soil and climate give it a comparative advantage in potato cultivation? What part did culture and tastes play? The Irish cultivated the potato as a garden crop from the outset, but in parts of Europe the potato seems to have been introduced first mainly as a fodder crop. Did this delay its adoption as food for humans in certain areas? When did the potato become the staple food of the Irish poor? These are difficult questions, but several able scholars have been offering some of the answers (Bourke 1993a; Whelan 1995; Solar 1989b; Dickson 1997; Daly 1997; O'Rourke 1991a; Turner 1996). A full understanding requires paying more attention to the history of the potato in other places.

Comparative perspectives

In his contribution to the series of public lectures jointly organised by Teagasc (Ireland's agricultural education and research authority) and University College Dublin in September 1995, Peter Solar noted that the failure of the potato after 1845 produced hardship and indeed deaths in other parts of Europe too: excess mortality was considerable in Belgium and the Netherlands, for instance. Solar ranged far and wide across Europe's potato regions, tackling from a novel perspective the question of why so many died in Ireland. The uniquely high rate of potato consumption in Ireland is part, but only part, of the answer. Peter Gray introduced a further comparative note, by comparing famine relief and welfare regimes in Ireland, France and the Low Countries in the 1840s. Both Solar and Gray argued that the Irish poor faced a particularly harsh ideological climate, which constrained relief spending and increased mortality.[6] Thirdly, the links drawn between the Irish famine and modern famines prompted me to compare aspects of the two. My analysis shows that while the horrific symptoms of famine have changed little since the 1840s, the dimensions and the causes have altered significantly. Most important, perhaps, Ireland before the Great Famine was a peaceful place, but most of today's famines stem from the disruption caused by post-colonial wars. A comparative perspective highlights the enormity, relatively speaking, of the Irish famine in the world history of famines.[7]

Regional and local studies can offer, implicitly or explicity, another comparative perspective. Only a selection of the huge number of studies done over the last few years can be listed here.[8] Taken together, these studies show that no county in Ireland was immune from the famine. They are a reminder too of how well documented the Irish famine is, and a reflection of the considerable local interest in it. That local interest led to the creation in 1991 of the Irish Famine Network, a forum for famine researchers all over Ireland to present their findings and exchange ideas.[9] On the whole, the promise offered by doing local studies in a comparative framework has yet to be fulfilled.

Landlords

Irish landlords were very much the scapegoats of British policy makers and public opinion during the famine. On the one hand, they were expected to face up to their responsibilities to the stricken tenantry; on the other, the authorities in London saw the crisis as a means of purging the country of its less viable holdings and less competent proprietors. The record yields instances of landlords who met the crisis with brutality and irresponsibility, and of others who were bewildered and overwhelmed by it. Evictions on a mass scale were an important part of the story. Evictions might be rationalised as a precondition for agricultural improvement, but landlords with disproportionate numbers of smallholders had an added incentive for getting rid of them, because they were liable for their rate payments. W. E. Vaughan has put the number of families evicted by legal process during the famine and its aftermath at 70,000, while James S. Donnelly Jr numbers the victims of involuntary surrenders of their holdings 'almost certainly' at more than half a million.[11]

However, the impact of the famine on landlord behaviour and on landlord fortunes has not been rigorously studied. Donnelly's classic 1975 work on Cork contains an excellent account of the situation in that county, but Maguire's analysis of the Downshire estates ends in 1845 and Vaughan's masterly interpretation of 'mid-Victorian' landlord-tenant relations begins with the 1850s (Donnelly 1975; Maguire 1972; Vaughan 1994). So perhaps it is too soon to generalise about landlords.

The recent crop of studies includes Stephen Campbell's account of events leading up to the assassination in 1847 of Denis Mahon, absentee landlord of Strokestown, Robert Scally's lucid analysis of a rent-strike on the nearby crown estate of Ballykilcline, and Tom Yager's study of evictions on the remote Mullet peninsula in west Mayo. None of the landlords profiled in these studies distinguished themselves during the famine. Indeed, Scally's *The End of Hidden Ireland* highlights the parasitical character of landlordism as represented by the lessor of Ballykilcline, Lord Hartland. Hartland's insanity in the mid-1830s had no obvious impact on farming on the estate, and the tenants benefited by being left alone and paying no rents for several years. Ironically, in the wake of a standoff which lasted almost a decade, the crown treated its tenants better than the majority of Irish landlords did – but in part because it could afford to do so (Campbell 1994; Scally 1995; Yager 1996).

The traditional historiography emphasised the drastic impact of the famine on estate turnover. For decades before the late 1840s few estates had changed hands, but this was partly because the law made it very difficult for creditors to lay claim to insolvent property. The Incumbered Estates Court was established in 1849 to ease the transfers of such property. The timing makes the impact of the famine on Irish landed proprietors difficult to separate from the creation and early history of the Court. Such an institution had been recommended by the famous Devon Commission in 1845 and would have been created in due course in any case, but in the early years clearly some of the Court's business was linked to the problems posed by the famine. How much is a moot point. A survey of the standard accounts suggests that the timing of the Court's creation has confused the impact of the famine *per se* on landlords. Here are two examples from well-known sources:

> The rise in poor-rates and the decline in rent receipts served to send many proprietors into the Incumbered Estates Court once its operations began in 1849. (Black 1960: 130)

> Under the shock of that disaster many of the old landlords had broken, succumbing to the crushing burden of paying vast sums in poor relief at a time when rents drastically diminished. Post-famine legislation, notably the Encumbered Estates Act of 1849, enabled numbers of them to dispose of their estates to a new type of owner who knew the value of money. (Lyons 1973: 26)

However, analysis of the Incumbered Estates Court's business in its early years shows that neither the decline in rent receipts nor the rise in outgoings explain more than a fraction of the debt due on estates presented to the Court. It is clear from the debt profile of those presented that most of the landlords who succumbed would have been in deep trouble in any case, once legislation like that enacted in 1849 allowed creditors to claim what was their due.[12]

Emigrants

The famine migration occurred just before steamships won out over sail on the north Atlantic route. Much has been written about the terrible conditions and high mortality endured by Ireland's 'economic refugees' on the long crossing. Robert Scally (1995: 218) offers an eloquent summary:[13]

> The miserable epic of the Atlantic crossing in these years has been told so often and well that it hardly seems necessary to recount its dreadful details. Flanked

by Skibbereen and Grosse Isle at either end of the voyage, the 'coffin ship' stands as the central panel of the famine triptych, depicting bondage and fever in the steerage, wailing children and mothers' pleas from the darkness below decks, heartless captains and brutal crews, shipwreck, pestilence, and burial at sea. In its own smaller scale, the memory of the emigrant steerage has long been held, like the slaves' 'middle passage' and the trains of the Holocaust, as an icon in Ireland's oppression.

Such accounts are reminders of the harsh conditions faced by many passengers, and of the exploitation endured by some at the hands of unscrupulous ship-owners and agents en route. Yet they do not prepare one for the important point that most Irish emigrants made it safely to the other side during the famine years. Raymond Cohn (1984, 1987) has inferred migrant mortality on the passage between Europe and New York from 1836 to 1853 from a sample of contemporary passenger lists. What is most remarkable about his findings is that neither the Irish as a group nor the famine years stand out; the record of German ships in 1847 and 1848 was much worse, and curiously 1849, not 1847, produced the highest mortality overall. While the death rate out of Liverpool, the departure point for most of the New York-bound Irish, was higher in 1847–3 than in 1845–6, the mean mortality rate was still less than two per cent. Admittedly, the New York passenger lists do not tell the full story. In Black '47 mortality on the Canadian route, serviced mainly by old timber hulks, was very much higher, and that route accounted for a significant proportion of the outflow in that horrible year. Thereafter, it was the American ports that dominated and, given the tragic and chaotic contexts of the journeys, it is the low overall mortality which is significant.

In March 1847, in a frequently cited passage, the *Cork Examiner* noted that 'the emigrants of this year are not like those of former ones; they are now actually *running away* from fever and disease and hunger, with money scarcely sufficient to pay passage for and find food for the voyage' (Ó Gráda 1999: 107). Nonetheless, though hard data distinguishing between the socio-economic backgrounds of those who died and those who emigrated are lacking, it seems fair to assume that the latter were mostly people of some modest means.[14] For most of the landless poor, with no savings or liquidated assets to fall back on, the cost of a passage remained too high. An account in the *Freeman's Journal* (8 May 1847) of a Roscommon woman who had sought refuge for herself and six children in a night asylum in Dublin, is illuminating in this respect. She had been put into custody by the keeper for failing to account for a large sum of money in her possession. The magistrate evinced surprise at the family's condition, 'while she had so much money about her'. The following is the woman's account:

> She lived in the county Roscommon, and her husband held about ten acres of land, but he died last Shrovetide; she had no means of sowing a crop, and she gave up the place to a collector of poor rate, who gave her £15 for it; she got £5 for a mare, and £4 for a cow, 10s. for a cart and harrow, and more money for other things, and this made up all she had; she was about going to America, but she would not be taken with her children for less than £27.

When her eldest boy, a 13-year old, corroborated her story, the magistrate deemed it 'evidently true', and discharged her.

In a paper that assesses the impact of emigration on the famine, Kevin O'Rourke and I argue[15] that it was by no means an ideal substitute for other forms of famine relief in the 1840s. On the whole only those with some stake in the land could afford to emigrate, and such people were not at greatest immediate risk from starvation. The timing of the migration – heavier after rather than before the worst of the mortality crisis – also suggests that it was not ideally tailored to relieving the worst-hit. In the words of Robert Murray, general manager of the Provincial Bank of Ireland, 'the best go, the worst remain'.

Still, emigration reduced famine mortality. Moreover, though it did not target the poor as effectively as soup kitchens or even the public works, unlike them, its effect went well beyond mere crisis-management. In sum, though the famine emigration was part of the famine tragedy, mortality during the crisis would have been even higher without it, and in the long run it played an important role in increasing the living standards of those who stayed behind.[16]

Medicine men and fishers of men

In Ireland, medical historians traditionally devote far more attention to the doctors than to their clients. The famine fits the pattern: Sir William MacArthur and even more so Peter Froggatt[17] dwell on the commitment and heroism of medical personnel, at the expense of the fundamental point that medicine succeeded in saving few lives. The work of Laurence Geary, Joel Mokyr, and Joseph Robins[18] signals an overdue shift in focus from the medics to their patients and those who were too poor to pay them. Relatively few died of literal starvation during the Great Famine; dysentery, typhus, typhoid fever, and other hunger-induced infectious diseases did most of the damage. There was little that doctors could do. They understood the importance of cleanliness in the homes and yards of the poor and stressed the link between contaminated food or water and dysentery. Isolation in fever hospitals was their main institutional remedy for fever. But that was common sense, hardly science. The Dublin practitioner who mused in print whether 'the epidemic, like the ague, owes its origins to terresterial miasms' was closer to the truth than the editorial in the *Dublin Medical Press* that claimed that 'it could easily be shown that famine and destitution are more frequently the effect than the cause of fever' – but that is akin to comparing witchdoctors and alchemists. Indeed it was because Ireland's medicine men had no cure for infectious diseases that they died in large numbers themselves. How much difference would better medicine have made? Mokyr (1995) surmises that had the blight delayed its visitation by a few decades, the breakthroughs of Koch and Pasteur 'might have saved hundreds of thousands of lives'. But given the shortage of food, would the famished not simply have perished of something else?

In modern famines deaths are rare among doctors, clergymen and others concerned with relief. Not so in Ireland in the 1840s. The famine struck at a time of evangelical revival and renascent Catholicism in Great Britain and in Ireland. The resulting sectarian tensions were bound to influence charitable efforts in Ireland. In their contributions to Radio Éireann's series of famine lectures, Patrick Hickey and Irene Whelan offered new perspectives on the trade in food for souls by evangelical supporters of the established church, or 'souperism', but both conceded its limited extent. In some remote pockets, fierce competition between fishers of men may have benefited the poor, temporally if not spiritually. The unpleasant business of souperism has been adequately analysed by now, but more work on the role of the churches and the clergy as voices for the poor and distributors of relief funds is needed. In its analysis both of ecclesiastical high politics and of priestly action and activism at grassroots level Donal Kerr's study of the Catholic Church during the famine breaks new ground.[19]

Winners and losers

Research on the famine is still dominated by historians, with economic analysis playing second fiddle. The balance has been shifting, however (e.g. Mokyr 1985; McGregor 1989; Ó Gráda 1993: ch. 3; 1994a: ch. 8; O'Rourke 1991a, 1991b; Rosen 1999; Solar 1989a, 1989b). One of the most interesting analytical

contributions of 1995 was Amartya Sen's address to the international conference on famine and hunger organised by Ireland House, New York University
in May.[20] It turns out that Sen's entitlements model, which stresses the role of
distributional shifts instead of the lack of food in the aggregate in causing famine,
receives mixed support from the Irish case. In its simplest form, the model
implies a zero sum game. But a winners-and-losers approach to Ireland in the
1840s highlights the difficulty of identifying any substantial socio-economic
group of gainers *during* the crisis. The fate of the labouring and cottier classes
was death and emigration. The impact of the famine on landlords, though
often exaggerated, was also undoubtedly negative in the short run. Export data
suggest that farmers specialising in livestock were little affected by the potato
failure, but the majority of farmers, reliant on tillage and on potato-fed labour
and pigs, were surely hurt.[21] One group – that heterogeneous and numerous category straddling urban traders, small-town shopkeepers, and moneylenders – so
far remains almost untouched by serious research on the famine. Given the
antipathy to the mealmonger and the gombeenman in literary accounts, and
contemporary claims that some traders made fortunes during the famine, the
neglect is surprising. In an unpublished paper[22] that combines evidence from
business records with theoretical inferences based on market price data for
potatoes and grain I have suggested, tentatively, that traders and moneylenders
as a group did not thrive in the late 1840s.

Though few can have gained while the famine was raging, the emphasis in
Sen's model on the distributional impact is still useful, since suffering was by
no means equally shared. The privations of some better-off groups (landlords
and traders and farmers) provoked them into inflicting much greater suffering
on others (cottiers and labourers). Moreover, some, like workers and employers
in urban, export-oriented industries escaped lightly. The point needs making,
because sometimes the commemorations seemed to make vicarious victims of
the entire population of Ireland in 1995. Finally, the appeal of the entitlements
approach is boosted by placing Ireland in its contemporaneous United Kingdom
context. Despite the relatively poor grain harvest of 1846, in arithmetical terms
the problem of food availability in the United Kingdom as a whole was far less
serious, and contemporary data imply that the Irish crisis had very little impact
on overall public spending or long-term interest rates.[23]

Few would deny that once economic life returned to normal in the early
1850s, most famine survivors became winners in the material sense. Real
wages rose significantly in the wake of the crisis; for farmers, there were vacant
holdings, and the competition for land was less fierce than before; the

emigrants who were forced to leave were materially better off where they went. Folklore suggests that the gains were accompanied by feelings of loss, resentment, and guilt.

Representations

Though Edwards and Williams's classic *The Great Famine* (1956) included an excellent chapter by the literary scholar Roger McHugh on the famine in folk memory, its editorial introduction nonetheless reflected the reluctance of Irish historians to invoke folklore as evidence. Kevin Nowlan, who ghost-wrote the introduction, faulted folklore for representing 'the failure of British government...in a sinister light'. I have argued (in Ó Gráda 1994b) that the biases of the material gathered by the Irish Folklore Commission in the 1930s and 1940s are really quite different. Its concerns are almost exclusively local, and its antipathies are mainly local too. Folklore is rich in anecdotal detail, and very revealing on aspects of the famine such as excess mortality, conflicts between neighbours over food, and the potato before the blight. Moreover, its silences and confusions and evasions, when detectable, are also telling (compare Passerini 1979). Folklore, then, has something distinctive to contribute to our understanding of the Great Irish Famine.

The sesquicentennial prompted the broadcaster and folklorist Cathal Póirtéir to provide book-length compendia of famine folklore in English and in Irish. Most readers of both languages will agree that, page for page, the Irish-language material is more evocative and more informative.[24] Contributions by Terry Eagleton, Christopher Morash, and Margaret Kelleher explain how the famine is represented in Anglo-Irish literature.[25] While Eagleton notes a virtual 'silence' in the literature of the Anglo-Irish revival, Morash has drawn attention to many obscure works on the famine dating from the period before Yeats, Gregory and the rest. Morash's reminder that novelist and short story writer William Carleton's background was not as modest as implied in the boast that 'I have risen from a humble cottage and described a whole people' is a fruitful starting point for a compelling interpretation of how the famine transformed or transfixed Carleton's writing. Carleton's background explains his constant idealisation of the 'prosperous small farmer'. However, the famine switched him from being sympathetic to suspicious of the 'vagrant, gypsy brood' of labourers and beggars who outnumbered the small farmer in Ireland before the famine, and who would be the famine's main victims. And yet villains from such backgrounds provided Carleton's most memorable characters, and even in his post-1845 works they are often decent people.

When the famine struck, Carleton (1794–1869) worried that his depictions of it would lead to accusations of 'exaggeration' and 'fanaticism'.[26] In the event, though his reputation as a writer had rested on his 'authenticity', his muse failed him when it came to the famine. For Carleton the famine marked what Morash dubs 'the end of writing'. Morash's sophisticated journey through representations of the famine in literature ends with the warning that 'there can be no innocent narrative of the Famine'. A salutary warning to even historians who disagree.

To the chagrin of designers of book covers, contemporary representations of the famine in art are few. Perhaps this is because the famine silenced painters and illustrators, as it silenced Carleton. The much-reproduced engravings in the *Illustrated London News* offer an obvious exception. Their depictions of evictions, funerals and deserted villages ring true, though Margaret Crawford has analysed the failure of some of them to capture the horrors of the famine, remarking on the 'anatomical sturdiness' of the figures as reproduced. Yet perhaps a more plausible reason for the artists' failure was the thin market for graphic, disturbing images of suffering. Nor should the failure be exaggerated: Peter Gray's and Noel Kissane's search for illustrations yielded a surprising amount of unfamiliar material. Gray has also scrutinised the rhetoric behind contemporary cartoons, particularly those in *Punch* and similar periodicals.[27]

In 1995 the George Moore Society organised an interesting exhibition of modern representations of the famine in painting and sculpture. In his introduction to the exhibition catalogue, the art critic Brian Fallon mused that 'in some cases the connection may not be immediately obvious, in fact it may not be obvious at all'. Though the exhibition contained several striking and evocative images, it is probably fair to say that it was too pretty to convey the obscenity of famine.[28]

Ideology and relief

Amartya Sen has often argued (e.g. in Sen 1995b) that modern famines would be easy to prevent, given the political will. But was it that simple in Ireland in the late 1840s? Today the issue of the efficient transmission of relief from the centre to those at risk is a recurrent one in current discussions of disaster management. In a series of papers Mary E. Daly has made the case for such an understanding of the Irish famine, emphasising the victims' lack of 'voice' or influence in some of the worst-affected regions and widespread corruption and favouritism at local level (Daly 1986, 1995; but also Fewer 1995; Kerr 1994; Fitzpatrick 1995b). However, her support for such an 'agency' interpretation is tempered and, on the whole, the new famine history holds that for Ireland the problem was less institutional than ideological. Ireland in the 1840s was not Somalia; it was a peaceful place, and its police, coastguard, and civil service were almost corruption-free.

New research on the links between ideology and relief, in particular work by Christine Kinealy and Peter Gray, powerfully reasserts their role in Ireland in the late 1840s. Kinealy's exhaustive study of the operation of poor relief during the famine confirms that from 1847 on a combination of dogma, fiscal prudence, and 'a zealous determination to use the calamity to bring about long-term improvements in the economy of Ireland' won out over the requirements of those at immediate risk. In the 18 months following the transfer of responsibility to Irish Poor Law in mid-1847, London's contribution to Irish relief was minimal; its response to continuing mortality in 1849 was transfers from the richer regions of Ireland to the poorer. Kinealy links the increase in 'mortality, evictions, emigration, spiralling taxation and financial indebtedness' to the transfer to local responsibility.

One of the novel features of Gray's analysis of political ideology and the power of ideas is its emphasis on the providentialist aspect. With both God and Malthus on their side, influential ideologues like Charles Wood and Charles Trevelyan felt few qualms about minimalist intervention. Gray's conclusion, supported by a close reading of the evidence, is as unambiguous as it is brave. It is that the charge of culpable neglect is 'indisputable'; policy amounted to a 'death sentence on many thousands' (Kinealy 1994, 1995b; Gray 1994, 1995a: 103).

How many lives might have been saved in Ireland by a less constrained policy stance? Nobody had the answer in 1995, and we probably will never know precisely. In the circumstances, excess mortality was unavoidable. Yet in different ways the new scholarship of Kinealy, Gray, Solar, and others[29] reminds us that policy did matter, and that the human cost of policy failure in Ireland during the famine was considerable.

A 'no fault famine'?

Students of recent and contemporary famines are not shy about pointing the finger at 'guilty' parties. Amartya Sen blames moneylenders and speculators for famine in Bengal in the 1940s and Martin Ravallion blames them for exacerbating the crisis in Bangladesh in the 1970s. Alex de Waal notes that some 'analysis' of famine in Mozambique in the 1980s amounts to 'little more than a catalogue of Renamo vandalism'. Michelle McAlpin shows how timely public action prevented famine in Maharashtra in the 1970s, but Jean Dreze and Sen blame inept policy in Kenya for making things worse (Sen 1981: 76–7, 159; Ravallion 1987: 57; de Waal 1993: 33; McAlpin 1987; Drèze and Sen 1989: 91). And while Mengistu Miriam's Dergue is often, and rightly, blamed for the Ethiopian famine of 1982–4, a US congressman admitted in 1986 that it was partly America's fault too: 'the fact of the matter is, we made some tragic errors'.[30]

In Ireland, the issue of responsibility for the famine continues to raise some hackles and misunderstandings. Nationalist sentiment about the tragedy runs deep, and in 1995 Irish opposition leader Bertie Ahern and President Mary Robinson both argued that some form of retrospective apology or recognition of guilt on the part of the United Kingdom would help improve Anglo-Irish relations. Their pleas echo an abiding sense that the British policy-makers and British public opinion were to blame for the Irish famine.

Commentary on the famine has skirted around this issue of blame for half a century or so. The 'revisionist' reaction, beginning with Edwards and Williams (1956), offered a useful antidote to the wilder claims of 'genocide'. Yet in retrospect, and particularly in the light of the research findings of the last decade or so, the apologetic subtext of the 'revisionist' enterprise has also become clearer. In 1967 in a classic statement of the 'revisionist' position the late Rodney Green described the famine as 'primarily a disaster like a flood or an earthquake'. The comparison was hardly apt, not least because excess mortality in the wake of even the worst floods and earthquakes does not last for several years. Green invoked the analogy to suggest that there was little state intervention could have done, but he also emphasised the 'ramshackle' nature of Irish agriculture in 1845. Third, he defended administrative economy on the moral relativist grounds that 150 years ago parsimony and callousness were 'exhibited as much to the English as to the Irish poor'. As in most 'revisionist' analyses of the famine, Green combined arguments about administrative powerlessness, agricultural backwardness, and relativism with a tendency to question or talk down what was to be explained – the true death toll of the famine. In sum, the Irish famine was a no-fault famine (Green 1984: 273–4).[31]

Recent interpretations, based on more thorough research, support the finding that elites and policy makers could have done much more for the Irish poor. It does so in two steps: first it establishes the inept and equivocal character of Westminster's response to the famine and the lack of sympathy among middle-class Britons for the Irish, and second, it shows that these mattered. Moreover, as Gray, Kinealy, Kerr and others reminded us in 1995, criticism of the government was by no means limited to firebrand nationalists such as John Mitchel and William Smith O'Brien or to their supporters among later generations. Many humane contemporaries pleaded that more could and should be done. On this defining humanitarian issue, it is only fair to note that it is Mitchel and Smith O'Brien – for all their other warts – who emerge well, not the public opinion leaders or politicians of the day.[32]

Conclusion

The sesquicentennial commemorations clearly prompted a remarkable amount of research activity into the Irish famine. With few exceptions, the research reflected what I called some years ago a post-revisionist approach to the famine: placing the tragedy in its context of economic backwardness, but shedding the somewhat apologetic and sanitised stance of an earlier literature. The 'dry as dust' tone is gone. In other ways, the style has not changed that much: students of the Irish famine still prefer the narrative approach to the analytical, and tend to identify more with the humanities than the social sciences. Important exceptions such as Mokyr, Solar and Morash tend to be foreigners.

In approaching the true anniversary of Black '47, Irish famine research was in good health. Both the supply of and the demand for fresh information and new interpretations was greater than ever before. A few aspects are worth special attention. First, a good deal has been written about the political context, but we still know little about evolving popular attitudes during and after the famine (Daly 1986: 86–7, 114; Connolly 1995; Ó Tuathaigh 1995; Eiríksson 1997b.). The sources are plentiful: folklore, contemporary verse, letters, newspapers, and visitors' impressions offer ample scope for systematic content analysis.[33] Second, some of the gaps in our knowledge of famine demography are being filled by the study of parish registers, burial records, and hospital and workhouse lists. Yet much about the timing of excess mortality in different parts of the country remains a blank. Similarly, the complementarity or substitutability of mortality and emigration in the late 1840s deserve further study. Thirdly and more generally, Irish famine research stands to benefit from being more explicitly comparative, and from studying and experimenting with approaches applied elsewhere.

Notes

Introduction

1   Michael Ellman (2000) usefully distinguishes between FAD1 (FAD = Food Availability Decline) and FAD2 famines. Mortality during FAD1 famines is largely unavoidable, whereas alternative policies could reduce, if not prevent, the mortality associated with FAD2 famines. By this reckoning the Irish famine was a FAD2 famine.

2   For an excellent recent survey see Donnelly 2001.

3   The Irish Famine Network held a number of workshops and published Lindsay and Fitzpatrick 1993; Eiríksson and Ó Gráda 1995.

4   The sesquicentennial commemorations prompted the publication of dozens of local accounts of the famine, the best of them of very high quality indeed. Here is a sampling: Hickey 1993, 1995, 2002; Grant 1997, 2000; Ó Murchadha 1998; Grace 2000; Marnane 1996–7; Murphy 1996; Ó Canainn 1995; O'Neill 1997; McAtasney 1997a, 1997b; Cowman and Brady 1995; Ó Cathaoir 1994; Kinealy and Parkhill 1997; Kinealy 1996; Curtin 2000; Fitzgerald and Kennedy 1995; Swinford Historical Society 1995; Swords 1999; Cork Archives Institute 1996; Stewartstown and District Historical Society 1996; Ó Fiannachta 1997; Kinsella 1995.

5   Chapter 5 of Ó Gráda 1999 describes the impact of the famine on Dublin.

6   See also Guinnane and Ó Gráda 2002b; Guinnane et al. 2004.

7   For perspectives on famine emigration see Scally 1995; Laxton 1997.

8   A shorter version of the essay, with more references, appeared in Ó Gráda 1998. See also Ó Gráda 1995a.

9   Readers with a knowledge of Irish may compare Ó Gráda 1994b; Póirtéir 1996. See also Donnelly 1996b; Ó Ciosáin 2000.

10   The New History of Ireland Archive (c/o Dictionary of Irish Biography, Earlsfort Terrace, University College Dublin); Ó Gráda 2001c: 210. I am grateful to Richard Hawkins for allowing me to inspect the New History of Ireland material. On the history of the *Agrarian History* see Ó Gráda 2001c: 210.

11   Chapters 5 and 6 in the present volume both result from my own involvement in that Project, however, as do a study of the Enniskillen workhouse, co-authored with Tim Guinnane and Des McCabe (see note 6 above), and portions of *Black '47 and Beyond* (Ó Gráda 1999). The methodology behind Guinnane and Ó Gráda (2002b) was also inspired in part by the Project. The Enniskillen and North Dublin Unions were two of eight unions analysed in detail by the Project. Digitised versions of the workhouse studies conducted by NFRP

associates are soon to be mounted on the website of the Humanities Institute of Ireland at University College Dublin.

12 For other glosses on history writing in the 1940s and 1950s see Cullen 1997; Lee 1997.

Chapter One: Ireland's Great Famine

1 For new research on the origins of potato blight see Ristaino et al. (2001); Dwan (2004).

2 Malthus believed that cannibalism 'must have had its origin in extreme want, though the custom might afterwards be continued from other motives' (1826: Book 1, ch. 4). However, hard evidence of survivor cannibalism during famines is scarce. Its incidence remains an unresolved and controversial issue for historians, archaeologists, and anthropologists. It did happen: at the height of the Leningrad siege-famine between December 1941 and mid-February 1942 nearly 900 people were charged with cannibalism. The number of cases declined thereafter, and none was reported in 1943 or 1944 (Belozerov 2005: 223–4). However, culture mattered: at the height of the almost contemporaneous Bengali famine of 1943–4 the destitute in Calcutta refused even the bully-beef proffered by soldiers. The one instance of cannibalism described by a traveller through famine-stricken India in 1896–97 referred to a female member of an obscure flesh-eating caste who had been surviving on corpses left floating in a river, and it caused tremendous publicity in the area in which it happened (Merewether 1985: 213–24). The reductionist argument that cannibalism's absence in India is explained by the fact that destroying cattle would be destroying the community's capital ignores the strong free-rider context of famine.

3 Majendie had worked with Senior on the Poor Law Report of 1834.

4 The scandal of the 'Temple wage' (named after Sir Richard Temple, then Governor of Bombay) in India in the late 1870s offers an apt parallel (Hall-Matthews 2005: 192, 204).

5 I am grateful to Kevin Whelan for providing me with a copy of the Clare data. There was also a marked decline in the number of rapes recorded during the famine (Ó Gráda 1994a: 203).

6 Of course the increase in the number of workhouse inmates in the interim accounts for much of the rise.

7 This relative advantage of females during famines is a near-universal phenomenon (Macintyre 2002; Ó Gráda 2007: ch. 5).

Chapter Two: Poor and getting poorer?

The authors would like to acknowledge the suggestions of Robert Allen, Mary E. Daly, James S. Donnelly Jr, David Johnson and Peter Solar.

1 Recent work on real wages in Britain seems to indicate that an improvement was in fact taking place. See especially Williamson and Lindert (1983).

2 Bowley (1899) presented a series of Irish agricultural money wages for the century between 1791 and 1892. But for the pre-Famine period these data are based on scattered and incomplete information. Bowley relies on Arthur Young for 1777, the Dublin Society's *Statistical accounts*

for 1801–10, and various Parliamentary Commissions for 1830, 1836, and 1845. The figures were interpolated and 'adjusted' rather arbitrarily for unemployment. The accuracy and internal consistency of Bowley's series are thus in doubt. For what they are worth, they show that the unadjusted data are more or less trendless, so that declining prices after 1815 would have resulted in higher real wages. The data adjusted for unemployment present a far more pessimistic picture.

3   Recall, for example, Mill's devastating comments on British living standards, made in 1848. Mill (1929: 751) provides no quantitative basis for his claim.

4   See *Report of the Commissioners for inquiry into the condition of the poorer classes in Ireland* (PP 1836, xxxiii), p. 113.

5   Ibid., p. 121.

6   *Census of Ireland for the year 1841* (PP 1843, xxiv) (hereafter *1841 census*), p. 433.

7   Two other variables, the wage level of the poor and the quality of housing were also used as proxies for income. These variables were strongly correlated with the two reported in table 2.2 and gave qualitatively similar results.

8   This is not to say that the relation between changes in economic welfare and the prevalence of rural industry was invariant. Kennedy has argued that the plight of the linen weavers before 1840 has been exaggerated because they were able to make up for their reduced earnings by increased work hours. See Kennedy 1985: 8–9.

9   It stands to reason that the income-type variables measuring the level of poverty were endogenous to the other exogenous variables, thus introducing a simultaneous equation bias in the regressions. We therefore re-estimated the regression, using an instrumental variable technique in which we used all the exogenous variables plus population growth between 1821 and 1841, the proportion of population living in cities, and the proportion of land under cultivation (as a proxy for land quality) as instruments. The results leave the conclusions above unaffected, but suggest that when we obtain a correct coefficient on an income-type variable (e.g table 2.2, col. 6), the result is probably spurious.

10   O'Connell, 'Fourth letter on the repeal of the Union', NA, HO 100/L35/181.

11   For earlier attempts along these lines – with contrasting conclusions – see Martin (1840: v); O'Brien (1921: 575). After the first draft of this essay was completed, we learned of an unpublished paper by David Johnson, 'Consumption in pre-Famine Ireland'. Dr Johnson has graciously allowed us to use his paper and some of the arguments below were much improved by his work.

12   See O'Brien (1921: 36) and sources cited there. The extensive survey of tillage in Wakefield's *Account of Ireland* (1812) does not mention tobacco though there are brief descriptions of some minor crops like furze and onions. There is no mention of tobacco growing either in Mason's roughly contemporary *Statistical account* (Mason 1814–19). A witness before the 1830 Select Committee on tobacco growing confirmed that no tobacco was cultivated in Ireland before 1825. In 1829 about 500 Irish acres were devoted to tobacco: *Report from the S.C. on the growth and cultivation of tobacco* (PP 1830, x), p. 549. This figure is about consistent with that given in *A return of the number of acres of land under cultivation for the produce of tobacco in Ireland* (PP 1830, xxvii), pp. 93–8 which gives a figure of 461 acres. Output per English acre of marketable dried tobacco was 800–1,200 lb (PP 1830, x, pp. 557–8, 659), so that total domestic production was at most one million lb in 1829, which was about 25 per cent of legal imports. A

contemporary guess puts total Irish output at 840,000 lb in 1829 (ibid., p. 645, testimony of W. K. Dehany).

13 In 1812 Wakefield (1812: 11, 31) noted that tobacco was 'an article of great consumption in Ireland'. See also Mason (1814–19), *Statistical survey* (vol. 11, pp. 156, 363; vol. 111, pp. 448–9). The Poor Law Inquiry of 1836 included a special survey on the 'expenditures' of the labouring classes which mentioned tobacco as a necessary and common item in workers' budgets. One County Leitrim witness even claimed that he knew of 50 cases of labourers smoking common turf because they could not afford tobacco! See *Reports of Commissioners for inquiry into the condition of the poorer classes in Ireland* (PP 1836, XXXI), p. 24.

14 According to Newenham (1805: 325–6), 'With the exception of the labouring poor in and near Dublin, it [tea] is not to be found in one house out of one hundred belonging to that description of people in Ireland, nor in one house out of fifty belonging to the small farmers, nor in one house out of fifty belonging to farmers who hold a hundred acres.' References to tea-drinking in the 'drink' and 'expenditure' surveys of the Poor Law Inquiry are very rare. A few references to tea can be found in the Mason surveys, compiled in the 1810s. In most of these, the authors are quite explicit about tea being a luxury good. See Mason (1814–19), *Parochial survey* (vol. 111, pp. 194, 243–4).

15 An account of the number of hundred weights of sugar which paid duty for home consumption in Ireland from 5 Jan. 1780 to 5 Jan. 1830 (PP 1830, x); Customs and excise duties (PP 1829, xv), p. 378.

16 After 1789, tobacco was subject to the 'survey and permit system' by which the duties paid consisted primarily of excise taxes rather than customs. The advantages were allegedly a reduction in smuggling and better quality control. As a consequence, the collection occurred in the various parts of the United Kingdom, so that continuous import statistics exist for Ireland (and for Scotland) between 1790 and 1850. The separate series for tea and sugar end in 1829 and 1827, but the Drummond Commission reported Irish import data for a single year, 1835. See *Report of the Commissioners appointed to consider a general system of railways in Ireland* (PP 1837–8, XXXV). The Railway Commission data have been criticised in some detail in Solar (1979). Although Solar does not discuss the import statistics, his advice to check these figures against other sources seems to apply here as well. Such a check yields inconclusive results. The Commission reported data for 1825 as well as for 1835, and at least the former can be compared to other sources. The figures for tea and tobacco are equal or very close to the British custom statistics. The figure for imported refined sugar is the same as the custom statistics, but that for imported foreign sugar is about 8 per cent too low. The figures reproduced by the Railway Commission imply a decline of 33 per cent in Irish sugar consumption between 1825 and 1835. There is thus serious doubt about the reliability of these figures.

17 Johnson, 'Consumption', p. 2.

18 Before 1814 the Irish duty was lower than the British. After 1814 the duties were the same, but the bureaucratic nuisance of importing duty-paid tea into Ireland was compounded by the confusing alternation of the collection agency. In 1819 the duty on tea in Great Britain became an excise duty, and stayed so until 1834 when it was returned to the customs. In Ireland it switched from custom duty to excise in 1825 and back in 1834. See *Customs tariffs of the UK from 1800 to 1897* (PP 1898, LXXXV), p. 200. Later in the century, with the concentration of overseas

trade in Britain and the growing integration of the two countries, the problem of the importation of duty-paid goods may have become more serious, but since our sugar and tea consumption series end in the late 1820s and since the import of tobacco was not affected by this, there seems little reason for concern.

19 PP 1898, LXXXV, p. 184; Johnson, 'Consumption', pp. 6–7.

20 The general formula is B = (bk+i/e), where: B is the bias in the growth of income (measured as the percentage increase in measured Y when actual Y is constant and the quality of the good in terms of consumption value per lb increases one per cent); e is the income elasticity of demand; b is the negative own price elasticity; k is the proportion of quality improvement that is reflected in higher prices; o < k < I.

21 Prices based on a mean of the January and July prices as reported in the microfilmed appendix of Gayer et al. 1953. Tariffs from Great Britain, *Customs tariffs of the United Kingdom* (PP 1898, LXXXV), pp. 190–1, using the tariff on British plantation or American tobacco. Irish tariffs were substantially lower than British in the 1790s but were gradually equalised after 1800, and in 1811 the rates were the same.

22 'To those who bothered to peruse the statistics, it was quite clear that the amount of tobacco passing through the Irish customs, far from keeping pace with the great increase in population, was in fact declining. Yet nobody doubted that smoking was becoming more popular . . . this pointed to a vast trade in smuggled tobacco' (Williams 1959: 175).

23 Legal imports in 1793 were 1,777,000 lb; in 1794 they were 5,043,000 lb.

24 The full details of this estimation procedure are presented in an appendix, omitted here. See Mokyr and Ó Gráda 1988: 231–4.

25 The assumptions made were: (a) that *total* income in Ireland grew at the rate of growth of *total* income in Britain between 1790 and 1815 (reflecting Irish prosperity during the Napoleonic wars) and at the rate of population growth thereafter; (b) that income *per caput* grew throughout the period at the same rate as in Britain; (c) that income *per caput* in Ireland was dominated by population growth so that income *per caput* declined at a rate proportional to population growth; (d) that income *per caput* was constant. We also postulated income elasticities of 0.5 and 1.0.

26 The price data are calculated as follows: tobacco, tea and sugar prices computed as averages of January and July prices of the prices reported in the microfilm data appendix in Gayer et al. 1953. They are deflated by the 'best guess' consumer price index computed by Williamson and Lindert (1983).

27 An average decline is indicated by only one series, that for tobacco using version I of our smuggling procedure, a price elasticity of -0.2 *and* omitting the period 1790–4/1795–9. Since this series is triply biased in the pessimistic direction, it must be regarded as the ultimate lower bound for our estimate.

28 On this compare the *1821 Census*, pp. 29, 35 (2), 59, 61, and Brenan 1935: 210, 264–5, 277, 281, 314.

29 J. Logan, 'Schooling and literacy in the nineteenth century', unpublished paper presented to the Irish Social and Economic Society Conference on education and literacy, May 1983, p. 3.

30 *1841 Census*, p. 370 and *passim*. An added problem in making comparisons is that the pre-1841 data include a small but unspecified number of pupils in industrial schools.

31 *Second Report of the Commissioners of Public Instruction* (PP 1835, xxxiv). The commissioners' report gave enrolment and attendance for thousands of schools. A large sample suggested a ratio of 0.7.

32 *1821 Census*, p. xxx; *1841 Census*, p. 440. In 1841 deputies and assistants accounted for about one fifth of the total. It is assumed that in 1821 these were included in the total for teachers.

33 Indirect evidence of emigrants does not confirm major differences between emigrants and those who stayed behind. See Mokyr and Ó Gráda 1982.

34 The improvement in Leinster is roughly the same in rural and urban areas, though the *level* of illiteracy in rural areas was about fifty per cent higher than in urban areas. Because urbanisation was not very important, little in the movement in illiteracy is attributable to shift-effects.

35 On the importance of the Irish in the British army see Carsten 1983.

36 NA, ADM 139/1–89. Only Irish sailors were extracted from ADM 139/39–63. All 6,503 observations pertain to men measured between July 1853 and February 1854.

37 India Office Library, Files L/MIL/9/29–L/MIL/9/46.

38 For details of the samples and the computation methods used, see Mokyr and Ó Gráda, 'Living standards in Ireland and Britain; the East India Company army data', paper presented to the Social Science History Association meeting, St Louis, Oct. 1986.

39 The standard errors of the difference of means tests were .062 for the 21–30 age-group and .092 for the 21–40 group. A regression on a third-degree polynomial in age with a nationality dummy (Irish=1; non-Irish=0) yielded the following regression:

$$HEIGHT = 27.94 + 3.52AGE - 0.102AGESQ + 0.00093AGECUBED + 0.396IRISH$$
$$(38.27)\ (-31.84)\qquad (23.17)\qquad\quad (3.93)$$
$$R^2 = 0.4126;\ F(4,6498) = 1141.2$$

Figures in parentheses are t-statistics.

40 R. Floud, 'New dimensions of the industrial revolution', paper presented to the Social Science History Association meeting, St Louis, Oct. 1986; Mokyr 1988.

41 Despite the potato's fearsome reputation and the undeniable forebodings which some contemporaries felt about a possible pending disaster, food crises before 1845 were typically short lived and produced few excess deaths. See e.g. Ó Gráda 1993: ch. 1.

42 For instance, the Cork provision industry entered a period of decline after 1815. See Donnelly 1975: 45–6. The replacement of the processed meat and pork exports by live cattle exports after 1815 constituted a severe setback to these industries.

43 For a similar conclusion, based on the single parish of Killashandra, Co. Cavan, see O'Neill 1984: 97–8, 115–24.

44 A similar conclusion is reached by Kennedy 1985: 36.

OFFICIAL PUBLICATIONS CITED:

Abstract of the Answers and Returns . . . (of the 1821 Census) (PP 1824, XXII)

Customs and Excise Duties (PP 1829, XV).

Report from the Select Committee on the Growth and Cultivation of Tobacco (PP 1830, X).

An Account of the Number of Hundred Weights of Sugar which Paid Duty for Home Consumption in Ireland from Jan.8, 1780 to Jan. 5, 1830 (PP 1830, X).

A Return of the Number of Acres of Land under Cultivation for the Produce of Tobacco in Ireland (PP 1830, XXVII).

Second Report of the Commissioners of Public Instruction (PP 1835, XXXIV).

Report of the Commissioners for inquiry into the condition of the poorer classes in Ireland (PP 1836, XXXIII).

Report of the Commissioners Appointed to Consider a General System of Railways in Ireland (PP 1837–8, XXXV).

Census of Ireland for the year 1841 (PP 1843, XXIV).

Customs Tariffs of the United Kingdom from 1800 to 1897 (PP 1898, LXXXV).

Chapter Three: Bankrupt landlords and the Irish famine

We are grateful to L. M. Cullen, James S. Donnelly Jr, and W. E. Vaughan for their comments on an earlier draft.

1   No precise number is possible. An appendix to a House of Lords Inquiry into the Irish Poor Law in 1849 (BPP 1849 vol. XVI) returned a total of 21,437 estates, but over half of these were valued at less than £300.

2   e.g. Donnelly 1974–5: 106–7; 'Report of Richard Bourke, 15 July 1847', in *Papers Relating to the Relief of Distress*, 4th series (1847), 67 (reprinted in Irish University Press, *Famine Relief in Ireland*, vol. 2 (1968), 74).

3   The reference is to Mary Martin, who inherited the estate when her brother Thomas died from famine fever. Thomas had caught the fever when visiting former tenants in the workhouse. See Tim Robinson's introduction to Scott 1995: xi. An account in the archive of the Irish Folklore Commission describes 'a landlord named Freeman Dave of Castle Cor, Kanturk [who] is believed to have given all he had to feed the poor. His property was sold after the Famine' (Irish Folklore Commission Archive, Dublin, vol. 1,068, pp. 235–39).

4   *Thom's Commercial Directory* 1851; also BPP, 1845 App. 98.

5   Large 1966; Curtis 1980: 337; for an interesting case study of one hard-pressed landed family see O'Neill 1996–7.

6   A breakdown of the underlying data by barony is given in Eiríksson and Ó Gráda 1996.

Chapter Four: Famine diseases and famine mortality

This is an abbreviated and considerably amended version of a paper given at a conference on famine demography held at Les Treilles, France, 25 April–9 May 1999. The longer version is available as Mokyr and Ó Gráda 1999.

1   In his introduction to the Tables of Death (on which more below), William Wilde defined 'starvation' as 'Want, Destitution, Cold and Exposure, Neglect, Want of Necessities of Life', in Irish *Gorta*. He also suspected that some of those reported to have died of 'infirmity, debility and old age' belonged in the same category. See BPP 1856a: 518.

2   In this regard Ireland's good roads may have been a double-edged sword: although they made it possible to rush relief food supplies to starved regions, they facilitated the flows of disease-spreading famine refugees.

3   The instructions given to enumerators stipulated (BPP 1856b: cxxix) that 'the enumerators will observe the period over which the inquiry extends, in order to enter with accuracy the various persons who have died since the 6th June 1841, but who would, if now alive, be reckoned among the members of the existing families as relatives, lodgers, or servants, &c'. Since the form (p. cviii) stipulated that those 'who died while residing with the family' be included, institutional deaths should not have been included. It would be surprising if none were, but we don't deem this a major problem.

4   This follows from the fact that the death rate in a typical year in Ireland before the famine was about 24 per thousand. See Mokyr 1980.

5   The same phenomenon is illustrated by the report of cholera deaths; although cholera only reached Ireland in December 1848, the census reported 1,376 cholera deaths in the years 1841–7 (plus a further 2,502 in 1848). This must be in part a reflection of faulty dating, but it is also possible that some survivors confounded the epidemic with some other disease. The *1841 Census* similarly reports a steady stream of cholera deaths in the 1830s.

6   For a fuller account of the underlying assumptions, see Mokyr and Ó Gráda 1999.

7   This view is confirmed by simple regressions in which the various estimates of the degree of under-reporting are regressed on measures of the sum of mortality and outmigration and in which the coefficients were consistently significant and negative. The value of X is strongly and negatively correlated with total mortality, which suggests that death was a main determinant in the incidence of under-reporting, but because of errors in measurement and the appearance of the estimated people dead in terms on both sides of the equation, these estimates are suspect.

8   Thus in Thane, near Bombay, an Indian woman who had already lost two children through water-borne illnesses pointed out that 'to boil water consistently would cost the equivalent of $4.00 in kerosene, a third of her earnings'. In Nigeria in the early 1970s (when GDP per capita was £100–150) the cost per patient of fluids for treating diarrhoeal diseases was £4 using locally made fluids and £20 using commercial fluids. The greatest problem was getting the fluid to the patient or the patient to the fluid. See *International Herald Tribune*, 9 Jan. 1997; Brycesok 1977: 111; World Bank 1979: tables 1 and 2.

9   It bears noting that though the Irish famine killed mainly very poor people, many who were by no means poor succumbed as well. Indeed, the poor had built up some immunity to diseases such as mild typhoid fever, so that during the famine when fever struck the higher classes they were just as likely to succumb. At greatest risk were people such as clergymen, relief workers, and medical practitioners, whose work involved frequent contact with the diseased. In Ireland as a whole nearly 200 doctors and medical students died in 1847, three times the pre-famine average. Catholic and Protestant clergymen also died in large numbers (MacArthur 1956: 311; Froggatt 1989: 148–50; Kerr 1996: 22–5).

10   A good example of the state of medical science is provided by Wilde's analysis of scurvy. Wilde recognised the possible importance of the change in diet and the use of hard, dry-grain instead of fresh vegetables, but then added immediately that the two peculiar causes that more

than others contributed to induce scurvy were fluctuations in humidity and temperature and the 'moral depression coupled to inactivity'. See BPP 1856a: 513–14).

Chapter Five: Mortality in the North Dublin Union during the Great Famine
We thank Catherine Cox, Margaret Preston, and Peter Solar for suggestions and for sharing data, and Colin Pan for research assistance. Carolyn Moehling provided valuable comments on an earlier draft. We also thank seminar participants in the economic history workshop at UCLA for comments and suggestions. The underlying databases form part of the Irish National Famine Research Project. This paper was revised while Guinnane was a Visiting Scholar at the Russell Sage Foundation.

1   For more on this see Besley et al. 2004.

2   Comparing the total number of deaths in workhouses in 1845 (5,979) and 1846 (14,662) with those in 1847 (66,890), 1848 (45,482), 1849 (64,440), and 1850 (46,721), is instructive in this respect. On the early history of the poor law in Ireland see O'Brien 1982–3, 1985.

3   For more on this see Guinnane and Ó Gráda 2002b.

4   In mid-March 1847 the entire country contained workhouse accommodation intended for 93,860 inmates, 3,069 hospital places intended specifically for fever patients, and extra accommodation for 6,630. At that time there were about 120,000 inmates in the workhouses, including over 8,000 fever patients and another twelve thousand sick inmates. See BPP, HC 1847 vol. LV, 'Copies or Extracts of Correspondence Relating to the State of Union Workhouses in Ireland', 3rd series, 86–7.

5   Nicholls 1856: 325–6; BPP, HC 1847 vol. LV [863.], 'Copies or Extracts of Correspondence Relating to the State of Union Workhouses in Ireland', 2nd series, 7–13.

6   For a case study see Eiríksson 1998. That of the North Dublin Union (or NDU) is one of 17 surviving registers (and one of only five of them from outside Ulster) to cover the entire famine period. For a guide to surviving workhouse-related material see Lindsay and Fitzpatrick 1993.

7   NAI, BG78*, NDU board minutes 14 Mar. 1849. For more on the South Dublin Union see Burke 1987. For conditions in Dublin generally during the famine see Corrigan 1975–6; Cox 1996; Callaghan 1971; Ó Gráda 1999: ch. 5.

8   The Mendicity was located at Moira House, Usher's Island. It had previously been the home of Lord Moira, whose family let it to the Mendicity Society in 1826. After the takeover 'the upper story of the edifice was removed, the handsome gardens covered with offices; and every measure adopted to render it a fitting receptacle for the most wretched paupers' (Gilbert 1903: vol. 1, 400). Richard Hall, assistant poor law commissioner, claimed that the health of Mendicity paupers had improved when they were moved to the NDU (*Saunders' Newsletter*, 21 Oct. 1841).

9   Only four workhouses were admitting paupers before the end of 1840. They were Cork city (1 Mar. 1840), the South Dublin Union (24 Apr. 1840), the NDU (4 May 1840), and Londonderry (10 Nov. 1840).

10   Nicholson 1927: 6; NDU minutes, 12 Dec. 1845; 26 Nov. 1845.

11 At the outset the board had a protestant majority (*Saunders Newsletter*, 28 Oct. 1841). Alleged proselytism in both city workhouses was a recurring theme. On 6 May 1846 two North Dublin Union guardians proposed that 'the Roman Catholic religion not being the true religion we object to pay for the teaching of its doctrine'. See also Burke 1987: 87–92.

12 NDU minutes, 19 May 1842; *Saunders' Newsletter*, 4 Mar. 1841, 29 July 1841, 22 Oct. 1846.

13 In December 1841 a motion in favour of a beef dinner was passed by a big majority. See *Freeman's Journal*, 16 Dec. 1841.

14 Ó Murchadha 1998: 22, also pp. 158–60, 209–12; NLI, MS 7850.

15 Thus Clifden workhouse did not open its doors to paupers until March 1847 even though 'their special attention had been called to some recent deaths in Clifden from starvation', while in Castlebar the guardians blamed a lack of funds for their refusal to admit inmates while the workhouse contained only one-sixth of its capacity. See 'Copies or Extracts of Correspondence', 2nd series, 8–9; *Tenth Annual Report of the Poor Law Commissioners*, 43–4, 59–64.

16 'Copies or extracts of correspondence', 3rd Series, 10–11, 172–3.

17 NDU minutes, 20 Jan 1847; NDU minutes, 14 Apr. 1847.

18 The weekly data are given in the NDU minutes for the period (see note 10).

19 For an earlier application of duration methods in Irish economic history see Guinnane 1992. The model used in the present paper differs in some important respects.

20 Proportionality is itself an assumption; the model is semi-parametric rather than non-parametric. In applications such as ours, where a large fraction of all observations are censored, there is good reason for concern about whether the proportionality assumption is satisfied. David Shoenfeld (in 'Chi-squared goodness of fit tests for the proportional hazards regression model', *Biometrika* 67 (1989): 145–53; and 'Partial residuals for the proportional hazards regression model', *Biometrika* 69 (1982): 239–41) develops a widely used method for testing the proportionality assumption. The so-called Schoenfeld residual is the actual value of a covariate at the time of failure minus its expected value. If the proportionality assumption holds, the Schoenfeld residuals will not be correlated with duration. Schoenfeld, 'Chi-squared goodness of fit tests', reports formal tests of proportionality based on his residuals, and notes that these tests can be done graphically by examining the residuals for patterns of correlation with time. We have both computed the formal tests and examined the residuals graphically. With only one exception we reject the null of correlation with duration at the 99 per cent confidence level, and for the remaining covariate can reject the null of correlation with time at the 95 per cent confidence level.

21 The most likely cause for a correlation between the risk of death and the desire to leave would be some unobserved quality of the workhouse itself. For example, if we had a sample of individuals from multiple workhouses, and did not know which one they were in, this would be a real problem. Given that we have just the one workhouse's population this is not a problem.

22 We thank a referee for helping us to clarify our thinking on this matter.

23 Formally, this amounts to inducing seven strata. Inmates admitted in 1844 are in the first strata, those admitted in 1845 are in the second, etc. We initially worked with two strata, one for those admitted before the famine and one for those admitted after. The specification we report is a less constrained version of this approach, and, as we shall see, warranted by our findings. We discuss the details below.

24 We experimented with several specifications of age and other effects, and discuss these alternatives below.

25 Our data refer to burials in the 'general' plots. Our thanks to John Kinahan, secretary of Glasnevin cemetery, for allowing us to consult the relevant records.

26 On 1 July 1846 the guardians ordered an end to the use of potatoes in the workhouse (NDU minutes).

27 Our potato price data, which we owe to Peter Solar, are bi-monthly, but we assume that the price in even-numbered months is equal to the price in the preceding month. Solar collected a 'high' and 'low' series: ours is the average of the two, though this choice does not materially effect the outcome. The correlation over our period of the average price of potatoes with the average price of oats is 0.65 and with the average price of maize, 0.62.

28 That is, a test for the null hypothesis that all month dummies are jointly zero yields a very low chi-square value; for the version we report in table 5.2 it is 12.12 (p=.35).

29 The chi-square statistic for the likelihood-ratio test that age, age squared, and the dummy for elderly are jointly zero is 28.5 (p=o). There are two other blocks of variables included in our specification where some individual effects are not statistically significant, but we include them because they are part of a block of variables that is collectively significant. These are the health status dummies (chi-square = 29.7, p=o), the place of birth dummies (chi-square=17.5, p=0.00).

30 On the issue of gender and famine in Ireland and more generally see Fitzpatrick 1997; Ó Gráda 1999: 101–4; Macintyre 2002.

31 Guinnane and Ó Gráda 2002b puts the North Dublin Union and its experience in the context of all the poor law unions of Ireland.

Chapter Six: The market for potatoes in Dublin in the 1840s

Most of the underlying data were collected in connection with the National Famine Research Project in the mid-1990s. An earlier version of this paper was presented at the CORN/UCD Conference on 'The mid-19th century European subsistence crisis' held at the Humanities Institute of Ireland, December 2003. I am grateful to David Dickson, Ingrid Henriksen, and Peter Solar for help on various points.

1 Salaman 1947; Cullen 1968; Connell 1951; Bourke 1993a; Hoffman and Mokyr 1984; Mokyr 1981; Rosen 1999; Dwyer and Lindsay 1984; Solar 1989a, 1989b, 1997; Ó Gráda 1994, 1999; Mokyr and Ó Gráda 1996.

2 Before the famine Cork city held six regular potato markets, some of which operated almost daily. See Ó Gráda 1999: 147–9. For a general discussion of the potato before the famine see Bourke 1993a: chs 1–2.

3 Thackeray [1843] 1888: 129, 152. Thackeray's book includes four sketches of potato sales (pp. 90, 114, 130, 153).

4 Swift 1948: 364–5; *Post Office Dublin Directory and Calender for 1847* (Dublin, 1847), 547–8; Shaw 1850. In 1850 Dorset Street (Upper and Lower) contained six bakers, Francis Street four, North King Street six, and Patrick Street four.

5   *Statistisk Tabelvaerk, Ny raekke, 3. Bind* (Copenhagen, 1851) [reporting 98 employers or self-employed bakers, and 430 'helpers']; *1851 Census of Great Britain*; BPP 1852–3, vol. LXXXVIII (Part I) [c. 1691–I), 1, 8, 15 (for London); LXXXVIII (Part II) [c. 1691–II), 944, 1,018 (for Edinburgh). In the late 1840s there were about 250 bakers in Brussels paying the 'patent' tax, a charge that varied with the size of the business. Brussels had a population of 208,000 *c.*1850 (private communication from Peter Solar, 3 Sept. 1998).

6   T. C. Speer, 'Medical report containing an inquiry into the causes and character of the diseases of the lower orders in Dublin', *Dublin Hospital Reports*, vol. III (1822), 180 (as cited in J. Prunty 1999: 34).

7   Warburton et al., *Dublin*, vol. II, p. 1131.

8   At the height of the famine (16 October 1847) a market report in the *Freeman's Journal* contrasted the two or three dozen sacks on supply with a norm of 'three or four hundred' before the crisis.

9   *FJ*, 21 Dec. 1846; *DEM*, 21 Aug. 1846.

10 *DEM*, 21 Aug. 1840. However, as David Dickson has reminded me, they must have been mainly small-time operators since only one is described as such in *Slater's Directory* for 1846.

11 The *Mail*, a four-page broadsheet, appeared on Mondays, Wednesdays and Fridays. The *Freeman's* appeared daily, Sundays excepted.

12 Dwyer and Lindsay 1984; Rosen 1999.

13 *DEM*, 1 May 1840, 12 May 1843; 3 Nov. 1843; 14 Mar. 1845.

14 *DEM*, 25 June 1846, 30 Nov. 1846, 30 July 1847, 10 Sept. 1847.

15 *FJ*, 2 Sept. 1846; 16 Sept. 1846, 28 Oct. 1846, 21 Feb. 1849; *DEM*, 19 May 1848.

16 *DEM* (23 Oct. 1840) refers to dairy owners now requiring 'a great deal of coarse potatoes'.

17 Bourke 1993a: 107–8.

18 *DEM*, 26 Sept. 1845.

19 NAI, NDU minutes, 26 Nov. 1845 and 12 Dec. 1845.

20 *DEM*, 26 Sept. 1845; 25 Aug. 1848; 6 Sept. 1848. See also Bourke 1993a: 107.

21 The point about price elasticity must not be exaggerated, however. Note that in microeconomic theory, the sum of the own and cross price elasticities must equal the negative of the income elasticity of demand. Other evidence suggests that the income elasticity of demand for potatoes was low if not indeed negative (some have argued that the potato is a Giffen good). Presumably it was not as low in Dublin as in rural Ireland. Nonetheless, significantly positive cross elasticities would be needed to allow the demand elasticity for potatoes to be significantly less than zero.

22 Bowden 1967: 818; Flinn 1977: 492–3; Ó Gráda 2001b; de Maddalena 1950: 157–9; Ravallion 1987: 14; Ó Gráda and Jean-Michel Chevet 2002. For prices in Malawi in 2001–2 see www.fews.net/Malawi.

23 *DEM*, 24 July 1840, 17 Sept. 1840, 21 Oct. 1842, 4 Nov. 1842; *FJ*, 19 Feb. 1845.

24 *DEM*, 26 May 1841, 4 June 1841, 25 Feb. 1842, 4 Mar. 1843, 18 Mar. 1843.

25 *DEM*, May 1842, 16 Dec. 1842; 17 Jan. 1845; *FJ*, 24 Jan. 1849.

26 *DEM*, 30 Sept. 1842, 2 Oct. 1846, 11 Nov. 1846.

27 *DEM*, 7 Aug. 1846; *FJ*, 29 Oct 1847, 3 Dec 1847.

28 Hoffman and Mokyr 1984.

29 Ibid.; *Thom's Directory* 1848, 155.
30 Note too Bourke (1993a: 104–5) on the export trade in potatoes.
31 In Knight 1984: 94.
32 *DEM*, 23 Oct. 1846, 30 Oct. 1846.
33 For accounts of potato varieties before the Famine see Tighe 1801: 234–5; Bourke 1993a: 33–9; Ó Gráda 1994a: 86–9.
34 Bourke 1993a: 45; *DEM*, 10 Nov. 1848.
35 *FJ*, 9 Oct. 1840, 24 Nov. 1841. On the latter date Lumpers were quoted at 1s 6d to 1s 10d, droppers at 1s 8d to 2s. Perhaps 'dropper' referred to quality rather than variety. The *New Shorter Oxford Dictionary* defines 'dropper' as 'a shoot growing downwards from base of a bulb and itself developing a bulb at the apex'.
36 *DEM*, 19 Mar. 1841, 8 July 1842, 29 Nov. 1844.
37 *DEM*, 23 Feb. 1844; 29 Nov. 1844; 2 May 1845; 30 May 1845; 21 Feb. 1846; *FJ*, 25 May 1843.
38 *DEM*, 10 June 1845.
39 *DEM*, 19 Sept. 1845, 7 Nov. 1845, 14 Nov. 1845, 5 Dec. 1845.
40 Compare Ó Gráda 1993: ch. 3; McCloskey and Nash 1984.
41 Compare Bourke 1993a and Mokyr 1981.
42 *FJ*, 9 Sept 1846. However, Alexander Somerville, in his *Letters from Ireland during the Famine of 1847*, claimed that 'the disease is peculiarly a lumper disease – they have all failed' (1994: 37). See also Bourke 1993a: 39.
43 In the sense of George Akerlof 1970.
44 *DEM*, 21 July 1848, 1 Sept. 1848; *FJ*, 1 Sept. 1848. On 10 August the *FJ* cited *The Banner of Ulster* to the same effect. The *Banner* described the Lumper as a variety that 'a few years since [was] scarce fit for human food, but which high cultivation has greatly improved'.

Chapter Seven: Mass migration as disaster relief
1 Cited in Mokyr (1985: 38).
2 Ireland's population grew from 5 million c.1800 to 8.2 million in 1841 (Mokyr and Ó Gráda 1984).
3 The following few paragraphs are based on Ó Gráda (1999).
4 Mokyr (1985) used excess mortality rates, but these cannot be calculated at the baronial level.
5 The wage data were generously provided by Liam Kennedy. The excess mortality data are as described on pp. 131–3. County Dublin was omitted from the regression, for reasons given on p. 131.
6 A remarkable feature of the famine emigration is that women were about as likely as men to 'better themselves' through leaving, a pattern that has endured in Ireland till today. In the Third World today crisis migrations typically involve adult males; some abandon their families, but most offer a crucial lifeline in terms of remittances (Drèze and Sen 1989: 77–9).
7 The population had grown at just over this rate during the previous decade.
8 Adding potato variables to equation (1) on p. 128 above adds nothing to the regression: these variables are completely swamped by the wage variable, are completely insignificant, and in some cases have the wrong sign.

9   As a partial check on the sensitivity of our results to the emigration estimates, we also calculated emigration rates on the assumption that 200,000 births were averted during the crisis. These averted births have to be subtracted from our emigration estimates; the averted births were allocated between counties in proportion to deaths, and emigration figures were again calculated as residuals. On these assumptions, the correlation between emigration and deaths was -0.015, and the correlation between emigration and the emigration/death ratio was 0.726. Emigration was more weakly correlated with the explanatory variables in table 7.2 than before; otherwise the results were unaffected.

10   We ran the regression in equation (1), adding the log of the emigration rate to the right hand side. Controlling for wages, the partial impact of emigration on death rates was indeed negative, although the elasticity was low (0.1) and the coefficient only weakly significant (a t-ratio of -1.13). In addition, there is clearly a great deal of simultaneity in the data, which is why we do not want to lean on this analysis in the text.

11   Ó Gráda (1999: ch. 5) shows that mortality rates increased in Dublin during the famine, following the influx of immigrants from the countryside. For an analysis of how the famine emigration affected Lancashire, see Neal (1995).

12   There are other reasons why the famine had permanent effects on the Irish economy: for example, the potato blight persisted, reducing potato yields and increasing their variability for decades (Solar 1989a). This amounted to a negative productivity shock that reduced the demand for agricultural labour (O'Rourke 1994). Nonetheless, it is the pull of overseas labour markets rather than the push of domestic conditions that explains post-famine Irish emigration (O'Rourke 1991b).

13   Hatton and Williamson (1993) also find that it was the poorest who left after the famine, in a multiple regression framework.

14   The wage data are taken from Bowley (1899) and Fitzpatrick (1980), except those for 1836, for which we thank Liam Kennedy. Bowley's 1870 estimates for Clare and Roscommon were replaced by more plausible numbers.

15   For the pre-famine figure, see Mokyr (1985: 35); for the post-famine period, see Hatton and Williamson (1993: 575).

16   Although age-specific emigration makes such percentages difficult to interpret.

17   For further analysis of the connection between emigration and long-run demographic trends in Ireland, see Guinnane (1997).

Chapter Eight The New York Irish in the 1850s

1   The populations of the main cities in the US (in thousands) in 1800 and 1860 were:

	1800	*1860*
New York	60	814
Philadelphia	41	566
Baltimore	25	212
Boston	27	178
Brooklyn	5	267

On European cities see de Vries (1984: 270–8).

2 'John Burke memoir', New York Historical Society; Ellis 1960: 387–94; Eliza Quinn to her parents, in 'Letters from Irish emigrants and others', BPP 1849: 128; Mary Brown to Mary ?, NLI, Arnold Schrier collection.

3 For details see Ruggles and Sobek 1997; Duncan 1961.

4 The following are the mean OCCSCORES for male workers aged twenty and over:

Age	Irish	German	New York
20–29	26	24	28
30–39	23	26	28
40–49	23	26	28

5 In Joseph Ferrie's sample of antebellum immigrants, which links passenger lists and manuscript census data, less than one fifth of the Irish who arrived in the port of New York between 1840 and 1850 remained there on census day in 1850. See Ferrie 1997: 44–5; Ernst 1949: 188; Mooney 1850: 83–4, 93–4.

6 Details in *Tables showing the arrival of Alien Passengers and Immigrants in the US from 1820 to 1888* (Washington, DC: Treasury Dept., Bureau of Statistics: 1889).

7 Presumably unmarried parishioners would have been more mobile.

8 Stern 1997; Degler 1952: ch. 9; Ferrie 1997; *The Irish-American*, 26 Aug. 1849, cited in Ernst 1949: 62; Maguire 1868: 214–15, cited in O'Donnell 1999: 271.

9 Steinberg (1989: ch. 6) admits the role of marital status, but also claims that Irishwomen's choices were 'far more limited'. Service was merely 'a temporary expedient to allow them to forge new lives' (p. 166).

10 Diner 1983: 79–94; compare Lintelman 1991; Handlin 1941: 66–7; Byrne 1873: 37; Maguire 1868: 319. Infant mortality in tenements was twice that in private dwellings in which most servants lived (Citizens' Assocation of New York, *Report of the Council of Hygiene and Public Health* (New York, 1865).

11 Christine Stansell (1987: 157) claims that 'servants were, in fact, the only women workers who saved money'.

12 Charles Dickens, *American Notes for General Circulation* (London, 1842); George Foster, *New York By Gas Light* (New York, 1850); 'Ladies of the Mission', *The Old Brewery and the New Mission House* (New York, 1854), p. 34; Richardson 1970: 27; Stansell 1987: 74, 201; Gilfoyle 1992: 36–41; Hill 1993: 188–92.

13 Citizens Association of New York, *Report of the Council of Hygiene and Public Health* (New York, 1866), 77. This takes no account of tenement houses used by prostitutes. Thirty-five per cent of William Sanger's large sample of New York prostitutes were Irish. Some sense of the family backgrounds of the city's prostitutes may be gained from his finding that though two thirds of them were aged under 25, fewer than one in three had a father living, and fewer than two in five a mother living. See Sanger 1858.

14 Citizens Association, *Report*, 77; Groneman Pernicone 1973.

15 Ten of the 15 grooms from Tuosist married women from the same parish, and three more women from the neighbouring parishes of Bunnawn and Kenmare. Eleven of the twenty-nine grooms from Ahamlish married women from the same parish, and another four married women from neighbouring Drumcliff.

16　The rules of canon law seem to have been enforced, if not too harshly. About one couple in eleven had to produce a baptismal certificate or certificates, but several couples were also given dispensations for consanguinity or a mixed marriage.

17　Coale and Treadway 1986: 88, 105. I_f in New York State was 0.279, uncorrected.

18　As distinct from those assisted through rent rebates or sums granted in return for giving up their holdings.

19　Fitzpatrick 1984: 17–21.

20　On Strokestown and Ballykilcline compare Campbell 1994; Scally 1995; and Harris 1996.

21　Heather Griggs, 'Emigrant Bank and Transfiguration Church records as suplementary historical sources: a statistical analysis' (typescript, 1996), 37. Griggs's archaeological research concentrated particularly on a block of tenement houses in the Sixth Ward.

22　Ernst deemed the censal information 'of little statistical value, for obvious reasons'. Compare Ernst 1949: 217; Sanger 1858: 33–4, 576; Stansell 1987: 173.

23　An alternative measure of age-heaping, Whipples's index (defined as $P_{15} + P_{20} + \ldots + P_{35} + P_{40})/0.2(P_{14} + P_{15} + \ldots P_{42} + P_{43})$, also highlights the Irish tendency to age-heap. The apparent female advantage is an artifact of the female populations being younger. See Shryock and Siegel 1978: 116–17.

	Male	Female
Irish	1.98	1.79
German	1.44	1.37
New York	1.29	1.24

24　Isabella Bishop (*The Englishwoman in America* (1856), cited in Richardson 1970: 53) declared that 'probably in no civilised city of the world is life so fearfully insecure'. See too Snyder 1995: 298; Burrows and Wallace 1999: 637–8, 757–7, 838–40; Gorn 1987: 402–3; Monkkonen 1995, 2001; Gerrard 1853; David T. Courtwright, 'Violence in America', *American Heritage* 47 (1996), 38–51; Silberman 1978; Anbinder 1992: 107–8; Gurr 1989. For England and Ireland see Gatrell 1980: 342–3; *1841 Census*, 'Report upon the tables of death', 192–3.

25　New York Municipal Archives, Police Court Cases Dismissed, 21 July 1854–30 Sept. 1854 (Roll no. 165).

26　Monkkonen 2001: 143; Ernst 1949: 202–5; Board of Aldermen, *Documents*, 21 (2) (Dec. 1854), 970; Stott 1990: 251–3.

27　Ernst 1949: 57, 240; Richardson 1970: 90, 111–12; Gerrard 1853: 9; Monkkonen 2001: 128–30; *1841 Census*, 18, 22.

28　In 1852 a Cork-born carpenter, who had arrived in New York about two years previously, was able to earn $15 to $20 a week in piecework making packing boxes, allowing him to save $100 a year. However, his son shared the work with him. Another immigrant, Thomas Garry, was earning 8s a day in 1848 working on the railway in upstate New York. A Corkwoman wrote home in 1850 that carpenters could earn 7s British a day in New York. Taken together, these numbers imply earnings of $10–$12 a week for immigrant tradesmen or semi-skilled workers. John Burke arrived in New York in May 1847. He obtained work in a store where he was earning $9 a week some months later, 'which was rated very good wages'. See Ernst 1949: 67 (citing *Young America*, 24 Jan. 1846), 77–8; *NY Herald*, 30 Apr. 1854 (cited in Degler 1952: 74); Thomas Garry to his wife,

8 Mar. 1848 (in App. X, 'Letters from Irish emigrants and others', Gore-Booth letters in BPP 1849: 129); 'Letters from emigrants', *Annalecta Hibernica*; 'John Burke Memoir', NY Historical Society.
29 For anthropometric corroboration see Costa and Steckel 1997: 50–3.
30 Albion 1939: 418. In their report for 1855 the Commissioners of Emigration (*Annual Reports of the Commissioners of Emigration of the State of New York from the Organization of the Commission, May 5 1847 to 1860* (New York, 1861), 173–4) refer to the fall off in emigration in that year. For the case that anti-immigrant sentiment played a part in the decline see Cohn 2000.
31 Gallman 1969; Soltow 1975a, 1975b; Conley and Galenson 1998; Galenson 1998; Herscovici 1993; Ferrie 1997, 1999.
32 Walker 2000: table 3.

Chapter Nine: The famine, the New York Irish and their bank

I am grateful to Mr Donald Kelly, Vice-President, for access to the Emigrant Savings Bank archives at head office on 41st Street, to Tyler Anbinder, Marion Casey and Heather Griggs for sharing their knowledge of New York history with me, and to Máire Ní Chiosáin, Antoin Murphy, Des Norton, and Renée Prendergast for comments on an earlier draft. Most of the primary material referred to here is held in Room 238 of the New York Public Library. Some of this chapter describes the beginnings of a project on which I am engaged with Eugene N. White of Rutgers University.

1 See e.g. Boyer (1997: 65–8), and the sources cited there.
2 Black (1969) is an indispensable source on the pamphlet literature on the provision of saving and credit facilities for the Irish poor.
3 The property belonged to John Milhau, one of the original trustees. The contract was for a rent of $2,100 annually, with an option to purchase for $30,000. The Emigrant Savings Bank bought the property from Milhau in 1852.
4 Ernst (1994: 133) refers to one deposit of $10,000 in 1856, which I have so far been unable to locate.
5 The kind of information described here is does not exist for British (or Irish) savings banks in this period (compare Johnson 1985: 98).
6 This section contains material also published in different form in Ó Gráda 1999: ch. 3.
7 Citations are provided in Ó Gráda 1999: ch. 3.
8 I am grateful to Heather Griggs for a copy of this database.

Chapter Ten: The Great Famine and other famines

1 Mary Robinson's perspective on the Irish Famine is well captured in Robinson 1994.
2 Dublin-born Geldof was the leading light behind Band Aid, a charity organised by 169 popular musicians in support of Ethiopian famine victims.
3 For more on the famine in Dublin see Ó Gráda 1999: ch. 5.
4 For more on these issues see the various contributions in Dyson and Ó Gráda 2002.
5 For my own contribution to this debate see Ó Gráda 1999: ch. 2.

Chapter Eleven: Famine, trauma and memory
This is a slightly amended version of a paper read to a meeting of An Cumann le Béaloideas Éireann, 6 November 2000. An earlier draft was presented at the Dublin City University Conference on Cultural Trauma and National Identity, 28–29 April 2000. My thanks to Guy Beiner, Michael Laffan, Sarah Maza, Niall Ó Ciosáin, Tim O'Neill, Máire Ní Chiosáin, Brendan Walsh, and Nicholas Williams for helpful comments and to Professor Séamas Ó Catháin, head of the UCD School of Irish, Celtic Studies, Irish Folklore and Linguistics, for permission to cite manuscript material in his care.

1 Two of Mary Robinson's keynote addresses on famine commemoration are available online: http://www.irlgov.ie/oireachtas/Addresses/02Feb1995.htm; http://gos.sbc.edu/r/robinson.html.

2 On the issue of post-famine famines see O'Neill 1995.

3 BPP, 'Fifteenth report of the commissioners of national education for Ireland (for the year 1848)', [1066.] xxiii (1849), 3.

4 Compare Fentress and Wickham 1992.

5 Avril Doyle, in EC Humanitarian Office, *Ireland's Famine: Commemoration and Awareness*, Brussels 1996, 3, 7; id., 'Caint an Aire', in *Comhdháil an Chraoibhín 1996*, 6; *The Detroit News*, 20 Aug. 1995; Kevin Whelan, http://new-brunswick.net/Saint_John/irish/irish2.html.

6 *The Detroit News*, 20 Aug. 1995 (Michael Collopy); *Parliamentary Debates Seanad Éireann* (*PDSÉ*), vol. 152, no. 16, 27 Nov. 1997 (David Andrews); *Boston Herald*, 7 May 2000 (Stephen Jackson).

7 Doyle, 'Caint an Aire', 7; id., EC Humanitarian Office, 8; *Parliamentary Debates Seanad Éireann*, vol. 152, no. 16, 27 Nov. 1997.

8 Department of Foreign Affairs, *Irish Aid: Consolidation and Growth: A Strategy Plan*. Dublin, 1993: 10 (I am grateful to Monica O'Connor of the Department for a photocopy). The sums (in £1,000s) received by Trócaire and Concern in donations and church door collections, as given in their annual reports, were as follows:

Trócaire		*Concern*	
Year	Collected IR£	Year	Collected IR£
1993–4	4,937	1990	4,430
1994–5	5,299	1991	7,368
1995–6	4,920	1992	16,434
1996–7	4,936	1993	9,013
1997–8	6,377	1994	13,491
1998–9	7,541	1995	6,764
		1996	7,478
		1997	8,190

Note: Trócaire accounting years end on 28/29 February

9 Note, however, how in November 1963 Muintir Mhuigheo organised a lecture by Cecil Woodham-Smith about her experiences in writing *The Great Hunger* in aid of the Irish Freedom from Hunger Campaign (see chapter 12 below, note 32).

Chapter Twelve: Making famine history in Ireland in the 1940s and 1950s

I very am grateful to Kevin B. Nowlan, Thomas P. O'Neill, Ruth Dudley Edwards, Joyce Padbury and Patrick Lynch for sharing their reminiscences and for correcting me on several points. Austin Bourke, Louis Cullen, David Dickson, Ronan Fanning, Tom Garvin, Patrick Higgins, Michael Laffan, James McGuire, Peter Neary, Tim O'Neill, Gearoid Ó Tuathaigh and Kevin Whelan provided useful comments. The standard disclaimer applies with greater force than usual.

1   R. Dudley Edwards's academic diary, Dec. 1954. I am very grateful to Ruth Dudley Edwards for allowing me to consult and quote from her father's diary. Subsequent references are to the diary are given as 'RDE'.
2   NAI, D/T S. 13626.
3   Ibid.
4   On Oliver MacDonagh's academic career, see Tom Dunne's tribute in F. B. Smith (ed.), *Ireland, England and Australia: Essays in Honour of Oliver MacDonagh* (Cork and Canberra, 1991), pp 1–13. On Kevin Nowlan, *Report of the President, University College Dublin 1985–6*, pp 159–60; on Roger McHugh, *Report of the President, University College Dublin 1977–8*, pp 125–6; on Rodney Green, see the memoir by R. D. C. Black in *Irish Economic and Social History* 8 (1981), 5–7. Moody had invited Michael Yeats, then a student in TCD, to participate, but Yeats opted for a legal career instead.
5   Moloney had completed his MA in history before embarking on medical studies. MacArthur's lecture to the Irish Historical Society on 'The identification of some pestilences recorded in the Irish Annals' (subsequently published in *Irish Historical Studies* 6 (1948–9), 169–99) was not quite germane to the Great Famine, but he had recently published 'Famines in Britain and Ireland', *Journal of the British Archaeological Association* 3rd ser. 9 (1944), 66–71.
6   Comhairle le Béaloideas Éireann, Annual Report 1945–6, p. 4; minutes of meetings, 22 June 1945 and 1 Feb. 1946. The replies are to be found in Irish Folklore Commission MSS 1068–75 and 1136. I am grateful to Séamas Ó Catháin for showing me the relevant CBÉ files.
7   James Carty, a member of ICHS, probably provided the link with Cahills. His brother Francis, later editor of *The Sunday Press* and *The Irish Press*, worked for the firm at the time.
8   NAI, D/T S. 13626. T. Ó Raifeartaigh to An Rúnaí, Roinn an Taoisigh, 17 Aug., 1950.
9   From this time on, the famine project would become basically a UCD affair, while Moody's colleagues and students would monopolise the Faber & Faber series of monographs. I am grateful to Gearoid Ó Tuathaigh for pointing this out.
10 On the proposed school of historical research see Edward MacLysaght, *Changing Times* (Gerards Cross, Bucks, 1978), pp 167–70.
11 'Tenth Annual Report of the ICHS', *IHS* 6 (1948–9), 67. O'Doherty, a friend of Dudley Edwards and editor of the *ICHS Bulletin*, was clever and by all accounts a kind man; he died in Strabane in May 1954. On Williams see James McGuire's Obituary in *Irish Historical Studies* 26 (1988) 3–7; on Edwards, Aidan Clarke's in ibid., 121–7.
12 RDE, 22 Dec. 1951.
13 RDE, 29 Oct. 1952. Green's footnotes suggest that he consulted no manuscript sources. Edwards also noted (15 Dec. 1953): 'Reading Rodney Green's section on Agriculture one can

now see precisely how much better it could have been if he had attempted to reconstruct the sources. It is clear enough in talking to him that he realises this and as he says no one has yet attempted a systematic study of an Irish estate so that the work suffers from being a study surveyed before the real ground work has been surveyed.' T. P. O'Neill recalls being asked to rephrase a few sentences in response to Connell's comments.

14 RDE, 23 Dec. 1954.

15 Much of it was published elsewhere, e.g.: 'The Society of Friends and the Great Famine', *Studies* xxxix (1950), 203–13; 'Sidelights on proselytism', *Irish Ecclesiastical Record* (1951).

16 RDE, 23 Oct. 1951; 21 July 1955.

17 R.B. McDowell remembers a genial meeting with James Meenan in a Dublin club to discuss the allocation of subject matter. Meenan mirthfully conceded all requests from McDowell for topics that the latter wanted included in his own chapter.

18 RDE, 17 Nov. 1951, 22 Dec. 1951. Moody had suggested Duncan and Black ('now lecturing in economics in Queen's and a TCD prodigy ten years ago') to Edwards. Edwards (23 Oct. 1951) had also considered including a brief section on education from W. J. Williams, recently retired professor of education in UCD, and father of Desmond Williams.

19 *IHS* 8 (1952–3), 162.

20 See the memoir of Maureen McGeehin by Tom Dunne in Gerard O'Brien (ed.), *Catholic Ireland in the Eighteenth Century: The Collected Essays of Maureen Wall* (Dublin, 1989).

21 Lee 1990: 590, incorrectly attributes the 'short, brilliant introduction' to Williams and Edwards.

22 I owe this reference to the late T. P. O'Neill.

23 RDE, 22 Dec. 1954.

24 Edwards and Williams, pp vii, 126, 255, 312. This is noted in Mokyr 1983: 263. The issue of excess mortality has been addressed several times since; see Mokyr 1980; Boyle and Ó Gráda 1986.

25 Several accounts of how the footnotes went 'missing' survive, but I am assured by Paddy Lynch that this is the correct one! Margaret Crawford tells me that MacArthur derived much of his information from articles by William Wilde in the *Dublin Quarterly Journal of Medical Science* (vii (1849), 64–126, 340–404; viii (1849), 1–86, 270–339), and Wilde's better-known contributions to the 1851 population census. Crawford's own 'Epidemic diseases in the Great Famine of Ireland 1845–50' (presented at the Famine and Disease Conference, Christ's College, Cambridge, July 1991) builds on and in part supersedes MacArthur chapter. MacArthur was accorded every facility while working on his chapter in Dublin. Two cartons of the Chief Secretary's papers were temporarily transferred from the State Papers Office to the National Library for his use, but he hardly used them in the end.

26 It is clear from his diary that Dudley Edwards in these years worried a good deal about writer's block. James McGuire tells me that Edwards later on would recommend a work diary as a cure for this problem.

27 The reference is to the works by Canon O'Rourke (1902) and W. P. O'Brien (1896).

28 e.g. in the *Irish Times*, 11 Jan.1957 by F. S. L. Lyons; in *IHS* 11 (1958–9), 60–4 by Nicholas Mansergh; in *History* 42 (1957), 155–6 by Norman Gash; in the *American Historical Review* 63 (1957–8) by Helen Mulvey; in the *English Historical Review* 73 (1958), 316–18 by W. L. Burn.

29 D/T S.13605.

30 I am grateful to the late T. P. O'Neill for this information.

31 By 1987 hardback sales in Britain had reached 45,225, book clubs sales 5,634, and export sales 4,304 (letter from Hamish Hamilton to author, 16 Mar. 1987). In the United States, Woodham-Smith topped *Time Magazine*'s bestseller list for several weeks. Penguin issued a new reprint in 1991.

32 The lecture was organised by Muintir Mhuigheo in aid of the Irish Freedom from Hunger Campaign (*Irish Times*, 9 Nov. 1963). The Woodham-Smiths had been frequent visitors to Mayo from the 1940s. For de Valera's views on Woodham-Smith I am grateful to T. P. O'Neill and Máirtín Ó Flatharta (de Valera's private secretary for several years).

33 Ireland had featured largely in *The Reason Why: A Behind-the-Scenes Account of the Charge of the Life Brigade* (London 1953), and indeed Woodham-Smith's interest in the Famine was prompted by her study of the papers of Lord Lucan of Crimean War fame. Michael Egan, custodian of the Lucan papers in Castlebar, also introduced Woodham-Smith to some Mayo workhouse material. The oversimplified model of the pre-famine economy presented in *The Reason Why* reappears in *The Great Hunger*. Though not an academic historian, Woodham-Smith was a formidable researcher. Much of her work was based on previously unused archival material.

34 It was therefore rather churlish of Leland Lyons to take Woodham Smith to task for singling out Dudley Edwards in her acknowledgements, and ignoring Williams. Edwards was an old friend by 1962, while Williams could hardly claim to be an authority on the famine. See F. S. L. Lyons, review of *The Great Hunger*, *IHS* 14 (1964–5), 76.

35 RDE, 31 Oct. 1955; see also 3 Jan. 1954.

36 Woodham-Smith stuck to her guns: 'the Famine left hatred behind. Between Ireland and England the memory of what was done and endured has lain like a sword' (1962: 412).

37 Australian academic historians have made analogous criticisms of another 'epic international bestseller', Robert Hughes's *The Fatal Shore: A History of the Transportation of Convicts to Australia 1787–1868* (London 1987).

38 Roy Foster, 'We are all revisionists now', *Irish Review* 1 (1986), 3; Ó Gráda (1989: 10–11).

39 F. S. L. Lyons, reviews of Edwards and Williams, *The Great Famine*, in the *Irish Times*, 21 January 1957, and of Cecil Woodham Smith, *The Great Hunger*, in *IHS* 14 (1964–5), 76–78. Woodham-Smith is not cited at all in Lyons's *Ireland Since the Famine* (London 1971). *The Great Hunger*, a 'trade' book, was less widely reviewed in the professional journals than *The Great Famine*. See, however, the reviews by Kevin Nowlan, *Studia Hibernica* 3 (1963), 210–11; Francis Finnegan, *Studies* 52 (1963), 329–31; E. A. J. Johnson, *Journal of Economic History* 24 (1964), 120–1.

40 The usefulness of parish registers as a source for historians had recently been brought home by Domhnall Mac Cárthaigh, 'Marriage and birth rates for Knockainy Parish, 1882–1941', *Cork Historical and Archaeological Society Journal* XLVII (1942).

41 Compare J. A. Robins, 'Charter school and poor law records', *Irish Archives Bulletin* 3 (1) (1976): 2–6.

42 As T. P. O'Neill recounted to the author: 'To get access to any official papers was an achievement and one was hemmed in by regulations. All my notes had to be left behind to be

"vetted" by the Keeper of State Papers before I could take them out of the building. What I was allowed to take was censored. This happened in regard to information regarding a landlord who refused to subscribe to a local relief committee – he was Lord Conyngham who held vast estates in Donegal and Clare as far as I recollect' (T. P. O'Neill to author, 6 June 1991).

43 Edwards and Williams (1956: xv).

44 Dunne, MacDonagh tribute, pp. 2–3 (see note 4 above).

45 RDE, 20 Jan. 1952. The reference to 'Butterfield' was to Herbert Butterfield of Peterhouse, Cambridge.

46 RDE, 27 July 1952. E. C. Large, *Advance of the Fungi* (London 1940).

47 The references here are to William Carleton, *The Black Prophet* (Dublin 1847) and Liam O'Flaherty, *Famine* (London, 1937).

48 RDE, 11 Sept. 1952.

49 RDE, 5 Mar. 1954. The reference is to T. O'Herlihy CM., *The Famine 1845–1847: Ravages and Causes* (Drogheda 1947).

51 RDE, 28 Dec. 1954.

52 A recent case in point: Rionach Uí Ogáin's *An Rí Gan Choróin* (Dublin 1987), the most comprehensive study to date of 'the Great Dan' in folklore, has been ignored by historians.

53 T. P. O'Neill to author, 6 June 1991.

54 Edwards and Williams 1956: viii; Brendan Bradshaw, 'The emperor's new clothes', *Fortnight* (Supplement on 'Free Thought in Ireland'), no. 297 (1991), 18.

55 Timothy P. O'Neill, 'The famine of 1822' (unpublished MA thesis, UCD, 1965); Maurice A. Trant, 'Government policy and Irish distress 1816–19' (unpublished MA thesis, UCD, 1965); Dennis M. O'Sullivan, 'The causes, development and relief of distress in Mayo in 1831' (unpublished MA thesis, UCD, 1968).

Chapter Thirteen: Making famine history in Ireland in 1995
I wrote this paper while Visiting Professor at Ireland House, New York University, in spring 1996. The useful comments of David Dickson, Jim Donnelly, Joseph Lee, and Kevin Whelan on an earlier draft are gratefully acknowledged.

1 The BBC and RTÉ each produced a useful documentary series, and they co-produced a teledrama. RTE's documentary series attracted a weekly audience of nearly half a million, and a book based on Radio Éireann's series of lectures on the famine is now in its fourth printing. The music ranged from a popsong by Sinéad O'Connor to a famine suite by Charlie Lennon.

2 John Boland in the *Sunday Business Post*, 26 Nov. 1995; Eddie Holt in the *Irish Times*, 30 Dec 1995

3 The sesquicentennial also prompted the reprint of a classic study of the famine (Edwards and Williams 1956) in 1994, and the appearance in book form of Alexander Somerville's *Letters from Ireland during the Famine of 1847* (Somerville 1994).

4 Sen 1995a; Boyce 1982: 170. I am grateful to Joseph Lee for alerting me to Boyce's claim. On the earlier historiography see chapter 12 above. The excellent magazine *History Ireland* has run several short pieces on the famine and famine historiography, e.g. Gray 1993; Donnelly

1993; Kinealy 1995b. 'Revisionist' textbooks now have some catching up to do, though certainly no more than the unreconstructed supporters of 'genocide' interpretations of the 'Great Starvation' active in the United States. The range is represented by Boyce 1990: ch. 4, and Ray O'Hanlon, 'Famine curriculum taking roots in States', *Irish Echo*, 21–27 Feb., 1996.

5   Until very recently, Bourke and the late T. P. O'Neill were the only historians in Ireland to focus their researches for more than a short period on aspects of the famine. Niall Ó Ciosáin's trawl of the pre-1960 literature (Ó Ciosáin 1995–6) yielded only Edwards and Williams's commissioned volume, which would not have emerged at all but for government funding and repeated prodding from civil servants, and a series of articles by O'Neill.

6   Solar 1997; Gray 1997.

7   Robinson 1994; McClean 1988; Ó Gráda 1998.

8   Cowman and Brady 1995; Grant 1990; Hickey 1993, 1995: Kierse 1984; McAtasney 1997; Vincent 1992; Ó Gráda 1995b; Ó Canainn 1995; Yager 1996. Also relevant is O'Neill 1995.

9   The Network published two source guides for researchers: Lindsay and Fitzpatrick 1993, and Eiríksson and Ó Gráda 1996. See also Cosgrove 1995.

10   The project directors were David Dickson, David Fitzpatrick, Mary E. Daly, and this writer.

11   Donnelly 1975, 1989, 1995; Eiríksson and Ó Gráda, chapter 3 above; Vaughan 1994: 28.

12   Eiríksson and Ó Gráda: chapter 3 above; Lyons 1993; see also Robinson (ed.) 1995.

13   See also Ó Laighin 1995.

14   For more on the migrants see Glazier et al. 1989; MacDonagh 1956.

15   Reprinted as chapter 7 above.

16   Hatton and Williamson 1993; Fitzpatrick 1995a. See also the special issue of *New York Irish History*, 9 (1995), 'The Great Hunger's impact on New York City'.

17   MacArthur 1956; Froggatt 1989; 'Doctors in the Great Famine', *The Recorder* 8 (2) 1995: 1–9.

18   Geary 1995, 1997; Mokyr and Ó Gráda 1999; Robins 1995: chs 6–10.

19   Whelan 1995; Kerr 1994; Hatton 1994; Goodbody 1995; on the Irish Christian Brothers, see Ó Cearbhaill 1996.

20   Sen 1995a; see also Sen 1981.

21   This leaves out of account the impact of largely exogenous shocks such as high corn prices in late 1846 and early 1847 and an outbreak of liver fluke in 1848.

22   'Traders and the Great Famine'.

23   Reflecting the historian Brian Inglis's judgement that 'if the British chose not to consider Ireland as part of Britain, when such an emergency arose, they could hardly complain if the Irish did likewise' (1956: 140).

24   Póirtéir 1995b, 1996. See also Lysaght 1996; Cumiskey 1994–5. The impact of the famine on the fate of the Irish language is a topic that would repay further study. See de Fréine 1995. Though certainly in relative decline, the number of Irish speakers in 1845 was probably at an all-time high.

25   Eagleton 1995; Kelleher 1995; Morash 1995, 1989. Nic Eoin (1995) offers an excellent survey of literature on the famine in Irish.

26   Ironically, graphic accounts of famine suffering by Cecil Woodham-Smith and Robert Kee would lead to similar accusations over a century later. On Carleton see also King 1995.

27 Gray 1993, 1995; Kissane 1995; see also Whelan 1995b.

28 Crawford 1994; The George Moore Society, *Famine* (n.p., 1995). Compare the paintings produced in 1945 to mark the famine's centenary, reproduced in Ó Gráda 1994b. For some scepticism on the broader theme of silence see Ó Ciosáin 1995–6.

29 Kinealy 1994; Gray 1994, 1995, 1997; Solar 1997. Post (1985) links variations in excess mortality to differences in relief regimes.

30 Representative Howard Wolpe of Michigan, cited in J. Shepherd, 'Some tragic errors': American policy and Ethiopian famine, 1981–5', in J. O. Field (ed.), *The Challenge of Famine: Recent Experience, Lessons Learned* (Hartford, Conn., 1993), p. 88.

31 Compare Mary E. Daly's plea (1986: 113) that 'it does not appear appropriate to pronounce in an unduly critical fashion on the limitations of previous generations' and similar claims in Boyce 1990: ch. 4.

32 The print media are full of examples; two from the Tory *Cork Constitution* must do here. Variants of the plea made at a meeting of Fermoy Union in early November 1846 that ministers 'gave twenty million to emancipate the slaves, who were never so much to be pitied as the people of this country are at present' were commonplace at the time (*Cork Constitution*, 7 Nov. 1846). The Skibbereen correspondent who 'could not help thinking how much better it would be to afford [the poor] some temporary relief in their own homes during this severe weather, than thus to sacrifice their lives to carry out a miserable project of political economy' (*Cork Constitution*, 17 Dec. 1846) was anticipating the criticisms of modern historians such as Kinealy and Gray. See also Kerr 1994: 63; Ó Gráda 1993: 104, 132–3; Kinealy 1994: 348; PRO, T.64.366.A, 21 Jan 1849. For recent glosses on Mitchel see Morash 1995: 59–75; Ó Ciosáin 1995; Newsinger 1996.

33 Some of whom detected hatred and anger (for example, Balch 1850: 206, 214; Osborne 1850: 201–5).

Bibliography

Adamets, S. 2002. 'Famine in nineteenth and twentieth century Russia: mortality by age, cause and gender', in Dyson and Ó Gráda, *Famine Demography*, pp. 158–80.

Adams, William Forbes. 1932. *Ireland and Irish Emigration to the New World from 1815 to the Famine*. New Haven: Yale University Press.

Akenson, D. H. 1970. *The Irish Education Experiment*. London: Routledge & Kegan Paul.

Akerlof, George. 1970. 'The market for lemons: quality uncertainty and the market mechanism'. *QJE* 84: 488–500.

Albion, Robert G. 1939. *The Rise of New York Port, 1815–1860*. New York: Scribner.

Alter, George, Claudia Goldin and Elyse Rotella. 1994. 'The savings of ordinary Americans: the Philadelphia Saving Fund Society in the mid-nineteenth century', *JEH* 54 (4): 735–67.

Anbinder, Tyler. 1992. *Nativism and Slavery: The Northern Know Nothings and the Politics of the 1850s*. New York: OUP.

Anbinder, Tyler. 2001. *Five Points: The Nineteenth-century New York City Neighbourhood that Invented Tap Dancing, Stole Elections and Became the World's Most Notorious Slum*. New York: Free Press.

Anbinder, Tyler. 2002. 'From famine to Five Points: Lord Lansdowne's tenants encounter North America's most notorious slum', *American Historical Review* CVII (2): 351–87.

Anon. 1854. *Brief Notes of a Short Excursion in Ireland, in the Autumn of 1852, by the Editor and Sole Proprietor of the Hull Advertiser*. London: Whittaker.

Ashton, T. S. 1948. *The Industrial Revolution*. Oxford: OUP.

Balch, William Stevens. 1850. *Ireland as I Saw It: The Character, Condition, and Prospects of the People*. New York: Putnam.

Barber, John and Andrei Dzeniskevich. 2005. *Life and Death in Leningrad, 1941–44*. London: Palgrave Macmillan.

Beiner, Guy. 1999. 'Bodhaire Uí Laoghaire: oral history and contemporary Irish historiography', *PaGes: Postgraduate Research in Progress* 6: 9–21.

Belozerov, Boris. 2005. 'Crime during the siege', in Barber and Dzeniskevich, *Life and Death in Leningrad*, pp. 213–28.

Bennett, William H. 1932. 'A chronological history of the Emigrant Industrial Saving Bank' (Emigrant Savings Bank Archives, New York).

Bertrand, Marianne, Erzo F. P. Luttmer and Sendhil Mullainathan. 2000. 'Network effects and welfare cultures', *QJE* 115 (3): 1019–55.

Besley, T., S. Coate, and T. W. Guinnane. 2004. 'Understanding the workhouse test: information and poor relief in nineteenth-century England', in T. W. Guinnane and W. Sundstrom (eds), *History Matters*. Stanford: Stanford UP, pp. 245–70.

Bishop, Isabella. 1856. *The Englishwoman in America*. London: John Murray.

Black, R. D. C. 1960. *Economic Thought and the Irish Question 1817–1870*. Cambridge: CUP.

Black, R. D. C. 1969. *A Catalogue of Pamphlets on Irish Subjects Published between 1750 and 1900 and Now Housed in Irish Libraries*. New York: Kelley.

Borch-Jacobsen, M. 2000. 'How a fabrication differs from a lie', *London Review of Books*, 22 (8), 13 Apr.: 3–7.

Borjas, Geroge. 1995. 'Ethnicity, neighbourhooods, and human capital externalities', *American Economic Review* LXXXV: 365–90.

Boss, L. P., M. J. Toole, and R. Yip. 1994. 'Assessments of mortality, morbidity, and nutritional status in Somalia during the 1991–1992 famine', *Journal of the American Medical Association* 272: 371–6.

Bourke, P.M.A. 1968. 'The use of the potato crop in pre-famine Ireland', *JSSISI* XII (6): 72–96.

Bourke, Austin. 1993a. *The Visitation of God? The Potato and the Irish Famine*. Dublin: Lilliput.

Bourke, Austin. 1993b. 'The Irish grain trade, 1839–48', in Bourke, *Visitation of God*, pp. 159–69.

Bourke, A. and H. Lamb. 1993. *The Spread of Potato Blight in Europe in 1845–6 and the Accompanying Weather Patterns*. Dublin: Meteorological Office.

Bowden, P. 1967. 'Agricultural prices, farm prices and rents', in J. Thirsk (ed.), *The Agrarian History of England and Wales*, vol. IV, Cambridge: CUP, pp. 593–695.

Bowley, A. L. 1899. 'The statistics of wages in the United Kingdom during the last hundred years (Part III). Agricultural wages – Ireland' *JRSS* LXII: 395–404, 555–70.

Boyce, D. G. 1982. *Nationalism in Ireland*. London: Croom Helm.

Boyce, D. G. 1990. *Nineteenth Century Ireland: The Search for Stability*. Dublin: Gill & Macmillan.

Boyce, D. G. 1992. *Ireland 1828–1923: From Ascendancy to Democracy*. Oxford: Blackwell.

Boyer, George. 1997. 'Poor relief, informal assistance, and short time during the Lancashire cotton famine', *EEH*, 34: 56–76.

Boyer, G. R., T. J. Hatton, and K. H. O'Rourke, 1994. 'Emigration and economic growth in Ireland, 1850–1914', in T. J. Hatton and J. G.Williamson (eds), *International Migration and World Development*. London: Routledge, pp. 221–39.

Boyle, P. P. and C. Ó Gráda. 1986. 'Fertility trends, excess mortality, and the Great Irish Famine', *Demography* 23: 543–62.

Brenan, M. 1935. *Schools of Kildare and Leighlin, 1775–1835*. Dublin: Gill.

BPP. 1843. Reports of the commissioners appointed to take the census of Ireland for the year 1841. [504] vol. xxiv.i. BPP (1856a). The census of Ireland for the year 1851, Part V: Tables of Death, vol. I, [2087–I], vol. xxix. 261.

BPP. 1845. 'Report from H.M Commissioners to Inquire into the State of the Law and Practice in respect of the Occupation of Land in Ireland' (*Devon Commission*) (672) vol. XXII [.I].

BPP. 1847–8.'Abstract of Return from the Registrar's Office of the Court of Chancery in Ireland', (in 226) vol. LXII [.213].

BPP. 1849. 'Colonization from Ireland: 3rd Report from the Select Committee of the House of Lords', vol. xi (86).

BPP. 1852a. 'Return of savings banks in the United Kingdom that have failed, stopped payment or been discontinued since the year 1844', vol. 28 [.471], 749.

BPP. 1852b. 'Return from each savings bank in the United Kingdom . . .', vol. 28 [.521], 757.

BPP. 1854–5. 'Report of H.M Commissioners Appointed to Inquire into the Incumbered Estates Court . . . with an Appendix Containing Evidence and Returns'. (1938) vol. XIX [.527].

BPP. 1856a. 'The Census of Ireland for the year 1851, Part v (2): Tables of Death', [2087–II], vol. XXX.I.

BPP. 1856b. 'The Census of Ireland for the year 1851, Part VI: General Report', [2134], vol. XXXI.i.

Brycesok, A. D. M. (1977). 'Rehydration in cholera and other diarrhoeal diseases', *Technologies for Rural Health*. London: Royal Society.

Burger, G. C. E., J. C. Drummond and H. R. Stanstead (1948). *Malnutrition and Starvation m the Western Netherlands, September 1944–July 1945*, Part I. The Hague.

Burke, Helen. 1987. *The People and the Poor Law in Nineteenth-century Ireland*. Dublin: IPA.

Burrows, Edwin G. and Mike Wallace. 1999. *Gotham: A History of New York City to 1898*. New York: Oxford University Press.

Byrne, Stephen. 1873. *Irish Emigration to the United States*. New York, Catholic Publication Society.

Callaghan, Olwen. 1971. 'A study of Dublin 1845–50: the impact of the Great Famine on a city' (Undergraduate thesis, Department of Modern History, UCD).

Campbell, Stephen. 1994. *The Great Irish Famine: Words and Images from the Famine Museum Strokestown Park*. Strokestown: Irish Famine Museum.

Carmichael, A. 1983. 'Infection, hidden hunger, and history', in Rotberg and Rabb, *Hunger and History*, pp. 51–66.

Carsten, P. 1983. 'Irish soldiers in the British army, 1792–1922; suborned or subordinated?', *Journal of Social History* 17: 31–64.

Casey, Marion R. 1996. 'Friends in need: financing emigration from Ireland, the Irish Emigrant Society and the Emigrant Industrial Savings Bank', *Seaport Magazine*, May.

Christiansen, E. 1997. *The Northern Crusades* (new edn). Harmondsworth: Penguin.

Cipolla, C. M. 1965. *Literacy and development in the West*. Harmondsworth: Penguin.

Clark, Dennis. 2005. *The Irish in Philadelphia: Ten Generations of Irish Experience*. Philadelphia: Temple University Press.

Clarkson, L. E. and E. M. Crawford. 2001. *Feast and Famine: Food and Nutrition in Ireland 1500–1920*. Oxford: OUP.

Coale, A. J. and Roy Treadway. 1986. 'A summary of the changing distributions of overall fertility, marital fertility, and the proportion married in the provinces of Europe', in A. J. Coale and S. C. Watkins (eds), *The Decline of Fertility in Europe*. Princeton: PUP, pp. 31–80.

Coelho, Philip R. P. and James F. Shepherd. 1976. 'Regional differences in real wages: the United States, 1851–1880', *EEH* 13 (2): 551–91.

Cohn, Raymond L. 1984. 'Mortality on immigrant voyages to New York, 1836–1853', *JEH* 44: 289–300.

Cohn, Raymond L. 1987. 'The determinants of individual mortality on sailing ships, 1836–1853', *EEH* 24: 371–391.

Cohn, Raymond L. 2000. 'Nativism and the end of the mass migration of the 1840s and 1850s', *JEH* 60 (2): 361–83.

Cole, W. A. 1975. 'Trends in eighteenth-century smuggling', *EHR*, 2nd ser. x: 395–410.

Concern Worldwide. 1995. *'A Glimmer of Light': An Overview of Great Hunger Commemorative Events.* Dublin: Concern.

Cohn, R. L. 1984. 'Mortality on Immigrant voyages to New York, 1836–1853', *JEH* 44: 289–300.

Conley, T. G. and D. W. Galenson. 1998. 'Nativity and wealth in mid-nineteenth century cities', *JEH* 58: 468–93

Connell, Kenneth H. 1951. *The Population of Ireland 1700–1845*, Oxford: OUP.

Connolly, S. J. 1995. 'The Great Famine and Irish polities', in Póirtéir, *Great Irish Famine*, pp. 34–49.

Cork Archives Institute. 1996. *Great Famine Facsimile Pack.* Cork: CAI.

Corrigan, F. 1975–6. 'Dublin workhouses during the Great Famine', *Dublin Historical Record* 29: 59–65.

Cosgrove, Marianne. 1995. 'Sources in the National Archives for researching the Great Famine: the Relief Commission Papers', *Irish Archives Bulletin*, Autumn: 3–12.

Costa, Dora L. and Richard H. Steckel. 1997. 'Long-term trends in health, welfare, and economic growth in the United States', in R. H. Steckel and R. Floud (eds), *Health and Welfare during Industrialization.* Chicago: Chicago University Press, pp. 47–90.

Cousens, S. H. 1960. 'Regional death rates in Ireland during the Great Famine from 1846 to 1851', *PS* 14: 55–74.

Cowman, D. and D. Brady (eds). 1995. *Teacht na bPrátaí Dubha: The Famine in Waterford 1845–1850.* Dublin: Geography Publications.

Cox, Catherine. 1996. *Dead Dubliners: The Effects of the Famine in the North Dublin Union.* Dublin: National Famine Research Project.

Crawford, E. M. (ed.) 1989. *Famine: The Irish Experience.* Edinburgh: John Donald.

Crawford, M. 1988. 'Scurvy in Ireland during the Great Famine', *Journal of the Society for the Social History of Medicine* 1: 281–300.

Crawford, M. 1994. 'The Great Irish Famine: Image versus Reality', in R. Gillespie and B. Kennedy (eds), *Ireland: Art into History.* Dublin: Townhouse, pp. 75–88.

Crews, Frederick. 1998. *Unauthorized Freud: Doubters Confront a Legend.* Harmondsworth: Penguin.

Crotty, Raymond D. 1966. *Irish Agricultural Production*, Cork: Cork UP.

Cullen, L. M. 1968. 'Irish history without the potato', *P&P* XL: 72–83.

Cullen, L. M. 1968–9. 'The smuggling trade in Ireland in the eighteenth century', *PRIA* 67 (c): 149–75.

Cullen, L. M. 1981. *The Emergence of Modern Ireland, 1600–1900.* London: Batsford.

Cullen, L. M. 1998. 'The politics of the famine and famine historiography', in Breandán Ó Conaire (ed.), *The Famine Lectures: Léachtaí and Ghorta.* Boyle: Comhdháil an Chraoibhín, pp. 166–88.

Cumiskey, M. 1994–5. 'Folk memories of the famine', *Creggan: Journal of the Creggan Local History Society*, no. 7: 57–60.

Curtin, Gerard. 2000. *A Pauper Warren: West Limerick 1845–49.* Midleton, Cork: Sliabh Luachra Books.

Curtis, L.P. Jr. 1980. 'Incumbered wealth: landed indebtedness in post-famine Ireland', *American Historical Review* 85 (2): 332–67

Cutler, David M. and Edward L. Glaeser. 1997. 'Are ghettos good or bad?', *QJE* CXII (3): 827–72.

Cutler, David M., Edward L. Glaeser, and Jacob L. Vigdor. 1999. 'The rise and decline of the American ghetto', *JPE* 107 (3): 455–506.

D'Alton, Ian. 1980. *Protestant Society and Politics in Cork 1812–1844.* Cork: Cork UP.

Daly, Douglas C. 1996. 'The leaf that launched a thousand ships', *Natural History*, January, pp. 24–32.

Daly, Mary E. 1980. 'The development of the National School system, 1831–40', in A. Cosgrove and D. McCartney (eds), *Studies in Irish History presented to R. D. Edwards.* Dublin: UCD, pp. 150–63.

Daly, Mary E. 1981. *Social and Economic History of Ireland since 1800.* Dublin: Educational Company.

Daly, Mary E. 1986. *The Famine in Ireland.* Dundalk: Dundalgan Press.

Daly, Mary E. 1995. 'The operations of famine relief, 1845–47', in Póirtéir, *Great Irish Famine*, pp. 123–34.

Daly, Mary E. 1997. 'Farming and the famine', in Ó Gráda, *Famine 150*, pp. 29–48.

Daly, Mary E. 2006. 'Recent research on the Great Famine', in Ó Gráda et al., *When the Potato Failed.*

Davies R. W. and S. Wheatcroft. 2003. *The Years of Hunger, 1931–33.* London: Macmillan.

De Fréine, Seán. 1995. 'An Gorta agus an Ghaeilge' in Póirtéir, *Gnéithe*, pp. 55–68.

Degler, Carl. 1952. 'Labor in the economy and politics of New York City, 1850–1860' (unpublished PhD dissertation, Columbia University).

De Maddalena, Aldo. 1950. *Prezzi e aspetti di mercato in Milano durante il secolo XVII.* Milano: Malfasi.

De Vries, Jan. 1984. *European Urbanization 1500–1800.* London: Methuen.

De Waal, Alex. 1993. 'War and famine in Africa', *IDS Bulletin* 24 (4): 33–40.

Degler, Carl. 1952. 'Labor in the economy and politics of New York City, 1850–1860' (unpublished PhD dissertation, Columbia University).

Denecke, Dietrich. 1976. 'Innovation and diffusion of the potato in Central Europe in the seventeenth and eighteenth centuries', in R. Buchanan, R. Butlin and D. McCourt (eds), *Field, Farms, and Settlement in Europe.* Belfast: Institute of Irish Studies, pp. 107–17.

Devereux, Stephen. 2000. 'Famine in the twentieth century', IDS Working Paper 105, University of Sussex (available at http://www.ids.ac.uk/ids/bookshop/wp/wp105.pdf).

Dickson, David. 1997. 'The potato and diet before the famine' in Ó Gráda (ed.), *Famine 150*, pp. 1–27.

Dickson, David. 1998. *Arctic Ireland: the Extraordinary Story of the Great Frost and the Forgotten Famine of 1740–41.* Belfast: White Row Press.

Diner, Hasia R. 1983. *Erin's Daughters in America: Irish Immigrant Women in the Nineteenth Century.* Baltimore: Johns Hopkins Press.

Dirks, R. 1993. 'Famine and disease', in Kenneth F. Kiple (ed.), *The Cambridge World History of Human Disease.* Cambridge: CUP.

Dolan, Jay. 1983 [1975]. *The Immigrant Church: New York's Irish and German Catholics 1815–1865.* South Bend: University of Notre Dame Press.

Donnelly, James S. Jr. 1974–5. 'The journals of Sir John Benn-Walsh relating to the management of his Irish estates, 1823–64'. *Journal of the Cork Historical and Archaeological Society,* LXXIX: 86–123; LXXX: 15–42.

Donnelly, James S. Jr. 1975. *The Land and People of Nineteenth-Century Cork.* London: Routledge & Kegan Paul.

Donnelly, James S. Jr. 1988. 'The Kenmare estates during the nineteenth century', *Journal of the Kerry Historical and Archaeological Society* XXI: 5–41.

Donnelly, James S. Jr. 1989. 'Landlords and tenants', in W. E. Vaughan (ed.), *The New History of Ireland,* vol. 5, Oxford: OUP, pp. 334–349.

Donnelly, James S. Jr. 1993. 'The Famine: its interpreters, old and new', *History Ireland,* 1:3.

Donnelly, James S. Jr 1995. 'Mass eviction and the Great Famine', in Póirteir 1995a: 155–73.

Donnelly, James S. Jr 1996a. 'Irish property must pay for Irish poverty': British public opinion and the Great Irish Famine', in C. Morash and R. Hayes (eds), *'Fearful Realities': New Perspectives on the Famine.* Dublin: Irish Academic Press, pp. 60–76

Donnelly, James S. Jr 1996b. 'Constructing the memory of the Famine in Ireland and the Irish diaspora, 1850–1900', *Éire-Ireland* XXXI (1–2): 26–61.

Donnelly, James S. Jr 2001. *The Irish Potato Famine,* London: Sutton Publishing.

Drèze, Jean and Amartya Sen. 1989. *Hunger and Public Action.* Oxford: OUP.

Duncan, Otis D. 1961. 'A socioeconomic index for all occupations', in A. Reiss Jr (ed.), *Occupations and Social Status.* New York: Free Press, pp. 109–38.

Dupâquier, J. 1975. 'Population' in P. Burke (ed.), *The New Cambridge Modern History.* Cambridge: CUP.

Dwan, Berni. 2004. 'Famine bug search moves to South America'. *The Irish Times,* 13 May.

Dwyer, Gerard P. and Cotton M. Lindsay. 1984. 'Robert Giffen and the Irish potato', *AER* LXXIV, 188–92

Dyson, T. 1991a. 'On the demography of South Asian famines: Part 1', *Population Studies* 45: 5–25.

Dyson, T. 1991b. 'On the demography of South Asian famines: Part 2', *Population Studies* 45: 279–97.

Dyson, T. and C. Ó Gráda (eds). 2002. *Famine Demography: Perspectives from the Past and Present* Oxford: OUP.

Eagleton, T. 1995. *Heathcliff and the Great Hunger.* London: Verso.

Edwards, R. Dudley and T. D. Williams. 1956. *The Great Famine: Studies in Irish History 1845–52.* Dublin; Browne & Nolan (new edn: Lilliput, 1994).

Eiríksson, Andrés. 1997a. *The Great Famine in Ennistymon Poor Law Union.* Dublin: NFRP.

Eiríksson, Andrés. 1997b. 'Food supply and food riots', in Ó Gráda, *Famine 150*, pp. 67–93.

Eiríksson, A. 1998. *Ennistymon Union and Workhouse during the Great Famine: A Statistical Report.* Dublin: NFRP.

Eiríksson, Andrés and Cormac Ó Gráda. 1997. *Estates Records of the Irish Famine: A Second Guide to Famine Archives.* Dublin: DFN.

Ellis, E. 1960. 'State-aided emigration schemes from crown estates in Ireland c.1850', *Annalecta Hibernica* 22: 329–94.

Ellman, Michael J. 2000. 'The 1947 Soviet famine and the entitlement approach to famines', *Cambridge Journal of Economics* 24 (5): 603–30.

Erickson, Kai. 1994. *A New Species of Trouble: The Human Experience of Modern Disasters,* New York: Norton.

Ernst, Robert. 1949. *Immigrant Life in New York City 1825–1863.* New York: King's Crown Press.

Famine Inquiry Commission. 1945. *Report on Bengal.* Delhi: Government of India Press.

Farmar, Tony. 2002. *Believing in Action: The First Thirty Years of Concern 1968–1998.* Dublin: A&A Farmar.

Fentress, James and Chris Wickham. 1992. *Social Memory.* Oxford: OUP.

Ferrie, Joseph P. 1994. 'The wealth accumulation of antebellum immigrants to the U.S. 1840–1860', *JEH*, 54: 1–33.

Ferrie, Joseph P. 1997. *'Yankeys Now': Immigrants in the Antebellum U.S., 1840–60.* New York: Oxford University Press.

Fewer, T. G. 1995. 'Poverty and patronage: responses to the famine of the Duke of Devonshire's Lismore Estate', in Cowman and Brady, *Teacht na bPrátaí Dubha*, pp. 69–100.

Findley, S. E. 1994. 'Does drought increase migration? A study of migration from rural Mali during the 1983–1985 drought.' *International Migration Review* 28: 539–53.

Fishlow, Albert. 1961. 'The Trustee Savings Banks, 1817–1861', *JEH* 21: 26–40.

Fitzgerald, Patricia and Olive Kennedy. 1995. *An Gorta Mór i gCill Alaidhe (The Great Famine in Killala).* Killala: the authors.

Fitzpatrick, David. 1980. 'The disappearance of the Irish agricultural labourer, 1841–1912', *IESH* 7: 66–92.

Fitzpatrick, D. 1984. *Irish Emigration 1801–1921.* Dundalk: Dundalgan Press.

Fitzpatrick, David. 1989. 'Emigration, 1801–70', in W. E. Vaughan (ed.), *A New History of Ireland,* vol. 5. Oxford: Oxford University Press. pp. 562–622.

Fitzpatrick, D. 1995a. 'Flight from famine', in Póirtéir, *Great Irish Famine*, pp. 174–84.

Fitzpatrick, David. 1995b. 'Famine, entitlements, and seduction: Captain Edmond Wynne in Ireland, 1846–51', *English Historical Review* CX: 596–619.

Fitzpatrick, David. 1997. 'Women and the Great Famine', in M. Kelleher and J. H. Murphy (eds), *Gender Perspectives on Nineteenth-Century Ireland.* Dublin: Irish Academic Press, pp. 50–69.

Flinn, Michael et al. 1977. *Scottish Population History from the Seventeenth Century to the 1930s,* Cambridge: CUP.

Floud, R. and K. Wachter, 1982. 'Poverty and physical stature; evidence on the standard of living of London boys, 1770–1870', *Social History* 6: 422–52.

Fogel, R. et al. 1983. 'Secular changes in American and British stature and nutrition', *JIH* xiv: 445–81.

Fogel, R. W. 1991. 'The conquest of high mortality and hunger in Europe and America', in P. Higonnet, D. S. Landes and H. Rosovsky (eds), *Favorites of Fortune: Technology, Growth, and Economic Development since the Industrial Revolution*. Cambridge, MA: Harvard University Press, pp. 33–71.

Foster, R. L. 1988. *Modern Ireland 1600–1972*. London: Allen Lane.

Froggatt, P. 1989. 'The response of the medical profession to the famine', in Crawford, *Famine*, pp. 134–56.

Galenson, D. 1998.'Ethnicity, neighbourhood, and the school attendance of boys in antebellum Boston', *Journal of Urban History* 24 (5): 603–26.

Gallman, Robert. 1969. 'Trends in the size distribution of wealth in the nineteenth century: some speculations', in L. Soltow (ed.), *Six Papers on the Size Distribution of Wealth and Income*. New York, pp. 1–30.

Gatrell, V.A.C. 1980. 'The decline of theft and violence in Victorian and Edwardian England', in V.A.C. Gatrell, B. Lenman, and G. Parker (eds), *The Social History of Crime in Western Europe since 1500*. London: Europa, pp. 238–370.

Gayer, A. D., W. W. Rostow and A. Schwartz, 1953. *The Growth and Fluctuations of the British Economy, 1790–1850*. Oxford: Clarendon.

Geary, L. M. 1995. 'Famine, fever, and the bloody flux', in Póirtéir, *Great Irish Famine*, pp. 74–85.

Geary, L. M. 1996. 'The late disastrous epidemic: medical relief and the Great Famine', in C. Morash and R. Hayes (eds), *Fearful Realities: New Perspectives on the Famine*. Dublin: Irish Academic Press.

Geary, L. M. 1997. 'What people died of during the Famine', in Ó Gráda *Famine 150*, pp. 95–111.

Gerrard, J.W. 1853. *London and New York: Their Crime and Police*. New York: W. C. Bryant.

Gilbert, Sir John Thomas. 1972. *A History of the City of Dublin*, 3 vols. Shannon: Irish Academic Press [facsimile of Dublin: McGlashan & Gill edn, 1854–9].

Gilfoyle, Timothy J. 1992. *City of Eros: New York City, Prostitution, and the Commercialization of Sex 1790–1920*. New York: Norton.

Gillis, J .R. (ed.) 1994. *Commemorations: The Politics of National Identity*. Princeton: PUP.

Glasco, Laurence A. 1980. *Ethnicity and Social Structure: Irish, Germans and Native-born in Buffalo, N.Y., 1850–1860*. New York: Arno Press (reprint of 1973 SUNY Buffalo PhD dissertation).

Glazier, I. A. 1984. *The Famine Immigrants: Lists of Immigrants Arriving at the Port of New York, 1846–1851*. Baltimore: Genealogical Publishing Company.

Glazier, Ira, D. Mageean, and B. Okeke. 1989. 'Socio-economic characteristics of Irish emigrants, 1846–1851', in Klaus Friedland (ed.), *Maritime Aspects of Migration*. Cologne: Bölau Verlag, pp. 243–78.

Goodbody, Robin. 1995. *A Suitable Channel: Quaker Relief in the Great Famine*. Bray: Pale Publications.

Gorn, Elliott J. 1987. '"Good-bye boys, I die a true American': homicide, nativism, and working class culture in antebellum New York City', *Journal of American History* 74 (2): 388–410.

Grace, Daniel. 2000. *The Famine in Nenagh Poor Law Union.* Nenagh: Relay Press.

Grant, James. 1990. 'The Great Famine and the poor law in the province of Ulster: the rate-in-aid issue of 1849', *HIS* 105: 30–47.

Grant, James. 1997. 'The Great Famine in County Down', in Lindsay Proudfoot (ed.), *Down: History & Society.* Dublin: Geography Publications, pp. 327–352.

Grant, James. 2000. 'The Great Famine in County Tyrone', in Charles Dillon and Henry A. Jeffries (eds), *Tyrone: History & Society.* Dublin: Geography Publications, pp. 587–616.

Gray, Peter. 1993. 'Punch and the famine', *History Ireland* 1: 2.

Gray, Peter. 1994. 'Potatoes and providence: British government's responses to the Great Famine', *Bullán: An Irish Studies Journal,* no. 1: 75–90.

Gray, Peter. 1995a. 'Ideology and the Famine', in Póirtéir, *Great Irish Famine,* pp. 86–103.

Gray, Peter. 1995b. *The Irish Famine.* London and New York: Thames & Hudson.

Gray, Peter. 1997. 'Famine relief policy in comparative perspective: Ireland, Scotland and North Western Europe 1845–49', *Eire-Ireland* 32 (1): 86–108.

Gray, Peter. 1999. *Famine, Land, and Politics: British Government and Irish Society 1843–50.* Dublin: Irish Academic Press.

Green, E. R. R. 1956. 'Agriculture', in Edwards and Williams, *The Great Famine,* pp. 89–128.

Green, E. R. R. 1984. 'The Great Famine', in T. W. Moody and F. X. Martin (eds), *The Course of Irish History.* Cork: Mercier Press (first published in 1967), pp. 263–74.

Greil, H. 1998. 'Age- and sex-specifity of the secular trend of height in East Germany', in John Komlos and Joerg Baten (eds), *The Biological Standard of Living in Comparative Perspective.* Stuttgart: Steiner Verlag, pp. 467–83.

Gribben, Arthur. 1999. *The Great Famine and the Irish Diaspora in America.* Amherst: University of Massachusetts Press.

Griggs, Heather. 1997. 'Emigrant Bank and Transfiguration Church records as supplementary historical sources: a statistical analysis', Foley Square archaeological project, mimeo.

Groneman, Carol. 1978. 'Working-class immigrant women in mid-nineteenth century New York: the Irish women's experience', *Journal of Urban History* 4: 255–73.

Groneman Pernicone, Carol. 1973. 'The 'Bloody Ould Sixth': a social analysis of a New York City working-class community in the mid-nineteenth century' (unpublished PhD dissertation, University of Rochester).

Guinnane, T. W. 1992. 'Age at leaving home in rural Ireland, 1901–1911', *JEH* 52 (3): 651–74.

Guinnane, T. W. 1997. *The Vanishing Irish: Households, Migration and the Rural Economy in Ireland, 1850–1914,* Princeton: Princeton University Press.

Guinnane, T. W. and C. Ó Gráda. 2002a. 'Mortality in the North Dublin Union during the Great Famine', *Economic History Review* LV (3): 487–506.

Guinnane, T. W. and C. Ó Gráda. 2002b. 'Workhouse mortality and the Great Irish Famine', in Dyson and Ó Gráda, *Famine Demography,* pp. 44–64.

Guinnane, T. W, Desmond McCabe, and C. Ó Gráda. 2004. 'Agency and famine relief: Enniskillen workhouse during the Great Irish Famine', downloadable at www.ucd.ie/economic/workingpapers/wp04.15.pdf.

Gurr, Ted Robert. 1989. *Violence in America, vol. 1, The History of Crime.* Newbury Park: Calif, Sage.

Häkkinen, Antti. 1992. 'On attitudes and living strategies in the Finnish countryside in the years of famine 1867–68', in idem (ed.), *Just a Sack of Potatoes? Crisis Experiences in European Societies, Past and Present.* Helsinki, pp. 149–166.

Hall-Matthews, David. 2005. *Peasants, Famine and the State in Colonial West India.* London: Palgrave Macmillan.

Handlin, Oscar. 1941. *Boston's Immigrants 1790–1865: A Study in Acculturation.* Cambridge, Mass: Harvard UP.

Harris, Ruth-Ann. 1996. 'Ballykilcline and beyond', *Irish Studies Review* 15 (Summer), 39–42.

Hatton, Helen E. 1994. *The Largest Amount of Good: Quaker Relief in Ireland.* Kingston: McGill-Queens University Press.

Hatton, T. J. and Williamson, J. G. 1993. 'After the famine: emigration from Ireland, 1850–1913.' *JEH* 53: 575–600.

Hatton, T. J. and Williamson, J. G. 1994. 'What drove the mass migrations from Europe in the late 19th century?' *PDR* 20: 1–27.

Hayden, Tom (ed.) 1997. *Irish Hunger: Personal Reflections on the Legacy of the Famine.* Boulder: Roberts Rinehart.

Herscovici, Steven. 1993. 'The distribution of wealth in nineteenth century Boston: inequality among natives and immigrants', *EEH* 30 (3): 321–35.

Herscovici, Steven. 1994. 'Ethnic differences in school attendance in antebellum Massachussets: evidence from Newburyport, 1850–1860', *Social Science History* 18: 471–96.

Herscovici, Steven. 1998. 'Migration and economic mobility: wealth accumulation and occupational change among antebellum migrants and persisters', *JEH* 58 (4): 927–56.

Hickey, Patrick. 1993. 'Famine, mortality and emigration: a profile of six parishes in the Poor Law Union of Skibbereen', in Patrick O'Flanagan and Cornelius G. Buttimer (eds), *Cork: History and Society.* Dublin: Geography Publications, pp. 873–918.

Hickey, Patrick. 1995. 'The famine in Skibbereen Union (1845–51)', in Póirtéir, *Great Irish Famine*, pp. 185–203.

Hickey, Patrick. 2002. *Famine in West Cork: The Mizen Peninsula Land and People, 1800–1852.* Cork: Mercier Press.

Hill, Marylin Wood. 1993. *Their Sisters' Keepers: Prostitution in New York City 1830–1870.* Berkeley: U. of California Press.

Hionidou, V. 1995. 'The demography of a Greek famine: Mykonos, 1941–19', *Continuity & Change* 10: 279–99.

Hionidou, V. 2002. 'Send us food or send us coffins: the 1941–42 famine on the Aegean island of Syros', in Dyson and Ó Gráda (eds), *Famine Demography*, pp. 181–203.

Hobsbawm, Eric and T. Ranger (eds). 1983. *The Invention of Tradition.* Cambridge: CUP.

Hoffman, Elizabeth and J. Mokyr. 1984. 'Peasants, potatoes and poverty: transactions costs in prefamine Ireland', in Gary Saxonhouse and Gavin Wright (eds), *Technique, Spirit and Form in the Making of the Modern Economy: Essays in Honor of William N. Parker.* Greenwich, Conn: JAI Press, pp. 115–45.

Hoppen, K. T. 1989. *Ireland since 1800: Conflict and Conformity* (London)

Hough, Franklin B. 1857. *Census of the State of New York for 1855.* Albany: Charles van Benthuysen.

Iliffe, John. 1987. *The African Poor: A History.* Cambridge: CUP.

Inglis, Brian. 1956. *The Story of Ireland.* London: Faber and Faber.

Johnson, Paul. 1985. *Saving and Spending: the Working-class Economy in Britain 1870–1939,* Oxford: Oxford University Press.

Kane, Robert. 1845. *The Industrial Resources of Ireland.* Dublin: Hodges & Smith.

Katz, E. and Stark, O. 1989. 'International labour migration under alternative informational regimes: a diagrammatic analysis.' *European Economic Review* 33: 127–42.

Katzman, David M. 1978. *Seven Days a Week: Women and Domestic Service in Industrializing America.* New York: Oxford University Press.

Kelleher, M. 1995. 'Irish famine in literature', in Póirtéir, *Great Irish Famine,* pp. 232–47.

Kennedy, Liam. 1985. 'The rural economy, 1820–1914', in L. Kennedy and P. Ollerenshaw, (eds), *An Economic History of Ulster, 1820–1914.* Manchester: MUP, pp. 1–61.

Kerr, Donal A. 1982. *Peel, Priests, and Politics: Sir Robert Peel's Administration and the Roman Catholic Church in Ireland 1841–46.* Oxford: OUP.

Kerr, Donal A. 1994. *A Nation of Beggars? Priests, People, and Politics in Famine Ireland 1846–1852.* Oxford: Clarendon.

Kerr, Donal A. 1996. *The Catholic Church and the Famine,* Dublin: Columba.

Khoroshinina, Lidiya. 2005. 'Long-term effects of lengthy starvation', in Barber and Dzeniskevich, *Life and Death in Leningrad,* pp. 197–212.

Kierse, S. 1984. *The Famine Years in the Parish of Killaloe 1845–1851.* Killaloe.

Killen, J. 1995. *The Famine Decade.* Belfast: Blackstaff.

Kinealy, Christine. 1994. *This Great Calamity: The Irish Famine 1845–52.* Dublin: Gill & Macmillan.

Kinealy, Christine. 1995a. The role of the poor law during the famine', in Póirtéir, *Great Irish Famine,* pp. 104–22.

Kinealy, Christine. 1995b. 'Beyond revisionism: reassessing the Great Famine', *History Ireland* 3: 4.

Kinealy, Christine. 1996. 'The response of the poor law to the Great Famine in Galway', in Gerard Moran and Raymond Gillespie (eds), *Galway: History and Society.* Dublin: Geography Publications, pp. 375–94.

Kinealy, Christine. 1999. 'The Great Irish Famine: a dangerous memory?', in Gribben, *The Great Famine,* pp. 239–53.

Kinealy, Christine and Trevor Parkhill (eds). 1997. *The Famine in Ulster.* Belfast: UHF.

King, Sophia Hillan. 1995. 'Pictures drawn from memory: William Carleton's experience of famine', *Irish Review* 17/18: 80–9.

Kinsella, Anna. 1995. *County Wexford in the Famine Years.* Enniscorthy: Duffry Press.

Kissane, Noel. 1995. *The Irish Famine: A Documentary History.* Dublin: NLI.

Kniffin, William H. 1918. *The Saving Bank and its Practical Work.* New York: Bankers Publishers Company.

Knight, Denis (ed.) 1984. *Cobbett in Ireland: A Warning to England.* London: Lawrence & Wishart.

Kohl, J. G. 1844. *Travels in Ireland.* London: Bruce & Wyld.

Kotre, John. 1996. *White Gloves: How We Create Ourselves Through Memory.* New York: Norton.

Kozlov, Igor and Alla Samsonova. 2005. 'The impact of the siege on the physical development of children', in Barber and Dzeniskevich, *Life and Death in Leningrad*, pp. 174–96.

Kumar, G. 1987. 'Ethiopian famines 1973–85: a case study' WIDER Working Paper No. 26: Helsinki.

Lachiver, Marcel. 1991. *Les Années de misère: la famine au temps du Grand Roi*. Paris: Fayard.

'Ladies of the Mission'. 1854. *The Old Brewery, and the New Mission House at the Five Points*. New York: Stringer & Townsend.

Lane, P .G. 1972. 'The Encumbered Estates Court Ireland, 1848–49', *ESR* III: 413–53.

Lane, P. G. 1981–2. 'The impact of the Encumbered Estates Court upon the landlords of Galway and Mayo', *Journal of the Galway Archaeological and Historical Society* 38: 45–58.

Lannie, Vincent P. 1968. *Public Money and Parochial Education*. Cleveland, Ohio: The Press of Case Western Reserve University.

Large, David. 1966. 'The wealth of the greater Irish landowners, 1750–1815', *Irish Historical Studies* 15 (57): 21–44.

Laxton, Edward. 1997. *The Famine Ships*. New York: Henry Holt.

Lee, J. J. 1990. *Ireland 1912–1985*. Cambridge: CUP.

Lee, J. J. 1997. 'The famine as history', in Ó Gráda, *Famine 150*, pp. 159–75

Lee, J. J. 2000. 'Irish history', in Neil Buttimer, Colin Rynne, and Helen Guerin (eds), *The Heritage of Ireland*. Cork: Collins, pp. 117–36.

Lenihan, Pádraig. 1997. 'War and Population, 1649–52', *IESH* XXIV: 1–21.

Lindsay, Deirdre and David Fitzpatrick. 1993. *Records of the Irish Famine*. Dublin: Irish Famine Network.

Lintelman, Joy K. 1991. '"Our serving sisters": Swedish-American domestic servants and their ethnic community', *Social Science History* 15 (3): 381–95.

Litton, H. 1994. *The Great Famine: An Illustrated History*. Dublin: Wolfhound.

Livi-Bacci, M. 1991. *Population and Nutrition: An Essay on European Demographic History*. Cambridge: CUP.

Locke, John. 1852. *Ireland, Observations on the People, the Land, and the Law in 1851*. Dublin.

Logan, J. 1983. 'Schooling and literacy in the nineteenth century', unpublished paper presented to the Irish Social and Economic Society Conference on education and literacy, May.

Long, Clarence D. 1960. *Wages and Earnings in the US, 1860–1890*. Princeton: PUP.

Lumey, L. H. 1998. 'Reproductive outcomes in women prenatally exposed to undernutrition from the Dutch famine birth cohort', *Proceedings of the Nutrition Society* 57: 129–35.

Lynch, Patrick and John Vaizey. 1960. *Guinness's Brewery in the Irish Economy 1759–1880*. Cambridge: CUP.

Lyne, Gerard J. 1992. 'William Steuart Trench and post-famine emigration from Kenmare to America, 1850–55', *Journal of the Kerry Archaeological and Historical Society* 25: 51–137.

Lyne, Gerard J. 2001. *The Lansdowne Estate in Kerry under the Agency of William Steuart Trench*. Dublin: Geography Publications.

Lyons, F. S. L. 1973. *Ireland since the Famine*. London: Collins.

Lyons, Mary. 1993. *Illustrated Encumbered Estates, Ireland 1850–1905, Lithographic and Other Illustrative Material in the Incumbered Estates Rentals*. Whitegate, Co. Clare: Ballinakella Press.

Lysaght, Patricia. 1996. 'Women and the Great Famine: voices from the Irish oral tradition', in A. Gribben (ed.), *Famine Legacy: An Interdisciplinary Collection of Essays in Commemoration of the Great Hunger in Ireland*. Champaign: University of Illinois Press, pp. 21–47.

Lysaght, Patricia. 1996–7. 'Perspectives on women during the Great Irish Famine from the oral tradition', *Béaloideas* 64/65: 63–130.

MacArthur, W. A. 1956. 'Medical history of the famine', in Edwards and Williams (1956).

MacAtasney, Gerard. 1997. *'This Dreadful Visitation': The Famine in Lurgan/Portadown*. Dublin: Beyond the Pale.

MacCarthy, R. B. 1993. *The Trinity College Estates, 1800–1923* (Dundalk).

MacDonagh, Oliver. 1956. 'Irish emigration to the United States of America and the British colonies during the famine', in Edwards and Williams, *The Great Famine*, pp. 319–90.

Macintyre, Kate. 2002. 'Famine and the female mortality advantage', in Dyson and Ó Gráda, *Famine Demography*, pp. 240–60.

MacLysaght, E. 1950. *Irish Life in the Seventeenth Century*, 2nd edn. Cork: Mercier.

Maguire, J. F. 1868. *The Irish in America*. London: Longman's Green.

Maguire, W. A. 1972. *The Downshire Estates in Ireland 1801–1845*. Oxford: OUP.

Maguire, W. A. 1976. 'Lord Donegal and the sale of Belfast: a case study from the Encumbered Estates Court', *EHR* 29 (4): 570–84.

Maharatna, A. 1996. *The Demography of Famines*. Delhi: Oxford University Press.

Malthus, T. R. 1970. *Essay on the Principle of Population*, ed. A. Flew. Harmondsworth: Penguin.

Manning, James Hilton. 1917. *Century of American Savings Banks*, New York: B. F. Buck.

Margo, Robert A. 1999. *Wages and Labor Markets in the United States 1820–1860*. Chicago: University of Chicago Press.

Marnane, Dennis. 1996–7. 'The famine in south Tipperary', *Tipperary Historical Journal* 9: 1–42; 10: 131–50.

Martin, R. M. 1848. *Ireland Before and After the Union with Great Britain*, 3rd edn. London, Dublin: J. B. Nichols.

Mason, W. S. ed. 1814–19. *A Statistical Account or Parochial Survey of Ireland*, 3 vols. Dublin: Graisberry & Campbell.

Maxwell, Constantia. 1946. *Dublin under the Georges*. London: Harrap and Dublin: Hodgis Figgis.

McAlpin, M. B. 1987. 'Famine relief policy in India: six lessons for Africa', in Michael H. Glantz (ed.), *Drought and Hunger in Africa: Denying Famine a Future*. Cambridge: CUP, pp. 393–413.

McArthur, John. 1854. *Incumbered Estates Court Ireland: Summary of Proceedings*. Dublin.

McAtasney, Gerard. 1997a. *Leitrim and the Great Hunger, 1845–1850*. Carrick-on-Shannon: Carrick on Shannon and District Historical Society.

McAtasney, Gerard. 1997b. *This Dreadful Visitation: The Famine in Lurgan/Portadown* Belfast: Beyond the Pale Publications.

McCartney, Donal. 1987. *The Dawning of Democracy: Ireland 1800–1870*. Dublin: Helicon.

McClean, Raymond. 1988. *A Cross Shared Ethiopia-Derry: Famine in Ethiopia, a Personal Perspective*. Ballyshannon: Donegal Democrat.

McCloskey, D. N. and John Nash. 1984. 'Corn at interest: the extent and cost of grain storage in medieval England', *AER* 74 (1): 174–87.

McGregor, Patrick. 1989. 'Demographic pressure and the Irish famine: Malthus after Mokyr', *Land Economics* 65: 228–38.

McGregor, Patrick. 2004. 'Insufficient for the support of a family: wages on the public works during the Great Irish Famine', *Economic and Social Review* 35 (2): 219–39.

McHugh, R. 1938a. 'William Carleton: a portrait of the artist as propagandist', *Studies* XXVII: 47–62

McHugh, R. 1938b. 'Maria Edgeworth's Irish Novels', *Studies* XXVII: 556–70.

McHugh, R. 1938c. 'Charles Lever', *Studies* XXVII: 247–60.

McHugh, Roger. 1956. 'The famine in folklore', in Edwards and Williams, *The Great Famine*, pp. 391–406.

McParlan, J. 1802. *Statistical Survey of the County of Donegal.* Dublin: Graisberry & Campbell.

Mercer, A. 1992. 'Mortality and morbidity in refugee camps in El Fasher, Sudan 1982–89', *Disasters* 16 (1): 28–42.

Merewether, F. H. S. 1985 [1898]. *A Tour through the Famine Districts of India.* New Delhi: USHA.

Mill, J. S. 1929. *Principles of Political Economy.* London: Longmans.

Miller, David W. 2000. 'Mass attendance in Ireland in 1834', in S. J. Brown and D.W. Miller (eds), *Piety and Power in Ireland 1760–1960: Essays in Honour of Emmet Larkin.* Belfast: Institute of Irish Studies, pp. 158–79.

Miller, Kerby. 1985. *Emigrants and Exiles: Ireland and the Irish Exodus to North America.* New York: Oxford University Press.

Mitch, D. F. 1982. 'The spread of literacy in nineteenth-century England' (unpublished PhD thesis, University of Chicago).

Monahan, W. Gregory. 1993. *Year of Sorrows: The Great Famine of 1709 in Lyon.* Columbus, Ohio: Ohio State UP.

Mokyr. J. 1980. 'The deadly fungus: an econometric investigation into the short-term demographic impact of the Irish famine, 1846–51', *Research in Population Economics* 2: 429–59.

Mokyr, J. 1981. 'Irish history with the potato', *IESH* 8: 3–29.

Mokyr, J. 1985. *Why Ireland Starved: An Analytical and Quantitative History of the Irish Economy 1800–1850*, 2nd edn. London: Allen & Unwin.

Mokyr, J. 1988. 'Is there still life in the pessimist case?', *JEH* 48: 69–92.

Mokyr, J. 1995. 'Famine disease and famine mortality: lessons from the Irish experience'. Presented at the New York University/Ireland House Conference on Famine and World Hunger.

Mokyr, J. and Ó Gráda, C. 1982. 'Emigration and poverty in pre-Famine Ireland', *EEH* XIX: 360–84.

Mokyr, J. and Ó Gráda, C. 1984. 'New developments in Irish population history, 1700–1850', *EHR* 2nd ser. 47: 473–88.

Mokyr, J. and C. Ó Gráda. 1988. 'Poor and getting poorer ? Irish living standards before the Famine', *EHR* 51: 209–35.

Mokyr, J. and C. Ó Gráda. 1996. 'Heights and living standards in the United Kingdom, 1815–1860'. *EEH* Apr., 1–27.

Mokyr, J. and C. Ó Gráda. 1999. 'Famine disease and famine mortality: lessons from the Irish experience', Working Paper 99/12, UCD Centre for Economic Research.

Mokyr, J. and C. Ó Gráda. 2002. 'What do people die of during famines? The Great Irish Famine in comparative perspective', *EREH* 6 (3): 339–64.

Mokyr, J. and Rebecca Stein. 1997. 'Science, health and household technology: the effect of the Pasteur revolution on consumer demand', in Robert J. Gordon and Timothy Bresnahan (eds), *The Economics of New Goods*. Chicago: University of Chicago Press and NBER, pp. 143–205.

Monkkonen, Eric H. 1995. 'New York City homicides', *Social Science History* 19: 201–14.

Monkkonen, Eric H. 2001. *Murder in New York City* Berkeley: University of California Press.

Mooney, Thomas. 1851. *Nine Years in America; in a Series of Letters to His Cousin, Patrick Mooney, a Farmer in Ireland*. Dublin: Pattison Jolly.

Morash, C. 1989. *The Hungry Voice: The Poetry of the Irish Famine*. Dublin: Irish Academic Press.

Morash, C. 1995a. *Writing the Irish Famine*. Oxford: OUP.

Morash, C. 1995b. 'Spectres of the famine', *Irish Review* 17–18 (Winter): 74–9.

Murphy, Ignatius. 1996. *A People Starved: Life and Death in West Clare 1845–1851*. Dublin: Irish Academic Press.

Murphy, Maureen. 1983. 'The Irish Emigrant Society', in Michael F. Funchion (ed.), *Irish American Voluntary Organisations*. Greenwich, Ct., pp. 171–3.

Murray, C. J. L. and A. D. Lopez. 1994. 'Global and regional causes of death patterns in 1990', *Bulletin of the World Health Organization* 72: 447–80.

Neal, Frank. 1995. 'Lancashire, the famine Irish and the poor laws: a study in crisis management', *IESH* 22: 26–48.

Neal, Frank. 1996. 'The famine Irish in England and Wales', in Patrick O'Sullivan (ed.), *The Irish Worldwide: Heritage, History and Identity*, vol. 6, *Meaning of the Famine* (London: Leicester University Press), pp. 56–80.

Neal, Frank. 1998. *Black '47: Britain and the Famine Irish*. London: Macmillan.

Newenham, T. 1805. *An Inquiry into the Progress etc. of the Population of Ireland*. London: Baldwin.

Newsinger, John. 1996. 'The Great Irish Famine: a crime of free market economies', *Monthly Review*. 11–19

Nic Eoin, Máirín. 1995. 'Ar an trá fholamh: an gorta mór i litríocht Ghaeilge na haoise seo', in Póirtéir, *Gnéithe*, pp. 107–30

Nicholas, S. and P. Shergold, 1987. 'Human capital and the pre-famine Irish emigration to England.' *EEH* 17: 22–43.

Nicholls, Sir George. 1856. *History of the Irish Poor Law*. London.

Nicholson, Asenath. 1927. *The Bible in Ireland*. New York.

Nora, Pierre. 1979. 'Between memory and history: *les lieux de mémoire*', *Representations*, no. 26.

Norton, Desmond. 2005. 'On landlord-assisted emigration from some Irish estates in the 1840s', *AgHR* 53 (1): 24–40.

Novick, Peter. 1999. *The Holocaust in American Life*. New York: Houghton Mifflin.

O'Brien, G. A. P. 1921. *The Economic History of Ireland from the Union to the Famine*. London: Longmans Green.

O'Brien, Gerard. 1982–3. 'The establishment of poor law unions in Ireland, 1838–43', *IHS* 33: 97–120.

O'Brien, Gerard. 1985. 'The New Poor Law in pre-famine Ireland: a case history', *IESH* 12: 33–49.

O'Brien, W. P. 1896. *The Great Famine in Ireland*. London: Downey.

Ó Canainn, S. 1995. 'An Gorta i nDún Fionnachaidh', in Póirtéir, *Gnéithe*, pp. 164–91.

O'Carroll, P. 2000. 'Re-membering 1798', in E. Slater and M. Peillon (eds), *Memories of the Present: A Sociological Chronicle of Ireland, 1997–1998*. Dublin: IPA, pp. 15–23.

Ó Cathaoir, Eva. 1994. 'The poor law in County Wicklow', in Ken Hannigan and William Nolan (eds), *Wicklow: History and Society*. Dublin: Geography Publications, pp. 503–80.

Ó Cearbhaill, S. E. 1996. 'Na Bráithre Críostaí Agus an Gorta Mór', *Comhar*. 13–6.

Ó Ciosáin, Niall. 1995. 'Dia, bia agus Sasana: An Mistéalach agus íomhá an ghorta (God, Food, and England: Mitchel and the Image of the Famine)', in Póirtéir, *Gnéithe*, pp. 151–63.

Ó Ciosáin, Niall. 1995–6. 'Was there a "silence" about the famine?', *Irish Studies Review* 13: 7–10.

Ó Ciosáin, Niall. 2000. 'Famine memory and the popular representation of scarcity', in Ian McBride (ed.), *History and Memory in Early Modern Ireland*. Cambridge: CUP, pp. 95–117.

O'Donnell, Edward T. 1999. 'How the Irish became urban', *Journal of Urban History* 25 (2): 271–86.

Ó Fiannachta, Pádraig (ed.). 1997. *An Gorta Mór*. An Daingean: An Sagart.

Ó Giolláin, Diarmuid. 2000. *Locating Irish Folklore: Tradition, Modernity, Identity*. Cork: Cork University Press.

Ó Gráda, C. 1974. 'Agricultural head rents, pre-famine and post-famine', *Economic and Social Review* 5 (3): 385–92.

Ó Gráda, C. 1983. 'Across the briny ocean: some thoughts on Irish emigration to America, 1800–1850', in T. Devine and D. Dickson (eds), *Ireland and Scotland: Parallels and Contrasts in Economic and Social Development*. Edinburgh: Donald, pp. 118–30.

Ó Gráda, C. 1984. 'Malthus and the pre-Famine economy', in A. Murphy, (ed.), *Economists and the Irish Economy*. Dublin: Irish Academic Press, pp. 75–95.

Ó Gráda, C. 1985. *Éire roimh an nGorta: an Saol Eacnamaíoch* Dublin: An Gúm.

Ó Gráda, C. 1989. *The Great Irish Famine*, London: Macmillan.

Ó Gráda, C. 1991. 'The height of Clonmel prisoners, 1840–9', *IESH* 18: 38–47.

Ó Gráda, C. 1993. *Ireland before and after the Famine: Explorations in Economic History 1800–1925*, 2nd edn. Manchester: MUP.

Ó Gráda, C. 1994a. *Ireland: A New Economic History 1780–1939*. Oxford: OUP.

Ó Gráda, C. 1994b. *An Drochshaol: Béaloideas agus Amhráin*. Dublin: Coiscéim.

Ó Gráda, C. 1995a. 'Was the Great Famine just like modern famines?', in Póirtéir, *Great Irish Famine*, pp. 248–58.

Ó Gráda, C. 1995b. 'An Gorta san Ardchathair', in Póirtéir, *Gnéithe*, pp. 164–75.

Ó Gráda, C. 1996. 'Making Irish famine history in 1995', *History Workshop Journal*, no. 42: 87–104.

Ó Gráda, C. 1997a. 'The Great Famine and other famines', in Ó Gráda, *Famine 150*, pp. 129–57.

Ó Gráda, C. (ed.) 1997b. *Famine 150: The Teagasc/UCD Lectures*, Dublin: Teagasc.

Ó Gráda, C. 1997c. 'Immigrants, savers, and runners: the Emigrant Industrial Savings Bank in the 1850s', Institute of Economics, University of Copenhagen, Discussion Paper 97–24.

Ó Gráda, C. 1998. 'Was the Great Famine just like modern famines?' in Helen O'Neill and John Toye (eds), *A World without Famine?* (London, 1998), pp. 51–71.

Ó Gráda, C. 1999. *Black '47 and Beyond: The Great Irish Famine in History, Economy, and Memory*. Princeton: PUP.

Ó Gráda, C. 2001a. 'Famine, trauma, and memory', *Béaloideas* 69: 121–43.

Ó Gráda, C. 2001b. 'Markets and famines: evidence from nineteenth-century Finland', *Economic Development and Cultural Change* 49 (3): 575–90.

Ó Gráda, C. 2001c. 'Farming high and low, 1850–1914', *AgHR* 49 (11): 210–18.

Ó Gráda, C. 2005. 'Markets and famines in pre-industrial Europe', *Journal of Interdisciplinary History* 36 (2): 143–66.

Ó Gráda. 2007. *Famine: A Brief History*. Princeton: PUP.

Ó Gráda, C. and Jean-Michel Chevet. 2002. 'Famine and market in *ancien régime* France', *JEH* 62 (3): 706–33.

Ó Gráda, C. and Kevin H. O'Rourke. 1997. 'Mass migration as disaster relief: lessons from the Great Irish Famine', *EREH* 1 (1): 3–25.

Ó Gráda, C., Richard Paping and Eric Vanhoute. 2006. *When the Potato Failed: Causes and Effects of the 'Last' European Subsistence Crisis*. Turnhout: Brepols.

O'Hanlon, Ray. 1996. 'Famine Curriculum Taking Roots in States', *Irish Echo*, 21–27 Feb.

Ó Laighin, P. B. 1995. 'Grosse-Isle: Samhradh an Bhróin, 1847', in Póirtéir, *Gnéithe*, pp. 192–225.

Olmstead, Alan L. 1976. *New York City Mutual Savings Banks, 1819–1861*. Chapel Hill: University of North Carolina Press.

Ó Murchadha, Ciarán. 1998. *Sable Wings over the Sand: Ennis, County Clare, and its Wider Community during the Great Famine*. Ennis: Clasp Press.

O'Neill, K. 1984. *Family and Farm in pre-Famine Ireland*. Madison: University of Wisconsin Press.

O'Neill, Thomas P. 1956. 'The organization and administration of relief', in Edwards and Williams, *Great Famine*, pp. 207–59.

O'Neill, Timothy. 1995. 'The persistence of famine in Ireland', in Póirtéir, *Great Irish Famine*, pp. 204–18.

O'Neill, Timothy P. 1996. 'Minor famines and relief in Galway, 1815–1925', in G. Moran and R. Gillespie (eds), *Galway: History and Society*. Dublin: Geography Publications, pp. 445–87.

O'Neill, Timothy P. 1996–7. 'The Rices of Mountrice: solicitors' records of an epigonal family', *Journal of the Kildare Historical and Archaeological Society* XVIII (3): 351–66.

O'Neill, Timothy P. 1997. 'The famine in Offaly', in Timothy P. O'Neill and William Nolan (eds), *Offaly: History & Society*, Dublin: Geography Publications, pp. 681–732.

O'Neill, Timothy P. 2000. 'Famine evictions', in Carla King (ed.), *Famine, Land and Culture in Ireland*. Dublin: UCD Press, pp. 29–71.

Orcutt, William Dana. 1934. *The Miracle of Mutual Savings: As Illustrated by One Hundred Years of the Bowery Savings Bank*, New York: Bowery Savings Bank.

O'Rourke, John. 1902. *The History of the Great Irish Famine of 1847*, 3rd edn. Dublin: Duffy.

O'Rourke, K. H. 1991a. 'Did the Great Irish Famine matter?', *JEH* 51: 1–22.

O'Rourke, K. H. 1991b. 'Rural depopulation in a small open economy: Ireland 1856–1876', *EEH* 28: 409–32.

O'Rourke, K. H. 1992. 'Why Ireland emigrated: a positive theory of factor flows', *Oxford Economic Papers* 44: 322–40.

O'Rourke, K. H. 1994. 'The Economic impact of the famine in the short and long run', *American Economic Review (Papers and Proceedings)* 84: 309–313.

O'Rourke, K. H. and J. G. Williamson. 1997. 'Around the European periphery 1870–1913: globalisation, schooling and growth', *EREH* 1 (2): 153–90.

Osborne, S. Godolphin. 1850. *Gleanings from the West of Ireland*. London: Boone.

O'Shea, John. 1989. '"Thurles Savings Bank 1829–71', in William Corbett and William Nolan (eds), *Thurles, the Cathedral Town*. Dublin: Geography Publications, pp. 93–116.

Ó Tuathaigh, Gearóid. 1995. 'An Gorta Mór agus an Pholaitíocht', in Póirtéir, *Gnéithe*, pp. 26–40.

Passerini, Luisa. 1979. 'Work, ideology and consensus under Italian Fascism', *History Workshop* 8: 82–108.

Payne, Peter L. and Lance E. Davis. 1956. *The Savings Bank of Baltimore, 1818–1866: A Historical and Analytical Study*. Baltimore: Johns Hopkins Press.

Percival, J. 1995. *The Great Famine: Ireland's Potato Famine*. London: BBC.

Pim, Jonathan. 1855–6. 'Address delivered at the opening of the eighth session of the Dublin Statistical Society', *Journal of the Dublin Statistical Society* 1: 6–34.

Pitkänen, Kari. 1992. 'The patterns of mortality during the Great Finnish Famine in the 1860s', *Acta Demographica 1992*. Heidelberg: Physica-Verlag, pp. 81–102.

Pitkänen, Kari. 1993. *Deprivation and Disease: Mortality during the Great Finnish Famine of the 1860s*. Helsinki: Finnish Demographic Society.

Pitkänen, Kari. 2002. 'Famine mortality in nineteenth-century Finland: is there a sex bias?', in Dyson and Ó Gráda, *Famine Demography*, pp. 65–92.

Póirtéir, C. (ed). 1995a. *The Great Irish Famine*. Cork: Mercier.

Póirtéir, C. (ed.). 1995b. *Gnéithe den Ghorta*. Dublin: Coiscéim.

Póirtéir, C. 1995c. *Famine Echoes*. Dublin: Gill & Macmillan.

Póirtéir, C. 1996. *Glórtha ón nGorta*. Dublin: Coiscéim.

Pollard, Sidney. 1973. 'Industrialization and the European economy', *EHR*, 2nd ser. XXVI: 636–48.

Pollard, S. 1978. 'Labour in Great Britain' in P. Mathias and M. M. Postan (eds), *The Cambridge Economic History of Europe* VII (1). Cambridge: CUP, pp. 97–179.

Porter, W. H. 1849. 'Savings banks: a review of papers dealing with savings banks', *Dublin University Magazine* 34: 127–38.

Post, J. D. 1985. *Food Shortage, Climatic Variability and Epidemic Disease in Preindustrial Europe: the Mortality Peak in the early 1740s*. Ithaca: Cornell UP.

Prager, Jeffrey. 1998. *Presenting the Past: Psychoanalysis and the Sociology of Misremembering*. Cambridge, Mass.: Harvard UP.

Pratt, John Tidd. 1845. *Progress of Savings Banks from 1829 to 1844 . . . Extracted from the Official Returns.* London.

Proudfoot, Lindsay J. 1995. *Urban Patronage and Social Authority: the Management of the Duke of Devonshire's Towns in Ireland, 1764–1891.* Washington, DC: Catholic University of America Press.

Prunty, J. 1999. *Dublin Slums 1800–1925: A Study in Urban Geography.* Dublin: Irish Academic Press.

Purcell, J. 1938. 'The Irish Emigrant Society of New York', *Studies* XXVII (108).

Quinlan, Carmel. 1996. 'A punishment from God? The famine in the centenary folklore questionnaire', *Irish Review* 19: 68–86.

Ravallion, Martin. 1987. *Markets and Famines.* Oxford: OUP.

Richardson, James. 1970. *The New York Police: From Colonial Times to 1901.* New York: Oxford University Press.

Ridge, John T. 1996. 'Irish county societies in New York, 1880–1914', in Ronald T. Bayor and Timothy J. Meagher (eds), *The New York Irish.* Baltimore: Johns Hopkins Press, pp. 275–300.

Ristaino, J. B., C. T. Groves, and G. R. Parra. 2001. 'PCR amplification of the Irish potato famine pathogen from historic specimens', *Nature* 411: 695–7.

Robins, Joseph. 1995. *The Miasma: Epidemic and Panic in Nineteenth Century Ireland.* Dublin: IPA.

Robinson, Mary. 1994. *A Voice for Somalia.* Dublin: O'Brien Press.

Robinson, Mary. 1995. 'Keynote address'. Ireland House/New York University Conference on Famine and World Hunger, 19–20 May.

Robinson, O. 1962. 'The London companies as progressive landlords in the nineteenth century', *EHR* 15 (1): 103–18.

Robinson, Tim. 1995. *Connemara after the Famine. Journal of a Survey of the Martin Estate, 1853 by Thomas Colville Scott.* Dublin: Lilliput.

Rosen, Sherwin. 1999. 'Potato paradoxes', *JPE* 107 (6): S294–S313.

Rotbert, Robert I. and Theodore K. Rabb. 1983. *Hunger and History.* Cambridge: CUP.

Roth, M. and Charles G. Salas (eds). 2001. *Disturbing Remains: Memory, History, and Crisis in the Twentieth Century.* Oxford: OUP.

Royle, Stephen A. 1984. 'Irish famine relief in the early nineteenth century: the 1822 famine on the Aran Islands', *IESH* 11: 44–59.

Ruggles, Steven and Mathew Sobek. 1997. *Integrated Public Use Microdata Series. IPUMS-98, Version 2.0.* Social History Research Laboratory, Minneapolis: Department of History, University of Minnesota (www.ipums.umn.edu).

Salaman, Redcliffe N. 1947. *The History and Social Influence of the Potato,* Cambridge: CUP.

Salisbury, Harrison. 1969. *The 900 Days: the Siege of Leningrad.* New York: HarperCollins.

Sandberg, L. 1979. 'The case of the impoverished sophisticate; human capital and Swedish economic growth before World War I', *JEH* XXXIX: 225–42.

Sandberg, L. and R. Steckel, 1980. 'Soldier, soldier, what made you grow so tall?' *Economy & Society* 23: 91–105.

Sanger, William W. 1858. *The History of Prostitution.* London: Sampson Row.

Sarkar, Nikhil. 1998. *A Matter of Conscience: Artists Bear Witness to the Great Bengal Famine of 1943*. Calcutta: Punaschka.

Scally, R. J. 1995. *The End of Hidden Ireland: Rebellion, Famine and Emigration*. New York: OUP.

Schofield, R. S. 1973. 'Dimensions of illiteracy, 1750–1850', *EEH* 10: 437–54.

Schrier, Arnold. 1958. *Ireland and the American Emigration, 1850–1900*. Minneapolis: University of Minnesota Press.

Scott, Thomas Colville. 1995. *Connemara after the Famine: Journal of a Survey of the Martin Estate, 1853*, ed. Tim Robinson. Dublin: Lilliput.

Seaman, J., S. Leivesley, and C. Hogg. 1984. *Epidemiology of Natural Disasters*. Basel: Karger.

Seaman, John. 1993. 'Famine mortality in Africa', *IDS Bulletin* 2 (4): 27–32.

Sen, A. K. 1981. *Poverty and Famines*. Oxford: OUP.

Sen, A. K. 1995a. 'Starvation and political economy: famines, entitlement, and alienation', address to the NYU/Ireland House Conference on Famine and World Hunger, New York, May.

Sen, A. K. 1995b. 'Starvation and political economy'; 'Nobody need starve', *Granta* 52 (Winter).

Sennett, Richard. 1998. 'Disturbing memories', in P. Fara and K. Patterson (eds), *Memory: The Darwin College Lectures*. Cambridge: CUP.

Shaw, Henry. 1850. *New City Pictorial Directory*. Dublin.

Shears, P., A. M. Berry, R. Murphy, M. Aziz Nabil. 1987. 'Epidemiological assessment of the health and nutrition of Ethiopian refugees in emergency camps in Sudan', *British Medical Journal* 295: 314–18.

Sherman, Franklin J. 1934. *Modern Story of Mutual Savings Banks*. New York: Little & Ives.

Showalter, Elaine. 1997. *Hysteries: Hysterical Epidemics and Modern Culture*. New York: Columbia University Press.

Shryock, Henry S. and Jacob S. Siegel. 1978. *Methods and Materials of Demography* (condensed version). New York: Academic Press.

Silberman, Charles E. 1978. *Criminal Violence, Criminal Justice*. New York: Random House.

Smyth, George Lewis. 1844–9. *Ireland, Historical and Statistical*, 3 vols. London: Whittaker.

Snyder, Robert W. 1995. 'Crime', in Kenneth T. Jackson (ed.), *The Encyclopedia of New York City*. New Haven: Yale UP.

Solar, P.M. 1979. 'The agricultural trade statistics in the Irish Railway Commissioners' Report', *IESH* 6: 24–40.

Solar, P .M. 1989a. 'Harvest fluctuations in pre-famine Ireland: evidence from Belfast and Waterford newspapers', *AgHR* xxxvii (2): 157–65.

Solar, P .M. 1989b. 'The Great Famine was no ordinary subsistence crisis', in Crawford, *Famine*, pp. 112–131.

Solar, P. M. 1997 'The potato famine in Europe', in Ó Gráda, *Famine 150*, pp. 113–27.

Soltow, Lee. 1975. *Men and Wealth in the United States, 1850–1870*. New Haven: Yale University Press.

Somerville, Alexander. 1994. *Letters from Ireland during the Famine of 1847*, ed. K. D. M. Snell. Dublin: Irish Academic Press.

Stansell, Christine. 1987. *City of Women: Sex and class in New York 1789–1860*. New York: Knopf.

Steckel, R. 1983. 'Height and *per capita* income', *Historical Methods* XVI: 1–7.

Steinberg, Stephen. 1989. *The Ethnic Myth: Race, Ethnicity, and Class in America*, 2nd edn. Boston: Beacon Press.

Stern, William J. 1997. 'How Dagger John saved New York's Irish', *City Journal* 7 (2) [http://www.city-journal.org/html/7_2_a2.html].

Stewartstown and District Historical Society (1996) *The Famine in East Tyrone*. Stewartstown: Stewartstown & District Historical Society.

Stott, Richard B. 1990. *Workers in the Metropolis: Class, Ethnicity and Youth in Antebellum New York City*. Ithaca: Cornell University Press.

Summers, R. and A. Heston. 1991. 'The Penn World Table (Mark 5): an expanded set of international comparisons, 1950–1988', *QJE* 106: 327–68.

Swift, John. 1948. *History of the Dublin Bakers and Others*, Dublin: Irish Bakers, Confectionery & Allied Workers Union.

Swinford Historical Society. 1995. *An Gorta Mór: Famine in the Swinford Union*. Swinford: SHS.

Swords, Liam. 1999. *In Their Own Words: The Famine in North Connacht, 1845–49*. Blackrock, Co. Dublin: Columba Press.

Taylor, C. E. 1983. 'Synergy among mass infections, famines, and poverty', in Rotberg and Rabb, *Hunger and History*, pp. 285–304..

Thackeray, W. M. [1843] 1888. 'Irish Sketchbook', in idem, *Works*, vol. 18. London: Smith, Elder.

Thomas, Brinley, 1985. 'Feeding Britain in the industrial revolution' in J. Mokyr (ed.), *The Economics of the Industrial Revolution*. Totowa, NJ: Rowman & Allenheld, pp. 137–50.

Thom's Irish Almanac and Official Directory (annual), Dublin: Alexander Thom.

Tighe, William. 1801. *Statistical Account of the County of Kilkenny*. Dublin: Graiseberry & Campbell.

Todaro, M. P. 1969. 'A model of labor migration and urban unemployment in less developed countries', *AER* 59: 138–148.

Toole, M. J. and R. J. Waldman. 1988. 'An analysis of mortality trends among refugee populations in Somalia, Sudan, and Thailand', *Bulletin of the World Health Organization* 66: 237–47.

Turner, M. 1996. *After the Famine: Irish Agriculture, 1850–1914*. Cambridge: CUP

Vaughan, W. E. (ed.) 1989. *The New History of Ireland*, vol. 5. Oxford: OUP.

Vaughan, W. E. 1994. *Landlords and Tenants in Mid-Victorian Ireland*. Oxford: Clarendon.

Vaughan, W. E. 1995. 'Reflections on the Great Famine'. *Ulster Local Studies* 17 (2).

Vaughan, W. E. and A. Fitzpatrick, 1978. *Irish Population Statistics*. Dublin: Royal Irish Academy.

Verling, Máirtín. 1999. *Béarach Mná ag Caint: Seanchas Mhairéad Ní Mhionacháin*, Indreabhán: Cló Iarchonnachta.

Vincent, J. 1992. 'A political orchestration of the Irish Famine: County Fermanagh, May 1847', in M. Silverman and P. H. Gulliver (eds), *Approaching the Past: Historical Anthropology Through Irish Case Studies*. New York: Columbia UP, pp. 75–98.

Von Braun, J., Teklu, T. and Webb, P. 1998. *Famine in Africa: Causes, Responses and Prevention*. Baltimore: Johns Hopkins Press.

Wakefield, Edward G. 1812. *An Account of Ireland, Statistical and Political*, 2 vols. London: Longman.

Walker, Thomas R. 2000. 'Economic opportunity on the urban frontier: wealth and nativity in early San Francisco', *EEH* 37 (3): 258–77.

Warburton, J., James Whitelaw and Robert Walsh. 1818. *History of the City of Dublin*, 2 vols. London: Cadell & Davies.

Watkins, S. C. and J. Menken. 1985. 'Famines in historical perspective.' *PDR* 11: 647–76.

Wegge, Simone. 1998. 'Chain migration and information networks: evidence from nineteenth-century Hesse-Cassel', *JEH* 58 (4): 957–86.

Wheatcroft, S. G. 1981a. 'Famine and factors affecting mortality in the USSR: the demographic crises of 1914–1922 and 1930–33'. Discussion Paper no. 20, Centre for Russian and East European Studies, University of Birmingham.

Wheatcroft, S. G. 1981b. 'Famine and factors affecting mortality in the USSR: the demographic crises of 1914–1922 and 1930–33: Appendices'. Discussion Paper no. 21, Centre for Russian and East European Studies.

Wheatcroft, S. G. 1983. 'Famine and epidemic crises in Russia, 1918–1922: the case of Saratov', *Annales de Demographie Historique*, pp. 329–52.

Whelan, Irene. 1995. 'The stigma of Souperism', in Póirtéir (ed.), *Great Irish Famine*, pp. 135–54.

Whelan, Karl. 1999. 'Economic geography and the long-run effects of the Great Irish Famine', *ESR* 30 (1): 1–20.

Whelan, Kevin. 1995a. 'Pre- and post-famine landscape change', in Póirtéir, *Great Irish Famine*, pp. 19–33.

Whelan, Kevin. 1995b. 'Immoral economy: interpreting Erskine Nichol's *The Tenant*', in Boston College Museum of Art, *America's Eye: Irish Paintings from the Collection of Brian P. Burns*, Boston, pp. 57–67.

Williams, N. 1959. *Contraband Cargoes: Seven Centuries of Smuggling*. London: Longman.

Williams, N. J. A. (ed.) 1981. *Pairlimint Chloinne Tomáis*. Dublin: Institute of Advanced Studies.

Williamson, J. G. 1986. 'The impact of the Irish on British labor markets during the industrial revolution', *JEH* 46: 693–720.

Williamson, J. G. 1995. 'The evolution of global labor markets since 1850: background evidence and hypotheses', *EEH* 32: 1–54.

Williamson, J. G. and P. H. Lindert. 1983. 'English workers' living standards during the industrial revolution: a new look', *EHR*, 36: 1–25.

Willis, Thomas. 1844. *The Social and Sanitary Condition of the Working Classes of Dublin City*. Dublin: O'Gorman.

Winnick, Myron. 1994. 'Hunger disease: studies by Jewish physicians in the Warsaw ghetto', *Nutrition* 10: 365–80.

Woodham-Smith, Cecil. 1962. *The Great Hunger: Ireland 1845–49*. London: Hamish Hamilton.

World Bank. 1979. *World Development Report 1979*. Washington, DC: World Bank

Wright, W. 1882. *The Chronicle of Joshua the Stylite, Composed in Syriac AD 507*. Cambridge: CUP.

Wrigley, E. A. and R. Schofield. 1981. *The Population History of England, 1538–1871: A Reconstruction*. London: Arnold.

W. T. H. 1850. *The Encumbered Estates of Ireland*. London.

Yager, Tom. 1996. 'Mass eviction in the Mullet peninsula during and after the Great Famine', *IESH*, XXIII: 24–44.

Yamin, Rebecca. 1997. 'New York's mythic slum: digging lower Manhattan's infamous Five Points', *Archaeology*, Mar./Apr.: 45–53.

Index

Index

Koch, Robert, 80, 84, 259
Kohl, Johann, 91–2
Kotre, John, 224, 231
Kozlov, Igor, 23
Kumar, Gopalkrishna, 198

labour force, decline in, 19
Labour Rate Act, 94
Lachiver, Marcel, 218, 223
Ladies of the Mission, 193
Lamb, H., 253
land sales, 49
landlords, *see also* under emigration, 3, 17–18,
    48–60, 207, 219, 255, 260
  bankruptcies of, 49–51
  debts of, 56–8
  extravagance of, 58
  income of, 21
land mines, 205
Lansdowne estate (Kerry), 162–3, 192
Land War (1879), 59
Lane, P. G., 49, 58
Lannie, Vincent P., 165
Large, David, 52
Large, E. C., 247
Lee, J. J., 5
Lenihan, Pádraig, 16
literacy, *see also* illiteracy, 37, 45
Litton, H., 252
Livi-Bacci, M., 4, 81
living standards, pre-famine, 24–47
  measures of: biological, 42–4, 45;
      consumption of goods, 31–7;
      education, 37–42
  provincial, 125
  source material, 25–31
Lloyd, David, 228–9
Locke, John, 49
Long, Clarence D., 169
Lopez, A. D., 83
louse, human, 77

Lynch, Patrick, 19
Lyne, Gerard J., 162–3
Lyons, F. S. L., 50–2, 245–6
Lysaght, Patricia, 224–5

McAlpin, Michelle, 264
MacArthur, W. A., 67, 77, 236–9, 242, 258
MacCarthy, R. B., 48
McCartney, Donal, 50
McClean, Raymond, 196, 204
Mac Coitir, Séamus, 204
MacDonagh, Oliver, 131, 236–7, 239, 242
McDowell, R. B., 236–9, 244
McGregor, Patrick, 13, 86, 259
McHale, John, 248
McHugh, Roger, 223, 236–7, 239, 249, 261
MacLysaght, E., 32
McParlan, J., 38
Maguire, J. F., 153
Maguire, W. A., 48, 58, 255
Maharatna, A., 65, 80, 215
Maher, Joseph, 239
Mahon, Denis, 163, 255
malaria, 81
Malthus, Thomas, 42, 124, 263
Malthusian theory, 15
Manning, James Hilton, 177–8
Mansergh, Nicholas, 246
marasmus, 15, 64, 69, 78
Margo, Robert, 169
Martin, F. X., 5
Marx, Karl, 17
Matsell, George, 164, 168
Maxwell, Constantia, 90
medical
  ignorance, 79
  knowledge, 202–4
  personnel, 19, 77–9, 258–9
Meenan, James, 239
Mendicity Institution, 215
Menken, Jane, 21, 121, 135–7, 140

320